DEVON AND CORNWALL RECORD SOCIETY

New Series

Volume 60

Early fourteenth-century model book folio – Christ's Passion and The Three Living and The Three Dead – recycled as the cover of the first general receivers' book. (© The British Library Board, BL, Add MS 32244, inside back cover)

STRATTON CHURCHWARDENS' ACCOUNTS, 1512–1578

EDITED BY

JOANNA MATTINGLY

DEVON AND CORNWALL RECORD SOCIETY

THE BOYDELL PRESS

First published 2018
Reprinted 2021

A publication of the
Devon and Cornwall Record Society
published by The Boydell Press
an imprint of Boydell & Brewer Ltd
PO Box 9, Woodbridge, Suffolk IP12 3DF, UK
and of Boydell & Brewer Inc.
668 Mt Hope Avenue, Rochester, NY 14620–2731, USA
website: www.boydellandbrewer.com

ISBN 978 0 90185 360 8

Series information is printed at the back of this volume

A CIP catalogue record for this book is available
from the British Library

Contents

Illustrations and Maps

Frontispiece

Colour plates
(between pp. 152 and 153)

Figures

(Note: maps by Peter Joseph)

Preface and Acknowledgements

This project is the culmination of over thirty years of study of Cornwall's late medieval churches and their records. Stratton churchwardens' accounts, which started out as those of the High Cross, were selected for transcription because they are continuous from 1512 to 1578 and mainly written in English. Two account books kept by Stratton's general receivers, the parish treasurers, survive for parts of this period, and the second runs to 1581. They are split between the British Library and the Cornwall Record Office. All throw considerable light on the continuing enlargement of Stratton church well into the Reformation period and the impact of sudden religious change on ordinary people's lives.

The project has been greatly assisted by a grant from the Q-fund which enabled photocopies to be made from the microfilm of Stratton churchwardens' accounts held at the Cornwall Record Office. Maps and illustrations were funded by a grant from the late Miss Isobel Thornley's Bequest to the University of London. I am grateful to Peter Joseph for his patience and good humour in producing the maps and improving some photographs for publication. Dan Mallett took photographs at the Cornwall Record Office, including the cover image. Archivists and librarians at the Cornwall Record Office, the British Library, The National Archives, the Courtney Library of the Royal Institution of Cornwall, the Institute of Historical Research and the Cornish Studies Library have been exceptionally helpful as always. The cover photograph and the 1583 Stratton marketplace plans are reproduced courtesy of Cornwall Record Office, while the British Library Board has given permission for the use of the frontispiece image and two of the colour plates. Alexis Jordan took one of the photographs of the parish church; other photographs were taken by the author. These are reproduced by permission of Stratton PCC and Wolborough PCC and the Churches Conservation Trust in the case of Torbryan.

My biggest debt of gratitude is to my editor Catherine Rider who has shared my enthusiasm for the project from the start. She also expanded all the Latin headings to make them more easily comprehensible to the general reader. I am grateful to Andrew Thorpe (Devon and Cornwall Record Society General Editor), Nicholas Orme, Christine and Colin Edwards, and Todd Gray for answering specific queries and for general advice about archival editing. Oliver Padel assisted me with place-name interpretations and Andrew Langdon with lantern crosses. David Thomas, archivist, and Lesley Trotter helped with some tricky readings and Angela Broome with the index. My brother David Mattingly gave technical advice at a critical stage. Lucy McCann and my husband Alex Hooper read and commented on drafts of the introduction. Clive Burgess, David Dymond and Joan Dils have generously shared their expertise on churchwardens' accounts and Linda Voigts her research on St Armel. Magnus Williamson and Matthew Cheung Salisbury identified the music, while Cathy Oakes, Michelle Brown, Athena Reiss, Miriam Gill and Ellie Pridgeon were among those who helped identify the possible early-fourteenth-century model book folio that was one of the most surprising discoveries of this whole project.

Abbreviations

Add MS	Additional manuscript
BL	British Library
bz	bushel
c	100 or hundredweight
C1–C3	The National Archive, Chancery Court cases
COED	*Compact Oxford English Dictionary*
CRO	Cornwall Record Office, Truro
DCNQ	*Devon and Cornwall Notes & Queries*
DCRS	*Devon and Cornwall Record Society*
E134	The National Archive, Exchequer Court case
f., ff.	folio, folios
JRIC	*Journal of the Royal Institution of Cornwall*
li	*libra* (a pound in currency or in weight)
L&P	*Letters & Papers of Henry VIII*
m	1,000
mems	membranes
MS	manuscript
ob	*obulus* (halfpenny)
OC	*Old Cornwall* journal
pers. comm.	personal communication
PROB 11	The National Archive, wills
qr	farthing
RCG	*Royal Cornwall Gazette*
REED	Records of Early English Drama
RIC	Royal Institution of Cornwall
SC2	The National Archive, manorial court records
TDA	*Transactions of the Devonshire Association for the Advancement of Science, Literature and Art*
TNA	The National Archive, Kew
v	verso

Introduction

Stratton High Cross and general receivers' accounts

The Stratton High Cross or churchwardens' accounts for 1512 to 1578 are made up of 104 paper folios and a parchment cover and are in the British Library collections.[1] Written mostly in English, they are significant because they are among only eighteen (of some two hundred) surviving sets of pre-Reformation churchwardens' accounts which cover the whole period 1535–70 when most Reformation change took place.[2] This allows us to track the progress of the Reformation in a single parish and its impact on the lives of ordinary people. Some of the other seventeen accounts have been published as edited volumes by county record societies or as extracts, with St Laurence's in Reading being the latest.[3] The Stratton accounts were published as cherry-picked extracts in 1880, but de-contextualised, and not always accurately or consistently transcribed.[4] Other comparable, but less complete, published sets of accounts used here include Mildenhall in Suffolk and Chagford in Devon.[5]

What makes Stratton a little more unusual, and arguably adds to its importance for Reformation historians, is the fact that there are also two general receivers' or stock wardens' account books covering parts of the same period.[6] Written mainly in English, like the High Cross wardens' accounts, these cover the periods 1534–49 (with half of a 1531 account) and 1557–81. The earlier of these two books, also at the British Library, is made up of twenty folios with a recycled, and very rare, early fourteenth-century model book folio as a cover.[7] It lists guild, store and other account returns regularly, including those of the High Cross which became churchwardens' accounts.[8] This gives us an overview of parish administration in Stratton, with at least thirteen groups accounting to the general receivers, who were effectively parish treasurers. These were six groups known as guilds, including the High Cross; four less elitist groups known as stores, who held goods and livestock; and

1 BL, Add MS 32243.

2 Hutton, 'Local Impact of Reformation', p.115, fn.3. For an introduction to churchwardens' accounts and their potential see Cox, *Churchwardens' Accounts*; Middleton-Stewart, 'Parochial Activity', pp.283–4; and Burgess, 'The Churchwardens' Accounts of St Andrew Hubbard', pp.61–6.

3 Dils, *Reading St Laurence Churchwardens' Accounts*. See also Binney, *Accounts of Morebath*; Duffy, *Voices of Morebath*; Hanham, *Churchwardens' Accounts of Ashburton*; Northeast, *Boxford Churchwardens' Accounts (to 1561)*; Price and Barnard, *Churchwardens' Accounts of the Parish of Badsey*; and Kitto, *St Martin-in-the-Fields Accounts*. Other complete 1535–70 accounts await full publication.

4 Peacock, 'Churchwardens' Accounts of the Parish of Stratton', pp.195–236.

5 Middleton-Stewart, *Records of the Churchwardens of Mildenhall*; Osborne, *Church Wardens' Accounts of St Michael's Church Chagford*.

6 BL, Add MS 32244; CRO, P216/25/208. Hereafter these are called general receivers' books 1 and 2.

7 Cathy Oakes, pers. comm., noted similarities with the de Lisle Psalter of c.1308–c.1340.

8 For guilds see Mattingly, 'Medieval Parish Guilds', pp.290–329; Westlake, *Parish Gilds of Mediaeval England*; Bainbridge, *Gilds in the Medieval Countryside*.

three miscellaneous groups called the Sextons, Our Lady Maidens and Robin Hood.[9] Apart from High Cross, none of their accounts has survived, but an idea of the likely content can be gained from good survivals elsewhere in Exeter diocese.[10] The High Cross wardens' accounts show that by 1531–32 a group known as 'the eight men' also accounted at Stratton.[11]

The second general receivers' account book, which is in the Cornwall Record Office, originally had forty unnumbered folios, but folios 37 and 40 are missing and 39 is very fragmentary. Parchment for the cover, a recycled folio of music from a Tudor breviary or antiphonal, seems to be part of the Easter service from a Benedictine abbey and includes lauds for Good Friday and matins for Holy Saturday.[12] This sheet was folded in half and stitched, and it cost 1d in 1557 when a quire of paper cost 4d. Further paper 'to put in this bocke' was bought for 1d in 1569–70.[13] Rents of church lands now take precedence in the receipts, and payments to the poor show the transition from manor to parish governance. Like the High Cross wardens' accounts, the Stratton general receivers' books attracted antiquarian attention and extracts were published.[14]

Stratton also has a parish archive connected with these accounts which has been used to clarify obscure points. Known as the Blanchminster Charity[15] records, this comprises 340 separate items including all the later general receivers' and some churchwardens' accounts for Stratton, a general pardon for the 1497 Cornish rebellion, the rood loft contract of 1531 (appendix 1), a chantry land case of 1554–55, the 1583 church house case (appendix 4) with its two plans, and many grants, feoffments and leases about church lands from the fourteenth to the nineteenth century.[16] Early-sixteenth-century tax lists, 4 sixteenth- and about 20 early-seventeenth-century wills and other probate material, 18 Westminster court cases and occasional manorial records shed further light on Stratton and its people.

There is a great deal of information in both sets of Stratton accounts about the building and enlargement of the church as parishioners strove to achieve the Cornish (and West Devon) ideal of a three-hall church with three similar width gables at the east end.[17] Documented building work over forty-five years includes the completion of the south aisle and the three-stage tower, a new rood screen and loft, the widening

[9] Some stores did have associated guilds, too; see 'Guilds, stores, parochial organisation, and chantries' section below.

[10] For Devon see Hanham, *Churchwardens' Accounts of Ashburton*; Osborne, *Church Wardens' Accounts of St Michael's Church, Chagford*; Binney, *Accounts of Morebath*. For Cornwall see Antony, St Breock, Camborne, Menheniot, North Petherwin, Poughill, and St Thomas Launceston, CRO, P7/5/1 (transcript), P19/5/1, P27/5/1, P144/5/2–3, P167/5/1, P192/5/1, P221/5/1–4. Bodmin is more comparable with Stratton as it has churchwardens', general receivers' and town receivers' accounts, but no guild accounts, CRO, B/BOD/245; /314/2–6.

[11] BL, Add MS 32243, f.23. At Poughill the six men's accounts were like Stratton general receivers' accounts, see CRO, P192/5/1, p.9.

[12] CRO, P216/25/208. Matthew Cheung Salisbury and Magnus Williamson identified the music, and Tavistock Abbey, Tywardreath Priory or Exeter, are the most likely sources.

[13] CRO, P216/25/208, ff.3v, 18.

[14] Peacock, 'Churchwardens' Accounts of Stratton', pp.232–6; Goulding, *Blanchminster Records*, pp.54a–60a, 65–71.

[15] The Blanchminsters of Binhamy were the main fourteenth-century family but not major donors of land to Stratton church.

[16] CRO, P216/25/1–340.

[17] Mattingly, *Looking at Cornish Churches*, p.25.

and heightening of the north aisle, and the complete demolition and rebuilding of the Lady chapel and chancel. The general receivers were the main contractors, with the High Cross wardens and other groups involved in fund-raising. Stratton church today retains walling, roof timbers and bosses and the majority of its original piers. Window frames appear to be Victorian copies of the originals. In 1887, arcades were rebuilt while pinnacles, tracery and the west window of the tower and its sculpture were replaced.[18]

Stratton accounts include entries on many non-religious matters like medieval fairs and entertainment where other sources can fill out the picture.[19] There is a complete account of the building of the former market cross in 1543–44 and a church ale brewers' draft account of 1559 (appendix 2.1). The Reformation is well covered, with no fewer than three inventories of church goods from 1559, 1570–71 and 1578 at the back of the High Cross wardens' accounts (appendix 3.1–3.3). The first shows Marian re-equipping of the church, the second includes the church house contents and the last details parish armour. Three other draft accounts partially survive. Cancelled drafts of the 1559 and 1575 High Cross wardens' accounts were partly recycled for inventories (appendix 2.2–2.3), while a damaged 1581 draft occurs at the back of the second general receivers' book.

Finally, the change from manorial to parish government can be tracked from 1557 on, especially in the general receivers' accounts. Parish responsibilities now included the poor, tax-raising subsidies, doles, musters, causeways or causeys, highways and bridges. Overseers of the poor, constables and highway wardens are sometimes noted. Lengthening lists of the poor, who had to be provided with shifts, shoes, shelter, surgery and shrouds, in 1570 included a shroud for the tinker's maid.[20] There are also four lists of parish poor from 1578 to 1581. The general receivers' accounts include bell casting in 1557–59, 1564–65 and 1577–78, and in 1571–78 bridge-building at Stratton rather than Hele. Fish caught in the bridge pool raised 6d for the latter project.[21]

The High Cross wardens' accounts were generally made on the Sunday before or after 2 February, the Purification of the Virgin Mary.[22] On one occasion, in 1540, the account was made on 1 June, with no explanation given. February accounting, usually on a Sunday towards the middle of the month, continued to be the norm in Elizabeth's reign. General receivers' accounts, by contrast, were autumnal. Where noted, the accounting day was October to November in 1531–49, apart from in 1547 when it was held late, on 1 January 1548. Between 1557 and 1568 no dates are noted and thereafter accounts were usually made up in mid-December. Such accounts would have been read aloud to the parishioners, hence Sunday was the usual choice.

[18] Stratton was not sashed-out like many Cornish churches in the late eighteenth century, and Victorian fenestration is mostly late Perpendicular and South Hams type. *RCG*, 22 January 1864, p.8, col.1 notes a concert to raise funds for a new roof and CRO, P216/2/71 summarises the 1887 restoration.

[19] Hays et al., *Records of Early English Drama*; Hutton, The Rise and Fall of Merry England. But see Duffy, *Voices of Morebath*, pp.66–7, for an attack on the Devon volume of REED's speculation about the form of Morebath's St George's revel and when it was held. Duffy may have a point in adhering strictly to what the record says, but rain has never deterred Padstow's Obby Oss or Helston's Hal-an-Tow in early May.

[20] Maid may mean daughter here, CRO, P216/25/208, f.17v.

[21] CRO, P216/25/208, f.21v. Henderson and Coates, *Old Cornish Bridges*, pp.120–1 noted Hele bridge as the full seamark or head of the estuary.

[22] The accounting day is not always given.

Scribes, of which there were more than thirty-five for the High Cross accounts and perhaps five or six for all the general receivers' accounts, were paid variable amounts. The High Cross scribes were paid between 4d and 8d and the general receivers' scribes between 8d and 12d.

Usually the High Cross wardens raised between £2 and nearly £11 per year. This money came from gifts, funeral expenses (including registering names on the bede or prayer roll), church ales and fairs up to 1547, with high mortality encouraging giving. The High Cross spend never exceeded £8, and the accounts were mostly kept in balance. Receipts dropped to just over £1 in 1552, but recovered to £4 or more thereafter and were over £13 in 1571. Church ales continued to raise funds, boosted by sales of church goods. In 1550 the High Cross wardens were called churchwardens for the first time, though until 1570 both terms, or simply the word wardens, were used interchangeably.

General receivers, also known as stock wardens, dealt with much larger sums of money than the High Cross wardens initially. This was due to their role as parish treasurers. Until 1547, receipts from guild and store profits were usually between £14 and £25, with a high of over £34 in 1531 when the rood loft was begun. The lowest receipt – £2 2s 7d – was recorded just after this, in 1548, after the abolition of the guilds.

When the accounts resume in 1557 rents from church lands form the main receipts. Church lands included former chantry property at Hele, Stonelands (alias Popes Place) at Bude,[23] parish meadows and the church house in Stratton, Millook in Poundstock, Exe in Week St Mary and Treburtle in Tresmeer near Launceston. These rents were augmented by large fines and heriots (the best beast, due on the death of each tenant or 'life') and high payments for reversionary leases for these properties.[24] Receipts tended to be lower than before 1548. The range for the general receivers or stock wardens in Elizabeth I's reign seems to have been between £6 and £20, with receipts over £23 only in 1571–72 (when expenses are missing) and 1575–76.

The parish of Stratton

Stratton parish lies in the far north of Cornwall, in a hundred of the same name which includes the historic market town of Stratton and the newer coastal resort of Bude. Comprising more than 2,617 acres on the Culm Measures, rather than granite, most land in 1842 was classed as fertile arable with some meadow and pasture and 28 acres of woodland.[25] Garlic was grown alongside corn and grass.[26] In 1820 Stratton was described as 'the principal entrance into Cornwall from Devon', and Stratton hundred was the earliest part of Cornwall to be colonized by the Saxons.[27]

[23] Probably just south of the Strand and north of Berries, see figure 1. Parish meadows have not been identified but the parish estate later was mainly at Hele and just north of Bude.

[24] For history of church lands see Goulding, *Blanchminster Records*, pp.2a–9a, 36a, 49a.

[25] In 1842, 1,700 acres were arable, CRO, TA/216. Unenclosed strips are shown on the tithe map at Poundfield, along the parish boundary between Burn and Stratton, CRO, TM/216. Polsue, *Complete Parochial History*, iv, p.190; Smith, *Leland's Itinerary*, i, p.316; Bere and Stamp, *Book of Bude and Stratton*, p.18; and Lysons, *Cornwall*, p.295. The Culm Measures is an area of heavy clay soils extending into Devon, in contrast to the lighter soils of the granite areas. See Balchin, *Cornish Landscape*, p.41.

[26] Bere and Stamp, *Book of Bude and Stratton*, p.18 claim that garlic was a medieval crop.

[27] Gilbert, *Historical and Topographical Survey of Cornwall*, p.544.

Stratton itself was in existence c.880 when it went by the Cornish name Straetneat or valley of the river Neet. Tun, meaning town, was added to the first element of the Cornish name by 1086 to give the more English-sounding Stratone, but as the earlier version shows, the original place name meant the river valley not town on the street.[28] St Andrew was patron saint of the church here by the mid-twelfth century and his feast days became the fair days.[29]

As well as being a market centre for the hundred, Stratton also benefited from sea trade via Bude. Originally, the main settlement near the haven was Efford on the southern side of the river Neet, with Bude appearing as a name only in 1400.[30] Bude's first quay dates from 1577, and in 1602 Richard Carew described it as 'an open sandie Bay, in whose mouth riseth a little hill, by euerie sea-floud made an Iland, and thereon, a decayed Chappell: it spareth roade onely to such small shipping, as bring their tide with them, and leaueth them drie, when the ebbe hath carried away the Salt-water'.[31] Limestone was a common import according to the church accounts, an essential ingredient of mortar and plaster. Wine came by sea, too, though communion wine came via Holsworthy later, and salt and other goods were exported.[32] Stratton was approximately the fifteenth wealthiest parish in Cornwall in 1545.[33] In 1525, Stratton people paid £10 3s tax, while the older market towns of Kilkhampton and Week St Mary raised £7 10s 8d and £5 18s respectively.[34] Stratton tax payments were a little less in 1543 at £9 17s 8d, with only Morwenstow paying more in Stratton hundred.[35]

Occupations recorded at Stratton in the sixteenth century included baker, blacksmith, butcher, carpenter, cook, crowder or fiddle player, cutler, draper, hatter, hellier or slater, joiner, mason, mercer, merchant, pedlar, schoolmaster, shoemaker or cordwainer, shopkeeper, tailor and thatcher. Skilled craftsmen like carvers, glaziers, stonemasons, vestment makers and bellfounders came from Bodmin, Launceston, the Tamar valley, west Devon, Exeter and perhaps as far away as Bristol. Surgeons, pedlars and tinkers were not local either, while foreigners included Irish men, women and children and an occasional Breton. Another sign of Stratton's increasing importance and urban status was the fact that it had a new clock in 1512–13, probably on its church tower like the one at St Austell.[36]

Stratton's population was rising as is shown by the increase in the number of taxpayers between 1525 and 1543 from fifty-five to ninety-seven. The parish then suffered a major setback in 1547 when no fewer than 153 deaths were recorded

[28] Padel, *Popular Dictionary*, pp.159–60; Stratton hundred was the most densely populated part of Cornwall at the latter date, Balchin, *Cornish Landscape*, p.77.

[29] Orme, *English Church Dedications*, p.118.

[30] Padel, *Popular Dictionary*, p.60.

[31] CRO, P216/25/208, f.28; Chynoweth et al, *The Survey of Cornwall*, f.118v.

[32] Kowaleski, *Havener's Accounts*, p.318, fn.8 notes imported wine sold at Kilkhampton in 1302; Balchin, *Cornish Landscape*, p.121 records ten saltpans at Stratton in 1086.

[33] Stoate, *Cornwall Subsidies*, pp.158–68.

[34] TNA, E179/87/130, mems i–v, Stratton 1525; Stoate, *Cornwall Subsidies*, pp.147–8.

[35] Stoate, *Cornwall Subsidies*, pp.141–2, 167 shows that Morwenstow paid £10 5s 6d in 1543 but less than Stratton in 1545.

[36] BL, Add MS 32243, f.3. Symonds, *History of English* Clocks, p.15 shows the spread from cities to towns and Brown, *Cornish Clocks*, p.15 notes a clock at Launceston in 1432. St Austell's surviving one-handed 24-hour clock is like that at Raunds, Northamptonshire, Rosewell, *Medieval Wall Paintings*, p.146, fig.159.

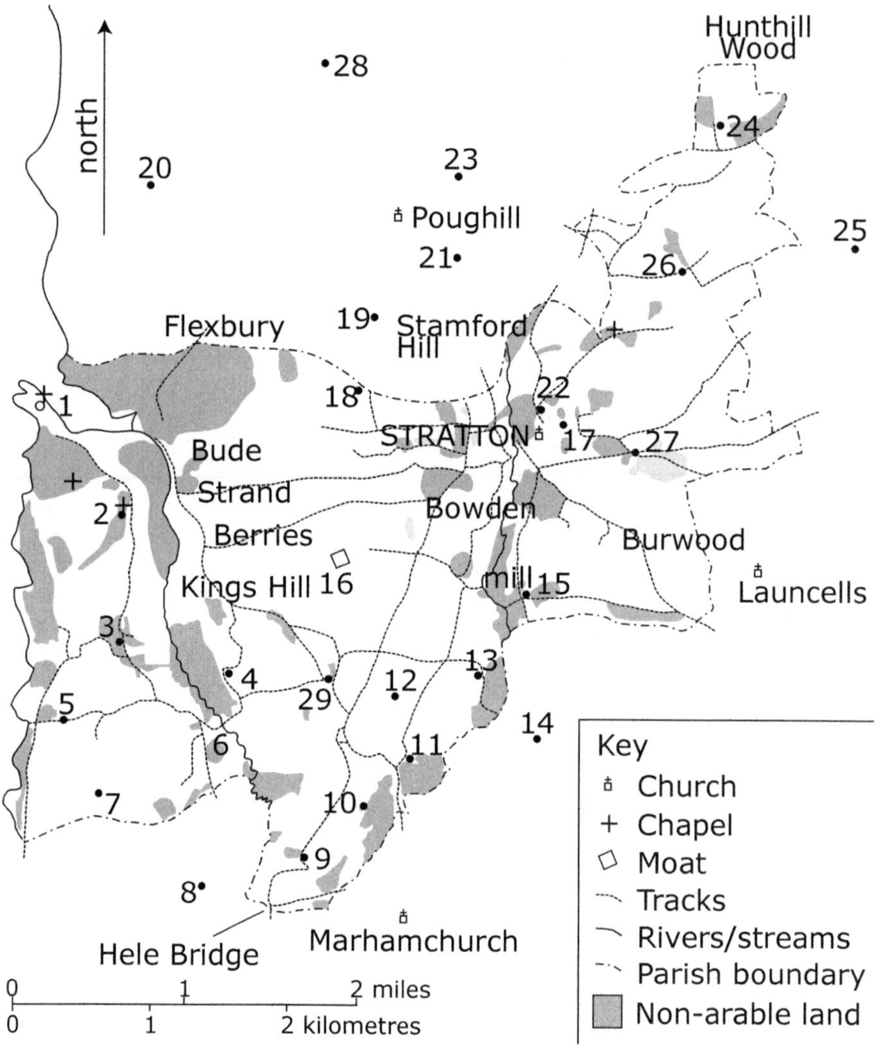

Figure 1 Stratton parish map, showing key places in medieval and later periods
Popes Place alias Stoneland was near the Strand, north of Berries
Stamford Hill is the site of the Civil War battle of 1643.

Key

1 Compass Point
2 Efford
3 Lynstone
4 Bagbury
5 Upton
6 Roddsbridge
7 Phillips
8 Whalesborough, Marhamchurch
9 Hele
10 Pollards
11 Pinch
12 West Grove
13 East Grove
14 Cann Orchard, Launcells
15 Howard
16 Binhamy
17 Sanctuary
18 Burn
19 Broomhill Manor, Poughill
20 Maer, Poughill
21 Burshill, Poughill
22 Cothill
23 Crabbe, Poughill
24 Herdbury
25 New Leigh, Launcells
26 Colebrook
27 Diddies
28 Northcott, Poughill
29 Thorn

during a localised plague or epidemic.[37] In the next year the chantry returns record four hundred communicants, suggesting a population of at least five hundred then.[38]

Markets, fairs and the church house

In 1540–43 John Leland described Stratton as 'a praty [pretty] market' which 'standith about a mile from the sea' and noted that 'ther is no very notable toun or building from Botreaux [Boscastle] by est north est a long apon the shore upper on Severn to Hertland point but Strettoun'.[39] John Norden in the 1580s described Stratton as 'a market towne verie well served of all kynde of necessaries', and in 1611–12 the market was recommended to residents of Eastway in Morwenstow and Boyton.[40] Yet Stratton is not included in the gazetteer of pre-1516 markets and fairs, unlike Kilkhampton and Week St Mary.[41] Stratton records confirm that in the 1500s its marketplace was 'a common filthy place' part-owned by John Trenger, with no 'standings or booths pitched upon the said lands before the building of the [church] house'.[42] By the late sixteenth century everything from fish to hats was sold in this small space, with the church house pentice, butcher's shambles and market house providing some protection from rain.[43]

1517 may mark the start of Stratton fair. At this date six messers or merchants rented stalls on a 14-foot-wide strip of land in front of the newly built church house. This area was marked out from the rest of the marketplace by three boundary stones.[44] Stratton's church house still stands on the west side of the marketplace, and was used for the tolswylt or weighing of yarn and wool. First noted in 1529, annual sums for this and stall rents within and without the church house became a regular source of income. Rental income greatly increased once the pentice was added to the front of the church house.[45] By 1530 at the latest Stratton had two annual fairs,

[37] Pool, 'Stratton', p.502 notes that in May 1547 there were 28 deaths, 38 in June and 87 in July which could suggest bubonic plague. Some 72 deaths are also noted in the High Cross wardens' account, with 1529–31, 1537–40, 1570–72 being other high mortality years, and a 1575–76 sickness was noted in the second general receivers' book. Kilkhampton escaped the 1547 localised epidemic, but at Poughill there were 20 deaths, the highest number for the sixteenth century and five times the norm: CRO, P102/1, p.168; P192/1/1. Bristol's 'great plague' was 1544–45, as elsewhere, see Slack, 'Local Incidence of Epidemic Disease', p.49 and Schofield, '"Crisis" Mortality', p.104, and sweating sickness hit Devon in 1551, Wylie, 'Observations', pp.101–15.

[38] Snell, *Chantry Certificates*, pp.7, fn.47 adds a quarter for those under fourteen years, but Goulding, *Blanchminster Records*, p.37a, notes five hundred communicants.

[39] Smith, *Leland's Itinerary*, i, p.176.

[40] Graham, *Topographical and Historical Description*, p.58; Fox and Padel, *Cornish Lands of the Arundells of Lanherne*, p.xcvi.

[41] Gazetteer of Markets and Fairs to 1516, Cornwall: www.history.ac.uk/cmh/gaz/cornwall.htmail.

[42] 1583 deposition of John Marys, gentleman, appendix 4.

[43] The pentice was added in 1567–69, and shambles, 1574–75: CRO, P216/25/208, ff.15, 16v; BL, Add MS 32243, f.91. The shambles were later converted into cottages, see photograph in Bere and Stamp, *Book of Bude and Stratton*, p.80. The vestry held on 17 April 1876 authorised demolition, CRO, P216/5/1.

[44] Trenger's land, BL, Add MS 32243, f.7v (1518 account) and appendix 4.

[45] At Burford in Oxfordshire the 1525 market-house is still known as the Tolsey, Catchpole et al., *Burford*, p.4. BL, Add MS 32243, ff.19v, 25 etc. and appendix 4.

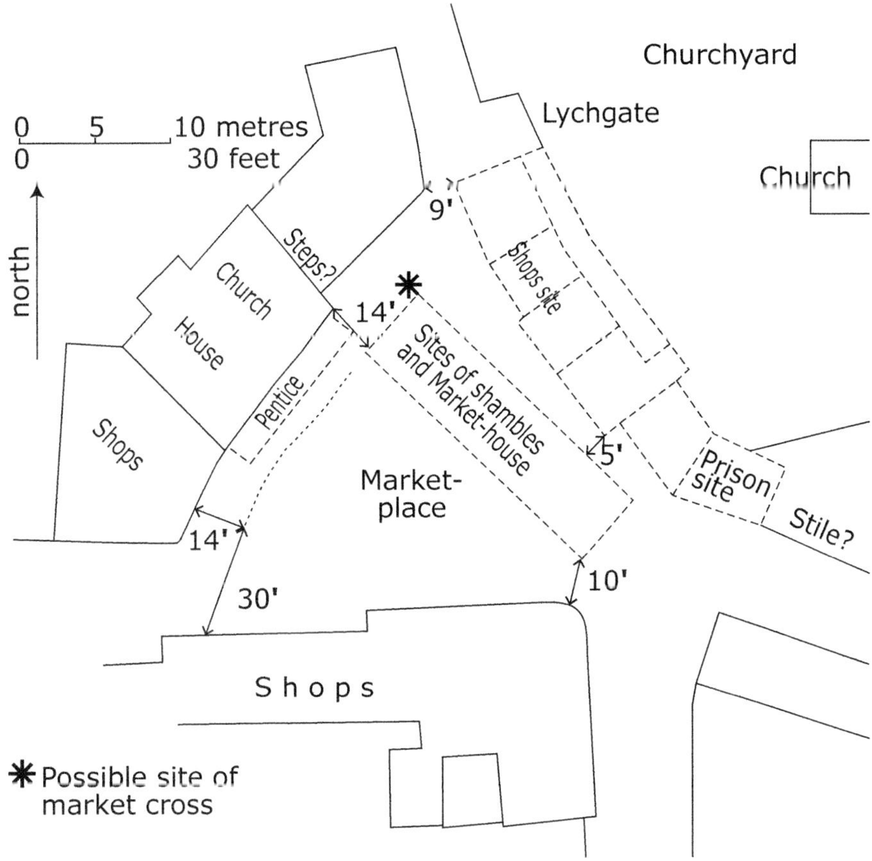

Figure 2 Map of marketplace and church house, Stratton.

held on 9 May and 30 November, St Andrew's feast days.[46] A third fair was later added on 11 December.[47] In 1565–66, when a clerk of the market, rather than the bailiff, ran the fairs, a book of assize of the statutes for weights and measures was bought.[48] Trestles for the assizers are noted in the 1570–71 church house inventory (see appendix 3.2). The renting of the market stalls was central to the 1583 church house dispute and two plans of the marketplace date from this time (appendix 4 and figures 7–8).[49]

Other market facilities included a new cross erected in 1542–43 by Bond, the mason. Very likely a stepped structure similar to the mid-fifteenth-century example surviving at Grampound, with a lantern head and religious imagery like the one at Launceston, the cross took a fortnight and four days to build and cost £5 8s 8d. Accounts show that the stone, lime and grit had to be sourced and fetched and that

[46] BL, Add MS 32243, ff.21, 23. St Andrew was patron saint of Stratton church.

[47] Lysons, *Cornwall*, p.295.

[48] CRO, P216/25/208, f.13v.

[49] CRO, P216/25/140a–b.

Figure 3 The lychgate, the marketplace and church house, Stratton.

mortar was made on site.[50] By 1545–46 'the crosse down yn ye strett' housed a further standing or stall at fair time, and in 1549 the hangman's scaffold was erected around it.[51] Its demise is charted in the general receivers' accounts of 1573–74 when stones were taken from the cross into the church house, perhaps for recycling for one of the town bridges. Lime 'occupied at the cross' presumably filled the socket in the base stone and prevented the cross's re-erection.[52]

The church house, where church ales were brewed and Whitsun feasts held, was probably built in 1515.[53] Church houses were usually two-storeyed buildings with a kitchen, a meeting room and a storeroom for brewing utensils downstairs. These rooms were generally separated by wooden partitions and in the first two cases were usually served by separate entrances. Upstairs was the feasting room with trestle tables and benches, accessed by an external stair, with a further storeroom beyond for play props like Robin Hood's house and costumes.[54] Stratton church house had a kitchen, a buttery and an external stair projecting 6 to 7 feet into the street, as well as a feasting room and storerooms.[55] In 1558–59 Stratton feasts

[50] BL, Add MS 32244, f.13v. Langdon, *Stone Crosses in North Cornwall*, p.44.

[51] BL, Add MS 32243, f.41; Pool, 'Stratton', p.502.

[52] CRO, P216/25/208, f.23. The base stone remained in 1753, Pool, 'Stratton', p.502.

[53] The date on the modern plaque on church house and the year when Trenger, the donor, and others were rewarded, BL, Add MS 32243, f.5v.

[54] Mattingly, 'Built to Last?', pp.107–18.

[55] Appendix 4. Stratton's feasting room, like Ashburton's, was later used as a school, Hanham, *Churchwardens' Accounts of Ashburton*, p.viii.

comprised bread, pies, roast meat and probably cheese, washed down with two strengths of hopped ale or beer (the weaker 'small' drink being from the second brewing), cider or wine. On Trinity Sunday of that year bacon was eaten and other feasting took place at Rogationtide, on guild feast days, as part of the Robin Hood festivities around May Day, at wedding breakfasts and funeral wakes or to celebrate the beginning or end of major building projects.[56]

Entertainment was provided from a church house base by gypsies in 1521–22 and 1558–61 at fair time and no doubt included bare-back riding, music, dancing, fortune-telling and perhaps pick-pocketing.[57] In 1525–26 a bear and bearwards visited, travelling players came in 1538–39 and four travelling musicians in 1579.[58] Home-grown entertainment in the 1520s and '30s was provided by crowders or fiddlers from the Jule family and by Robin Hood and his fellows.[59] By 1569–70 there was bull baiting, and archery practice took place at the churchyard butts.[60]

Manors and landowners

There were three main manors in Stratton: Binhamy, Efford and Stratton Bonamy.[61] Manorial lands were concentrated in and around Stratton. There was also a small rectorial manor called Stratton Sanctuary originally held by Launceston Priory to the north and east of the church, which included Crabbe in Poughill. This came into the hands of the Duchy of Cornwall.[62] There were manorial centres at Binhamy and Efford. Binhamy, a scheduled moated site with a c.12-foot-deep moat (now overgrown with trees and with no evident standing structures), was the thirteenth- and fourteenth-century powerhouse of Stratton, held by the Blanchminsters and later the Coleshills and Arundells.[63] A surviving late-thirteenth-century tomb effigy in Stratton church is likely to represent Reginald Blanchminster or his father Ralph the elder, not Reginald's son Ralph Blanchminster the younger who left money in 1348 to build a north aisle.[64]

Efford or Ebbingford, sited close to the harbour entrance at Bude, was the main gentry residence in the period covered by the church accounts. Held by the

[56] Appendices 2.1 and 4. Eggs and bacon were also consumed at Easter, see Winnington-Ingram, 'The Early Parish Registers of Stoke Edith', p.22.

[57] BL, Add MS 32243, ff.12, 62, 63v, 65. For historic background see Fraser, *The Gypsies*, pp.111–15, 130–3 which strongly suggests that the Act against 'Egyptians' of 1562 deterred further Stratton visits. For gypsies at Brereton in 1548 and Malpas in 1575, see Richards, *Old Cheshire Churches*, pp.70, 408; and twelve Egyptians were given 1s 6d at Uplyme, Devon, 1649, DRO, 303A/PW1.

[58] BL, Add MS 32243, ff.14v–15, 32v; CRO, P216/25/208, f.33v.

[59] BL, Add MS 32243, f.10 and 32244, f.4v. For Robin Hood see BL, Add MS 32244, ff.4, 5v, 6v and 13v for the sale of the wood of his house and Holt, *Robin Hood*, pp.194–7 for context. Robin Hood still features in the revived Hal-an-Tow at Helston Furry Day.

[60] CRO, P216/25/208, ff.16v–17.

[61] Humphreys, *List of Cornish Manors*. Bonamy must be a corruption of Binhamy and whether it really was a separate manor is uncertain.

[62] Orme, *History of Cornwall, Religious History to 1560*, pp.218–19. For Stratton Sanctuary see Stoate, *Cornwall Manorial Rentals and Surveys*, p.41 and Pounds, *Parliamentary Survey of the Duchy of Cornwall*, pp.163–4 which gives the bounds.

[63] Gilbert, *Historical and Topographical Survey of Cornwall*, p.546 includes further observations about the site and finds made there.

[64] Goulding, *Blanchminster Records*, p.11a; Orme, *Cornish Wills*, p.29.

Wamfords and Durants originally, it then passed by marriage to the Arundells of Trerice, a younger branch of the family based at Lanherne.[65] Associated with Efford were a free chapel dedicated to St Leonard, the chapel of the Holy Trinity and St Michael on the rock at the harbour entrance, a household chapel and a chapel of St George in the parish church.[66] A key Lancastrian supporter – Sir John Arundell the elder – was probably born at Efford around 1470 and was listed to attend upon the king's grace in 1492 at the reception of several French lords when peace was made with France.[67] He went on to marry Jane Grenville from Stowe in Kilkhampton parish, produced three sons and a daughter who lived into adulthood and died in 1511.[68] It is likely that he brought the cult of St Armel, King Henry VII's favourite saint, to Stratton and that it was continued there by his widow.

Armel was the patron saint of the sweating sickness, also known as 'sudye', a new disease that arrived in England in 1485 with Henry VII. That it was prevalent in Cornwall is clear: 'sudye' was recorded as the cause of death on the brass of John and Anne Mohun of Lanteglos-by-Fowey. Mohun husband and wife died within twenty-four hours of showing symptoms in September 1508.[69] Armel, a Breton saint of Welsh birth, is usually shown as a priest, sometimes wearing a chasuble over armour, leading a dragon by his stole. An image of Armel appears on the Devon rood screen at Torbryan (plate 4a) where the saint is shown leading a crowned dragon by a chain. Stratton High Cross wardens' accounts record the blessing of St Armel's chalice in 1512, and in 1531 a new altar and image of St Armel are noted in the rood loft contract (appendix 1). The general receivers' accounts show that St Armel's store was the wealthiest of the parish stores and guilds, and an anniversary or obit of St Armel was held on 16 August 1545 by the vicar.[70] Armel's altar stood next to the chapel of St George, a saint known for plague cures, and directly under that saint's mounted statue in the south aisle. Added kudos for Armel's cult came from the incorrect belief, recorded by at least one fifteenth-century source, that the saint was born in north Cornwall.[71]

After the death of Sir John Arundell the elder the manor passed to John Arundell the younger, who was born in about 1496 at Efford, came of age in 1517 and was knighted in 1534. Unable or unwilling to make Efford his main home (his mother Jane had remarried by 1513 and lived there until her death in 1551), John Arundell the younger settled at Gwarnick in St Allen parish, home of his first wife Mary Beville. He had little to do with Stratton apart from witnessing a feoffment of church lands in 1529 and being buried at Stratton in late November 1560. Stratton church house was rented on this latter occasion for 6s 8d for his funeral wake and 3s 4d was paid for his grave in the north-east or Lady chapel as befitted the heir to the Blanchminster estate.[72]

65 Gilbert, *Historical and Topographical Survey of Cornwall*, p.547.

66 Hingeston-Randolph, *Register of Edmund Stafford*, pp.43, 270; Pool, 'Stratton', p.500. The south aisle was the Efford aisle and the north belonged to Binhamy.

67 I am grateful to Linda Voigts for this and other references to the Arundells and St Armel.

68 Vivian, *Visitations*, pp.11–13.

69 Dunkin, *Monumental Brasses of Cornwall*, pp.34–5, plate xxx.

70 BL, Add MS 32243, f.2v; 32244, f.2 on, 17.

71 The entrance to the rood stair was to the right of the altar. Voigts, 'Plague Saints'.

72 Stoate, *Cornwall Subsidies*, p.60 shows lands worth £80-£133 6s 8d in 1525–43; Goulding, *Blanchminster Records*, pp.26–7; BL, Add MS 32243, ff.63v–4. Dunkin, *Monumental Brasses of Cornwall*, p.34 gives correct date of death as brass is a year out.

The role of resident lords of the manor fell to the Chamonds who were christened, married, buried, held funeral wakes and obits and made bequests there. Rushes to sweeten the church were bought for a Chamond wedding in 1532–33 and for Sir John Chamond's obit in 1545.[73] Sir John Chamond also bequeathed a gown in 1544 for conversion to vestments for Arundell chapel use.[74] He was assessed for tax in 1543 on £100 of lands. As befitted his rank and local status, lengthy knells accompanied him to his grave. Unusually, the parish paid for the ringers' feast afterwards.[75] When John's widow Dame Jane Chamond made her will on 1 January 1551 she asked to be buried between her Arundell and Chamond husbands in the south aisle. Her household at that time included her servant John Kempthorne and chaplain John Lyll, then vicar of Plymtree in Devon.[76] Edward and Richard Arundell, Jane's younger sons who both died in 1527, may also have been buried at Stratton.[77]

Other rising gentry with an interest in Stratton church included Dame Chamond's servant John Kempthorne the younger of Tonacombe and Master Thomas Arundell of Ley in Morwenstow.[78] In 1537 they acquired a forty-year lease of the rectorial tithes of Stratton and Poughill from the last prior of Launceston.[79] Thomas Arundell then became a major benefactor to Stratton church, giving a suit of vestments in 1539–41 when he was rewarded with a dinner. In 1541–42 one of his daughter's was married at Stratton with fresh rushes underfoot. Honouring his rectorial responsibilities in 1545, Thomas gave 26s 8d towards the new chancel, probably with Kempthorne. He is later found purchasing pieces of velvet, perhaps from the vestments he had given, while Kempthorne paid for some token repairs to the chancel roof in 1557.[80]

St Andrew's church and its building projects

Excavations during the 1888 restoration revealed traces of an earlier cruciform church of Norman and Early English date. This was conjectured to have an apsidal end.[81] In Cornwall transepts tend to be secondary additions of thirteenth- or fourteenth-century date added to churches of chancel-and-nave plan. Designed as the burial place of wealthy families, the north transept housed a late-thirteenth-century stone effigy of either Sir Reginald Blanchminster or his father Ralph.[82] In 1348, Sir Ralph Blanchminster, the son of Reginald, left 10 marks (£6 13s 4d) towards

73 BL, Add MS 32243, ff.24, 40.

74 We only know about this gift because the parish had to pay for the fur to be ripped out, BL, Add MS 32243, f.39v.

75 Stoate, *Cornwall Subsidies*, p.142; BL, Add MS 32244, f.14v.

76 RIC, Henderson Calendar 66, p.144. The original will does not survive.

77 Payments for knells and the bede roll were made by Lady Arundell, probably Elizabeth their unmarried sister, BL, Add MS 32243, ff.15v, 17v.

78 Waddon-Martyn, 'Our Family History', pp.6–10 shows that Kempthorne was a land agent with links to most of north Cornwall's wealthiest families including the Chamonds, who inherited Tonacombe manor by marriage. Arundell was a cousin of the Arundells of Efford.

79 This is the earliest deed in the Tonacombe archive. See Waddon-Martyn, 'Our Family History', p.7. Kempthorne was under-steward of Launceston priory then. BL, Add MS 32243, f.36v.

80 BL, Add MS 32243, ff.34v, 35v; 32244, ff.15v, 19; 32243, ff.47v, 57.

81 Taylor, *Parish Church of St Andrew*, pp.1–2.

82 Mattingly, *Looking at Cornish Churches*, p.22. Reginald died in 1277×83 and Ralph I in 1267×77; see Goulding, *Blanchminster Records*, pp.11a–15a.

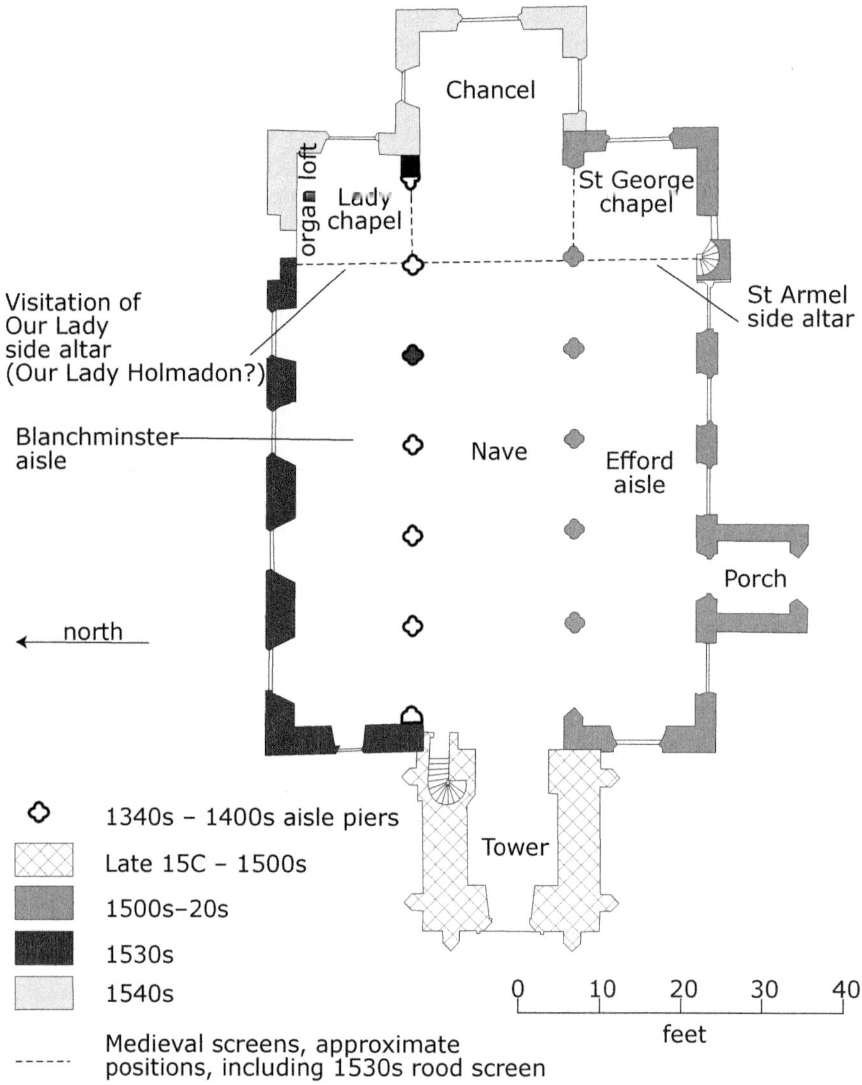

Figure 4 Stratton church, showing the medieval building phases.

the making of a narrow north aisle, and also timber for the lean-to aisle roof. This timber was brought from Downrow Wood in Whitstone parish and Polyphant stone for arcade pillars came from the Lewannick quarry. A pair of vestments was supplied for the altar which stood at the east end of the new aisle in the taller Lady chapel there.[83] This north aisle was later widened and heightened, before being restored to something like its fourteenth-century form in the Victorian period.

[83] Orme, *Cornish Wills*, p.29 and fn.7. An 1870s photos from the RIC photographic collections shows that the late-fourteenth-century pillar and respond of the Lady chapel were taller than those in the rest of the aisle.

Stratton's three-stage tower with set-back buttresses appears to date from the first decade of the sixteenth century on stylistic grounds, but might have been begun at the end of the fifteenth century. The clock was made at a cost of 10s in 1512–13, perhaps just after the tower's completion. Work on pinnacles, an east tower window and a door onto the leads is noted in 1533.[84] An early-sixteenth-century-style west window with an elaborate ogee arch and an integral west door, like that at Lewannick, were replaced with Ham Hill stone replicas in the nineteenth century.[85]

Perpendicular-period aisles with enough height for processions around the church before Sunday mass, and sufficient width to house side altars, came next (see plate 4b). The south chapel and aisle were added in the 1500s–10s, with granite piers of Cornish standard type. The carved abaci to the capitals feature simple flowers like the similarly dated south aisle at St Neot. By 1512, old timber was being sold off, probably from a demolished south transept. In the same year a gallon of wine was given to the bishop of Exeter, Hugh Oldham, when, announced by the vigorous ringing of the church bells, he came in person to bless five altar cloths, a process essential to getting the east end of the church working again. Putting lead on the roofs had to wait until 1514 and work was still going on in 1517 when a thatched shelter was made 'to set the church timber in'. At this date, quantities of lime, two wains or waggon loads of moorstone (south aisle pillars or window frames?), scaffold timber etc. totalled 17s 1d. Included in this sum were 4d for a gate to the moor (Bodmin Moor) and 5d for a supper for those who carried the lime, presumably from Bude. Costs were almost certainly much higher, but the general receivers' accounts, which might have filled out the picture, do not survive for this period. In 1525–26 ridge tiles and slate were bought to repair the church.[86]

The next major phase of building work, including the Perpendicularisation of the north aisle, is much better documented. It coincided with, or was prompted by, the creation of a new rood loft for which the detailed specification survives (see appendix 1). On 29 May 1531, John Daw, carver of Lawhitton, and John Pares, carver of Northlew in Devon, made a contract with Sir John Chamond knight, the vicar and five leading Stratton parishioners. As well as the rood screen, loft and rood or crucifix, the carvers agreed to make two side altars, images, parclose screens, pews, an organ loft and windows to light the rood loft, as well as setting desks or lecterns up in the choir. All this work was to be finished within the space of seven years. Daw and Pares also agreed to post and raise the wall plates and roofs to make a throughway along the loft and to correctly season and bring in timber. Payment was fixed at £2 6s 8d for a foot of work to include side screens etc., Stratton church being just under 49 feet wide. Receipts on the back of the contract suggest that £113 13s 4d was actually paid (the final £6 6s 8d being paid after 10 November 1538).[87]

To secure this contract, Daw and Pares had to find sureties from yeomen neighbours and Richard Daw, carver, probably John's brother, and to make a bond for £200 (roughly double the value of the contract) to ensure satisfactory finishing of

[84] BL, Add MS 32243, ff.2–v, 25–6.

[85] Beacham and Pevsner, *Cornwall*, pp.304, 623 describes Lewannick's tower as late fifteenth to early sixteenth century, while implying, incorrectly, that Stratton's tower is fourteenth century. Taylor, *Parish Church of St Andrew*, pp.6–7 suggests Somerset masons built this tower, as at Probus.

[86] BL, Add MS 32243, ff.2–v, 5v; 7–v; 15.

[87] CRO, P216/25/215. Only five of about 150 dated screens and lofts in Norfolk churches are as late as this, see Cotton, 'Medieval Roodscreens in Norfolk', pp.44–54.

the work.[88] John Daw did the on-site work as he received the regular payments from the general receivers each year. Pares seems to have concentrated on Devon, working at Chagford in 1529 and at Atherington, where part of his rood loft survives, in c.1544–47 or a little earlier.[89]

For each aspect of the Stratton project an appropriate model was identified. Thus St Kew was the model for the screen, loft and side altars; Liskeard for the crucifix 'with Mary and John'; St Columb Major for the parclose screens, and, nearer to home, Week St Mary for the rood loft windows. For the organ loft in the north chapel, Daw and Pares were recommended to take advice from the organmaker. These models and the Stratton screen itself do not survive, but Atherington gives a good idea of what the rood loft at Stratton may have looked like, and screen footings survive at Week St Mary.

A mason called John Rowclyff was employed by Stratton parish at this time to work on the tower and north aisle, but his contract has not survived. It is likely that he came from Kings Nympton, Devon, some 25 miles away.[90] In 1534–35 a moorstone pillar (now part of the war memorial) was brought from Efford. Probably carved on Bodmin Moor like the earlier granite pillars which it resembled, this was most likely carried by wain or waggon to Boscastle to arrive by ship at Efford.[91] It replaced a shorter fourteenth-century Polyphant pier, the second from the east. This new pier was on a level with the fourteenth-century Lady chapel pier and together they raised the height of the arcade enough to allow men to pass freely along the loft, albeit with some ducking of heads.[92] In 1537–40, granite windows with Tintagel rag-slate roofs, iron bars, leading and glazing were made to light the loft and a vice or staircase was squeezed in on the south side, where St Armel's altar stood. Boards to floor the loft were brought from Padstow, but there is no reference to the carving of the rood figures or the statue of St George.[93] The finishing of the side altars is indicated by the arrival of images in 1538–39 and 1541–42. Daw returned briefly in 1543, to mend faults in the rood loft and receive a reward.[94]

Work on creating a wider and higher Perpendicular-style north aisle included John Daw's setting of the north roof in 1534–36. He received two pairs of gloves and £1

[88] CRO, P216/25/216; a Richard Daw of Lezant, carver, made the chancel roof at Altarnun in 1534–36; see, Harvey, *English Medieval Architects*, p.79.

[89] CRO, P216/25/215; Osborne, *Church Wardens' Accounts of St Michael's Church Chagford*, p.122; Williams, 'Medieval English Roodscreens', pp.105, 129, 398. For Atherington see Bond and Camm, *Roodscreens and Roodlofts*, i, plates XXXVB, XXXVII–VIII; ii, plates LXXV–VII, XCIIIB–IV, fig.103 (p.274), p.291; Vallance, *English Church Screens*, plates 107, 244–5; and Gray, *Devon's Fifty Best Churches*, pp.39–41.

[90] Stoate, *Devon Lay Subsidies 1543–5*, pp.77–8. At Biddenham, Bedfordshire, in 1522 a mason came 30 miles to build the north aisle; see Byng, 'The Contract for the North Aisle', p.254.

[91] Transport was always a major cost, with sea and river routes considerably cheaper than overland and Stratton was well placed to take advantage of sea routes. See Coldstream, *Medieval Craftsmen*, pp.42–3.

[92] See the 1870s photograph of the church interior in the RIC collection. At Hartland, Devon, and elsewhere doorways or creep-throughs at loft level were preferred.

[93] St Nicholas' church, Ipswich, Suffolk still has its rood windows. BL, Add MS 32243, ff.30–33v; 32244, ff.8–v; 32243, f.32v. St George's store accounts would have included the latter costs.

[94] BL, Add MS 32244, f.8v; 32243, f.37; 32244, f.13.

for this work so it may have been a separate contract.[95] Rowclyff made a new north window in 1535 and Robert Hayne made the wall over this. Synterns, wooden semi-circular frames used to form arches, were bought second-hand from Kilkhampton and the arches of the arcade remade with new walling above but retaining the old Polyphant piers. In 1536–37 masons were paid a further 12s 3d for making the north aisle.[96] The north aisle pillars and altars were fixed in place and steps were made in the aisles to bring the Lady chapel and St George's chapel up to the same level as the chancel. Six crests or ridge tiles noted in 1539 indicate that the aisle was nearing completion.[97]

Chancel rebuilding came next, as in other Cornish churches at this time.[98] Technically the chancel was the responsibility of the rector of the parish, but following the dissolution of Launceston Priory in 1539, the rectory was in Henry VIII's hands with John Kempthorne and Thomas Arundell collecting the great tithes. This explains why, in 1541, John Marys rode to Exeter to meet the king's collectors about the chancel. The original Lady chapel and chancel were demolished, and stone from the former was carried to the church house for potential re-use.[99] Kempthorne brought the king's contribution of £5 6s 8d in 1544, while Thomas Arundell gave 26s 8d the following year.[100] New masons were chosen, one Stawford, probably from Devon, and George Jule from Poughill, who both also worked on Poughill tower at this time.[101] Stones were drawn from Bodmin Moor, lime came via Bideford, St Dominick and Launceston, laths from Holsworthy and lead from Hartland, perhaps recycled from the former abbey there.[102] Floors were tiled, the tiles perhaps coming from Barnstaple by sea via Bude. Thomas Hewett, a Bodmin glazier, glazed three chancel windows having put in the ironwork first, and John Cholwyll made the chancel roof. Plastering of the chancel went on throughout 1545, with a licence to carry granite from the moor bought then.[103] Like many Cornish and west Devon parishes, Stratton was still building its church well into the Reformation period.

Catholic Stratton

Clergy and services for the dead

In 1512 Stratton church had five altars served by a vicar, at least one or two other priests and a clerk. Three vicars cover the period of these accounts, but the first two were probably non-resident. Richard Carlyon was vicar for almost fifty years from 1492 to 1541, Gerens John from 1541 to 1556 and William Martyn from 1556 to

[95] BL, Add MS 32244, ff.4v, 6; 32243, f.29. Three roof bosses with heads of young men in the north aisle may be Daw's work, while similar, but less well-carved, versions occur in Poughill's north chapel.

[96] BL, Add MS 32243, f.29; 32244, ff.5, 6; 32243, f.30v. Victorian windows in distinctive South Hams style may be copies of Rowclyff's window. See Colvin, *Essays in Architectural History*, pp.22–51.

[97] BL, Add MS 32243, ff.29, 33. In 1536 work was also being carried out on the nave roof.

[98] This work was intended to create a uniform east end of three gables with similar width, height and windows.

[99] BL, Add MS 32244, ff.11, 12, 13, 14v.

[100] BL, Add MS 32244, ff.14, 15v.

[101] BL, Add MS 32244, f.14v; CRO, P192/5/1, p.72.

[102] BL, Add MS 32243, f.40v; 32244, ff.15, 16. Recycling material from former religious houses is noted elsewhere; see Duffy, *Voices of Morebath*, p.90.

[103] BL, Add MS 32244, ff.14v, 16. For Hewett see Mattingly, 'Who Made the St Neot Windows?', pp.227–32.

1581/2. The first two were career clergy who held other livings and were successively resident canons of Glasney College near Penryn.[104] William Martyn, the last vicar, was Carlyon's curate at Stratton in the 1530s and deputised for Gerens John in 1548.[105] He was then appointed vicar of Linkinhorne in 1550 by the Chamonds and six years later exchanged this living for Stratton.[106]

Stratton's vicar was responsible for the annual recitation of the bede roll from the pulpit and choreographed requiem masses and annual obits or mind days. References to the black suit of vestments or hiring the ornaments of the church indicate requiem masses. A priest, Thomas Constabell, asked for bells as well as ornaments in 1512–13, while John Moreman, rector of Menheniot and canon of Exeter, paid for the black suit in 1534–35, perhaps for a Hartland relative's funeral.[107] My Lady Parcyvale's mind day in 1513 involved four priests with bread and ale given by the High Cross wardens.[108] Sir John Chamond knight was similarly remembered or minded a year after his death in 1545, and a St Armel obit was held on 16 August in the following year. Two parish benefactors, John Trenger and William Nordon, were commemorated in a more regular way in 1522–23 and until 1547 in Nordon's case.[109]

Chaplains and curates included William Martyn, later the vicar, and Walter Dromond; both read the bede roll on one occasion. Nicholas Gyst and John Lyll may also have started their careers at Stratton. Lyll was later chaplain to Dame Jane Chamond and vicar of Plymtree, Devon. In 1522–23 he put his parents' names on Stratton bede roll, paid for his mother's burial in the church, left 20s to the church when he died in 1554 and was honoured with a knell. He also claimed cousinship with Nicholas Judd of Stratton and Sir John Judd, vicar of Launcells.[110] Other clergy noted in the accounts mostly served neighbouring parishes. At the end of the period Sir William Palmer acquitted the parishioners concerning an Act to protect the cap-making trade and kept the registers in 1577–78. The following year, the parish was visited by Mr Johnes, a minister, who preached twice and borrowed money, which he swiftly repaid.[111]

Clerks are not noted in the early accounts, but their presence is attested by frequent references to the holy water bucket from which they sprinkled the congregation. Rochets (a type of surplice) were given for one Palmar in 1532–33 and for a bedesman in 1556–57 so that they could assist the vicar at services. References to the bedesman continue well into Elizabeth's reign. John Bedner is named as the old parish clerk in 1561–62, and his successor William Orchard was responsible for the clock which was then new-made. A clerk's chamber is noted by this time.[112] After the Reformation, the new position of choir-master came into being as communal singing

[104] Peter, *Glasney*, pp.99, 165, 170–1.

[105] RIC, Henderson MS 10, p.359 and possibly BL, Add MS 32243, f.24; 32244, f.19.

[106] The Clergy of the Church of England Database, 1540–1835, www.kcl.uk/artshums/depts/history/research/proj/clergy.aspx (accessed 2 February 2017) for this and other entries.

[107] Duffy, *Voices of Morebath*, pp.37–8. BL, Add MS 32243, ff.3, 26v; Rose-Troup, *The Western Rebellion*, p.107.

[108] BL, Add MS 32243, f.3. For Lady Parcyvale's Dick Whittington-like rise see Chynoweth et al., *Survey of Cornwall*, ff.119r–v, Hull, 'Endowment of a Grammar School', p.25.

[109] BL, Add MS 32243, f.40; 32244, f.17; 32243, ff.12 onwards.

[110] Gyst was vicar of St Winnow 1538–45; RIC, Henderson MS 66, p.144; BL, Add MS 32243, ff.12, 53–v; TNA, PROB 11/36.

[111] BL, Add MS 32243, ff.98v, 101; CRO, P216/25/208, ff.26v, 33v, 34v and /224.

[112] BL, Add MS 32243, ff.24, 57v, 65; CRO, P216/25/208, ff.8, 13v, 28v.

became established. A 'querman' to help the choir is noted at Stratton as early as 1562–63, with Thomas White the younger holding this post in 1571–73. Singing boys helped the choir at Christmas, Easter and Whitsun and by 1576–77 were known as singing scholars.[113]

Guilds, stores, parochial organisation and chantries

Stratton had at least six guilds or fraternities, dedicated to All Hallows, St Andrew, Christ, the High Cross store, Our Lady and St Thomas in the period 1530–47. The total may have been higher as organisations known as stores sometimes had associated guilds, just as the High Cross did. At Stratton there were four other stores, dedicated to St Armel, St George, Our Lady Holmadon and the Trinity.[114] The Trinity store may date back to 1348 when Sir Ralph Blanchminster left money for two priests to celebrate for his soul, one being for the Trinity. The earliest identified guild, in the absence of any surviving fourteenth-century guild returns, is the fraternity of the store of the High Cross, which existed by 1486. The store of St Armel, a Breton saint, which may well have included a guild, was founded shortly before 1512.[115] A process of amalgamation before the Reformation is suggested by references to a joint store of Our Lady and St George in the 1540s. There was probably one guild or store for every forty adults at Stratton, though most guilds only had between twelve and twenty-four male and female members.[116] There was also a Robin Hood group and another two men were known as the Sextons, probably raising funds for the gravedigger's salary.

Three more single-gender – and in two cases age-specific – groups are commonly found elsewhere, namely those for young men, maidens and wives of the parish. Young people's groups for those aged about fourteen to twenty-six were like the Scouts, Guides or Sea Cadets, while wives' groups can be seen as the medieval equivalent of Women's Institutes. At Stratton, Our Lady's Maidens occur with young women as wardens, while St Armel's store may have been the young men's group. The wives have left no trace in surviving records, unlike at Poughill, which also had a young men's store dedicated to St Mark and St Anthony.[117] Robin Hood activities there and at Stratton involved both young men and maidens.

All these stores, guilds and groups raised money for the benefit of Stratton church, or their part of it. They spent this on lighting candles before images or altars, helping with repairs and rebuilding, and giving vestments and ornaments. Guild members expected prayers to be said for their souls in return.[118] Church ales were fund-raising and communal feasting opportunities and the High Cross ale at Whitsun was not the only one. The lack of reference to a brewing kettle in surviving accounts strongly suggests that another store or guild was responsible for that.[119]

113 Gant, *O Sing unto the Lord*, pp.108ff. for context; BL, Add MS 32243, ff.68v, 85, 87–v, 98v.

114 The claim that there were no guilds at Morebath may need reviewing in light of this, though single-gender groups are not guilds; see Duffy, *Voices of Morebath*, pp.26, 66.

115 Orme, *Cornish Wills*, p.29; CRO, P216/25/10 and Goulding, *Blanchminster Records*, pp.4–6; BL, Add MS 32243, f.2v.

116 Mattingly, 'Medieval Parish Guilds', pp.295, 308.

117 CRO P192/5/1, pp.17, 49 wives' money, 1539.

118 Mattingly, 'Medieval Parish Guilds', p.290.

119 Rogation Sunday drinkings (appendix 4), weddings, wakes, guild feasts etc. At Chagford the brewing kettle belonged to the Blessed Virgin Mary store in the churchyard chapel, Osborne, *Church Wardens' Accounts of St Michael's Church Chagford*, p.26.

The chantry chapel to the north of the chancel housed the Our Lady guild and probably the patronal guild of St Andrew and the store of Trinity, too. The Our Lady Holmadon store, and perhaps the Our Lady Maidens, presumably looked after the Visitation altar whose back was the rood screen. On the opposite side of the church, St George's store had its altar in the south chapel, with St Armel's altar just outside the rood screen in the south aisle. The High Cross guild and store focused on keeping candles, including the Pascal candle, lit in honour of the crucifix on the rood beam or loft. The All Hallows, Christ and St Thomas guilds may have supplied candles before nave images or shared space in any of the four chapels. It is also possible that Christ's guild funded an additional Friday mass.[120]

All these groups accounted to the general receivers annually, but only if they were in profit. The High Cross wardens' accounts show how this worked. On the day of the general receivers' account, usually in October or November but in one case on 1 January of the next year, the High Cross wardens handed over all the money that 'remained clear' from their previous year's account. They usually received back a small amount of up to 10s to start off the next year. Only in 1536 and 1547 were the High Cross wardens not included in the general receivers' accounts and this was because their surpluses were only 18d and 14d respectively as a result of the group's funding of the rood loft and chancel. Similarly, the absence of other guilds and stores from the general receivers' accounts at different times may be due to overspend not guild failure. Thus in 1539 St George's store's failure to account is likely to be due to the high costs of providing a mounted image of St George for the new loft.[121]

A hierarchy of guilds and stores is often evident due to the competitive nature of such organisations. Taking average annual profit recorded in the general receivers' accounts as an indicator, St Armel's store was the wealthiest with an average of over £3 16s per year. Next came the store (and guild) of High Cross with over 34s. St George's store, Our Lady Holmadon store and the guild of Our Lady all averaged between 20s and 25s profit per year, while the guilds of St Andrew, Christ and All Hallows, Trinity store, Our Lady Maidens and the St Thomas guild were in the range 10s to 17s. Probably not in the competitive running at all, were the Sextons with an average annual profit of only 2s 4d.[122] The poorest of the stores was that of Trinity, which by this date had only one warden, and the amalgamation of the St George and Our Lady Holmadon stores failed to raise St George's profits.[123]

In Stratton, almost a hundred surnames can be linked with store, stock or guild office. Between 1512 and 1581 over ninety-five men served in more than one office, while about eighty men served only once, like most maidens. In eighteen of the seventy-five cases where office-holding began pre-1548, the first office held was as warden of St Armel's store. William Wyll alias Hele was eighteen or nineteen when he took on this role in 1544–45 and William Hore may have been as young as fourteen

[120] Wolborough church, Devon (colour plate 4b) was a fully compartmentalised church, but Stratton's side altars were probably more like Ranworth, Norfolk. Blake et al., 'From Popular Devotion to Resistance', pp.176–7; Snell, *Chantry Certificates*, p.32.

[121] Rider and horse were removed from the loft eight or nine years later, BL, Add MS 32243, ff.44v, 48. At least one horse survived into the eighteenth century, Pool, 'St Issey', p.366.

[122] Bainbridge, *Gilds in the Medieval Countryside*, pp.125–6. Abnormal years where no profit was made are omitted from the calculations. However, if the missing years are included this does not significantly change the order.

[123] This store's failure coincided with the temporary loss of its side altar when the Lady chapel was demolished and rebuilt.

when he served in 1536–37, but each may have been paired up with an older warden like thirty-one-year-old Walter Rose who accounted for St Armel's in 1537–38. From being St Armel warden, the next step in parochial responsibility was to become a Sexton, guild or store warden, then High Cross or churchwarden and finally general receiver. Those truly addicted to office-holding might take on any of these roles again. Fourteen men were Sextons first and their ages range between twenty-five and thirty-eight, with High Cross wardens generally in their thirties or forties and general receivers in their forties to fifties.[124] Men who held office only once tended to be either very rich or poor, with nine of the ninety-seven Stratton taxpayers in 1543 being single-office holders. Most of the single-office holders were assessed for tax on £1 and none on more than £3 apart from Sir John Chamond knight who had lands worth £100. This contrasts with fifty-four taxpayers who held more than one office, with half assessed on £5 of goods or more.[125] Our Lady Maidens came from the frequent office-holding families in seventeen cases out of twenty-six, including a maid-servant, with four others not having recognisable Stratton names at all.

Stratton also had a north chantry chapel with its own chalice and priest. Probably dedicated to St Mary, this chantry was founded by William Nordon of Hele in 1476. Part of the priest's salary came from the 33s rent from Hele lands, and Nordon made the vicar John Langeston and five others feoffees. New feoffees were appointed in 1492. In 1523, after Nordon's death, a mind day or obit was annually celebrated in Stratton church by the vicar until the chantry's dissolution in 1548.[126]

Paraphernalia of Catholic worship: church plate, vestments, books

Stratton church had at least three chalices at any one time, though only one is noted in the 1559 inventory (see appendix 3.1). Chalices occur intermittently in the accounts, usually when they were blessed or mended. An interesting entry in 1533–34 relates to changing a chalice, and a case to house the new chalice was bought then for 3d.[127] Another chalice was given by Nicholas Gyst, vicar of St Winnow, in 1539–40, but the parish had to pay a bequest of 6s 8d to Poughill church on his behalf and 8d to those who brought the chalice.[128] Other church plate in the 1559 inventory included a ship for incense that cost 4s 8d in 1531–32, a copper-gilt cross and staff, mended in 1541–42, and a pair of candlesticks.[129] Marian replacement items included a basin, censer, pyx and lantern.

In contrast to the lost chalices, Stratton church still had at least eight sets or suits of vestments in 1559 (appendix 3.1). Suits of vestments usually comprised an alb or undergarment, chasuble, cope and stole. The black funeral vestments, including two copes, were in existence by 1512 and in 1514 the blue satin set, possibly satin of Bruges, is noted.[130] White damask vestments first appear in 1531 when mended by

124 For ages see appendix 4.

125 Stoate, *Cornwall Subsidies*, p.142.

126 Goulding, *Blanchminster Records*, pp.23–4; BL, Add MS 32243, f.12; Snell, *Chantry Certificates*, p.47.

127 Snell, *Edwardian Inventories*, pp.50, 54, notes the return of the two spare chalices in 1554; BL, Add MS 32243, ff.25v–26. Lanivet's leather chalice case is embossed with cross hatching, foliage and Gothic lettering and is on display at the Royal Cornwall Museum.

128 BL, Add MS 32244, f.10; CRO P192/5/1, p.52.

129 BL, Add MS 32243, ff.23v, 36v.

130 BL, Add MS 32243, ff.2, 5. In a poor parish it took years to get a black suit of vestments. See Duffy, *Voices of Morebath*, pp.37–9.

Hugh Courter, a Launceston tailor. New vestments were made after the finishing of the rood loft and remodelling of the east end. One set, given by Master Thomas Arundell in 1539–40, was brought from Exeter and blessed, but detail is lacking.[131] Master Chamond gave one of his gowns in 1544, probably for St George's chapel vestments after the fur had been removed, and the completion of the chancel and Lady chapel in 1545–46 merited a red velvet set. These cost £7 4s 8d including 24s 4d for two yards of material and 4d for the vestment maker's bargain or contract.[132] Other vestments listed in 1559 include sets of damask, Lewkes gold, velvet of unspecified colour and yellow silk with a matching altar frontal and side curtains. Seven surplices and four rochets were for clergy use, but there were only three more altar frontals, two of silk and one red. There were also nine altar towels which were laid on top of the altar.[133] Also for altar use were seven corporal cloth cases with three kerchers to wipe the chalice clean.

The entry for a pall for the hearse in the 1559 inventory could relate to two new biers made in 1540, while two cross banners with a streamer of silk are suggestive of St George. Banners were used for processing around the church before Sunday mass as well as for parish processions. One banner had a new staff in 1555.[134] The inventory also listed two houseling towels – long cloths used to catch crumbs of host at the annual Easter communion when Stratton's four hundred communicants knelt at the chancel step. A pair of font cloths were probably used at baptisms, a sacrament cloth covered the pyx, and the desk, rood and Lent cloths were all brand new.

Items not included in the 1559 inventory were the cruets and stand, the holy water bucket, the lych bell, the portable Easter sepulchre with its wooden taper frame, candle stands, a stone lamp possibly of cresset type like the one at Marhamchurch, the canopy over the altar, images and image cloths. Books are also left out, but the accounts show that these had included graduals or grails, a legend, manual, mass book, procession book and hymnal.[135]

Fixtures included a pulpit by 1545 with seges or seats first appearing a little earlier.[136] Five seges or pews were part of the carver John Daw's 1531 contract. Three were to be in the south aisle: one by the chancel door for a woman (Dame Jane Chamond?) and two outside the rood screen. The other two were to be made in the north aisle by the ceilure over the rood loft. 'Seges in the chancel' followed in 1546 with 'my Lady's pew', and a desk or lectern and others are noted in 1566–67, 1571–72 and 1580.[137]

Some thirty-five bench ends, all of standard type, survive. Most have symbols of the Passion of Christ or sacred monograms of Jesus and the Virgin Mary, sometimes crowned. St Andrew's saltire cross appears eight times, as well as a ship's rudder and a merchant's mark perhaps of the Taylour family. Heraldic shields relate to Arundell ancestors. Seven bench ends have initials, four being TM; if for Thomas

131 BL, Add MS 32243, ff.21v, 35v. Liturgical colours were not fixed and the best or newest vestments and altar cloths were used for the high altar and feast days. See Barton, 'The Ornaments of the Altar', pp.39–40 for use of York.

132 BL, Add MS 32243, f.39v; 32244, f.17.

133 Barton, 'The Ornaments of the Altar', pp.31–2

134 BL, Add MS 32243, ff.34v, 55.

135 See Wordsworth and Littlehales, *Old Service-Books.*

136 BL, Add MS 32243, f.40.

137 Appendix 1; BL, Add MS 32243, ff.42, 75, 76, 84v (for the eight men); CRO, P216/25/208, f.35v.

Marys rather than Thomas Martyn, these may be of 1530s date. A single bench with the initials NG might relate to Nicholas Gyst who provided plates and nails for the 1546 pews, while two with Andrew Sangwen's initials might be 1566–72 pews.

Bells and organs

Four bells were recorded at Stratton in May 1549–50 in an inventory taken by Sir Richard Grenville knight and Richard Chamond esquire.[138] Two sacring bells, a lych bell and a bedesman's bell also occur. Thought to ward off thunder and used to ring funeral knells, bells constantly required repair or new bell ropes. A reference to bell money in the 1535–36 general receivers' account could suggest a new bell or the recasting of an old one. The great bell was recast at Stratton in 1557–59 and a further bell in 1564–66 by John White, perhaps the Bristol bellfounder. Sums of £13 and £8 4s 3d are noted in the general receivers' accounts for this work and included the cost of making a thatched house for the bellfounder to work in.[139] As late as 1578–79 White was employed again to recast a bell for £15 13s 10d. This time a separate bell account was made, starting with 6d for a dinner for the bellfounder on Trinity Sunday, and a list of receipts including 16d from John Yeo for making an indenture which he 'gave towards the bell'.[140]

The organs are not referred to until 1525–26 when glue was bought to mend them. The 1531 rood loft contract stated that Stratton's organs were to be moved to a separate loft or stage attached to the rood screen on the north side of the Lady chapel. Glue to repair the organ and 'notis' occur in the accounts in 1545–46.[141] The organs continued in use well into the reign of Queen Elizabeth.

The Reformation in Stratton parish, 1534–81

In 1534–35, soon after becoming the archbishop of Canterbury, Thomas Cranmer held a 'metropolitical' visitation over the whole of southern England. Stratton wardens' expenses for attending came to 14d and the neighbouring parish of Poughill paid 2s 4d for this and a bishop's visitation.[142] Normally churchwardens attended only one visitation a year, generally that of the archdeacon, but from 1533 onwards 'churchwardens had repeatedly to receive or attend upon representatives of Crown, bishops and archdeacons who instructed and cross examined them'.[143] Two or more meetings a year were now the norm at Stratton as elsewhere. Archdeacon's visitations were often held at Launceston, though after 1550 Week St Mary and Bodmin were also used. Trips to Exeter, Honiton and even London had to be made. Such coercive and heavy-handed governance, combined with very high levels of taxation, led to eventual compliance with most of the changes introduced by the Reformation.

138 Snell, *Edwardian Inventories*, p.6.

139 BL, Add MS 32244, f.5v; CRO, P216/25/1, ff.4v–5v, 12v, 13v. John White of Bristol, bellfounder, occurs in Launceston accounts for 1543–44, Peter, *The Histories of Launceston and Dunheved*, p.185.

140 CRO, P216/25/1, 32, 33.

141 BL, Add MS 32243, ff.15, 41v and appendix 1, p.212.

142 Duffy, *Voices of Morebath*, p.83 described this as 'a cloud on their traditionalist horizon no bigger than a man's hand', but at Stratton it seems to mark the start of the Reformation. Part of a visitation enforcing royal supremacy, this event has been largely ignored by Reformation historians, BL, Add MS 32243, f.27; CRO, P192/5/1, p.32.

143 Hutton, 'The Local Impact', p.115.

Around the time of Cranmer's visitation, the Hartland-born vicar of Menheniot, Master Dr John Moreman, paid 4d for the use of Stratton's black vestments for a requiem mass. High Cross wardens had to make answer to the king's commissioners at Launceston for the church land and in the resulting *Valor Ecclesiasticus* of 1535 Stratton vicarage was assessed at £10 11s 8d.[144] But prayers for the dead and funeral knells continued to be said or rung and Catholic religious life continued.[145]

Saints' days were reduced in number in 1536 with dedication feasts moved to 1 October and holidays only on major saints' days. Basic prayers were now said in English not Latin. Stratton and Poughill's rectorial tithes were granted by the last prior of Launceston in 1537 on a forty-year lease to two Morwenstow gentlemen, Thomas Arundell and John Kempthorne.[146] In 1538 parish registers were introduced, causing alarm as 'the people in Devonshire and Cornwall … fear it means increased taxation'.[147] Injunctions passed in 1538 banned the cult of St Thomas Becket and the veneration of saints' images and relics. These injunctions were intended to introduce a Bible into every parish and to extinguish most side lights in churches, leaving only altar, rood loft and Easter sepulchre lights burning.[148] The guild of St Thomas at Stratton may have reinvented itself as the guild of the Apostle. A further injunction in 1541 led to the purchase of a Bible costing 6s 6d. In 1542–43 the Bible was chained to a desk or lectern.[149] Lights which had burnt at Easter and to a lesser extent Christmas were certainly extinguished at Stratton as payments for wax, once averaging 6s–8s a year, plummeted to 8d. For the next eight years payments for wax never rose above 4s 6d. The first phase of decluttering was at an end, and, as Hutton suggests, was not entirely unwelcome to parishioners keen to find places for new gifts in the church.[150]

Contrary to experiences elsewhere, two new images were brought to Stratton church in 1538–39 and 1541–42 despite the 1538 injunctions. As the latter was an image of Our Lady, these are likely to have been the images commissioned in 1531 from the carvers John Daw and John Pares.[151] St Armel's obit was celebrated by the vicar on 16 August 1545 for the first and last time, in front of this new statue, vestments continued to be made and lead for the chancel roof may have come from the dissolved abbey of Hartland a little earlier.[152] However, in 1545–46 Nicholas Judd and Richard Cory bought or sold unspecified silver plate for £6 2s 3d, suggesting that the parish was getting rid of its surplus church goods.[153]

References to parish armour and mustering also begin at this time, as at Morebath, and in 1546–47 two payments of a dole, related to a royal levy of November 1545,

[144] Moreman was imprisoned in the Tower of London for his Catholic traditionalist beliefs before the 1549 rebellion, Rose-Troup, *The Western Rebellion*, pp.107–9. BL, Add MS 32243, ff.26v, 28v; for *Valor Ecclesiasticus* see Polsue, *Complete Parochial History*, iv, p.163.

[145] Whiting, *The Blind Devotion of the People*, and Orme, *Cornwall and the Cross*, p.132, disappointingly downplay this vibrancy of traditional religion.

[146] Waddon-Martyn, 'Our Family History', p.7.

[147] *L&P*, 1539, I, no. 815, letter of 20 April from Sir Piers Edgcumbe to Cromwell.

[148] Orme, *Cornwall and the Cross*, p.136 suggests this impacted more in Cornwall where there were so many unique saints. Hutton, 'The Local Impact', p.116.

[149] BL, Add MS 32244, f.15v; 32243, ff.36v, 38.

[150] Hutton, 'The Local Impact', p.116.

[151] BL, Add MS 32244, f.8v; 32243, f.37 and appendix 1. Hutton, 'The Local Impact', p.117 missed these Stratton examples.

[152] BL, Add MS 32244, ff.15, 17.

[153] BL, Add MS 32244, f.16v.

helped finance Henry VIII's wars with Scotland and France.[154] By contrast, 'the affairs of the king' which brought the mayor of Launceston and others to Stratton in 1543–44 probably relate to nothing more sinister than chancel ownership, the crown having taken over the role of rector when Launceston Priory was dissolved in 1539.[155]

The 'final, panic-induced spate of registrations' on the Stratton bede roll in 1547 was not due to a premonition of where the Reformation was leading, but to plague.[156] There were 28 deaths in May, 38 in June and 87 in July, a total of 153 Stratton people in all, of whom at least 36 were recorded on the bede roll. Taking funeral knells, burial in the church and bequests as evidence, 72 deaths of better-off individuals are shown in the High Cross wardens' accounts at this time, though few are specifically named.[157] Poughill, Stratton's northerly neighbour, noted 20 deaths in its parish register of 1547–48 rather than its usual tally of between two and six deaths. Death was clearly the most pressing concern at Stratton at this time. The general receivers did not account that year until 1 January 1548, rather than in early November 1547 as would have been normal.[158]

The image of St George, part of an ensemble on the rood loft put up as recently as the late 1530s, was taken down at a cost of 4d in 1547, before the king's visitors arrived at Week St Mary in the autumn.[159] In the same accounts for 1547–48, the amount spent on wax was back to pre-1536 levels, but the parish failed to give enough wax for the tapers. Only 1s 10d was spent in 1548–49, and then nothing. St George's horse, the rood and two standings for other images, probably the attendant figures of St John and St Mary from the rood, came down immediately after a new order was sent in February 1548.[160] Stratton's guilds, stores, obits and lamp came to an end at Easter 1548, with only the High Cross store and Sextons continuing to account.[161]

At this critical juncture, there were major problems with Stratton's middle-aged vicar, Gerens John. Shortly before 5 February 1548, the large sum of 28s was paid for a compulsior and other charges about the vicar. Compulsiors were last-resort documents issued by bishops which compelled clergy to serve their cures on pain of suspension from office.[162] Gerens John had failed to hold the annual obit for William Nordon or read the bede roll, a high spot of the ritual year at Stratton, and his curate William Martyn was a late substitute.[163] The context for this odd behaviour was the

[154] BL, Add MS 32244, ff.17–v shows that Stratton paid at least 38s towards this tax, see Duffy, *Voices of Morebath*, pp.112–13. Stratton also sent soldiers, see p.160.

[155] Peter, *The Histories of Launceston and Dunheved*, p.185.

[156] Whiting, *The Blind Devotion of the People*, p.32.

[157] Toms, *Stratton Parish Registers*, p.viii (the originals are lost); BL, Add MS 32243, ff.44v–5v. On the reliability of knells as indicators of epidemics see Dils, *Reading St Laurence Churchwardens' Accounts*, p.xviii.

[158] CRO, P192/1/1; BL, Add MS 23244, f.17v.

[159] BL, Add MS 32243, f.46v; 32244, f.19. The king's visitors were at Week St Mary in autumn 1547, BL, Add MS 32244, f.19.

[160] As the taking down of the horse is the first entry in the accounts beginning on 6 February 1548, the word immediately seems appropriate, BL, Add MS 32243, f.48.

[161] Snell, *Chantry Certificates*, p.3.

[162] Snell, *Chantry Certificates*, p.37 gives Gerens age as forty-six. BL, Add MS 32243, f.46v and Dunstan, *The Register of Edmund Lacy*, p.6 for an example of a compulsior.

[163] BL, Add MS 32244, f.19.

impending closure of Glasney College, Penryn, where Gerens John was a resident canon. His salary there was between £10 2s 2d and £11 – rather more than the £5 he had in 'other promotions', probably meaning his Stratton salary less the cost of supplying a curate there. On 1 April 1548, Glasney College was dissolved and Gerens secured his pension of £6 13s 4d.[164] Four days later a rebellion started in Helston provoked by confiscations of church plate.

Recorded as the 'besynys that was in the west part' at Stratton and as 'the commosyon tyme' at St Thomas's Launceston, the Helston riots followed the murder of William Body, archdeacon of Cornwall, on 5 April 1548.[165] A general call up of men in east Cornwall and west Devon followed on 8 April 1548 and ten Stratton men rode west with the sheriff. Led by a former Robin Hood, John Marys aged forty-five, and thirty-five-year-old Richard Cory, the rest of the company were all young men. John Judd and Richard Olyver had recently been St Armel wardens and neither they nor Richard Call (smith), Thomas Martyn, John Davy (workman and pauper later), Roger Mayow, Robert Yeo and Nicholas Bond (mason) are noted in the 1543 tax returns. Each was paid a salary of 2s 8d (or 4d a day) with bread and cheese and provided with a horse.[166] They probably returned to Stratton around 16 April, possibly minus Nicholas Bond's horse.[167]

The company's paymaster was Master Thomas Arundell, and William Grove and Stephen Daw provided bread and cheese. The real causes of the rebellion were not widely known at this stage and serving the prince was the purpose of all the mustering and buying of parish armour.[168] Each parish was expected to provide its quota and this was a struggle for some east Cornwall parishes who resorted to selling off church plate.[169]

Commissions for the confiscation of chantry lands were granted on 17 April 1548 to John Grenville and others. At Stratton 16d expenses relating to 'the feoffers lands' in Master Richard Chamond's company and 'other of the parish' must relate to this.[170] The commissioners found certain lands called Helyn or Hele and claimed, incorrectly, that the churchwardens were the feoffees. Chantry lands were said to be worth 33s in rent and, after allowances, 30s 9d. There were also 6 ounces of plate, probably representing a chalice for the Lady chapel altar and this may well be the chalice and other stuff Master John Grenville demanded later that year. Richard Cory, one of the Stratton ten who had ridden west in 1548, was sent to Buckland Abbey to appease Grenville.[171] In 1548–49 the church house was used as a school and the schoolmaster could well have been the former chantry priest.[172]

[164] Snell, *Chantry Certificates*, pp.37, 39.

[165] BL, Add MS 32244, f.19; CRO, P221/5/2, p.30. Rose-Troup, *The Western Rebellion*, pp.75–80; Fletcher and MacCulloch, *Tudor Rebellions*, pp.52–3.

[166] BL, Add MS 32244, f.19v, Rose-Troup, *The Western Rebellion*, pp.82–3.

[167] He received compensation two years later, BL, Add MS 32243, f.50v.

[168] BL, Add MS 32244, f.19; Whiting, *The Blind Devotion of the People*, p.76 refers to those who put down the rebellion, rather unfairly, as loyalists, but as he shows on p.190 John Judd was a Bible-owning Protestant later.

[169] Snell, *Edwardian Inventories*, p.xix.

[170] Snell, *Chantry Certificates*, pp.2–3; BL, Add MS 32243, f.48.

[171] Snell, *Chantry Certificates*, p.47; BL, Add MS 32243, f.48v.

[172] BL, Add MS 32243, f.47v. The move of the Week St Mary chantry school to Launceston at this time may have created an opportunity, Hull, 'Endowment of a Grammar School', p.30.

Meanwhile Gerens John, the vicar, returned to the parish with two grail or mass books, perhaps ex-Glasney College, which the parish duly bought for 16s 8d.[173] These came from Penryn via Bodmin. A book called *The Paraphrases of Erasmus* was also bought for 12s. Pieces of velvet were sold to Master Thomas Arundell and the schoolmaster, and the rood or crucifix came down with the side altar pictures. Richard Cory is noted as buying half the pictures for 2s 8d in 1548–49.[174] Sir Richard Grenville knight and Richard Chamond, Stratton's resident esquire, confiscated the remaining plate at Stratton, apart from one chalice, on 6 May 1549. Making the king's inventory cost 7d including the paper and the list included two chalices (from the St Armel and St George altars?), a pyx and four bells. Eight cloths that had covered images during Lent were sold in 1549.[175]

The Prayer Book or Western Rebellion began at Bodmin on 6 June and continued until about 16 August 1549. Unlike at Morebath in Devon, there is no positive evidence of Stratton parishioners joining the rebels, though this is very likely. The rood or crucifix, recently taken down, was certainly set up again as an act of defiance during the rebellion.[176] Some Stratton parishioners probably knew Hartland-born Dr John Moreman whose release from prison was one of the rebels' demands. Then in 1549–50 the parish applied for a pardon.[177] After the rebellion Stratton was singled out as a place of punishment, due to its status as the major market town. John Moke made the gallows, probably around the market cross, and Thomas Clarke helped put them up. According to a later account, Simon Mourton, the vicar of Poundstock, was hung from the 'cross' by Stratton market-house on 13 October 1549 and left there for six days.[178]

This rebellion had other repercussions and it is at this point that the Stratton accounts briefly adopt the colloquial tone of the Morebath ones. Thus in 1549–50 William Rodde was paid 20s compensation 'for a mare, which the parish was content to pay for the mare if he had not his mare again' and for that 'he went to Launceston to have his mare and could not have her, his expenses and labour was 8d'.[179] In 1549–50 a payment of 2d was made for lacing the communion book and for three new books noted for matins and evensong, and matins in English.[180] The clappers were removed in autumn 1549 from all but the little bell as punishment, as elsewhere in the diocese. The churchwardens had to go to Week St Mary in 1551–52 to buy them back. The upside of this imposed silence was that payments for bell maintenance at

[173] BL, Add MS 32244, f.19; Wordsworth and Littlehales, *Old Service-Books*, pp.9, 203–6. Grails were among the books defaced or abolished in 1549–50, so Stratton got little use out of them.

[174] BL, Add MS 32244, f.19; 32243, ff.47v, 48v; 32244, f.19v.

[175] Snell, *Edwardian Inventories*, pp.5–6; BL, Add MS 32243, f.49. There is a similar entry at Boxford. See Northeast, *Boxford Churchwardens' Accounts*, p.xv.

[176] Fletcher and MacCulloch, *Tudor Rebellions*, pp.53–4, 59, 63; Duffy, *Voices of Morebath*, pp.127–41; Hutton, *The Rise and Fall of Merry England*, p.86. BL, Add MS 32243, f.49.

[177] For Moreman's Hartland origins see Rose-Troup, *The Western Rebellion*, p.107. BL, Add MS 32243, f.49.

[178] BL, Add MS 32244, f.20 and 1753 account quoted in Pool, 'Stratton', p.502. The latter seems to be based on the no longer extant Stratton parish register as it also notes Mourton's burial date as 18 October 1549. Rose-Troup, *The Western Rebellion*, pp.337, 499 included Simon Mourton among the rebels on the basis of a London ballad. She also noted a change of vicar at Poundstock by 16 January 1550.

[179] BL, Add MS 32243, f.49; Duffy, *Voices of Morebath*, pp.xiii–xiv.

[180] The English Prayer Book, BL, Add MS 32243, ff.49–v.

Stratton fell from 10s 3d per year to only 8d and no new bell ropes were needed until Mary came to the throne.[181]

Profits from church ales also plummeted from a few pounds a year to 13s 4d in 1550–51 due to the abolition of the practice. But unlike in most other places, church ales did not disappear altogether from Stratton. Sales of the Lent cloth, the great sepulchre cloth, four old painted cloths, two blue cloths, a rood cloth and other unspecified old cloths occur in the same account. The eight buyers had links to the St Andrew's and Christ's guilds and the St Armel and Our Lady Holmadon stores. Altars were pulled down and the stone sold for 4s 4d, the same as the resale value of the rood cloth. The church was whitewashed throughout and medieval wall paintings obscured.[182]

In 1552–53 there were sales of brass, a basin, old iron and a fire pan (used for building work). The second Prayer Book or communion book was bought for 4s 4d, along with wine and bread for the communion, or singing bread as it was soon to be called. The only chalice had to be mended, and the king's commissioners came to Lostwithiel.[183]

Payments for wax naturally resumed in 1553–54 with the return of Catholicism under 'the noble queen, her grace, reigning queen Marie'. This warm form of address suggests that Mary's return was welcomed by Stratton people.[184] In 1554, 1s of the 4s 10d spent on wax was for Candlemas, and in 1554–55 wax sales exceeded 10s. Christmas candles 'for the quiere' are noted in 1555–56 suggesting a return to business as usual, and in 1558–60 payments were back to pre-1536 levels again.[185] Two chalices with patens, confiscated in the previous reign, were returned after a royal warrant was signed on 1 September 1553, but not the pyx. Cloth of gold was bought back and the canopy over the sacrament and high altar with appropriate service books was restored.[186] The relatively large amount of 23s 4d for glazing in 1553–54 suggests that some windows may have been subject to some iconoclasm in the reign of Edward VI; probably heads of the Virgin Mary and Christ had been removed. Bell repairs of £3 11d in 1554–55 included the making of new bell clappers.[187]

The dissolved chantry, ironically, became the subject of further litigation in 1554–55 when its lands were said to be worth 73s 5d a year. The Court of Augmentations, acting on behalf of the king and queen, Philip and Mary, claimed six years of rent arrears from the churchwardens amounting to £23 17s 2½d. In the face of this outrageous claim, Stratton's churchwardens Thomas Jule and John Judd had to ride to London. On 21 October 1554 both appeared at the Court of Exchequer in Westminster Hall, and then returned to court again on 20 January and 9 February 1555 only to find that the sheriff had not sent the writ. It was then agreed to hold the enquiry before 28 April at Launceston and a decision in favour of the parish was recorded in Letters Patent on 3 July 1555. The churchwardens were able to prove that the chantry land

[181] BL, Add MS 32243, ff.51, 54. Rose-Troup, *The Western Rebellion*, pp.372–8 noted an order of 12 September 1549 demanding that all bells be taken down in the diocese apart from the least, which was later moderated to confiscation of the clappers.

[182] BL, Add MS 32243, ff.50–v. Hutton, *The Rise and Fall of Merry England*, p.87 found that sixteen of a sample of eighteen parishes gave up church ales completely at this time.

[183] BL, Add MS 32243, ff.52–v.

[184] Edward VI and Elizabeth were described as sovereigns.

[185] BL, Add MS 32243, ff.53v, 54v, 56v.

[186] Snell, *Edwardian Inventories*, pp.36, 50; BL, Add MS 32243, ff.53–v, 54v

[187] BL, Add MS 32243, ff. 53, 55.

had always been held by parish feoffees, not them, and so did not come under the terms of the Chantry Act. The churchwardens were away for four weeks and six days in all and John Judd's expense claim came to at least £3 3s with further sums also paid to him and Jule. Horse hire came to 6s 8d, legal fees were 15s-plus, with a further 2s 6d spent in Launceston, making a grand total of at least £5 10s 4d.[188]

Frankincense reappeared as expectations of a lengthy Catholic future began to fade, restoring a sensory dimension to services. A processional and an old manual book came from Exeter. Missing items like a latten basin, lych bell clapper and pyx were replaced. A banner staff and a holy water bucket were also bought. Vestments had a thorough overhaul in 1555–56 and candles were lit in the choir at Christmas. In 1556–57 a cord was needed to hang the Lent cloth across the chancel, and a pascal candle and taper were made. A new cloth to cover the rood, a holy water bucket in the porch, a sacrament box with lock and key and a censer were the items replaced, while stone was 'drawn' and the high altar made again.[189] In 1557–58 'eyers' or metal loops were made at the altar's end for suspending curtains, and two altar towels and a desk cloth were bought.[190] The bellfounder started work on recasting a bell and part of an old breviary or antiphonal was bought for 1d to cover the account in which his work was recorded.[191]

In 1558–59 a Lent cloth, a new hymnal, a painting of St Andrew, a Palm cross, an altar cloth, albs for vestments, candles to put on the banner staff and a holy water sprinkler were bought.[192] Some of these items appear in a 1559 inventory (see appendix 3.1). Probably this was the inventory made by John Avery for 18d rather than the first inventory made by Master Marys at a cost of 12d. A font lock, tapers to burn before the rood, new surplices and rochets were also supplied and much mending was done, including work on the silk banner. Two new coffers were bought and a carpet for the communion table.

Pascal tapers extend into Elizabeth's reign in 1559–60 and 3½ pounds of wax were burned before the rood then. Work on the wooden Easter sepulchre continued, with points and pins needed. Two procession books came in, but at the same time a new communion book was brought from Exeter, with a psalter book, and a new communion table was made.[193] References to table cloths and cushions for the latter occur often thereafter.

The 1559 injunctions were 'markedly more conservative than their Edwardine models', with some sympathy for retaining roods.[194] Unfortunately for Catholics at Stratton, as elsewhere, the injunctions were enforced by committed Protestants and were put into practice more quickly and aggressively than earlier ones. These injunctions were also followed up in 1560–61 by episcopal visitations which delved much deeper than those of 1538.[195] At Stratton in 1560–61, under a 'Jhesus' heading, the High Cross wardens' account noted that the Bible was laced up, communion

[188] Goulding, *Blanchminster Records*, pp.37a–38a, 89–91; BL, Add MS 32243, ff.54, 55v.

[189] BL, Add MS 32243, ff.54v–5, 56v–8.

[190] BL, Add MS 32243, f.59 and for 1555 'landings' at the altar ends, see Osborne, *Church Wardens' Accounts of St Michael's Church, Chagford*, p.180.

[191] CRO, P216/25/1, f.3v and see the cover of this book.

[192] BL, Add MS 32243, ff.60v, 63 and appendix 2.2.

[193] BL, Add MS 32243, ff.61, 62v–3.

[194] Duffy, *Stripping of the Altars*, pp.568.

[195] Duffy, *Stripping of the Altars*, pp.568–9, 571. Kempthornes and Arundells of Trerice were among the committed Protestants keen to put this into practice.

bread and a communion book bought, and the rood loft washed, while the general receivers' account noted the arrival of a new parish clerk at Whitsun.[196] After 1560, with the exception of 2d for candlelight in 1561–62, all candles were snuffed out for good. A calendar and commandments are noted in 1561–62 with the former restoring many saints' days. In 1562–63 houseling bread (another term for communion bread) and the first references to a choir of laymen and a choirman to help them occur.[197]

One of the most positive aspects of the Reformation was communal singing and choir-led music-making. This is well documented at Stratton, with the organ also remaining in use. In 1563–64 'pricking of [a] processional [book] in four parts' was done at Bodmin, where church songs were also bought. Five choir boys are noted in 1565–66 and seven in 1570–71 when a song of *Te Deum* was bought from a St Ives man.[198]

Gypsies returned to entertain three times at fairs held in 1559–61, and in 1563–64 and 1574–78 annual takings from church ales exceeded £3, a sign of their post-Reformation popularity. Peter's pence was revived in 1563–64 after being outlawed in 1534, but this went to the queen not the pope. Another bell was cast by John White in 1564–65 and a man was paid to tarry with him 'until he [the bell] was melt'.[199]

In 1563–64 glazing went on over the rood and organ loft, while pressure continued to be put on the parish to remove the rood loft. In this year John Marys had to make an answer about it. Reluctantly in 1564–65 concessions were made: the ceilure over the loft and the rood beam were taken down, but only after the parish had been excommunicated for failure to do so. Wine and good cheer for the bishop's servants were laid on by the parishioners when the excommunication was revoked.[200] The dismantling of the rood loft continued the next year, but still not to the commissioners' satisfaction. On Friday 20 October 1570, John Marys, Nicholas Yeo, William Bray and John Judd went to Launceston chapter court about the rood loft. Meanwhile William Rodde (Rad) took down the organ loft and organs, and a bargain was made for the sale of the rood loft in 1570–71.[201] The planching or floor of the rood loft was taken to the church house to be carefully stored and pieces were sold off in 1573–74 after two men had been paid more money to take the loft down.[202]

In 1566–67 communion wine was fetched from Holsworthy and seats were made for boy choristers. Mats were provided before the communion table, with the vicar getting his own kneeling mat later on. More enquiries about church lands came in 1567–68 from the queen's commissioners, while in 1569–70 the Bible had to be carried to Exeter and back.[203] While the Bible was away, John Judd lent his English Bible to the parish and he and other parishioners breakfasted at Prideaux Place, Padstow on church house business.[204] All these changes culminated in the sale of a chalice for 37s and the buying of a communion cup for £3 19s in 1570–71, the

[196] BL, Add MS 32243, ff.63v–4; CRO, P216/25/208, f.8.

[197] BL, Add MS 32243, ff.65v–6, 67v–8v. Duffy, *Stripping of the Altars*, p.567 for calendar.

[198] CRO, P216/25/208, f.11; 32243, ff.70, 73–v, 82v, 83v. Gant, *O Sing unto the Lord*, p.153 notes that a *Te Deum* was a canticle for morning use and Benham, *Latin Church Music*.

[199] BL, Add MS 32243, ff.62, 63v, 65, 70 (Peter's quarter), 72v; CRO, P216/25/208, ff.12v, 13v.

[200] BL, Add MS, 32243, ff.69v–70, 71; CRO, P216/25/208, f.12v. Marys and John Judd had to ride to Exeter to get the excommunication revoked.

[201] CRO, P216/25/208, f.18; BL, Add MS 32243, f.82.

[202] BL, Add MS 32243, ff.83v, 88–v.

[203] BL, Add MS, 32243, ff.75–v, 77, 80v.

[204] BL, Add MS, 32243, f.82v; CRO, P216/25/208, f.17v.

stockwardens giving £4 for this purpose. The latter is still extant and came from Exeter. It bears the maker's mark of the prolific communion cup-maker John Jons.[205] The parish bought a saucer for communion bread before it was able to raise the 17s 6d needed to buy the paten cover from Jons in 1576–77. John Yeo, merchant, brought this home.[206] A new font cover was made in 1572–73, and Bishop Jewell's *Apology for the Church of England* arrived in 1574.[207] The Ten Commandments were painted on boards by a painter called George, while John White was again employed to cast a bell in 1577–79, probably the great bell.[208]

Still the exodus of Catholic items from the church continued with cherubim, from heaven-representing roofs, and two pieces of old books going out in 1570–71. Other church stuff was sold to Mistress Mary Arundell for 20s in the same year, including some suits of vestments listed in colourful detail in the 1559 inventory.[209] In 1571–72, unspecified stuff was also sold to church use and an idea of this can be gained from the 1570–71 inventory (appendix 3.2), though the inventory omits the holy water bucket and ironware. Further sales in 1572–73 denuded the church of the rest of the 'Popish trash': two cruets, a coffer, a chest, a corporal cloth case, two candlesticks, more wooden angels and a basin.[210]

Iconoclasm is likely in the case of the market cross, which was taken down in 1573–74.[211] In 1574–75 the chancel step was removed and the chancel levelled. By 1577–78 silk laces were no longer needed for vestments but for touch boxes, part of the parish armoury. An inventory of church goods made in 1578 lists the parish armour in some detail and the church accounts are full of work needed to keep the archery butts in the churchyard upright. The final reference to the rood loft occurs as late as 7 August 1580 when Pears the joiner gave the final coup de grace. The screen was taken down and seats and pews put in its place, leaving the division between chancel and nave unclear.[212]

The poor and bereft

Payments to the poor occur soon after the stockwardens' account resume, in 1558, with a smock made 'for poor Johane' and bread and drink given for the poor on New Year's Eve. Comparison with Chagford in Devon suggests that this type of poor relief was a relatively new development.[213] As well as shirts, hose, shifts,

[205] BL, Add MS 32243, ff.82, 83; CRO, P216/25/208, f.17v. At Kilmington, Devon, Jons bought the medieval chalice and the same probably happened here. See Cornish, *Kilmington Church Wardens' Accounts*, p.39.

[206] BL, Add MS 32243, ff.83, 98v.

[207] BL, Add MS 32243, ff.87v, 93; CRO, P216/25/208, f.22.

[208] BL, Add MS 32243, f.98; CRO, P216/25/208, ff.32, 33. Bishop John Jewel of Salisbury's book was 'the standard defence of the new church', Duffy, *Voices of Morebath*, p.179.

[209] BL, Add MS 32243, f.82; CRO, P216/25/208, f.18v and appendix 3.1.

[210] BL, Add MS 32243, ff.84, 86 and colour plate 1.

[211] See 'Markets, fairs and the church house' section.

[212] BL, Add MS 32243, f.93v and appendix 3.3; CRO, P216/25/208, f.35v. Hanham, *Churchwardens' Accounts of Ashburton*, p.169 shows that Ashburton's rood loft was completely down by 1572.

[213] CRO, P216/25/208, f.4. At Chagford collections for poor people started on 16 January 1558, Osborne, *Church Wardens' Accounts of St Michael's Church, Chagford*, p.189. The first Elizabethan Poor Law Act was not passed until 1563, which suggests these may have been local initiatives, Palliser, *The Age of Elizabeth*, p.19. Carter and Thompson, *Sources for Local*

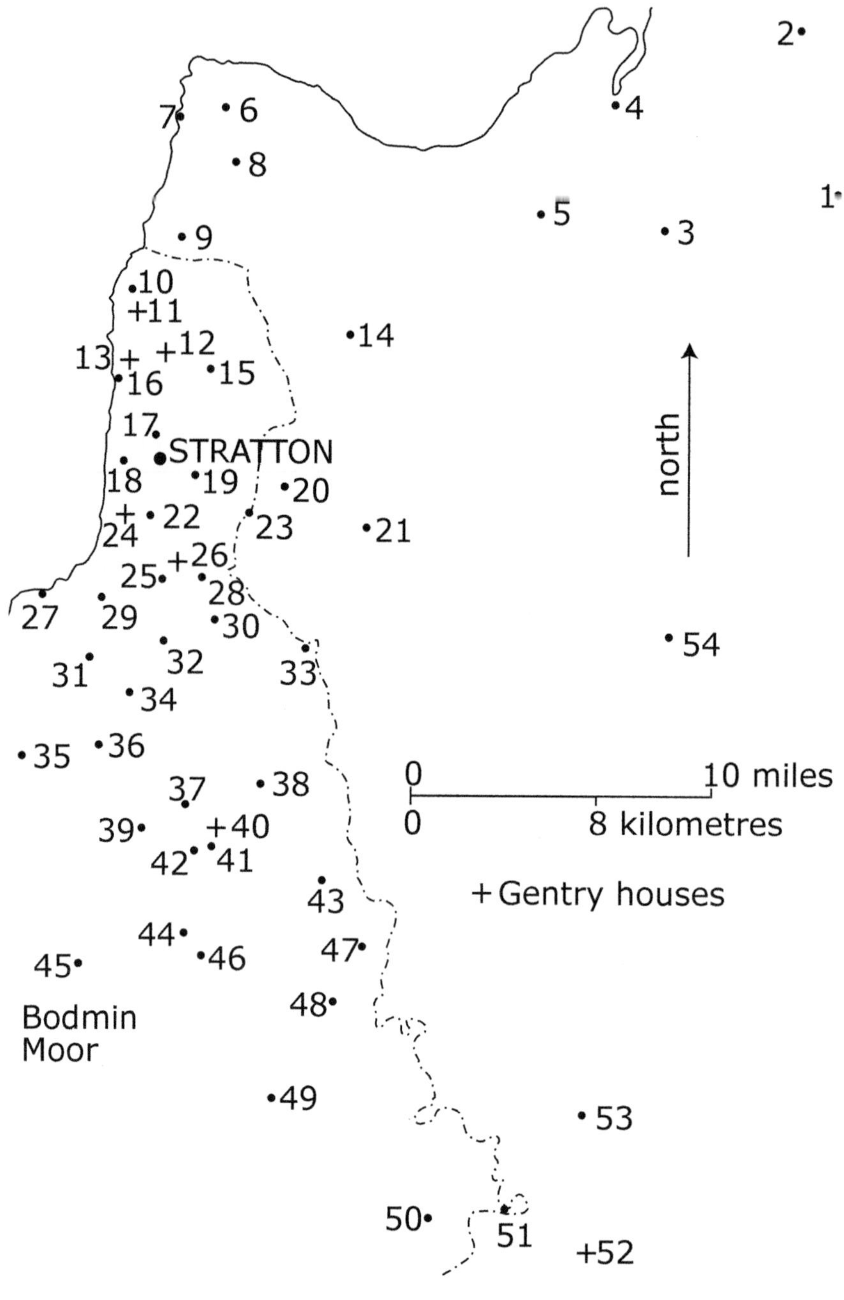

Figure 5 Stratton's local links.
In the key: a = churchwardens' accounts; b = brief for collection; c = craftsmen from; l = lands of Stratton church; m = musters; o = other residences; p = priest; r = rebellions; s = source of materials; v = visitations and church courts; w = work and models related to Stratton's rood loft; x = gentry houses

Key

1	Atherington	w
2	Tawstock	b
3	Taddiport	b
4	Bideford	s
5	Buckland Brewer	c
6	Hartland Abbey	c?
7	Hartland Quay	s
8	Philham	o
9	Welcombe	o
10	Morwenstow	c, o, p
11	Tonacombe	x
12	Ley	x
13	Stowe	x
14	Bradworthy	c
15	Kilkhampton	a, c, s
16	Combe	o
17	Poughill	c, o, p
18	Bude	s
19	Launcells	o, p, x
20	Pancrasweek	o
21	Holsworthy	s
22	Marhamchurch	o, p, v
23	Bridgerule	b
24	Whalesborough	o, x
25	Week Orchard	o
26	Marhays, Week St Mary	x
27	Millook, Poundstock	l
28	Downrow Wood	s
29	Poundstock	c, o, p, r
30	Whitstone	s
31	Jacobstow	m
32	Week St Mary	c, v
33	North Tamerton	c
34	Exe, Week St Mary	l
35	Otterham	s
36	Warbstow	b
37	Treburtle, Tresmeer	l
38	North Petherwin	a
39	Tresmeer	l
40	Penheale	x
41	Egloskerry	o
42	Badharlick, Egloskerry	o
43	Launceston	a, b, c, o, s, v
44	Polyphant	s
45	Altarnun	b
46	Lewannick	s, p
47	Lawhitton	c, p
48	Lezant	b
49	Linkinhorne	p
50	St Dominick	s
51	Calstock	b
52	Buckland Abbey	v, x
53	Tavistock	s
54	Northlew	c

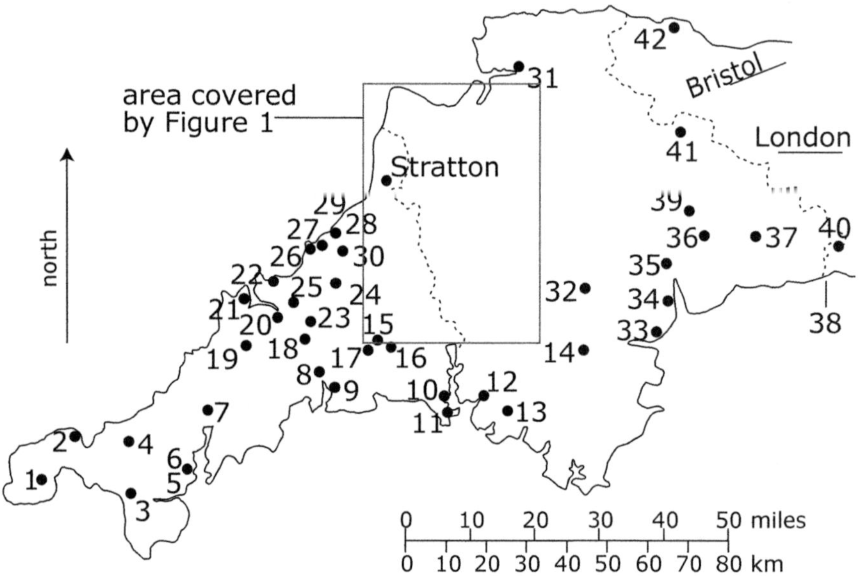

Key

1	St Buryan	b
2	St Ives	b, s
3	Helston	r
4	Camborne	a
5	Penryn	s
6	Glasney	p
7	Truro	b
8	Lostwithiel	c, v
9	St Winnow	p
10	Saltash	b
11	Antony and Millbrook	a, b
12	Plymouth	b
13	Plympton	b
14	Ashburton	a
15	Liskeard	w
16	Menheniot	p
17	St Pinnock	b
18	Bodmin	a, b, c, s, v
19	St Columb Major	w
20	St Breock	a
21	Padstow	b, s
22	Prideaux Place	v, x
23	Helland	b
24	St Breward	b
25	St Tudy and St Kew	b, w
26	Portquin	b
27	Tintagel	b, s
28	Boscastle	b, s
29	Minster	b?
30	Camelford and Lanteglos	b, v
31	Pilton	b
32	Chagford	a, w
33	Teignmouth	b
34	Powderham	p
35	Exeter	s, v
36	Plymtree	v
37	Honiton	v
38	Colyton Haven (Axmouth)	b
39	Cullompton	b
40	Kilmington	a
41	Morebath	a
42	Selworthy	p

Figure 6 Stratton's wider links.
In the key: a = churchwardens' accounts; b = brief for collection; c = craftsmen from or at; p = priest; r = rebellions; s = source of materials; v = visitations and church courts; w = work related to Stratton's rood loft; x = gentry houses. The map excludes: Totnes, near Ashburton (Devon), Bath, Bruton and Chard (Somerset), Portsmouth, Hastings, Oxford, Shrewsbury, foreign countries etc.

coats, waistcoats, aprons and shrouds, shoes were also made for paupers, and bed and board, nursing and surgeons paid for when necessary. By 1564 a sum of 6s 8d was set aside annually by the stockwardens 'to distribute amongst the poor people that be not sufficiently relieved with the gathering of the parish'.[214] This fund ran into trouble in 1574 when excess charges resulting from the building of the bridge meant that there was only 12d available for the poor. Perhaps because of this shortfall non-locals like William Whale and Joan Parterege and her child were given financial incentives to depart the parish, though they usually failed to go.[215] William Whale's wife Isott continued to be included in the poor relief lists in 1578–81. These three lists include the names of thirty-four people of whom twenty-four were women.[216] Most did not come from office-holding families, though some men had served in a single office as a Sexton or St Armel warden in the past. In about seven cases the pauper was an outsider. Husbands of two women had rented the church house kitchen or buttery and Richard Pery, who came from a family of office-holders, became a charge on the parish only after he hurt his leg. Pauper nicknames in the 1560s–70s include Red Robert, Lame Hellen (of Warbstow) and Old Bole, Mother Bole or Old Woman Bole.

The bereft included an increasing straggle of the dumb, lame and one-legged (though a blind priest sent a poor man to collect on his behalf), beggars including a Shrewsbury trio, poor men and the occasional poor woman or child including those robbed at sea and, in one case, an individual from London. Shipwrecked mariners, three from 'Cattya', maimed soldiers from the Irish wars, prisoners, the occasional man bankrupted by suretyships (standing pledge for another), people evicted by fire and an Oxford scholar also appear.

House fires are noted at St Breward twice, St Buryan, Jacobstow, Lezant and Millbrook in Cornwall and Tawstock in Devon, and collections were also made for the rebuilding of Chard in Somerset and for the havens of Colonton (Colyton, now Axmouth in Devon which occurs in other accounts), Hastings and Portsmouth. In the latter case receipts for 12d and 16d were sewn into the account.[217] Local havens like Tintagel, Bude and Porth Quin were not forgotten either and a collector for repairing the bridge at Wadebridge got 2s 6d – rather more than the usual 4d to 8d.[218] Others collected for hospitals and lazar houses, notably St Leonard's Launceston, St Laurence's (Bodmin) and St Martin's (possibly Looe) in Cornwall, Cullompton, Exeter (St Mary's, St Catherine's and a house of maimed men), Pilton, Plympton, Tadyport, Teignmouth and Totnes in Devon.[219]

More unusual entries include the poor man who went to the bath (presumably for a cure) and two women taken by Sir Richard Grenville, who spent three days in prison in early 1580 at a time when fears of spying were at a height.[220] In the period 1557–81 the number of collections in the church rose from about two a year to

History, p.86, note that the 1563 Act 'saw the compulsory payment of poor rates by householders'. For a payment to poor men in 1548 see p.89.

[214] CRO, P216/25/208, f.11v.

[215] CRO, P216/25/208, ff.23, 24–v.

[216] CRO, P216/25/208, ff.33A, 36, 38.

[217] CRO, P216/25/208, ff.36–v.

[218] Langdon, *Wade-bridge*, for context.

[219] St Martin's has not been identified, though Looe is possible.

[220] Rowse, *Sir Richard Grenville*, pp.157–77, for context.

eighteen. By 1579 the dates of collections are usually given. Stratton was evidently a good place to come to get a passport drawn up or to collect a begging licence. The parish also paid for the relief of plagued parishes in the west part of the country in 1579 and the ransoming of prisoners from overseas. Rates set by the justices of the peace were charged for St Ives on 8 March 1580 and to restore the old custom called 'Cornish heare' on 27 September 1581. If 'Cornish heir' is meant then this could relate to Cornish inheritance customs.[221]

[221] See Baker, *An Introduction to English Legal History*, pp.239–41 which shows inheritance cases were being changed around this time.

Editorial Method

Stratton's accounts are numbered by folio, apart from the final general receivers' accounts for 1557–81 where folio numbers have had to be assigned. In all cases v for verso has been added for the unmarked backs of each folio, which is abbreviated to f.; for example, f.1 is followed by f.1v. Folio numbers in square brackets are the editor's additions. With the exception of folios 4–4v of the High Cross wardens' accounts, all the accounts are in chronological order. The end of the 1532 account and the start of the 1533 account have been put back in their correct place. The draft brewing account of 1559 is included as appendix 2.1 and two other draft accounts which occur at the end of the High Cross wardens' accounts are appendices 2.2–2.3. Three inventories of church goods which can be dated 1559, 1570–71 and 1578, two being on the back of the draft accounts, are included as appendices 3.1–3.3.

The High Cross accounts from 1512 to 1578 and the general receivers' account books of 1531, 1534–49 and 1557–81 have been transcribed in full, with Latin headings and words indicated by italics extended but not usually translated. Headings are given in bold throughout as are subheadings. Marginal notations are occasionally commented on and sums in margins are usually footnoted. Entries relating to the standings at fairs are often indicated with a drawing of a hand or a cross in the margin, perhaps for the benefit of the clerk of the market. Non-payments are also shown in similar fashion.

Dating has been standardised as mistakes were often made by scribes, especially when the accounting day was not noted, and repetition of the previous year's date is common. In one case, news of the death of Henry VIII was received after the accounts had been made up.[1] This affects the dating of the High Cross wardens' documents most as their accounting day was usually around 2 February. Here modern dating has been used, taking the start of the year as 1 January rather than 25 March. This avoids the need for double dating. Fewer problems were encountered with the general receivers' or stockwardens' accounts apart from one, that of 1546–47, which was put in late on 1 January 1548 so that there are two 1548 accounts and none for 1547.

One of the major issues in editing the Stratton accounts is the frequent changes of scribe, especially for the High Cross wardens where thirty-five or more separate hands can be detected in a sixty-six-year period. This may be due to annual changes of High Cross wardens with, presumably, the older or more literate writing the account. Single scribes can be identified in 1519–25, 1535–49 (except 1541) and 1557–66 (except 1562 and 1564). The second of these scribes also wrote most of the first general receivers' account book. Another issue is that with each change of hand capitalisation and spelling are affected; 1529, 1533 and 1575 are particularly difficult accounts to read. An example of unorthodox spelling in 1529 and 1533 is 'matytt' for meat (workmen's food). The general receivers' or stockwardens' accounts are

[1] BL, Add MS 32243, f.42v where the account is dated to the regnal year 38 Henry VIII which only ran from 22 April 1546 to 28 January 1547 so the account which was made on 6 February 38 Henry VIII is technically from the first year of Edward VI.

generally more consistently written, probably by the parish clerk, as only two or three hands occur in each case.

Original spelling and clerical errors, mainly the duplication of words, have been left to reflect the character of the accounts. The old English letter thorn (*th*) is used occasionally and is here given as a *y*, the nearest letter form, while *z* is used for yoch (*g* or *gh*). A few examples are given in the glossary. *Ye* (the), *yr* (your), *yt* or *hytt* (it or that) have been kept as written because they are reasonably intelligible to modern readers. Also, the practice of genderising nouns or names with *hys* or *hyr* has been retained, as have Christian name and surname spellings. The archaic abbreviation *es* at the end of words has generally been given as *s* only. Here *j* has been substituted for *i*, *v* for *u*, double *f* reduced to a single *f* and split words like *un to* closed up. Divergent spellings of place names are footnoted on first occurrence but indexed by modern form. Text is sometimes modernised when quoted in the introduction and a standard form is used there for surnames.

Weights and measures have not usually been modernised in the transcripts. Bushel, a measure of volume, is often indicated as bz, li for *libra* can be £ or lb, ob for *obulus* is a halfpenny, but qr for farthing has usually been expanded as quarter. Also *di* has been expanded to *dimidia* meaning half, c = 100 or cwt, and m = 1,000. Other examples of weights and measures can be found in the glossary.

Roman numerals have also been kept in the transcripts throughout, though sometimes given as Arabic numerals in the introduction. This highlights the introduction of Arabic numerals into the accounts from 1568 as marginal notes and dates and as sums in the final 1578 churchwardens' account.

Capitalisation appears to be completely haphazard and usually scribally dictated with few letters apart from *R* and *S* having a distinctive capital form and large versions of *A* and *W* as likely to appear in the middle of a word as at the beginning. For these reasons, modern capitalisation has been preferred here. Capital letters have been used to indicate Christian names, surnames and place names, but not occupational names. Capitals have also been used for days and months (e.g. Trinity Sunday or November), saints, guild or store dedications (e.g. High Cross, Sextons, Maidens etc.) and some titles like Lord and Lady. Mr has been expanded to Master. King, queen and general titles like 'my lord bishop' have not been capitalised, partly to avoid possible confusion with surnames in the first and last case. Modern punctuation has been used in some cases.

Abbreviated words have been 'silently' expanded in most cases unless the expansion is unclear, and the occasional accidentally omitted letter supplied where the entry would not make sense otherwise, for example *wyndowe* rather than *wydowe*. In addition, the letter *e* has been added to the end of some words for clarity's sake, for instance *one* rather than *on*, and *to* is usually rendered as *two* when appropriate. Final letters have not been added where dialect studies suggest they may have been dropped deliberately, e.g. *menden* rather than *mendeng*.[2]

Editorial conventions used are: ^^ where scribes have made insertions above, at the end of a line or between lines. Crossed out words are included in square brackets with 'crossed out' following. [illeg.] is used for illegible words and ? for uncertain readings. Spaces left for further entries are noted in footnotes but not blank pages and torn edges, which are frequently found in the second general receivers' book, CRO, P216/25/208.

[2] See Hanham, *Churchwardens' Accounts of Ashburton*, p.xxi for Devon dialect.

Part I

High Cross Wardens' and Churchwardens' Book, 1512–78

[f.1]

The counte boke of the Hye Crosse wardenys of Stratton *anno domini* m ccccc xij [1512][1]

[f.1v] This book was begun in the 3rd year of the reign of king Henry the 8th AD 1512, and was ended in the 20th year of the reign of queen Elizabeth AD 1577[2]

f.2 [The counte of the Hye Crosstor crossed out]

The counte of the Hye Crosstore beyng wardenys Nycholas Hortop & John Payne, *anno regni regis Henricij octam tercio anno domini* m ccccc xij [1512][3]

Recetes

Memorandum recevid of John Regyll & John Hore	iijd
Item received for Symon Pole to be set a pone ye Hye Crosstor[4]	iijs iiijd
Item received of John Bond & John Coke, Sextyn men	xxd
Item received of John Getyn for his wyfe ys dafter to be put a pone ye Hye Crosstor	iijs iiijd
Item received of John Payne for olde tymber of the churchys	vjd
Item received of Walter Gyste for hys wyfys pytt[5]	iijs iiijd
Item received of Walter Langforth for a knyll	iiijd
Item received of Wylliam Gyste *junior* for a knyll	iiijd
Item received of John Wylle for a knyll	iiijd
Item received of Thomas Marys for the brack[6] sute	xvjd
Item received of Thomas Heyward & Rychard Lobbys for the black sute	xijd
Item received for the Hye Crosse ale yn owr tyme	xxxs iijd
Summa xlvjs[7]	

Expenses

Item for expenses at the visytacion at Lanceston	xiiijd
Item payd to John Wolfe for vij pownde of wex a genes Ester	iiijs viijd
Item paid payd for makyng of the same wex to Wylliam Gyste	iiijd
Item paid to Master Vycar	vs
Item for gress for the bellys	vjd ob
Item for a belrope	viijd
Item payde for yerd of bokeram to make iij new stolys	vijd
Item paid to Wylliam Jule for a stape to the stypyll dore	iijd
Item paid to Moris Taylour for makyng of iij new stoles mete & drynk & hyre	iiijd
Item paid payde for therd	jd
Item paid for blessing of v awter clothys [and iij new stolys crossed out]	xxiijd
Item paid for bred & drynk to ye ryngers to renge a gens my lord bosshopp[8]	ijd
Item paid for a gallon of wyne to geve my lord boshopp	ixd
Item paid for iiij new gerdelys	ijd
[Item paid illeg. word crossed out]	

1 BL, Add MSS, 32243.
2 Last account is 1578.
3 Covers most of 1511.
4 High Cross store, bede roll?
5 Church grave.
6 r used interchangeably with l.
7 John Yeo's signature added 1578.
8 Hugh Oldham, bishop of Exeter, visit?

[f.2v]

Item paid for the church dore kay	jd
Item paid for ij truss of rushes	vjd
Item paid for carying of ij treys	iiijd
Item paid [for crossed out] to Hare Gard ys labour to helpe carry ye treys	jd
Item paid to Wylliam Mathe for mendyng of olde belropys	ijd
Item paid to John Gyste for makying of ij collers	ijd ob
Item paid to John Hacker for hewyng of the churche tymber	iiijd
Item paid for the frethyng of the stypyll wyndows	iiijd
Item paid for iij pownd of wex ye price	xxiijd
Item for makyng of the same wex	ijd
Item paid [to crossed out] for mendyng of ij sacryng belys	ob
Item paid to Wylliam Gyst of Pozhyll[9] for makyng of ye church style mete & drynk	xiiijd
Item for makyng of a newe bere and mendyng the old bere	vjd
Item paid for making of a leche to church style	ijd ob
Item for scowryng of the sence	jd
Item paid for bressyng of Synt Armyll ys chalys	iiijd
Item paid to William Jule for mendyng of a claper	vjd
Item paid for makyng clene of the stypyll	jd
Item paid to William Boshop for mendyng of the belropys	jd
Item paid for x yerdes of clescloth to make iij rochets	vjs vijd
Item paid for makyng of the rochyots	xijd
Item for washeng of the church clothys	vjd
Item for makyng of thys cownte[10]	iiijd
Summa expenses xxvijs xd	

+*Et sic debet claro* – xviijs ijd *solute quietus est*
Jhesus

f.3

The cowmpte of the Hycrosse beying wardenys John Jule & Wylliam Gyste junior *anno domini millesimo* ccccc xiij ^1513^[11]

Recetes

Memorandum recevyd of Thomas Jerle[12] & John Payne beyng olde Wardenys	iiijs xd
Item received for Sir Thomas Constabell for the bells and oder ornaments[13]	xijd
Item received of Johan Paynter for iij namys whych be set a pone the bedroll[14]	xs
received item for a knell for Thomas Mares ys servant	iiijd
Item received for owr ale yn owr tyme	xxxvijs
Item received of Wylliam Cory for a olde coler for a bell	xd
Summa total liiijs	

Expenses

Memorandum payde for iiij belropys	iijs vjd
Item for expenses to the visi[t]acon at Lanceston	xiiijd
Item for vj pownd of wex a gense Ester	iiijs

9 Poughill, parish north of Stratton.
10 Space for three entries above.
11 Later addition.
12 Replaced Nicholas Hortope?
13 Black vestments?
14 First reference to bede roll.

Item for paid for my lady Parcyvale ys meneday[15] to iiij prists & for bred & ale	ijs ijd
Item paid for mendyng of an olde serpels	iijd
Item paid to Master Vicar	vs
Item paid for making of the clock[16]	xs
Item paid to Wylliam Pery to pay the prists wages	xs
Item paid for v pownd of wex a gens Crystysmas	ijs xjd
Item for gress to gress the bellys	ijd
Item for frankencens	ijd
Item paid for the makyng of the tapers	vijd
Item paid for iiij colers to ye bellys	ijs xjd
Item paid for xxxti vethem of cord	vjd
Item for washeng of the church clothys	vjd
Item for mendyng of ye bell ropys	jd
Item paid for a pownde of wex to make candelys	vijd
Item for gerdelys	ijd
Item for makyng of the cownte	iiijd
Summa xlvs	+ *sic debit* ixs *solute quiet*

[f.3v]

Recetes

The cowmpt of the Hyecross beyng wardenys Walter Langford & Robert Wade *anno domini millesimo* ccccc xiiij [1514]

Memorandum recevyd of the old wardenys Wylliam Gyst junior & John Jule	ixs
Item received for Genkyn Prist ys gyfte	xxd
Item of John Rose for Lamerton ys pytt	iijs iiijd
Item received of John Regyll for a knyll	[iiijd illeg. word crossed out] iiijd
Item received of Jhon & Harry Gard for ropys	vjd ob
Item received ofor the Hye Crosse ale yn owr tyme	xxviijs
Summa	xlijs xj[j crossed out]d ob

Expenses

Memorandum payd to Master Vicar	vs
Item for expens at the visi[t]acon at Lanceston	xiiijd ob
Item paid for mendyng of the church clothys	ijd
Item paid for a cord for ye sepulcar cloth	jd
Item paid for a pownd of frankyncens	ijd
Item paid for viij pownd of weke for making of tapers a gens Ester	iiijs viijd
Item paid for iiij pownd of wexe a gens Crystsmas to make ye tapers	ijs vijd
Item paid for a halfe a pownd of wexe to make candelys	iijd ob
Item paid for wekys [a pownd & di crossed out]	iijd
Item paid for makyng of ye wexe for ye hole yere	[ixd crossed out] vijd
Item for making of the colers for ye bell	jd
Item for putche, ter & gress to puche ye belropys	iiijd
Item paid to Robert Cuttyng for a days jorney for trussying of the bellys and for a man to helpe hym for ye mete & drynke & hyre	xd
Item paid for naylys	ob
Item paid for wyre to hong ye caneby	jd
Item paid a mendyng of the glasse	xvjd
Item paid for ij boshelys of lyme	xijd

[15] Obit for Thomasine Bonaventure, founder of Week St Mary School. See Hull, 'Endowment of a Grammar School'.

[16] First reference to the clock.

Item paid for lathenaylys ijd ob
Item paid for lathys ijd
Item paid for helyng stonys ijd
Item paid to the helyer for his wages vjd
Item for hys mete & drink iiijd
Item for the sodyer xvijd
Item paid for ij [boshull crossed out] ^semys^ of gravyll iiijd
Item for russhech vjd
Item mendyng of the belropys iijd

ff.4–v[17]

f.5
Item for gressyng of the bellys ijd
Item for paryng of ye treys ijd
Item for wassheng of the churche clothys vjd
Item for mendyng of v obys & wassheng of the same & mendyng of the copys & the b[r crossed out]lew sute & ye blacke sute viijd
Item paid for the makyng of the cownte iiijd

Summa xxiiijs ixd ob
+ so remaynyth yn ye honds xviijs jd
solut quietus est

The cowmpt of the Hye Crosse beyng wardenys Wylliam Woglow & Wylliam Davy *anno domini millesimo* ccccc xv [1515]

Memorandum recevyd of Master Langford & Robert Wade xviijs vd
Item received for Robert Wadyn ys grave & for his gyfte vjs viijd
Item received of Water Gyste for brokyn lyd vs
Item received of Wylliam Call for a dublet iijs vjd
Item received for a old bellrop of Mychael Myll jd ob
Item received of Ame Regyll for John Regyll ys grave iijs iiijd
Item received for Wylliam Gyste ys grave & for his gyft iiijs
Item received of Alsyn Heddyn for a knyll for a chyld iiijd
Item received for the Hye Cross ale xxvjs

Summa iijli vijs iiijd ob

[f.5v]

Expenses

Memorandum payd to John Wolfe for ix yerds of bocram to make howslyng towlys iijs iiijd
Item paid for the makyng of ye same towlys iijd
Item paid to Wylliam Gyst for viij pownd of wex to make tapers agens Ester iiijs viijd
Item paid for makyng of ye same wex & for candelys iiijd
Item for expenses at ye vysitasion at Lanston[18] xvijd
Item paid for a pownd of frankyncens ijd
Item paid for a plommer for a clothe of led & soder & warkmanshep xxjs ijd
Item paid for Trynger[19] ys costage & for his reward & for oder company ys coste iijs iiijd
Item for mendyng of the bellys vijd

[17] End of 1532, 1557 brewing account and start of 1533 inserted by mistake here. See 1532–33 accounts and appendix 2.1.
[18] Launceston.
[19] Church house benefactor.

Item for gress for the bellys jd
Item expenses at the visitasion of my lord boshopp xvjd
Item for iiij pownd of wex a gens Crystysmas ijs iiijd
Item for makyng of the same wex & for candelys for ye hole yer viijd
Item for washeng of the church clothys vjd
Item paid for bellropys xxti vathem xvd
Item for makyng of thys a count iiijd

Summa xlvjs ixd *solut quietus est*
+ *Et sic de claro* xxs vijd

f.6

Recetes

The cowmpt of the Hye Cross beyng wardenys Wylliam Call & Wylliam Olyver *anno domini millesimo* ccccc xvj [1516]

Memorandum recevyd of Wyllliam Woglow & Wylliam Davy olde Wardenys xxs vijd ob
Item received of Alsyn Puddener for her fader & here husbond to set y[he]m a pone the bedroll vjs viijd
Item received of Mychael Myll to set Rychard Pyle a pone ye beddroll iijs iiijd
Item received for a knyll for Gybbys iiijd
Item received of Wylliam Olyver for a walch bord iijd
Item received of the same Wylliam for ij yends of ropys iijd
Item received for owre ale clerely xxxvijs jd

Summa iijli viijs [v crossed out]jd ob

Expenses

Memorandum payd to John Cholwyll for a new whefyll for the gret bell & for mendyng of the other bellys iijs iiijd
Item paid for viij pownd of wex to Wylliam Gyste a gens Yester iiijs ixd
Item paid ^makyng of^ for the same wex & [candelys crossed out] iiijd
Item paid for wekes jd
Item for candelys ijd
Item paid for mendyng of the churches clothys iijd
Item paid to Wylliam Juyll for mendyng of a claper for the bell iijd
Item paid for naylys jd
Item paid for [paid fo crossed out] sylke to mend the vestements[20]
Item paid to Master Vicar for the bedroll
Item for expenses at the visitacion at Lanceston
Item for mendyng of vestements
Item paid for walche bord
Item for iiij boshells of lyme & the caryg &
Item for mendyng of ye clock
Item paid for a c of helyng stone
Item paid for a box to Wylliam Davy to set evydens
Item paid to a helyer for mendyng of the church f
sond & a server to serve the helyer
Item paid to the lords servants for makyng of the
Item for ij pere of hose clothys

[f.6v]

Item paid for gress & for gressyng of the bellys ijd ob
Item for iiij pownd of wex agens Crystesmas ijs vijd
Item for makyng of the same ijd
Item for mendyng of the stypyll wyndows & for mete & drynk ijs iiijd

[20] Page torn.

Item paid for naylys	viijd
Item paid for tymber to the same wyndows	xvjd
Item paid for washeng of the church clothys	vjd
Item for a cord for the Lent cloth	ijd
Item for makyng of ye a cownte	iiijd

Summa xlixs iijd ob

+ remaynyth [xixs iijd crossed out] xviijs xd *solut quietus est*

The cowmpte of the Hye Cross beyng wardens Nycolas Heddon & Nycolas Woglow *anno domini* mccccc xvjj [1517]

Recetes

Memorandum received of Wylliam Olyver for to set Margery Bylke apone ye bedroll iijs iiijd	
Item received for a knyll & for tapers for Avys	vijd
[Item received] of John Curtays for his wyfe ys pytt	iijs iiijd
[Item received] for owr ale yn owr tyme	xxxviijs

Summa xlvs iijd

f.7

Expenses

Memorandum payd for v pownd of wex agens Ester	iijs ixd
Item paid to John Wolfe for iij pownd of wex	ijs jd ob
Item paid to Wylliam Boshopp for candelys	ijd
Item paid for makyng of the tapers a gens Ester	ijd
Item paid for a kay to the vante	ijd
Item for expenses to the visitacon at Lanceston	xvjd
Item for the church dore kay	jd
Item paid to Recard for helyng of the church mete & dryng wages	viijd
Item paid to a server for his wages & mete & drynk	iiijd
Item paid for gravill	jd ob
Item paid to Master Vycar for the bedroll	vs
Item paid to John Hacker for possyng of Sangwen ys howse & for makyng of the howse to set the church tymber yn	iiijd
Item paid to John Jule for dachyng of the same howse	ijd
Item paid to Stephyn Smale to serve hym mete & drynke & wages	iiijd
Item paid to Alson Hoge for strekyng of the straw mete & wages	iijd
Item paid to Wylliam To wyll for scheryng of the church heg	ijd
Item paid to Water Maior for a truss arushees	iijd
Item paid for hye rent for the church howse[21]	iijd
Item paid for mendyng of the church clothes	jd ob
Item paid to Hew Prist for xv bosshelys of lyme	vjs
Item paid for candels	jd ob
Item paid to Nycholas Woglow for caryg of iiij bosshelys of lyme & *dimidia*	x[ij crossed out]d
Item paid for caryg of iij bosshelys & *dimidia* to Thomas Bryant	viijd
Item paid to John Wyll for iij bosshelys	viijd
Item paid to John Jule for iij bosshelys	viijd
Item paid to Nycholas Symon for iij bosshelys	viijd
Item for expenses for ther soper when they came home with ye lyme	vd
Item paid for a lanterne	vijd

[21] First specific reference to church house.

Item paid for iij ferdelys of lyme	vijd
Item paid to Thomas Marys for a reward to one of the lorde ys servants	iijs iiijd
Item paid to Isbyll Taylour for ij pownd of wex	xvijd
Item paid for makyng of the same tapers	ijd
Item paid to Ingeram for trussyng of the bells & mete & wages	xjd
Item for a man to helpe hym a day & a halfe mete & drynk	vd
Item for nayles & gress	ijd
Item for candelys	jd
Item for washessyg of [of crossed out] the church clothes	vjd
Item for makyng of the same cownte	iiijd

[f.7v]

Item paid to Nycholas Woglow for ij wenys of more stone	iijs viijd
Item paid to the same Nycholas for a yate to the More[22]	iiijd
Item for expenses the same tyme	ijd
Item paid for the fettyng of the schafyt tymber	vjd
Item paid for the fyllyng	iiijd
Item paid to John Payne for mak[yng], mete & drynk	iiijd

Summa xxxixs iiijd

\+ remaynyth vs vd *solut quietus est*

The compt of the Hey Crose beyng wardyns John Chamond esquyr & Thomas Marres *anno domini* m ccccc xviij [1518]

Recetes

Memorandum received of the olde wardyns Nycholas Heddon & Nycholas Uglow	vs vd
Item received for a borde yt was at Maryon Lyll ys &	
Item oure ale brueng	iijli
Item received for Jenyt Hore ys pyt	iijs iiijd
+Item received at the fayre[23] of vj messers	vjd

Summa iijli ixs iijd

Expences

Memorandum payed for iij bell ropys	iijs ixd
Item payed for expens at vysytacyon	xvjd
Item payed to the bucke bender	iijs iiijd
Item payed for mendyng of ij chalys	ijs viijd
Item payed for vj bz of lyme to Thomas Bryant	iijs viijd
Item for met & dryncke	iijd

f.8

Item to the hoper for mendyng of the framys	vjd
Item payd for the bede roll	vs
Item for frankensens	iiijd
Item for vj li of wex to Wylliam Gyste	iiijs vjd
Item to Allson Hoge for mendyng of churche clothyng	viijd
Item to John Gyste for makyn of ij colerys	iiijd
Item to Yengrum for mendyng of ye cloke	ijs
Item to Morton ys wyfe for mendyng of the serpyls	iiijd
Item payed for ix vethem of wyer for the cloke	ixd
Item payed for the trobell whyell	jd

22 Bodmin Moor.

23 Marginal note and first reference to a fair.

Item for blessyng of ij chalys iiijd
Item for trussyng of ij belles viijd
Item for iiij li of wex at Crystes mase ijs xd
Item for makyn of the taperes iiijd
Item for wekes ob
Item to John Hore for Bruzy xiijs iiijd
Item for rent for the churche house iijd
Item for feofers fynes of Stonelond & Hele iiijd
Item to Pynwell for helyng of ye churche viijd
Item for met & dryncke iiijd[24]

[f.8v]
Item payed to Heddon for ire for ye framys of the belles vijd
Item payed to John Bruzy for hys last paye ijs viijd
Item for wascheyng of ye church clothyng vjd
Item for makyn of ye compt iiijd
Summa expens lijs viijd ob
+ Remaynyth xvjs vjd ob
Et ^sic^ soluit quietus est

f.9
The a compte of the Hye Cross beyng wardens George Awnger & Michaell Myll *anno domini millesimo* ccccc xix [1519]

Recetes

Memorandum recevyd of John Chamond *armiger* & Thomas Marys beyng last wardens xvjs ^vjd ob^
Item received of Thomas Priste for the refusyng of the wardynshep[25] iijs iiijd
Item received for John Geton to be putt a pone the beddroll iijs iiijd
Item received for the Hye Cross ale yn [di crossed out] owr tyme xlviijs [v crossed out]jd ob
Summa iijli xjs [xjd crossed out] ijd

Expenses

Memorandum paid to Nycholas Heddon to pay the prists wages xiijs iiijd
Item payd for mendyng of the church clothys & for thred viijd
Item for frankyncens jd
Item paid to Wylliam Gyst for v pownd of wex a gens Ester iijs ixd
Item for the makyng jd ob
Item for expenses to the visitacon at Lanceston xijd
Item paid to Master Vicar vs
+Item paid for hye rent for the church howse iijd
Item paid to John Wolfe for wex a gens Crystesmas for iiij pownd ijs xd
Item paid for the makyng of the same jd ob
Item paid to John Payne for gress for the bell jd
Item paid to Cholwyll for mendyng of the bellys iiijd
Item paid for ij new crewytts xd
Item paid for pownd of wex to make candelys viijd ob
Item paid for ij ropys for the cholke vijd
Item paid for mendyng of the colers for the bells iiijd
Item for mendyng of the bell ropys jd

[24] *v[er]t'* added after the sum.
[25] A rare refusal to take office.

Item paid for whassyng of the church clothys vjd
Item paid for the makyng of thys a cownt iiijd

Summa xxxs xjd + remaynyth xls iiijd *Solut quietus est*

+ memorandum received of Myzhyll Myll for to sett iij namys a pone the bedroll the vaylour of xxxs jd yn ordinaments longyng to the churche J S

[f.9v]

The a compt of the Hyecross beyng wardens John Rose & Thomas Bryant *anno domini* mccccc xix[26] [1520]

Recetes

Memorandum recevyd of the parson of Selworth[27] for to sett John ^Payne of Lansow[28]^ a pone ye bedroll iijs iiijd
Item received of Myzhell Myll for a chandeler iiijd
Item received of John Gyst for occupying of the church hows ijd
Item received of Thomas Mares for occupying of the kechyn jd
Item received of Wylliam Gyst for the best cross iiijd
Item received of Wylliam Olyver for a halfe a peck of lyme jd
Item received of Sir Nycholas Gyst for to sett Flowr Durdon [to sett he[r] crossed out] a pon ye bedroll ^vjs viiijd^
Item received for a half a bosshell of zond jd
+Item received for stondyngs by the church howse ijs jd
Item received for Myzhell Myll ys grave & his gyft xs
Item received of John Carwetham for Avys Wadyn ys grave ^& for set her^ vjs viijd
Item received of John Trevelan for the browerse of the church haghe ijd
Item received of Alsyn Gilberd for a knyll for her son iiijd
Item received [of crossed out] for the Hye Cross ale yn owr tyme xlijs jd

Summa iijli xijs vd

f.10

Expenses

Memorandum payd to Wylliam Uglow for iij pownd of wex & a quarter ijs vjd
Item paid to Wylliam Gyst for iiij pownd of wex agens Crystesmas iijs [vjd crossed out] ijd
Item for makyng of the same ijd ob
Item paid to Wylliam Bosshepp for candeles ijd
Item paid for expenses at the visitacon at Launceston xvjd
Item paid for fronkencens iiijd
Item paid to Master Vicar vs
Item paid to a glasyer for mendyng of a glas viijd
Item paid to Nycholas Heddon for lyme iiijd
Item paid for ij truss of russhe vjd
Item paid for a busshell & di of lyme vijd ob
Item paid for caryg of the same frow Bedeford[29] vd
Item paid for ij zemys of zond ijd
Item for expenses at the visitacon at Lanceston xvjd
Item paid for schyllyng stonys to Thomas Maris iijd

26 Duplicate date to the last account, so the dating is now a year out.
27 Selworthy, Somerset, was an Arundell of Trerice benefice.
28 Launcells.
29 Bideford.

Item paid to Pynwyll for mendyng of the church for ij days & *dimidia* mete & drynk xvd
Item paid to Nycholas Heddon for mendyng of a claper iijd
Item paid to Nycholas Heddon for gerdelys ijd
Item for mendyng of the vestments jd
Item for a schowle xd
Item for mendyng for ^mendyng^ of ij locks ijd
Item for hy rent for the church howse iijd
Item for gressyng of the bells & mendyng of a coler ijd
Item for iij pownd of wex a gens Crystsmas ijs viijd ob
Item for makyng of the same jd ob
Item paid to W. Dromond for mendyng of the church jd
Item for a server ob
Item paid to Wylliam Jule crowder & unto W. To wyll for redyng of the church howse a day, met & dryng & hyre viijd

[f.10v]
Item paid to John Rose for wyrkyn at the same tyme iiijd
Item paid for strow v knogys jd
Item for wyr for the clock vjd
Item for mendyng of a coler ijd
Item for ij days werke to make the churche heg [ij days crossed out] iij men, mete & hyr ijs
Item for ij belropps ijs ijd
Item for expenses at the visitasion at Lanston xxiijd
Item for wassheg of the churche clothys vjd
Item for makyng of thys a cownt iiijd

Summa xxxjs vijjd ob

+So remaynyth clerly [xljs crossed out] xls v[x crossed out]jd? ob
sic solut quietus est

f.11

The a compt of the Hye Cross beyng wardens John Hayne & Thomas Jule *anno domini* m ccccc xx [1521]

Recetes

Memorandum recevyd of Tomsyn Blakhyll to set her husband a pone ye bedroll iijs iiijd
Item received of Sir John Lyll to set his fader & moder a pone the bedroll vjs viijd
+Item received of John Androw for a stondyng bi the church howse jd
Item received for the hyecross ale xxvjs viijd

Summa xxxvjs ixd

Expenses

Memorandum John Sonder payd to John Wolfe for vj pownde of wex a genst Ester vs vd
Item for makyng of the same iijd
Item paid for ij new bell colers xiiijd
Item paid for expenses at the visitacon at Lancestone xvijd
Item paid to Master Vicar for the bedroll vs
Item for gress for the bellys jd
Item paid hyerent for the church howse iijd
Item for scheryng of the church hagg ijd
Item paid to Yngram for mendyng of the bellys & the church style, mete & wages & to a man to help, his mete & wages xxjd
Item paid to Thomas Taylour for iij pownd of wex a genst Crystsmas ijs vjd
Item paid for a pownd & *dimidia* of wex to make candels xvd
Item for makyng of the sayd wex ijd

Item for caryng of zond iijd
Item for mendyng of ij colers ijd
Item for makyng of the church pekys iiijd
Item for mendyng of the church clothys iijd
Item for whasshyng of them vjd
Item for mendyng of the churchhowse ster jd
Item for makyng of ye a compt iiijd
^Item paid russhech[30] iijd^
Summa xx[vs jd crossed out]^iiijs ixd^
+ So remayneth xjs v[ij?]d
sic solute quietus est

[f.11v]

The a compte of Wylliam Jule smyzth & John Hacker wardens of the hyecross of the church of Stratton *anno* [rr crossed out] *domini* m ccccc xxj [1522]

Recetes

Memorandum recvyd for the Hyecross ale in owr tyme clerly[31] [xvjs xd ob crossed out]^xviijs vjd ob^

Expenses

Memorandum for expenses at the visitacon at Launceston xviijd
Item paid to Master Vicar for the bedroll vs
Item paid to Nycholas Heddon & Nycholas Lang recevers ixs xd ob
Item paid for wex to make candells vd
Item for mendyng of the bell colers & for gress iijd
Item for mendyng of a dext jd
Item paryng of the churche hagge jd
Item for [wh crossed out] wassheng of the church clothys vjd
Item for scowryng of [of crossed out] the grette chandlers jd
Item for rushes iijd
Summa expenses xviijs ob
remaynyth to the church vjd m
in John Hacker ys hondds

f.12

The a compt of Thomas Taylor junior & Nicholas Symon of Bowrwode wardens of the Hye Cross store *anno domini millimo* ccccc xxij [1523]

Recetes

Memorandum recevyd off Sir John Lyll for to sett his fader & moder a pone the bedroll vjs viijd
Item received of the same Sir John for his moder ys grave iijs iiijd
Item received of Johan Langford for her howsbond ys grave iijs iiijd
Item received of the Egyppcions[32] for the church howse xxd
Item received of Tomsyn Whythed ys be quethe iijs iiijd
Item received of Wylliam Dromond for poche for the yer a past xviijd
Item received of the same Wylliam & John Rose for ys yer ijs
Item received [of crossed out] for owr ale clerly xxxiijs iiijd
Summa lvjs iiijd

[30] Large space above.
[31] Space left for other entries.
[32] Gypsies.

Expenses

Memorandum payd to John Hayne for mendyng of the churche style	jd
Item paid for a truss of russhes	iijd
Item paid for gresse for the bellys	jd ob
Item paid for expenses to the visitacon at Launceston	iiijd
Item paid for a new bell rope	xvd
Item paid ij new bellcolers	xxiijd
Item paid for viij pownd of wex a genst Ester	vjs
Item paid for makyng of the same	iijd
Item paid for naylys to mend the church style	ob
Item paid for a belrope for the iij^de^ bell & a rope for ye lytyll bell	xvjd
Item paid to Master Vicar for the bedroll & Wylliam Northyn ys perpetual meneday[33]	vs
Item paid to John Cholwyll for trussyng of the greate bell & for a man to helpe hym	ijd
Item paid for wyr for the cloke	xviijd
Item paid for expenses for John Trenger ys meneday[34]	ijs jd
Item paid to a helyer for mendyng of ye church & for mendyng of ye towr	xd
Item paid to Nicholas Hedon for remeng of ye greate bell claper	iijd

[f.12v]

Item for mendyng of the bell colers	iijd
Item paid for lyme to hele the church	iijd
Item paid for nayles for mendyng of the towr	ob
Item for helyng stonys fore to mend the church	ijd
Item for to pownd of wex & *dimidia* a genst [Ester crossed out] Crystsmas	ijs jd
Item for makyng of the same	jd ob
Item for makyng of a kay for cofer yn the stypyll	iiijd
Item paid to Johan Morton for mendyng of ij syples	jd
Item paid to Margaret Martyn for mendyng of ye church clothys	iiijd
Item paid washeng of the church clothys	vjd
Item paid for hye rent for the church howse	iijd
Item for mendyng of a bell rope	ob
Item for making of a claper to the lytyll bell	vs vd
Item paid to Dromond for mendyng of the church	jd
Item paid W Gyst for lyme	jd ob
Item for making of ys a compt	iijd

Summa expenses xxxijs ixd
+ *Et sic de claro* xxiijs vijd
+ *Solut* Alexander Penvos & John Rose
principal rec[eivers] *quietus est*

f.13

The a compt of John Udy & Robert Bette, Hyecrosse wardens *anno domini millimo* ccccc xxiij [1524]

Memorandum recevyd of Alexander Penvos & John Rose genrall recevers	vijs viijd
Item received of Johan Prist to sett Thomas Prist and her a pone ye bedroll	vjs viijd
Item received of the same Johan Priste for her housbond ys grave	iijs iiijd
Item received of John Wolfe taylour for a knyll	vjd
Item received of Thomas Marys to sett Jamys Pole a pone ye bedroll	iijs iiijd
Item received of John Wolfe of Northcott[35]	xvjd

[33] Chantry founder's obit begins.

[34] Church house benefactor's obit.

[35] Poughill.

Item received for owr ale bruyng in owr tyme	xxxjs
Item received of Wylliam Dromond for huny and wex	xiijd
+^ Item received of a messer for stondyng agenst the church howse	ijd^

Summa [liiijs xjd crossed out] – lvs jd

Expenses

Memorandum payd for expenses to mylord besshep ys visitacon	ijs iiijd ob
Item paid for expenses at the last visitacon at Lanceston	[xviijd crossed out] xijd
Item for v pownd of wex agenst Ester	iiijs iiijd
Item for makyng of the same & for wekes	iiijd
Item paid to Master Vicar for the bedroll & Wylliam No[r]then ys meneday	vs
Item for mendyng of the church dor kay	ijd
Item payd to Nycholas Uglow for ij belropys	ijs ijd
Item paid for mendyng of the churche clothys	iiijd
Item for mendyng of ij bell colers	iiijd
Item payd to a plummer for mendyng of the church led	ijs vjd
Item paid for wex agenst Crystsmas	ijs viijd
Item for makyng of ye same	jd
Item for a halfe a pownd of frankencens	ijd
Item for gress for the bells	ijd
Item for washeng of the church clothys	vjd
Item for hye rent of the church howse	iijd
Item re[ceive]d [of W crossed out] for makyng of ys a compt	iiijd

Summa xxijs viijd ob rem[a]n clerly xxxijs iiijd ob

[f.13v]

The a compte of John Carwetham & Walter Maior Hyecross wardens *anno domini millesimo* ccccc xxv[36] [1525]

Recetes

Memorandum recevyd of Thomas Maris & Thomas Bryant generall recevers or stocke wardens	vjs viijd
Item received of George Awnger to sett iij namys apone the bederoll	xs
Item of Thomas Marys for Edmund Yate ys grave	iijs iiijd
Item received of Wylliam Sparke for his fader ys grave & hys gyfte to ye church	vjs viijd
Item received of John Sawnder to sett his moder apone the bede roll	iijs iiijd
Item received of Margery Betty for to sett her hosbond a pone the bederoll	iijs iiijd
Item received for a knyll for Alexander Raw	xd
Item received of Nycholas Heddon for broken yre	xviijd
Item received of Wylliam Dromond for poche & hony	xiijd
Item received of John Rose for hony & wax	xixd ob
Item received for the Hyecrosse ale	xxxijs iiijd

Summa iij li xjs viijd ob

Expenses

Memorandum payde to John Wolfe for viij pownd of wex a geste Ester	vjs iiijd ob
Item makyng of the same wex & for wekes	ijd ob
Item payd to a helyer for mendyng of [of crossed out] the church for mete & drynk and a man to serve hym	viijd
Item for halfe a c of helyng stone to Wylliam Olyver	ijd
Item paid for lathe nayle & for a pyn of yre for a poly	ijd ob
Item for expenses to the visitacon at Lanceston	xvjd

[36] Accounting year corrected.

Item for mendyng of a cofer to Wylliam Jule iijd
Item paid for a pownd of frankyncens iiijd
Item paid for iiij new belropys iijs viijd
Item for mendyng of all the old belropys iijd
Item payd for a new bell coler to Nycholas Uglow ixd

f.14
Item for mendyng of the church clothys ijd ob
Item paid to John Cholwyll for trussyng of the bellys ijs xd
Item paid for wex a genste Crytys mas one pownd ixd
Item for ij semys of gravyll & to helpe to trusse the bellys iijd
Item payde to Master Vicar for the bederoll & for Wylliam Northen ys perpetiall obytt or meneday vs
Item payd for the hye rent to the lords of Bynamy for ye church hows iijd
Item paid to John Gyste for mendyng of ye prists chamber ijs
Item for gress for the bellys ijd
Item paid to Nycholas Heddon for mendyng of ye claper of ye grete bell iiijd
Item for whassheng of ye church clothys vjd
Item for makyng of ys a compte[37] iiijd

Summa xxvjs xd

+ So remaynyth clerly to the churche
+ xliiijs xd ob & xiiijd obreceived for hony
+ *Et sic debit* xlvjs [iiijd crossed out] jd

Memorandum the sayd xlvjs jd payde to Nycholas Uglow & Richard Calygerne general recevers *Et sic quietus est*

[f.14v]

The accompt of Robert Uglow & John Puddner beyng hyecrosse wardens *anno domini millesimo ccccc xxvj* [1526]

Recetes

Memorandum recevyd of Wylliam Bosshep for a knyll for Lymscott ys wyfe iiijd
Item received for a knyll for Mawte servant to Master Chamond iiijd
Item received for a knyll for Thomas Blake ys dafter iiijd
Item received of Johan Myll for Johan Durdon iiijd
Item received of Magery Bette for ij knyllys viijd
Item received of John Dromond for a knyll iiijd
Item received of Master Harry Raynols for a buck of prikesong for a grave iijs iiijd
Item received of the berehurds & to have rome yn the churchhowse ijd
+Item received of marchands for stondyng a genst the church howse vjd ob
Item received of Richard Calygerne & Nycholas Woglow generall recevers xiijs vijd
Item received for owr ale yn owr tyme xxxiijs
Item received of Rychard Chyng for an olde belrop xd
Item received of Rychard Calygern & Nycholas Uglow generall recevers vjs viijd
Item received for hony & wex iijs

Summa lixs xd ob

Expenses

Memorandum paid for mendyng of the church clothys to Margaret Martyn iijd
Item paid to Nycholas Heddon for mendyng of a bell claper iiijd
Item paid for a pownd of frankyncens iiijd
Item paid for expenses at the visitacion at Launceston xvjd

37 Space above.

Item paid to Wylliam Gyst for ix yerds of dowles for to make serples iijs iiijd
Item paid to Nycolas Uglow for x yerds of dowles to make a new serples & to mend a olde serples iijs ixd
Item paid for makyng of ij new serples ijs vjd
Item paid for a lock for the vante[38] & mendyng of a olde yre vjd
Item paid for russhes for the church ixd
Item paid for ij new cruetts vjd

f.15
Item paid to Thomas junior for viij pownd of wex & *dimidia* a genste Ester at viijd a pownd vs viijd
Item for the making therof ijd
Item paid to Master Vicar for the bedroll & Wylliam Northen ys perpetuall menday vs
Item paid to John Cholwyll for to mend the bells jd
Item paid to Pynvyll for mendyng of the church & for a man to serve hym ij days & *dimidia* for mete & wages xx[j crossed out]jd
Item payd for a lanterne vijd
Item paid for a bhare ijd
Item paid to Robert Sparke for redyng a bowt the church howse iiijd
Item paid to Penwyll at a noder tyme for mendyng of the chuche vjd
Item paid for a pownd of wekys ijd ob
Item paid for mendyng of [a crossed out] colers iijd ob
Item for gresse for the bellys jd
Item paid to Wylliam Olyver for c of schelyng stonys iiijd
Item paid to Thomas Mares for vij c of schelyng stonys ijs iiijd
Item paid for hyerent for the church howse iijd
Item for fyne & sueyt of Hele & Stoneland iiijd
Item paid to Nycholas Jud for naylys jd ob
Item payd for a new bell coler ixd
Item paid to Penwyll for mendyng of the churche now lost vjs viijd
Item paid for mendyng of ij old syples vjd
Item paid to Symon Gyst for mendyng of the bell whevels ijd
Item paid for wex [a wex crossed out] a genst Ester payd to Wylliam Gyst ijs viijd
Item for makyng of the same ijd
Item paid to for zonde or gravell for the church [howse crossed out] iiijd
Item paid for lyme for the churche ijs vjd
Item paid for caryng of the same frow Bedeford ijs
Item paid to Nycholas Uglow for a xj crests xxijd
Item paid to the same Nycholas for ij new colers xviijd
Item paid to the same Nycholas for iij new belropys ijs xd
Item for making of ys accompte iiijd
Item paid for [gg crossed out] glue for mendyng of ye organs jd

[f.15v]
Item paid for whashyng of the church clothys viijd
Item paid for paid for a c of lathys vd

Summa lvs [viijd] ob
Summa [iijli jd ob crossed out]
Summa iiijs ijd

[38] Lockable font cover.

Thys a compte made the yer of owr lord God m ccccc xxvj of the wardenys of Hyecrosse Thomas Nicollson & Thomas Bray [1527]

Recetes

Memorandum recevyd of Robert Uglow & John Pudner wardenys the laste yer	vs
Item received of Nycholas Symon of Bowrwod to set hym a pone ye bedroll xxd	
Item received of John Udy & John Trevylion for to se Karitas Geton a pone the bedroll	iijs iiijd
Item received of my Lady Arondell for knyllys for Master Rychard Aronde[ll] & Master Edward	viijd
Item received for Wylliam Jule smyzthe to sett hym a pone the bedroll	iijs iiijd
Item received for stondyngs yn ye church howse of messers	ijd
Item received for a knyll for Mathe Rose his moder	iiijd
Item received of Wylliam Dromond for wex & hony	vjd
Item received of Wylliam Gysts wyfes grave	iijs iiijd
Item received for owr ale	xxijs viijd

Summa xljs

[f.16]

Expenses [margin]

Memorandum payd for iiij pownd of wex & *dimidia* to Wylliam Gyste a genste Ester	vs iiijd
Item for making of the same wex	ijd ob
Item paid for a pownd of frankencens	iiijd
Item for a yerd & halfe of blake reben sylke	jd ob
Item for iij quarters of crescloth for to cover the chalys	iijd
Item paid to John Kyng for the over plus of the crock yt was gevyn	xijd
Item for expenses of the aschedekyns wisitacon at Lanceston	xvjd
Item to Nycholas Woglow for ij boll ropys	ijs
Item to the same Nycholas for a coler for a bell	viijd
Item for thongs to mend ye colers	jd
Item paid to Master Vicar for the bedroll for Wylliam Northen his meneday	vs
Item paid to Nycholas Uglow for iij bellcolers	ijs ijd
Item paid for mendyng of the olde colers to Robert Uglow his servant	vd
Item for ij processinals	ijs ijd
Item paid for a manuell	ijs
Item paid for a yre for the holywater boket	iijd
Item paid to a tynker to mend & to bore ij holys yn the holywater bokett	ijd
Item paid to Thomas Spayver for schutyng of the bellropys	jd
Item paid for gresse for the bellys	jd
Item paid to John Cholwyll for mendyng of the frame of the bellys	viijd
Item paid for vj yerds of cressclothe to make awter clothys	ijs
Item paid [for crossed out] to Thomas Maris for blessying of the [chalys crossed out] ^same^	iiijd
Item for hemyng of them	jd
Item paid for mendyng of a chalys	vjd
Item paid for wex a genst Crystsmas iijli & di	ijs
^Item for making of the same	jd ob^
Item expenses of my lord besshepp his visitacon	xvjd
Item for whassyng of the church clothys	xd
Item for wekys	ob
Item for lyme to mend the churche	jd
Item paid to Hew Corter for mendyng of ye churche clothys	vjd

Item for making of ys a compte iiijd
Summa xxxijs viijd so remaneth to the church - viijs iiijd

[f.16v]
The accompt made the[39]

f.17

[f.17v]
The accompt of the Hyecros wardens John Pery & John Trevelan made yn the yer of owr lord God m ccccc xxvij *& anno regni regis H* viij, xix [1528]

Recetes

Memorandum recevyd of Thomas Nicolson & Thomas Bray wardens the yer past	viijs ^iiijd^
Item received of Sir John Grene for hony	vijd
Item received of Alson Pudner for hyr husbond is grave & to set hym a pone ye bedroll	vjs viijd
Item received of Sir Water Dromond to set Robert Besse is name a pone the bederoll	iijs iiijd
Item received of my Lady Arundell to set Master Rychard Arundell & Edward Arundell a pone the bederoll	vjs viijd
Item received of Nicholas Symon of Bowrwode for a croke yt Robert Heket gave to ye church for to set iij namys a pone the bedroll	xs
Item received of John Trevelan for John Morton ys grave	iijs iiijd
Item received of Nycholas Uglow for barrs of yre	iijs
Item received for owr ale	xxxvjs iiijd
Item received of the paynters for wyrkyng yn the church howse	xijd
Item received of the Rychard Ronell for occupying of the church howse & for a knyll	viijd
Summa iijli xixs xjd	

Expenses

Item paid for a pownd of frannkensens to Thomas Nicolson	iiijd
Item paid to Thomas Heket for a cofer key	iijd
Item paid to Nicholas Hedden for makyng off ij yres for cortens and for a yre for the holy water boket	vjd
Item for vj pownd of wex a genst Ester	iijs xd
Item for di yerd of satyn of burges ^for ye vestements^	xijd
Item for v quarters of grene tuke	vijd

f.18

Item paid to Mystras Grenfyld for rebens of sylke for to mend the vestements	xviijd
Item paid to the sayd Mystras Grenfyld for bradry gold	vjd
Item paid for thred	iijd ob
Item paid to John Peris for mendyng of the vestemetts	vs
Item paid to Master vicar for the bedroll & Wylliam Northyn is menedy	vs
Item paid to Cholwyll for makyng of a new whevyll for ye bellys & for the trussyng of them	iijs
Item paid to iij new belropys	iijs ijd
Item expenses to the visitacon at Lanceston	xiiijd
Item for mendyng of the ledd ^& for sawdre^	xxd

[39] Blotched.

Item paid for ij new rochetts ijs
Item to Glyn for makyng of old rochetts & mendyng of serpels iiijd ob
Item paid for Nycholas Judd for naylys for the whevels vjd
Item for wex a genst Crystsmas – iiij pownd ijs vjd
Item for making of the wex the hole yer iiijd
Item to Sir John Grene for washeng of the carperas jd
Item gresse [for crossed out] for the bells ijd
Item for mendyng of the old colers viijd
Item for scowryng of the chandelers iijd
Item for rushes for the church vjd
Item for washeng of the church clothys xd
Item for making a per of indentures[40]
Item for copyng of other wrytyng longyng to the church
Item paid to the paynter for payntyng of the Lent clothys for ymages xijd
Item for making of thys accompt iiijd
Item ij new colers for bellys xviijd

Summa xxxviijs ixd so *remanet*
xljs ijd *unde solute*
Receptoribuz xxxjs ijd & Nycholas Jude & John B[ond] *gardiani* xs

[f.18v]

The accompt of the Hyecros wardens John Bond & Nycolas Jud made yn the yer of owr lord God m ccccc xxviij *& anno regni regis H*viij, xx [1529][41]

Item we resevyd of John Pere & John Trevelyon xs
Item we resevyd of John Hollodner at Mekelmas xxd
Item we resevyd for the goyne vijs viijd
+Item we resevyd for standyn of the church hoys ijd ob
Item we resevyd for a quaartt of honny yt cum froo John Roos vijd
Item we resevyd for a pond of wex of John Roos vijd
Item we resevyd John Pere fo settyn Wyllyam Denys & Majere *uxorys eius* a pone the bedroll vjs viijd
Item we resevyd of Thomas Crymp for a knyll iiijd
Item we resevyd for owr ale xxxvijs iijd

The sum of the holl iijli iiijs xjd ob

[Memorandum John Bond & John Nycholas Judd ys in *debez* for the grave of a chyld of Harry Rayner iijs iiijd
& the grett bell for the same chyld iiijd crossed out]
Item paid for to Penwose for vij pownd of wex iiijs iiijd ob
& wykyes jd
Item paid for ye makyneg iijd
Item paid for ij pownd of frannkynsenc vd
Item paid to Thomas Talar for a quart[er][42] of wex ijd
Item paid to Nycollas Huglow for a bell collar ixd
Item paid fo Nycollas Huglow for halfe a powne of wex iiijd
Item paid to Nycollas Huglow for a bell rope xiiijd
Item paid to Thomas Tallar for halfe a powne of wex iiijd
Item paid fo Hamifre[43] Lang for makyng of the church styl[e] xjd

[40] Sums blank.
[41] Distinctive hand, erratic spelling.
[42] Of a pound.
[43] Humphrey?

Item paid for expencys to the vycytacyon	xiiijd
Item paid for the rent of the church hoys	iijd

f.19

Item paid ij nu bell ropys to Nycollas Hugllow	ijs vjd
Item paid for iij bz of lyem	xviijd
Item paid for a fonoue	ijd
Item paid for iiij dayes worc to the heller	xvd
Item paid for matytt & drync[44]	xijd
Item paid to Payllmar for sarvyn of the sayd heller matytt & drync	iiijd ob
Item paid to Nychollas Huglow for wyer for the cloyc	vijd ob
Item paid for a bz of lyem	vijd
Item paid for ij dayys to the heller	viijd
Item paid for matytt & drync	vjd
Item paid to Payllmar for sarvyn of them mayttytt & drync	ijd ob
Item paid for laytt naylys	jd
Item paid to John Gyst for stonys	iijd
Item paid for iiij pownd of wex	ijs vjd
Item paid wekys	ob
Item paid for thred for men[ding] of hobys & sety[n] of the peyryll	ob
Item paid to John Trevelon for makyn of the wex	ijd
Item paid to Thomas Clarartt[45] for mendyn of ij bell colar	ijd
Item paid to Wyllyam Moys for mendyn of iij colar & seyn the bellys yt claperys well hayng for the yeer	vjd
Item paid to Master Vycar for the bedroll & Wyllyam Northyn myndaye	vs
Item paid to Joger[46] Juyll for paryn of the churcherd hassyc	jd
Item paid for gressyn of the bellys	ijd
Item paid for a busyll of lyem to John Ude	vijd
Item paid for ruchys forhe church	vjd
Item paid for mendyng of the church mattytt & drync	ijd
Item paid for wassyn of the clothys	xd
Item paid fo makyn of the compt	iiijd

Summa expensys xxxis

& so we have payd to the nu wardens xs

sic remanet in manibus nostris de claro xxxiijs xid ob

[f.19v]

The compt of the Hye Crosse wardyns Nycholas att Wyll & John Dromond madd yn yere off our lord God [g crossed out] m cccccxxx *& anno regni regis Henri octto* xxi [1530][47]

Recetes

Memorandum recevyd fof Nycholas Judd & John Bonde being wardyns the last yere	x[xxiijs xjd ob]
Item off John Holodner of the gyft of Mawte Alyn	vs
Item recevyd off John Wad to bryng his brother a pone the bedroll	iijs iiijd
Item recevyd off Water Dromond to put ij namys apone ye bedroll	vis viijd
Item recevyd off John Bonde for ij knollys	viijd
Item off Richard Calygryne for a pitt & ij knells	iiijs

44 Meat and drink.

45 Clarke?

46 Roger?

47 Accounting year corrected.

Item off Thomas G Mares for a kneyll	iiijd
Item off John Braye for v kneyll	xxd
Item off John Schortt for a kneyll	iiijd
Item off John Pryst for a kneyl	iiijd
Item off Mathe Rose for ij knells	viijd
Item recevyd of William Regg for a knell	iiijd
Item recevyd of John Marys for kepyng of the tolswylt[48] yn the churche howse att Crystmasse	iiijd
+Item for standyng gainst the churche howse	jd
Item made with our ale att Wyttsonday clerely	xls
Summa tota recetes iijli xiijs ixd	

f.20

In expenses

In primis[49] payd for canvass to amend the cope	iiijd
Item for mendyng off the cope	ijs
Item paid to Nycholas Ugglow for bell roppe	xvd
Item paid to William Byschepe for vj pond off wex	iijs & vd
Item for wecks	ob
Item for makyn off the same wex	iijd
Item paid for frowkencens ij pond	vd
Item for thred to mende rotges & syrpyls	ijd
Item paid to Hew Corter for mend of the same rotghydds & syrpyls	iiijd
In ex pences att the archysdekyn ys vicitation at Lanston	xviijd
In ex pences att the byschepis vicitation	xd
Item paid to a glasyer	xxd
Item paid for a showle for the bedman	xijd
Item paid to Nycholas Heddyn for a crocke of yron	iijd
Item for paryng of churche agge	jd
Item for naylys to mende ye bells	jd ob
Item paid to a plommer & for sawder to amende ye ledd	iijs iiijd
Item paid to a man to helpe hem, for mett & drynge & wages	iiijd
Item paid to Nycholas Heddyn for mendyng of a showle	iijd
Item paid to Nycholas Uglow for new bell rope	xvjd
Item paid to ye same Nycholas for a bell colar	ixd ob
Item paid to Myzhellmass fayre[50] for nother new colar	xid
Item paid to Master Vicar for the general bedroll & Northyn ys mende	vs
Item payd to To Hekyth to repere the cloke	ijs
Item payd to Jo Cortes for carage of ye lytyll bell	xijd
Item payd to Nycholas Wgglow for a new bell rope	xvjd
Item payd bell colar	viijd

[f.20v]

Item payd for ix yerds off dowlys to make a syrpuls	iijs iiijd
Item for makyn off the same syrpils	xvjd
Item for a yerd off holand to make ij co[d crossed out]tidiall[51] cops	xijd
Item for the fyne & swtte off Hele & Stolonid[52]	iiijd

48 Weighing of yarn.
49 In the first.
50 Michaelmas fair?
51 Everyday copes.
52 Stoneland.

Item for the hye rent off the churche howse iijd

Item payd to John Trevelyon to make iiij tapers ayest Crysmasse ijd

Item paid to John Rose to redd the churche howse iiijd

Item paid to Nycholas Judd ^to make^ [sawdd crossed out] the bell claper iijs iiijd

Item payd to William Dromond to mende the churche mete & drynge & wages & for a man to serve hem the bozth viijd

Item for wasshong off churche clothyn xd

Item for makeng of thys compte iiijd

Item for vj pond wex a gynst Crystmas iijs iijd

Item payd for iij pycke of lyme vd

Item for gresse for the bells ijd

Item to John Roland to mende ^the^ colers & to mend the ropys & to pyke the j bellys vijd

Item for ruschys for the churche vjd

Item for thongs to mende colers jd

Summa expences xlvijs vjd ob

Sic remanet in manibus & nostris xxvjs ijd ob

Sic solim q' guardivit xs

receptoribus [xvjs ijd crossed out] Thome Taylar et Thome Bray

Sic [*q* crossed out] *quietus est*

f.21

The accompte of the Hey Crose wardens John Shorte & Rychard Chyng made yn the yere of our lord God *m^l^* ccccc xxx[53] *anno regis regni H* viij, xxij [1531]

Recetes

Item *in primis* recevyd of the olde wardens last past xs

Item received off Robert Uglow for iij namys [ux crossed out] apon the bedroll & a knyll xs iiijd

Item received of Matthy Roose for a name apon the bedroll iijs iiijd

Item received of John Heddon for a name apon the bedroll iijs iiijd

Item received of Rycherde Westlake for a name apon ye bedroll iijs iiijd

Item received of the for sayde Rycherd for a knyll which payd to the byyng off ye grett bell ijd nowe she gave for her knyll [besyd crossed out] that ijd

Item received of William Terbarfotte for a name apon ye bedroll iijs iiijd

Item received of Wylliam Gyst for hony xjd

Item received of Nycolas Symon for hony xd

Item received of Wylliam Gyst for a knyll iiijd

Item received of Garrett for ocupyyng of the kechyng yn ye chrych house with tesels[54] iiijd

Item received of the bayle off the toune for ocupyyng off the cryche house for ij ferrys viijd

Item received of Nycolas Heddon for a knyll iiijd

Item received of John Roose for a knyll iiijd

Item received of Thomas Hekett for ij knylls viijd

Item received of Master Thorne for ocupyng of ornaments of the cryche xijd

Item received of the forsayd Master Thorne for a [kyn crossed out] knyll iiijd

Item received of Matthy Roose for a knyll iiijd

Item received of John Bayall for a knyll iiijd

Item received of Stevyn Smale for a knyll iiijd

Item received of Johane Meryvyld for a knyll iiijd

Item received of Wylliam Whytte for [a knyll crossed out] the ornaments of the cryche xijd

[53] The date is a year out again.

[54] Teasels, for cloth finishing, were growing in John Rodde's garden at Lynstone in 1590, TNA, C3/229/33.

[f.21v]

Item received off John Shorte for a knyll	iiijd
Item received for a stondyng yn the cryche house	jd
Item received off Thomas Yerle for a knyll	iiijd
Item received off Rychard Chyng for a end off a rope	ijd
Item received for a pese of brase	jd
Item we made with the ale	xxxijs iiijd
Sum of the hole recetes [wt ye ale more xvjs xjd crossed out] iijli xvs iijd	

Expenses

Item in primis payd to Thomas Tayler for wax agen Ester	iiijs
Item payd to Nycolas Uglow for a bell rope	xvd
Item payd yn expensis att ye vysytocyon	xvjd
Item payd for makyn of a frame to sett tapers yn afore ye sepulker[55]	xijd
Item payd to Master Vycar for the generall bedroll	vs
Item payd to Nycolas Jude for makyn off rynggs for the Lentcloth	ijd
Item payd to Nycolas Uglow for cords to ye same Lentcloth	ijd
Item payd to Wylliam Gyst for cloth to mend ye whytte vestments	iiijd
Item payd to Nycolas Heddon for makyn of ye iar worke for the cryche stele	jd
Item ^payd^ for mendyng of ye same yate & for setting off ye same	jd
Item payd to Hu Corter for off [^dx^ crossed out] ^souyng^ ye cryche clothyis & mendyng off ij per of vestments	iiijd
Item payd to Thomas Tayler for ij pound of fronkasens	vd
Item payd to Nycolas Uglow for a cord for the lytell bell	iijd
Item payd to John Trevylyon for makyng of the wax agen Ester	iijd

f.22

Item [fo crossed out] payd for makyn of the herse	xijd
Item payd to Nycolas Heddon for nayls to the herse	jd
Item payd for hey rent for Stone lond	iijd
Item payd for ye hey rent of the cryche house	iijd
Item payd to Thomas Hykett for mendyng of the bedman ys bell	iiijd
Item payd to Thomas Tayler for wax agen Crystmas	xviijd
Item for makyn of ye vax to Trevylyan	ijd
Item payd to Thomas Hykett for kepyng of the cloke by the yere	ijs
Item payd to Elysander Penvos for russhys by the yere	vjd
Item payd for a key to the clarke ys cofer	ijd
Item payd to Thomas Hykett for a locke to the clokhouse	vd
Item payd for a bord yn the [towr crossed out] tower window	ijd
Item payd for paryng of the crych hegge	jd
Item payd for ^makyn^ of a pere of [sh crossed out] slevys to ye whytt vestments	jd
Item payd for [g crossed out] settyng of a vote to ye cryche yate	jd
Item payd to Wylliam y [sic] Moyys for mendyng of the bell colers by the yere	vjd
Item payd for thongs to the same	ijd
Item payd for shottyng of iij bellropis	jd
Item payd for a forme for the hey cryche house	iiijd
Item payd for a standyng for the [a crossed out] cruyts besyde Owr Lady of Holymondon	jd
Item payd for wekes by the yere	ob
Item payd for gresse for the bells	ijd
Item payd for waysshyng of ye cryche clothyng by the yere	xd

[55] Easter Sepulchre.

[f.22v]

Item payd of the gyft of Wylliam Whyte to Owr Lady ys wardens iiijd
Item payd for makyn of the compte[56] iiijd
Summa of the hole expensis xxiiijs vijd ob

Item a pese of iar of the cryche beyng viij^l^ pond which restyt with Nycolas Heddon at all nedes to be delyveryd
Item received a kercher of the gyft of Master Vycar which ys now here to be delyveryd
Now ther remaynyth yn owr honds clere with the ale mony ls vijd ob

f.23

The accompte of Stevyn Smale and Wylliam Baron beyng Hey Crose wardens made yn the yere of owr lord God m ccccc xxxj anno regni regis *H* 8 23 [1532]

Recetes

Item *in primis* recevyd of John Short & Rychard Chyng the old wardens ye laste yere pastxs
Item also received of the viij men ijs
Item received of John Marrys for stondyng yn the cryche howse Saynt Androw ys yn Maye[57] iiijd
Item received of Agnes Bryant for a name upon the bedroll iijs iiijd
Item received of Wylliam Moyse for a knyll iiijd
Item received of Johane Pryst for a name upon ye bedroll iijs viijd
Item received of John Wade for ij namys upon ye bedroll vjs viiijd
Item received of John Marrys for stondyng yn ye cryche howse Saynt Androw ys daye afore Crystmasse[58] iiijd
+Item received of certyn marchants for standyng by ye cryche howse ye same day iijd ob
Item received for wode of the toppyng of ye treys yn the cryche erth ijs viijd
Item received of John Edey for a name upon ye bedroll iijs iiijd
Item received of Nycholas Symon for a knyll iiijd
Item received of Johane Chope for an obytt vjd
Item received for owr ale xxxjs viijd
Summa of the hole recetes iijli vs jd ob

Expenses

Item fryst payd for wax to Thomas Tayler a gen Ester iiijs
Item paid for makyng thereof to Trevilyan iijd
Item paid for vj gerdels & for mendyng of a serpleys iiijd
Item paid for ij awter clothys for ye hey auter ijs vjd
Item paid for frannkasens iijd
Item paid for wasshyng of the cryche clothing xd
Item paid for a bell rope to Nycholas Uglow xvjd
Item paid to Kelly for beryng of the auter clothys to my lord of Bodmyn[59] jd

[f.23v]

Item paid to Sir Water Dromond for the bedreden[60] vs
Item paid to John Chollwyll for seyng to the bells the last yere past xvjd
Item paid to Cholwyll for nayl jd

[56] Space for two entries above.
[57] 9 May.
[58] 30 November.
[59] Thomas Vivian, Bodmin Prior.
[60] Reading bede roll.

Item paid for a shype[61] to hold frankasens iiijs viijd
Item paid for a new sense besyde ye old stuffe ijs
Item paid to Nycholas Jude for nayls to the bells ijd
Item paid to Wylliam Moyse for mendyng of the bell colers ijd
Item paid for v yards of cresse clothe to make racchyts for the clyler[62] xxd
Item paid for makyng therof to Glyan vd
Item paid to Cannyan the helyer for mendyng of the cryche howse iiijd
Item paid to Stevyn Smale for hys labor to serve hem ijd
Item paid for mete & drynke for them bothe vjd
Item paid for skowryng of the gret chandelers vjd
Item paid for skowryng of the senses ijd
Item paid to Thomas Heket for kepyng of ye cloke by the yere ijs
Item paid to Nycholas Uglow for a bell rope xiiijd
Item paid to Thomas Tayler for iij pownd of wax xviijd
Item paid to Trevilyan for makyng thereof ijd
Item paid for expenses at the vysitacion xxd
Item paid for russhys by the yere vjd
Item paid hey rent for the cryche howse iijd
Item paid for hey rent of Stone lond iijd
Item paid To Nycolas Heddon for makyng of a pycyse iiijd
Item paid to John Cholwyll for seyng to the bells by the yere xvjd
Item paid for grese to the bells ijd
Item paid for paryng of the cryche haggys jd
Item paid to Wylliam Moys to peke & g[r]esse ye bells by the yere vjd
Item paid to Wylliam Dromond for helyon of the cryche xijd

f.4[63]
Item paid for a busshell & a hafe of lyme & the bryngyn home therof xijd
Item paid for makyng of the accompte iiijd
Summa expenses xxxixs
Now ther remayneth yn owr honds xxvjs jd ob

[f.4v]
The accompte off Wyllyam Beschepp & Wyllyam Gyst beyn Hey Crosse wardens off all recetys & expensys doyn by them yn the yere off owr lord God m ccccc xx[xij ty crossed out]xv[64] *anno regni regis H 8 querto* [1533]

Recetes

Item received off Wyllyam Baron & Sthephyn Smale wardens the yer past xs
Item received off Johana Jeell to putt her hosbond a pond the bedroll iijs iiijd
Item received off Rycherd Aunger for her hosbond is grayff iijs iiijd
Item received off Rycherd Aunger for putt her hosbond & her a pond the bed roll vjs viijd
Item received off Nycholas Lang & Anneta *uxoryse ejus* for to be put a pon the bed roll vjs viijd
Item received of John Chohyll for to be set a pon the bed roll iijs iiijd
Item received of Robert Rygyll for his wyyff grayff iijs iiijd
Item received of Thomas Aprrys for the wyytys[65] yn chechersthos viijd

[61] Incense boat.
[62] Meaning unclear, possibly children.
[63] Folio misplaced. See also appendix 2.1, p.214.
[64] Misread as 1515.
[65] Weights for weighing yarn and wool.

Item received of John Pere for a knyll	iiijd
Item received of Wyllyam Sparca for a knyll	iiijd
Item received of John Wogllo for a knyll	iiijd
Item received of John TTrevellan for ropys	ob
Item received for horer alle yn horer yere	iijli ixs vijd ob

The *summa* of the holl recetes cum to vli viijs

expensye

Sum declaroys iijli ixs iiijd

f.24

Item payd for two bell ropys to Nycolas Wegllo	ijs iijd
Item payd for v pownd of wex agenst Ester vijd the pownd	ijs xjd
Item payd for wekes	ob
Item payd for the makyn	iijd
Item payd for a stape for a beell	iiijd
Item payd for a pownd of frankasense	ijd ob
Item paid for iij yerds of clothe to make Palmar a racchett	xd
Item paid for expenses att ij vycystacyons att Llanston	ijs viijd
Item paid for the bedroll to Master Vicarre for the yere	vs
Item paid for the last vysytacyon	ixd
Item paid for [of crossed out] mendyn of iij bokes of the cyrcheys	viijd
Item paid for keveryn of a mas boke	vd
Item paid for vij yerds ^of cloth^ & a garter for to make a hoyb to Sir Wylliams vestments	iijs jd
Item paid for iij yards of holland for the he auter	ijs vjd
Item paid to Nycolas Heddon for mendyn of the lytell bell claper	xijd
Item paid to John Moke for pare of the chyche hage	jd
Item paid to Thomas Heckytt for the cloytt for the yer	ijs
Item paid to John Ros for a matt for the wendo	ijd
Item paid to John Dromott for a dayys haylyn matytt & her	vd
Item paid for lyme for the same hellyer	iijd
Item paid for iij bell collars to Nycolas Woglo	ijs xd
Item paid to Palmor for mendyn of the chyrche floyr	jd
Item paid for a pownd of wex for to make candyls	vijd
Item paid to Thomas Morrys for the he rrentt of the chyche hos	iijd
Item paid to Thomas Morrys for the mor stonys	iijs
Item paid to Nycolas Woglo for a bell royp	xiijd
Item paid for suyttyn of a bell royp	jd
Item paid for mendyn of the legentt	iiijd
Item paid for mendyn of the chyche styyll to John Dromott	vd
Item paid for mendyn of the chyche to John Dromott	vd
Item paid for lyyme & stonys & latt	vijd
Item paid for ruscys for the chyche	vjd
Item paid for a pac of ruscys agen my lor[d] beschepp[66] cumyn	iijd
Item paid for a pac of ruscys agen Master Chamun weddy[n]	iijd
Item paid to Wyllyiam Moys to peke & gresse the bellys for the yer	xijd
Item for wassyn of the chyche clothyn by the yer	xd
Item paid for makyn of the accompte	iiijd

Summa expenses xxxviijs viijd

[66] Visit by John Veysey, bishop of Exeter.

[f.24v]
[mainly blank] [the acco crossed out]
By [me crossed out] me then
iij li vijs iijd ob

f.25

The accompte of John Jule & Thomas Hekytt wardens of the Hye Crosse *anno domini millimo & ccccc xxxiii & anno regni regis Henrici viij xxv* [1534]

Recetes

In primis recevyd off Wylliam Gyst & Wylliam Besshepp Hye Crosse wardens the yer past iij^li^ ixs ^iiijd^
Item received of Johan Hore for to sett Roger Hore herr husband a pone the bedroll iijs iiijd
Item received of John Jule of Lancels for to set Sir Rychard Denys parson of Powdram[67] a pone the bedroll & ij namys mor xxs
Item received of a glasyer for ledd xvjd
Item received of Margery Schorte to sett herr husbond & herr a pone the beddroll iijs iiijd
Item recevyd of Thomas Nycollson for a knyll for Emate Cole iiijd
Item received of John Rose for a quarte of hony vd
Item received of John Mares for occupying of the churche howse for wyztyng of yerne at ye fere tyme viijd
Item received of John Cholwyll for the occupying of the black sute for requiem[68]
Item received of John Wolfe for the same black sute
Item received for owr alle bruyng xxxvs v[i crossed out]jd
Item received of Wylliam Smyzth for occupying of the churche howse vjd
Item received of Thomas Rose for ye same howse iijd
Summa vj li xviijs iiijd

[f.25v]

Expenses

In primis payd for the changyng of a chalys[69] ixs iiijd
Item payd for viij yerds of lynclothe to make iiij new rochets ijs iijd
Item for makyng of the same rochets xijd
Item paid for ix pownd of wex a genst Ester vs iijd
Item makyng of the same wex iijd
Item paid for ij pownd of franken essens vjd
Item paid for scowryng of ye gret chandelers iijd
Item paid for ye mendyng of the stypell flowr viijd
Item paid to Master Vycar for the beddroll & Wylliam Northen ys meneday for the yer vs
Item payd for iij yerds of bokeram for to mend ye vestements xxjd
Item for thred for the same jd
Item for mendyng of ye [br crossed out] blew sute[70] mete, drynk & wages xijd
Item paid for ^iiij^ new bellropys & cord for ye clock paid to Nycholas Uglow [& a Lent ^cord^ crossed out] vs jd
Item paid for makyng of the claper of the grett bell vs
Item paid for viij bosshels of lyme ijs xd
Item paid for a pownd of wex to make candelys vijd
Item paid for expenses at the visitacion at Lanceston xviijd
Item for hye rent of the churche howse iijd

[67] Powderham in Devon.
[68] Sums left blank.
[69] At Baldock in c.1540 cruets were exchanged. See Palmer, *Tudor Churchwardens' Accounts*, p.60.
[70] Blue vestments, appendix 3.1–3.2.

Item paid for the makyng of the stypyll wyndow	vjs xd
Item paid for the yre for the same wyindow	iiijs
Item the glasyng of the same	xjs xd

f.26

Item for mendyng of the penakyls of ye stypyll	iiijs ^viijd^
Item paid for a bell color	ixd
Item for kepyng of ye clock	ijs
Item paid to a helyer for to mend the churche mete drynk & wages & for one to serve hym	xd
Item for schelyng stonys	iijd
Item for v [ij crossed out] pownd of wex a genst Crystsmas	ijs xjd
Item for makyng of the same	ijd
Item for ij trossys of rushes	viijd
Item for a cace for a chalys[71]	iijd
Item paid to John Cholwyll for ij yeres for taking hede of ye bells	ijs viijd
Item to Wylliam Moyse for mendyng of ye bell colers & gressyng of bells	xijd
Item paid for wasshens of ye churche clothys	xd
Item for gresse for the bellys	ijd ob
Item for paper	ob
Item paid for naylys for Dow	iijd
Item paid to Nycholas Judd for naylys	ijd
Item for a c of hache naylys to Dow	vd
Item for makyng of ys accompt	iiijd

Summa – iiijli iijs viijd
Remanet – liiijs viijd

[f.26v]

The acompt of John Payne & William Spark made the Sonday after the Purificacon of Owr Lady beyng Hycros wardens *anno domini millessimo* ccccc xxxiiij *et anno regni regis Henrici* viij, xxvj [1535]

Recetes

^Item received of Hoper of Berswyll[72]	xs^
In primis received of John Wulff to be set a pone ye beddroll	vjs ^viijd^
Item received off [Wylliam Gyst crossed out] ^Thomas Hyckyd^ & John Jule Hycrose wardens the yer past	xs
Item received of John Wulfe for the blacke sute	xxd
Item received of[73] Wodeward to set hym a pone the bedroll	iijs
Item received for a kertyll yt Esbyll Lyll gave to ye church	vjs iiijd
Item received of Wylliam for hys gyfte yt he gave to ye churche	vjs viijd
Item received of Isbyll Chyng for a knyll	iiijd
Item received of Master Doctor Morman[74] for ye black sute	iiijd
Item received of John Wyll alias Hele for a knyll	iiijd
Item received & made of owr ale	xlvs
Item received of Nycholas Symon of Bowrred[75] for ij knyllys	viijd
^Item received of Bere for the bellys	iiijd^
Summa – ^Item of Thomas Bryant	iiijd^

[71] Leather case?

[72] Burshill, Poughill.

[73] Blank for Christian name, probably William, a Poundstock priest.

[74] Vicar of Menheniot.

[75] Burwood.

Summa iiijli [xxd crossed out][76]
xjs viijd

f.27

Expenses

In primis payd to Hugh Corter for makyng of ij new lytyll surpels & mendyng of other surpels mete & wages viijd
Item payd to Master Vicar for ye bedroll & Wylliam Northyn is mynday vs
Item paid to Thomas Taylour for ix pownd of wex a gens Ester vs jd
Item paid to ye sayd Thomas for ij pownd of frankencens iiijd
Item paid to the same Thomas for wyre for ye clock iiijd
Item paid to John Rowland for makyng of ij bell colers iiijd
Item for expenses to the visitacion at Lanceston xvd
Item for ye church dore key jd
Item payd to a plummer for v pownd ^*dimidia*^ of zodry to mend the ledds ijs jd
Item paid to hym & to hys servant for ys wages to mend the ledds vjd
Item for ther mete & drynke vd
Item for naylys for trussyng of the bellys jd
Item paid to Thomas Clerke of ye bell ropys & the colers iiijd
Item paid for ij bushels of lyme at Bedeford xiiijd
Item for a busshell of lyme frow ye sowth parte[77] iiijd
Item for expenses to my lord of Cawnterbery is visitacon[78] xiiijd
Item for a cord to the clock vjd
Item payd to Hugh Corter for mendyng of the black sute & suuyng of the church clothing iiijd
Item paid to Nycholas Heddyn for twysts & crobe for ye church howse for the lytill dore yn the stypyll a bove ye lyd xxjd
Item paid to ye same Nycholas for yre for the est wyndow of the stypyll with ye old stuff ixs vijd
Item payd to Rowclyff yn parte of payment of his bargyn for the same est wyndow vjs viijd
Item paid to a warkeman to make a ragg & for ye same ragg iiijd
Item paid to Roger Sonder to make dor a boff yn ye stypyll & for ye wyndows yn ye church howse xd

[f.27v]

Item paid to Wylliam Gyst for a burd to make the same wyndow vijd
Item paid for iij burds more xijd
Item paid for a hoghed to set lyme yn xijd
Item paid for naylys for the lytill dore jd
Item paid for the glasyng of the stypyll wyndow for ye new glasse & the old glasse xs viijd
Item for a man to tend a pone the glasyer mete & drynke & wages to bryng hym stuff iiijd
Item payd to Nycholas Heddon for ye same wyndow & for ij buckells & ij nelys for ye bellys xijd
Item for kepyng of the clock paid to Thomas Hekytt ijs
Item paid to Master Vicar for ij sylver buttens for ye cope xijd
Item for a gerdyll for ye vestements jd
Item for a new belrope xijd
Item paid for iiij pownd of wex agenst Ester ijs iiijd

76 Erasings.

77 South Devon?

78 Archbishop Cranmer's visitation, see Introduction.

Item paid to a helyer for iiij days jurney a pone the church & ye church howse xvjd
Item for hys mete & drynke iiij days viijd
Item for a man to serve hym iiij days, mete & drynke & wages xijd
Item for wagges, a chesyll, naylys, ij new pyggs for ye secund bell xxijd
Item for a man to helpe Cholwyll a day mete & drynke & wages iijd
Item for mend^yng^ the rode loft to save the lyzt at Crystsmas ijd
Item for c of helyng stone to Calmady iiijd
Item for makyng clene of ye grett chandeler & ye sensys iijd
Item for whasheng of ye churche clothys xd
Item for a pound of wex to make candels vijd
Item for makyng of ij colers jd
Item for iij truss of russhes xd
Item to Chulwyll for mendyng of ye bellys for ye hole yer xvjd
Item paid to a helyer for a day & *dimidia* mete & wages xd
Item paid to a man to serve hym, mete & wages xd
Item paid to Nycholas Judd for a yre to a crok for ye church yate jd
Item for scheryng of ye church hag jd

f.28
Item paid for gres & pekyng of ye belys iiijd
Item paid to a man to helpe Cholwyll to trusse ye bells ijd
Item paid for a halfe a busshell of lyme iijd
Item for makyng of ys acompt iiijd

Summa iijli [xjs ixd crossed out] xijs iijd
[*Remanet* xixs xjd vjd xviijs ixd crosse d out]
Remanet xixs vd

[f.28v]
***Competus Johannis Hore & Mathei Rose gardianos Alti Crucis ecclesie Sancti Andrie de Stratton anno domini millessimo* ccccc xxxiiij [1536]**[79]

Recetes

Memorandum recevyd of John Payne and Wylliam Spark wardens ye yer past xs
Item received of John Marys for occupying of ye church howse for ij yer xvjd
Item received of Johan Blakehyll for settyng of hys[80] mother a pone ye bedroll iijs iiijd
Item received for a kertell yt Xrispian Elyt gave to the church vjs xjd
Item received of Thomas Taylour senior for his wyfe is grave iiijs iiijd
Item received of John Lang for a knyll iiijd
Item received of Thomas Bryant to sett his son a pone the bedroll whereof iiijd was payd before for a knyll iijs
Item [payd crossed out] received of Mathe Rose to set his mother a pone ye bedroll iijs
Item received of Mystras Marys for hyr husband ys grave iijs iiijd
Item received of Alson Bond to set [h crossed out] ys husbund a pone the bedroll iijs iiijd
Item received of Nycholas Yoe for a knyll iiijd
Item received of John Bryant for ij knyllys viijd
+Item received for a stondyng to the churche howse jd
Item received of Mathe Rose for a olde rope jd

[79] These accounts with Latin headings are by the same scribe as BL, Add MS 32244. Translates as 'The Account of John Hore & Matthew Rose wardens of the High Store of the church of St Andrew of Stratton the year of the lord 1534'. The date duplicates that of the previous account and is wrong.
[80] Her?

^Item received of Nycholas Symon for his brother knyll[81] vjd^
^Item received for owr ale [*Summa* crossed out] yn owr tyme xlixs vd [xlvijs xjd crossed out]^

Summa iijli [vjs jd crossed out] ixs

Expenses

Memorandum for expenses to the bysshepp is vistacon [at Lanceston crossed out] xd
Item paid to Thomas Taylour for vj pownd of wex iijs ixd ob
Item paid for the makyng of the same ijd
Item paid for frannkyn sens iijd
Item paid to Nycholas Uglow for iiij belropys iiijs
Item paid for a coler for a bell viijd
Item paid for thongs for to mend a bell coler ob
Item paid for a nother coler for a bell vjd
Item payd to ye arschedecon is visitasion xvjd
Item payd for expenses to Lanceston for to make awnswer to ye kyngs commyssinors for ye churche land xvjd

f.29

Item payd to Master Vicar for ye bedroll & Wylliam Northen is menedy vs
Item paid to John Rowclyff for makyn of ye northe wyndow xs
Item paid to Johan Langford for occupyng of hyr howse to drynk owr ale vjd
Item paid for a nwe manuell bock ijs
Item paid for a nwe procecinall bock xxd
Item paid to Thomas Taylour for stuff to ^make^ vj new stolys iijs vjd
Item for ye makyng of them to T Crympe vijd
^Item for blyssyng of ye same ijd^
Item paid to Nycholas Heddon for naylys yt John Dow occupyed xijd
Item paid for vij c of lathe nayls viijd
Item paid for ij per of glovys for J Daw ijd
Item paid to John Dromand for parmttyng & stoppyng of the holes & pynyng of the pylers yn ye northe syde xs
Item for whassheng of ye sowthe church[82] vjd
Item paid to Wylliam Dromand & John Dromand for makyng of the greces of the ij yeles & settyng of ye raggs xxd
Item paid to Alexander Penfos for iij truss of russhes xjd
Item paid to Thomas Bryant for a truss of russhes iijd
Item paid to Wylliam ^Dromand for^ pynnyng of ye aulters vd
Item paid for xj busshels & *dimidia* [of lyme crossed out] iiijs xd
Item paid for the cariage of the same lyme iijs
Item paid to the helyer for ye myddell church[83] xxijd
Item paid to ryngers for to ryng Crystian is knill iijd
Item paid to Thomas Taylour for v pownd of wex iijs iiijd
Item for ye makyng ijd
Item for gressyng & sutyng of bells ^ropes^ vjd
Item for gresse for ye bellys ijd
Item paid for hye rent for ye churchhows iijd
Item paid for a rope for ye lytill bell iijd
Item to Heddon for mendyng of ye panne yt beryth colys & ye pekes [iijs crossed out] vjd
Item paid to Nycholas Judd for makyng of a claper for ye grett bell vjs

81 Different scribe for late additions.
82 South aisle.
83 Nave.

Item for fetyng of ij zemys of gravell & for fettyng of ye synternys iijd
Item for whassheng of ye church clothys xd
Item paid to John Cholwyll for the kepyng of the bellys xvjd
Item paid to Thomas Hekytt for ye clock ijs

[f.29v]
Item payd to John Cholwyll for iij days jurney, mete & drynk xviijd
Item paid to Thomas Hekytt for a new schowle xijd
Item payd for ix yerds of clothe for to make a new serpels vs iijd
Item for the makyng of the same ^serpels^ & for mendyng of other serpels xxjd
Item makyng of ye accompte[84] vjd
Summa iiijli vijs vjd
Remaynet cler xviijd

f.30
***Competus Williami Call & Williami Olyver gardianos alti crucis factus Dominica post festum Purificationis Beate Marie anno domini millessimo* ccccc xxxvij [1537]**[85]

Recetes

Memorandum recevyd of John Hore & Mathe Rose wardens ye yere past xviijd
Item received of John Pery for hys gyft to sett hym & hys wyff a pone the bedroll vjs viijd
Item received of the same John for hys father ys grave iijs iiijd
Item received of John Payne & W. Besshep vijs vjd
Item received of John Rose for Wylson ys knyll iiijd
Item received for ij knyllys for Robert Uglow & his wyfe viijd
Item received of Sir Walter Dromond for to put on Johan Lang a pone the bedroll iijs iiijd
Item received for schellyng stonys jd
Item received for owr ale liijs ob
Item received of John Grendon ys grave iijs iiijd
Summa iij^li^ xixs ixd ob

Expenses

Memorandum payd to Heugh Cortyr for mendyng of the church style & church [howse crossed out] ^porche^ vd
Item paid for makyng of the greces of ye stypell & for mendyng of the alyers withowt the church for met, drynk & wages ^xvjd^
Item paid to a helyer & to his servant for mendyng & the church & the church howse ij halfe days, mete & drynk & wages xijd
Item paid to Thomas Hekytt for ye clock ijs
Item paid for ryddyng of the church wallys, met, drynk & wages xijd
Item paid to Thomas Clerke for gresyng & kepyng of ye bells vjd
Item paid to Master Vicar for ye bedroll & for Northen ys meneday vs
Item paid for frankencens [& a cord crossed out] vd ob
Item paid for gresse for ye bellys ijd
Item paid for wex viijd

[f.30v]
Item paid for expenses of the visitacon at Launceston xxd
Item paid to Wylliam Call & to Hugh Corter for makyng of ye church hegg & for werkyng a bowt ye church style, mete, drynk & wages xixd

[84] Space for three entries above.
[85] Duplicate date to the last account but correct.

Item paid to John Sonder [& crossed out] for makyng of ye churche yate & for tymber, mete, drynke & wages vjs viijd
Item paid to Thomas Hekytt for yre warke for ye same ijs iiijd
Item paid for wasshyng of ye church clothys xd
Item paid to Wylliam Olyver yt he payd to the masyns for for makyng of the northe church[86] xijs iijd
Item paid for ij resters iijd
Item for makyng of ys accompt[87] vjd

Summa – xxxviijs vijd ob
Remayneth cler to the church - xljs ijd

f.31

***Competus Nicholai Sutton in villa de Stratton et Johannis Lange gardianos Alti Crucis ecclesie Sancti Andrie appostoli de Stratton predictus factus Dominica post festum Purificationis Beate Marie Virginis anno domini millessimo* ccccc xxxvij[88] [1538]**

Recetes

In primis recevyd of Walter Bawden for a knyll for his daghter iiijd
Item received of John Greby for a knyll for mother iiijd
Item received for a kertell yt Mawte gave to be sett a pone the bedroll vs vjd
Item received of [Rogger crossed out] Nycholas Yeo to sett iiij namys a pone the bedroll xs
Item received of John Trevelan for a old staff of ye rodeloft jd
Item received of Nycolas Judd for old belropys xd
Item received of Mathe Rose to set [Gylberd Thomas crossed out] iiij namys a pone the bedroll vjs viijd
+Item received of Sir Walter Dromand for to sett Rychard Renell mylward a pone ye bedroll [iijs ^iiijd^ crossed out]
Item received of Wylliam Gyste for a knyll iiijd
Item received of Thomas Crymp for a knyll[89]
Item received of Xrispien Uglow vs
Item received of Walter Taylour ijd
Item received for owr ale xxxijs [vjd crossed out] ^ijd^
Item received of Margery Schorte for to sett a name apone bedroll iijs iiijd
Item for yre warke to Nycholas Judd iijs iiijd

Summa iijli iiijs viijd[90]

Expenses

Memorandum payd for wex a genst Ester ijs vd
Item paid for mendyng of a bell whevyll xijd
Item paid to Master Vicar for Wylliam Nothen ys meneday ^& ye bedroll^ vs
Item paid to Nycholas Uglow for iiij new belropys iiijs ijd
Item paid to T Clerke for mendyng of ij belcolers iijd
Item paid for *dimidia* pownd of wex iijd ob
Item paid for mendyng of iij belcolers to T Clerke iiijd ob
Item expenses to the visitacon at Lanceston xvjd
Item expenses at the kyngs visitacon at Lanceston xd
Item payd to a helyer for mendyng of the church mete drynke & wages vjd

86 North aisle.
87 Space for two entries above.
88 Date duplicates last account and is incorrect.
89 Sum left blank.
90 Accounting marks appear here and elsewhere in accounts.

Item for crests iiijd
Item ^me[n]dyng ^ of the sylkyn baners & a albe ijd
Item paid to Thomas Hekytt for makyng of the church dore kay & for mendyng of the lock viijd
Item paid to Cholwyll for mendyng of a frame of ye bellys jd

[f.31v]
Item payd for ij trusses of russhes viijd
Item paid to John Trevelian for *dimidia* busshell of lyme iiijd
Item paid for mendyng of the church lantron iijd
Item paid to John Payne for lether to make a bell coler vjd
Item paid to T. Clerke for makyng of ye coler ijd
Item paid for scowryng of the sences & ye chandeles jd
Item paid for gresse for the bellys ijd
Item paid to John Cholwyll for kepyng of ye bellys xvjd
Item paid for wassheng of the church clothys xd
Item paid for mendyng of serples ijd
Item for makyng of tapers jd
Item payd for makyng of ys accompt[91] vjd
Summa xxijs vd
Remanet xlijs vijd

f.32

[f.32v]
***Competus Williami Moyse & Johannis Maior gardianos Alti Crucis factus Dominica post festum Purificationis Beate Marie Virginis anno domini millessimo* ccccc xxxviij [1539]**

Recetes

In primis recevyd of Alson Meryfyld to sett ij namys a pone the bedroll xs
Item received of Walter Bryant for syttyng of hys mother a pone ye bedroll iijs iiijd
Item received of John Gyste for a knyll iiijd
Item received of Wylliam Lane for to sett Rychard Ronell apone ye bederoll iijs iiijd
Item received of Agnes Sangwen to sett Rychard Sangwen apone ye bederoll ijs vjd
Item received of John Barret to sett hym & hys wyff a pone the bedroll vs
Item received of the same John Barryt for a knyll iiijd
Item received of John Ede yn towne for a knyll iiijd
Item received of Sir Rychard Priste for to sett iij namys a pone the beddroll xiijs iiijd
Item received of Wylliam Moyse for a knyll iiijd
Item received of Nycholas Symon for a knyll iiijd
Item received of Mathew Rose for a knyll to sett a name apone ye bedroll ijs vjd
Item received of John Rowland junior for a gowne of the gyzfte of John Heddon xs
Item received of George Hacker a knyll iiijd
Item received of Mensyn Wulfe for the black sute viijd
Item received for the over plus yt was gaderyd for cariage of ye burds frow Padstow vd
Item received Master Vycar Rychard Carlyan to set Elyzabeth Carlyan apone ye bedroll ijs vjd
Item received of William Olyver for a knyll iiijd
Item received of Elyzabeth Dromond to sett Sir Water Dromond and Thomsyn Skyr a pone the bedroll vs
+Item received for standyng at ye church howse xd

[91] Space for two entries above.

Item received of players[92] at ye church howse iiijd
Item received of John Gyste for a knyll iiijd
Item received of Margery Schorte for a gefte yt sche hathe gevyn to the church iijs iiijd
Item received for owr ale bruyng xlijs
Summa vli vijs ixd

[f.33]

Expenses

Memorandum for expenses to my lord bysshepp ys visitacon xviijd
Item payd for blessyng of vj corporas xijd
Item paid for frankencens iijd
Item paid to a helyer for mendyng of the church, mete & drynk & wages vd
Item paid for lyme the same tyme iiijd
Item paid for mendyng of the church clothys viijd
Item paid to Wylliam Holmys for makyng of the grett bell claper xijd
Item paid for a potyll of ale the same tyme jd
Item paid for a man tho[93] helpe the belluter xijd
Item paid for makyng of a standyng to sett ye bokes apone vjd
Item paid for vj pound of wex agenst Ester iijs iiijd
Item for makyng of the same ijd
Item paid for iij busshels of lyme at Bedeforth xvd
Item paid for the caryage xijd
Item paid to Master Vicar for the bedroll & Wylliam Northen ys meneday vs
Item paid to Wylliam Gyste for tymber of ye vyce xd
Item for lathys for the same vyce iijd
Item for naylys for the same ijd
Item paid to a helyer mete, drynk & wages vjd
Item paid for a ryng with a boce & gemes & naylys for the vice dor xijd
Item expenses at Launceston to ye archedecon is visitacon xiiijd
Item paid to Rychard Curry for ix ropys for the scaffetts iiijd
Item paid for iij pound of metyll for ye grett bell ixd
Item paid to a man for to serve a masyn ij days mete, drynk & wages viijd
Item paid to Robert Regyll for caryng of gret to make for the wyndow ijd
Item paid to a helyer for helyng of the wyndow, mete, drynke & wages ijs
Item paid to John Bryant for fettyng of raggs to Tyndagyll[94] xxd
Item paid to the same John for servyng of a helyer, mete, drynk & wages viijd
Item paid to ij men for ryddyng abowte the church [howse crossed out], mete, dryng, wages vd
Item paid to Nycholas Uglow for vj crests xijd
Item paid for wassheng of the church clothys xd
Item paid to Nycolas Uglow for ij belropys ijs
Item paid for iiij bosshels & halfe of lyme xxiiijd
Item paid to Mathe Rose for caryage of the same xijd
Item for lathe naylys for the rodelozft wyndow iijd
Item paid to Master Vycar Rychard Carlyan for ledd for ye rodelozft wyndows vjs jd
Item paid to a helyer for mendyng of the church xd

[f.33v]

Item payd to John Dromand for hewyng of the pylers vjd

[92] Travelling actors.

[93] To.

[94] Tintagel, centre of the medieval slate industry.

Item paid for paper to make a lyer buck xd
Item paid to a helyer for mendyng of the church ijd
Item paid for glasyng of ij wyndows yn the rodelozfte ixs
Item for settyng of clapers yn sacryng bellys jd
Item for makyng greysys goyng yn to the churchhows dore & for ryddyng of the strette vd
Item paid to Thomas Hekytt for yryng of the wyndows yn ye rodeloft iiijs xd ob
Item paid to the same Thomas for ij locks & ij gemys xviijd
Item for makyng of the churche pykys iijd
Item paid to John Trevelan for a [ho crossed out] bushell of lyme viijd
Item paid for gres & kepyng of the bellys viijd
Item paid for ij trus of russhes to John Maior viijd
Item paid to John Cholwyll for mendyng & takyng hede of ye bellys xvjd
Item paid to John Cholwyll is son for settyng of ye tymber up for ye vyce iiijd
Item for makyng of thys accompte[95] vjd

Summa iijli iijs vijd ob

Remanet cler to the church xliiijs jd ob paid to William Lang & to Thomas Bryant generall receivers the same yere *quietus est*

f.34

***Competus Johannes Ede in villa et Williami Grove gardianos Alti Crucis ecclesie Sancti Andrie de Stratton factus Dominica proxima post festum Purificacionis Beate Marie Virginis anno domini millessimo* ccccc xxxviij[96] [1540]**

Recetes

In primis recevyd of James Kyng for a knyll iiijd
Item received for a knyll of John Cobeldick iiijd
Item received of John Beare for iij knyllys for hys chyldryn xijd
Item received of Wylliam Gest for iij knyllys xijd
Item received of Thomas Rose for iij knyllys xijd
Item received of John Davy for a knyll iiijd
Item received of John Wyett for a knyll iiijd
Item received of Nycolas Symon of Borwode for a knyll iiijd
Item received of Wylliam Beschepp for a knyll for his servant iiijd
Item received of John Ede for a knyll for hys servant iiijd
Item received of John Antony for iiij knyll for hys wife & chyldryn xvjd
Item received of Wylliam Lange for v knyllys xxd
Item received of John Trevelan for a knyll for Caprac ys dafter[97] iiijd
Item received of John Mares for the churche howse viijd
Item received of Johan Mayow for to hyr husband & hyr chyldryn apone ye bedroll vs
Item received of Thomas Bray to sett hys wyf a pone ye beddroll ijs vjd
Item received of John Antony to sett Wylliam Sangwen & hys chyldryn apone the bedroll iijs iiijd
Item received of Johan Blakehyll to John hyr broder apone the bedroll iijs iiijd
+Item received for standyng withowt the churchhowse vijd ob
Item received of Stephyn Daw for iiij yerds of whyt kersy yt the Iryshman gave to the church to be sett a pone ye bedroll & for his knyll iijs viijd
Item received of players for ye church howse jd
Item for a stranger for a standyng yr jd
Item received of Wylliam Beschep for to sett Leonard his servant apone the bedroll ijs vjd

95 Small space above.

96 Duplicate date to the last account, so this is two years out.

97 Space left below.

Item received of Thomas Bray for a kertell Thomas Wade is servant gave to the church for to sett hyr apone the bedroll vjs ijd
Item received for owr ale bruyng xxxj [ij crossed out] s ijd
Item received for a kertyll yt Peter Drinn ys wyffe gave to ye church[98]
Summa iijli ix [j crossed out]s iijd ob

[f.34v]

Expenses

Memorandum payd to Nycholas Mock for coveryng of the kyngs bock jd
Item paid for wex agenst Ester vj pound iijs vjd
Item paid for ij pound of frankencens iiijd
Item paid for iij new belropys ijs vijd
Item paid for ij new belcolers ijs
Item for expenses to the visitacon at Launceston xvjd
Item for mendyng of the church clothys vijd
Item paid for iij trussys of russhes xvjd
Item for mendyng of formis & trestels yn ye church howse iiijd
Item for makyng of wex vd
Item for makyng of ij new bears xiiijd
Item for scowryng of the gret chandelers jd
Item paid Master [va crossed out] Vicar for ye bedroll & W. Northen ys meneday vs
Item for mendyng of ye bell colers jd
Item paid to John Cholwell for [to] over se ye bells ye hole yer xvjd
Item paid to a helyer for mendyng of ye church & the churchehowse, mete, dryng, wages ij days and for a man to serve hym xxjd
Item for makyng of the church style for tymber & warkemenshep iijs xd
Item for mendyng of a lock of the church house ijd
Item paid to Thomas Taylour for vj yards of dowles & thred for to make a new albe for Master Chamond ys vestments & for lacyng for ye same iijs jd
Item paid for makyng & zowing of the same vestement vijd
Item paid for mete & dryng for he yt dyd werke apone the new albe & the old albe yt Master Arundell gave xiiijd
Item paid for a seme of zand jd
Item paid for gresse for the bellys [& for mendyng of the panns yt beryth coles jd crossed out] ^iijd^
Item paid for iij wheges for the bellys & for mendyng of the old panne jd
Item for kepyng of the bellys viijd
Item for wassheng of the church clothys xd
Item for wyke yerne ijd
Item so for mendyng of a masbocke iijs iiijd
Item for makyng of ys accompte[99] vjd
Summa xxxvjs ixd
Remanet xxxijs [ijs vjd ob crossed out] ixd

f.35

anno dominis millessimo ccccc xxxix

***Competus Nicolai Yoe & Williami Lang gardianos Alti Crucis factus primo die mensis Junij anno regni regis Henrici octavi tricesimo secundo sequente a festo Purificacionis Beate Marie* [1541]**

[98] Sum blank.
[99] Space above.

Item received of John Gyst[100] for his gyzst to the[m] & for his grave vjs viijd
Item received for a knyll for Alson Pyne[101]
Item received for a knyll for John Judd iiijd
Item received for a knyll Wylliam Moyse iiijd
Item received for a knyll of Nycholas Wyll iiijd
Item received of strangers for stondyngs agenste ye churchehowse xvd
Item received of John Marys for occupyyng of the churchehowse viijd
Item received of Thomas Rose for occupiyng of the churchehowse ijd
Item received for owr ale bruyng xliijs vd

Summa [xlvjs vijd crossed out] liijs ijd

[f.35v]

Expenses

Memorandum payd for vj pownd of wex a genst Ester iijs iiijd
Item paid for the blesyng of the sute of vestements yt Master Thomas Arundell gave to ye church xvjd
Item for the caryage of the same frome Exeter iiijd
Item paid for yre & naylys for mendyng of ye bells iijd ob
Item for scowryng of the grett chandeles & other chandeles ijd
Item for wykes & thred jd
Item for bokeram jd
Item for mendyng of the church pykes iijd
Item paid for expenses at the archedecon ys visitacon xvjd
Item for frankencens iiijd
Item for rushes xvjd
Item for makyng of tapers ijd
Item paid to John Cholwyll for the bellys xvjd
Item paid for a new boxe xixd
Item payd to Avery for mendyng of church & to a man to serve vjd
Item paid for mendyng of the holywater bokytt ijd
Item for iij boshels of lyme & *dimidia* & carag of the same ijs [ijd crossed out]
Item for mendyng of the church clothyng vjd
Item for stamyn & thred & gerdels vd ob
Item payde for viij yerds of dowles to make a serpelys & for makyng of the same vs
Item payde to Master Vicar for the bedroll & Wylliam Northen ys meneday vs
Item for whasheng of the churche clothys xd
Item for the kepyng of the bellys viijd
^Memorandum for a kertyll^[102]
Item paid for a new lanterne & ij new crewetts xviijd
Item paid to a plumer for mendyng of the ledds of ye gutters xxd
Item paid for wode for the same & for a man to helpe hym iijd
Item paid for a schowle xijd
Item paid for naylys ijd
Item paid for makyng of thys accompte[103] vjd

Summa xxxijs jd
Remanet cler to ye churche [xiiijs crossed out] xxjs jd

[100] Looks like Johan but clearly is not.
[101] Sum blank.
[102] Marginal entry; sum blank.
[103] Space left above; blotched entry.

f.36

***Competus Johannis Marys & Johannis Rose senior gardianos Alti Crucis ecclesie Sancti Andrie de Stratton factus Dominica post festum Purificacionis Beate Marie Virginis anno Christi* millessimo ccccc xlj *& anno regni regis Henrici octavi* xxxiij [1542]**

Recetes

In primis recevyd of Johan Olyver for hyr hosbond gyft to ye church vjs ^viijd^	
Item received of Rychard Jule for hys father ys grave	iijs iiijd
Item received of Rychard Calygerne for a knyll for hys wyff	iiijd
Item received of John Ede yn towne for the wode of the church erthe	xxijd
+Item received for stondyng a genst the church howse wall	iiijd
Item received of Margaret Symon for hyr husbond ys grave & for hys name to be regestryd a pone the comen bedroll	vjs viijd
Item received of Elizabeth Marys for ode of the church erthe	xjd
Item received of John Beys for Hockyn ys knyll	iiijd
Item received of Wylliam Bysshepp junior for Wylliam Bysshepp senior ys grave & hys wyffys grave	vjs viijd
Item received for stondyng a genst the churche howse wall on Sent Androw ys day	xvijd
Item received for a olde lanterne	iijd
Item received of Nycholas Mocke for olde lyncloth	xiijd
Item received of John Marys for wyztyng yn the church howse	viijd
Item received of Stephyn drynkyng of a canne of ale yn the church howse	jd
Item received of Nycholas Yerly for drynkyng of a can of ale yn ye same house	jd
Item received of Rychard Chyng for a knyll	iiijd
Item received of Margaret Symon for hyr sonne is grave	iijs iiijd
Item received Thomas Taylour for hys father ys grave	iijs iiijd
Item received of John Payne for a stone	jd
Item received for owr ale bruyng	xxxvjs
Summa iijli xiijs ixd	

[f.36v]

Expenses

In primis payd to for expenses to ye visitacon at Launceston	ijs
Item paid for vij pound of wex a genst Ester	iijs vjd
Item paid for the makyng of the same wex	ijd ob
Item expenses to the arschedecon ys visitacon	xxijd
Item paid for mendyng of the church lyd	iiijd
Item paid for one to serve hym	jd
Item paid for the bedroll & Wylliam Northyn ys meneday	vs
Item paid for wassheng of the church clothys	xd
Item paid to the organ maker	xijd
Item paid for hys drynkyn	ijd
Item paid to Nycholas Mock for mendyng of serples & rachetts	jd
Item paid for [iiij crossed out] ^v^ trussys of russhes	xxd
Item paid to Thomas Crymp for mendyng of vestements & for bokeram	viijd
Item paid to John Maior for a trusse of russhes a genst Master Arundell ys dafter was maryed	iiijd
Item paid for gerdels	iijd
Item paid to John Mock for mendyng of ye led yn ye chancel	iijd
Item paid to a man to help hym	jd
Item paid to Walter Byttyck for mendyng of the ledd	xijd
Item paid for the Bybyll	vjs vjd
Item paid for iij bosshels of lyme	xvd

Item paid for the caryag of the same lyme xd
Item paid to Water Byttyck for mendyng of the crosse viijd
Item paid for John Avery for poyntyng of ij churchys viijs
Item paid for zonde iijd
Item paid for a bosshell a lyme ixd
Item paid for makyng of candels jd
Item paid for iij new belropys iijs iiijd

f.37
Item paid to John Davy for ryddyng of the church howse gutter jd
Item paid for *dimidia* pound of frankenscens jd ob
Item paid for scowryng of ye grett chandelers & other chendeles ijd
Item paid for gres for the bellys jd ob
Item paid to John Cholwyll for to mend the bellys xvjd
Item paid to Wylliam Moyse for kepyng of the bellys xd
Item paid to John Deamond for caryng of a ymag of Owr Lady xijd
Item for makyng of ys accompt[104] vjd
Summa xlvs jd ob
Remanet cler to the church xxviijs vijd ob

^***Domine salva me sic Reginam nostram Elizabetham***[105]^

[f.37v]
***Competus Thome Wade et Johannis Beare gardianos Alti Crucis factus Dominica post festum Purificacionis Beate Marie Virginis anno Xpi millessimo* ccccc xlij *et anno regis Henrici* viij *tricesimo quarto* [1543]**

Recepts

In primis recevyd John Marys & John Rose senior wardens ye yer paste vjs viijd
Item received of John Wade for setting of hys syster a pone the bederoll iijs iiijd
Item received of Thomas Rose for a knyll for hys child iiijd
Item received of Johan Rede for hyr husbond ys knyll iiijd
+Item received of strangers for stondyngs a gens the church howse xvjd
Item received of John Marys for wyghtyng yn the church howse viijd
Item received of owr ale bruyng cler xliiijs vjd
Item received of John Comen for hys wife is knyll iiijd
Summa lvjjs [viijd crossed out] vjd

Expenses

Memorandum payd for a cord for the Lentcloth ijd
Item paid for scowryng of the grett chandelers ijd
Item paid for a new dext clothe & a towle xjd
Item paid for vj pounde of wex a genst Ester iijs iiijd
Item for makyng of the same iiijd
Item for mendyng of the churche clothys vjd
Item for mendyng of the albys iijd
Item for iij pound of frankyncens ixd
Item for expenses to the archedecon ys visitacon xxjd
Item for iiij trusse of russhes xvjd
Item for a corde for the organs ob
Item payd to Master Vicar for the bedderoll & Wylliam Northyn is meneday vs

[104] Space for three entries above.
[105] 'Lord save me and likewise our queen Elizabeth' in later hand.

Item paid for iij locks for the chauncel dores ijs
Item paid for bockeram to make the canabe for the sacrament viijd
Item for scowryng & makyng ijd
Item paid for wykes ob

f.38
Item for mendyng of the church ledde vijs
Item for a erthyn panne to hete ye metyll ijd
Item paid to the organ maker for hys fee xijd
Item payd for hys expenses & hys servant ij days xvjd
Item paid to a glasyer for mendyng of the church wyndows iijs
Item paid to John Mock for makyng of a ladder for the clock iijd
Item paid for a chayne for the Bybill iijd ob
Item paid to John Avery for setting of the tyle of ye church iiijd
Item paid for mendyng of the church pykes iiijd
Item paid to Thomas Hyckytt for mendyng of claper for ye bell ijs viijd
Item paid to Thomas Hekytt for kepyng of the clock ijs
Item paid to Wylliam Moyse for kepyng of the bellys xvjd
Item paid to John Cholwyyll for hys fee xvjd
Item paid for wassheng of the church clothys xd
Item paid for gresse for the bellys jd
Item paid for a chayne for the sens ijd
Item paid to Thomas Taylor for makyng for ye tyle jd
Item for makyng of thys accompt[106] vjd

Summa xlijs ob

Remaneth cler to ye church xvijs [xjd crossed out] ^xd^ ob

[f.38v]

***Competus Johannis Wade & Johannis Uglow factus Dominica post festum Purificacionis Beate Marie Virginis anno Xpi millessimo* ccccc xliiij *& anno regni regis Henrici* viij, xxxv *gardianos Alti Crucis ecclesie Sancti Andrie de Stratton* [1544]**

Receptes

In primis recevyd of John Maris & Nycholas Judde generall recevers vjs viijd
Item received of Heddon of Pancras Wyke[107] for the gyfte of Sir Rychard Carlyan vicar of ys church of late xiijs iiijd
Item received of Martyn Payle for an olde purse & xiiij botens of sylver & gylte iijs viijd
+Item received of strangers for standyngs by the church howse xxjd
Item received of Thomas Wyll for a knyll iiijd
Item received of John Marys for wyztyng yn ye church howse viijd
Item received for owr ale bruyng[108] xxxvjs viijd

Summa iijli iijs jd

Summa iijli iijs jd[109]

f.39

Expenses

Memorandum payd to Nycholas Mock for mendyng of ye church clothys mete drynk & wages vjd

[106] Space for two entries above.

[107] Space for Christian name blank; Pancrasweek, Devon.

[108] Space left above.

[109] Duplicate entry, as with many scribal errors.

Item payd for threde for ye same ob
Item paid for iij pownde of frankencens xd
Item payd for wexe ijs iijd
Item paid for expenses at the visitacon at Lanceston iiijs jd
Item paid to Master Vicar for the bederoll & for Wylliam Nordon ys obyte & oyer vs
Item paid for the scowryng of the grett chandelers ijd
Item paid for mendyng of ye bell colers & schotyng of ye ropys ijd
Item paid for naylys to mend the grett bell whefyll ob
Item paid for a cay for the cofer yt was of the gyft of Sir Rychard Carlyan ijd
Item paid to George Jule for drawyng of vj lode of [more crossed out] ^quary^ stone xviijd
Item paid for caryage of ye same vj lode iiijs vjd
Item paid for ij belropys xxjd
Item paid to Nycholas Heddon for a serpels xxd
Item paid for ij new belcolers to Thomas Clerke xxd
Item paid to John Mock for mendyng of ye church clothyng jd
Item paid to Thomas Clerk for mendyng of a coler jd
Item paid for gerdels for ye vestyments jd
Item paid to John Avery for mendyng of the church when ye plumer mendyd ye led vijd
Item paid to Basterd for caryng of iij lode of stone ixs
Item paid for drawyng of them ijs
Item paid to John Kyng for beryng of stonys owt ye strett to church howse ijd
Item paid for wyr for ye clock xijd
Item paid for expenses at the bysshep ys visytacon xxjd
Item paid for reryng of ye chancell to John Mock & Nycholas Mock xijd
Item paid for wassheng of ye church clothys xd
Item paid for gresse for ye bellys ijd
Item paid to Johan Wade for mete & dryngk for George Jule for makyng of ye guttyr of ye church howse & for John Wade for iiij days to helpe hym xxd
Item paid to Thomas Hyckytt for ye clock ijs
Item paid to John Cholwyll for the kepyng of ye bellys xvjd
Item paid to ye same John for makyng of a new bear xd
Item paid for iiij trusses of russhes to Nycholas Yeo xvjd

[f.39v]
Item payd for ryddyng of the backsyde of the church howse & ye beryng of [church crossed out] grete owt iijs
Item paid for Basterd ys mete & drynke when he brozft ij lode of morestone vd
Item paid to Thomas Clerke for mendyng of the bell colers & mendyng the colers now last vd
Item paid for naylys for mendyng jd
Item paid ryppyng of owt of ye fur of Sir John Chamond ys gowne[110] jd
Item paid for makyng of ys accompt vjd

Summa lijs ixd
Remaynyth cler to the churche xs iiijd

***Competus Georgegii Maior & Johannis Antonij gardianos Alti Crucis ecclesie Sancti Andric appostoli anno Xpi millessimo* cccc xliiij *factus Dominica proxima post festum Purificacionis Beate Marie Virginis in anno regni regis Henrici* viij, xxxvj [1545]**

[110] Recycling furred gown for vestments by removing fur.

Receptes

In primis recevyd of John Ede & Rychard Currye generall recevers ye yer past vjs viijd
Item received of Moyse for Xrispiana Uglow ys grave iijs iiijd
Item received for a knyll for Alson Meryfyld iiijd
Item received of Nycholas Wyll for to sett Johan Langdon a pone ye bedroll iijs iiijd
+Item received for stondyng a genst the church howse ijs iijd ob
Item received of John Mares for wyghtyng yn ye church howse viijd
Item received for Nycholas Heddon ys grave & hys geyfte to ye church vjs viijd
Item received of Wylliam Call for vj sponys of sylver the gyft of Xrispiana Uglow xxvjs viijd
Item received for Robert Regyll ys grave iijs iiijd
Item received of Johan Olyver for robell stonys vjd
Item received for owr ale bruyng xxxiijs [xjjd crossed out] ^xd^ ob
Item received of John Wyett for a knyll iiijd
Item received Nycholas Yeo for vj tresys ijd
Item received of T. Hyckyt ix hurdels xviijd
Item received for iij [tr crossed out] mores of treis xviijd
Item for a knyll iiijd

^*Summa* – iiijli x[s]^ iiij[d]

f.40

Expenses

Memorandum payd for ij new bel[ropys crossed out] ^colers^ ijs vd
Item paid for sope vjd ob
Item paid for wassheng of the church clothys vijd
Item paid for the thred to mende ye serpels jd
Item paid for the mendyng of the church clothys iijd
Item paid for ^naylys^ mendyng of the bellys ijd
Item paid to John Cholwill for mendyng of ye bellys xvjd
Item paid for settyng up of the lamp and mendyng ye yr ijd
Item for a trusse of russhes a genste Sir John Chamond ys meneday iiijd
Item for a days jurney to helpe make the pulpytt[III] & to dresse the church mete & drynke iiijd
Item for naylys for the pulpytt jd
Item paid for tymber for ye payse of the lamp jd
Item paid for viijli of wex a genst Ester ^& for wekes^ iiijs jd
Item for candels jd
Item paid for lyme & for helyng of the churche jd ob
Item paid for mendyng & scowryng of [ij at crossed out] ij saletts ijs
Item paid for cords for the clock iiijd ob
Item paid to Thomas Hekyt for the yre of the pulpytt & burds & for a ryng for the lamp xxd
Item paid to John Cholwyll for makyng of the pulpytt & for the payse of the lampe xd
Item for ij brassys for the bellys ijs vjd
Item for makyng of wex iiijd
Item paid for a key for the kechyn dore of the church howse & settyng ijd ob
Item for frannkencens jd ob
Item for a jerre of oyle for the lamp ixd
Item for ij trusse of russhes a genst Ester & Crystsmas viijd
Item paid for a locke & a kay for the rodelofte dore vjd
Item for expenses at the visitacon at Lanceston ijs ijd ob

III Pulpit.

Item paid for a zeme of tyle for the caryg frow Bede[112]	jd
Item paid for mendyng of the serpels	jd
Item paid for caryng of tyle with iiij horse ij days frow Bede, mete & drynk	iijs
Item paid for fettyng of ij barels of lyme & ij zemys of zonde	iiijd
Item paid to Thomas Hyckytt for a yre for the lampe	ijd

[f.40v]

Item payd to Nycholas Wyll for caryng of ij pere of harnys frow Lanceston	iiijd
Item paid to Mathe Rose for caryng of a zeme of zond	jd
Item paid to Sir Wylliam Wodeman for to dyscharge the parysch at a nother visitacon	viijd
Item payd for ij glassys for the lampe	iiijd
Item paid to Master Vicar for the bedroll & Wylliam Northen ys meneday	vs
Item paid for v busshels of lyme	ijs jd
Item for the caryage of the same	xxd
Item paid for xvij busshels of lyme frow Bedfowthe[113]	vijs ijd
Item paid to John Rowland junior for ij bords for caste ye led	vjd
Item payd for naylys for the same & trussyng of ye bellys	iijd
Item paid for a belrope	xvjd
Item paid for iij busshels of lyme	ijs iijd
Item paid for the caryag of iiij zemys of zond for caste the ledd	iiijd
Item paid for blessyng of a corporas	vjd
Item paid to Nycholas Will for a m^l^ of lathys	iijs ixd
Item paid for caryng of the same lathys frow Holseworthy	xd
Item paid for fettyng of xxj zemys of zonde	xxjd
Item paid for fettyng of ij m^l^ of schelyng stone frow Bede	xiiijd
Item for mendyng of the harnys & for poynts	ijd
Item paid for ij quarters lyme to Launceston	vjs
Item paid for fettyng of the same lyme at Launceston	ijs iijd
Item paid to Nycholas Gyst for naylys for ye chauncell	vd
Item paid for ix yerds of dowles to make a per of serpels	iiijs iiijd
Item paid to John Uglow for ij busshels of lyme	xxd
Item paid to John Avery for helyng of the church howse & his mete	xiijd
Item for a man to serve hym	viijd
Item paid for helyng stone	ijd
Item paid for makyng of a per of serpers & mendyng of the cope	xxd
Item paid to Georg Jule for settyng of tyle yn ye chauncell	iiijd
Item paid for ^wode for^ the glasyer	jd
Item paid for zayng of the churche tymber to John Bryant	vjs viijd
Item paid for thred	ob
Item paid to Thomas Clerke for kepyng of ye bellys & mendyng of ye ropes	xijd
Item paid for scowryng of the chandelers	ijd

f.41

Item for a pott	jd
Item paid for gresse for ye bellys	iijd
Item paid for helpyng to trusse the bellys	jd
Item paid to T. Hyckyt for the clock	ijs
Item for makyng of ys a compt	vjd

Summa iiijli ^vjs^ [ijd] ob

Remanet to ye church vs iijd ob

[112] Bude. 'iij he gave' added after sum.

[113] Bideford.

***Competus Radulphus Augere & Richardi Currye gardianos Alti Crucis Sancti Andrie ecclesie factus Dominica post festum Purificacionis Beate Marie Virginis anno domini millessimo* **ccccc xlv** *et anno regni regis Henrici* **viij** *trecesimo septimo* **[1546]**

Recept

In primis recevyd of Wylliam Lang for a knyll	iiijd

Recept

Item received for a remlett of damaske	xxd
Item received of Wylliam Bond for crocke of bras	xs
Item received of John Marys for the tymber of the chapell	xjs
Item received of Rychard Call for yron	iijs ixd
Item received for an olde lanterne	iiijd
+Item received for stondyng a genst ye churche howse wall	iiijs
Item received for stondyng apone the crosse down yn ye strett	iiijd
Item received for owr ale bruyng	xxxviijs ijd
Item received of John Marys for wyghtyng yn the churche howse	viijd
Item received for a knyll for Robert Pudener	iiijd
Item recevyd of John Payne for a per of beds[114] of ye gyft Agnes Clerk	ijs
Item received of Robert Hyghedone fo[r] a mote of a tre	vijd
^Item received for wode for^ *Summa* ^paryg of treys	iiijd^

Summa iijli xiijs vjd

[f.41v]

E^x^penses

Memorandum payd for mendyng of the church yate	ijd
Item payd for a halfe a pound of wex candels	iijd
Item paid for viij yerds of dowles for to make a per of serpels	iiijs
Item paid to Johan Coper for makyng of the same serpels	xviijd
Item paid for thred for the same	jd
Item paid for mendyng of ye churche clothyng Johan Rede ij days, mete, drynke & wages	vjd
Item for threde for the same	jd
Item for makyng clene of the harnys longyng to ye church	vijd
Item payd to Robert Hyghadon for mendyng of ye est church style	iijd [ob crossed out]
Item paid for viij pownd of wex	iiijs
Item paid for a halfe a pownd of frankencens	ijd
Item paid to Nycholas Jude for mendyng of iiij clapers for ye bellys	vs
Item paid to Nycholas Mock for sawyng of ye vestments	iijd
Item paid to the vicar for bedroll & Wylliam Nordon ys meneday	vs
Item paid to the same Thomas for ij holbarnes	iijs
Item paid for ij belropys	ijs vjd
Item paid to John Mocke for souuyng of ye church clothys & mendyng, mete & drynke	iiijd
Item paid for threde & lacyng	ijd
Item paid for a potyll of oyele for the lampe	vjd
Item payd to Mocke for makyng of dext & mendyng of ye ledd	xijd
Item paid for helyng stonys to John Payne & to Nycholas Judd	xijd
Item paid for lyme for the church	xijd
Item paid to John Avery for ij days & *dimidia* & a lad to serve hym, mete & wages	ijs jd
Item paid for poynts for ye harnys for iij mostryngs	iijd
Item paid to John Cholwyll for hys fee for kepyng of ye bellis	xvjd
Item paid to j plumer for mendyng of ye led	xiiijd
Item paid to John Mocke for glew ^& nowtis^for ye organs [ob crossed out]	jd

114 Rosary beads were usually described as a pair of beads.

f.42

Item paid for a bell coler	vjd
Item paid for a lanterne for ye church	xd
Item paid for ij trussys of russhes	viijd
Item paid to Thomas Hekytt for ye clock	ijs
Item for wyre for ye same	jd
Item paid to John Wyatt for settyng up [for crossed out] of ye payse of ye lampe	jd
Item paid for wassheng of the church clothys	xd
Item paid to Thomas Clerke for kepyn of ye bellys	xijd
Item paid for ij zemys of sonde	ijd
Item paid for gresse & thongs for ye bellys	iijd
Item paid for mendyng of the rachetts	jd
Item paid to Nycholas Gyst for naylys & for mendyng of ye scope for colys	iijd
Item paid for a corde for drawyng of ye clothe	jd
Item paid to Robert Cholwyll for makeng of ye seges yn ye chauncell	iiijs
Item paid for makyng clene of the grett chandelers	ijd
Item to Nycholas Gyst for plates & naylys for lady ys pew ^& for ye seges^ ixd	
Item paid for naylys for the dexts of chancell	ijd
Item to John Mocke for settyng up of my ladys pew	iijd
Item paid to John Avery for mendyng & parmttyng of the chauncell ye new loft	iijd
Item paid to John Wyll to serve hyme	ijd
Item paid to John Trevelan for makyng of wex	iijd
Item expenses at the visitacon at Launcestone	xviijd ob
Item paid for a schowle for the church	xiijd
Item paid to John ^Mocke^ for makyng of leggys for ye formys of ye church howse	jd
^Item paid to Nycolas Jyst for myddyng of a spyll of ye tyn[er] byll[115]	jd^
Item paid for [s crossed out] makyng of thys a compt	vjd
Summa lijs ixd ob	
Remanyth to churche xxs viijd ob	

[f.42v]

***Competus Johannis Rowland junior & Richardi Jule gardianos Alti Crucis ecclesie Sancti Andrie de Stratton factus Dominica post festum Purificacionis Beate Marie anno domini millessimo* ccccc xlvj *& anno regni Henrici* viij *dei gratia Anglia Francia & Hibernie regis defensoris fidei & in terris ecclesie Anglie & hibernie supremi capitis tricesimo octavo* [1547][116]**

***In primis* received**

received of Thomas Tayler & John Wade generall recevers ye last yer	xs
Item received of Georg Mayor for a knyll for Martyn Mayor	vjd
Item received of Master Larder for lenyng of ye black sute	viijd
+Item received for standyngs a genst ye church howse	iijs viijd
Item received for stondyngs a pone the crosse	iiijd
Item received of Master Beachamp for tyle	viijd
Item received for browse of the church hayge	ijd
Item received of John Lamerton for a knyll for lame Johan	iiijd
Item received of Wylliam Hore to set hys grandfather & grandmoder a pone the bedroll	vjs viijd
Item received of John Mares for wrztyng yn ye church howse	viijd
Item received for owr ale bruyng	xxxijs
Item received of Nycholas Bond for occupyng of ye church howse	ijd

[115] Tenor bell?

[116] News of Henry VIII's death was slow to reach Stratton, so the dating for this and the next account is odd.

Summa [liijs crossed out] lvs ^xd^ [vs viij crossed out]
f.43
^**Expenses**^ [Receptes crossed out]

In primis paid for a new bell rope	xxd
Item payd for a new bell coler	xijd
Item paid to John Cholwyll for ys fee for mendyng of ye bells	xvjd
Item paid to Thomas Hekytt for wyre for ye clock	xijd
Item for expenses at the archedecon ys visitacon	xxiijd
Item paid for ij pownd of francancens	viijd
Item paid to Bastyan for glewyng of the organs	jd ob
Item paid for selyng wex	jd
Item paid schuyng of a horse ryde to Launceston for ye churche	ijd
Item paid for a kay for ye chancell dore	ijd
Item paid to John Mocke for scowryng of ye grett chandelers & the other chandelers & sensys	vd
Item paid for viij li of wex a genst Ester	iiijs viijd
Item paid for the makyng	iiijd
Item paid for ye hyre of a horse to ryde to Launceston for ye churche busynes	iiijd
Item paid to Wylliam Payne & Rychard Curry for ther expensys to Launceston to the commyssinors for ye churche besynes	xxjd ob
Item paid to Master Vicar for ye beddroll & Wylliam Northen ys meneday	vs
Item paid to a glassyer for mendyng of ye glaswyndows	xviijd
Item paid to John Mocke to helpe hym	jd
Item paid to the organ maker for hys fee	xijd
Item paid for hys expenses	vjd
Item paid to a plumer to mende the ledde	xii[j crossed out]d
Item paid for a halfe a busshell of lyme	iiijd
Item paid to W. Lang & to John Rowland for helyng stone	iiijd
Item paid to John Averey for helyng of ye churche	iiijd
Item paid to a man to serve hym	ijd
Item for ther mete & drynke	vd
Item paid to Thomas Hekytt for the clock	ijs

[f.43v]

Item paid for ye kechyn dore	ijd ob
Item paid for ij trusse of ^rushes^	viijd
Item paid for mendyng of the church clothys ^& werkyng yn ye churche howse^	xiijd
Item paid for wassheng of ye church clothys & for sope	xd
Item paid to Thomas Clerke for mendyng of colers	iijd
Item paid to John Rowland, Thomas Clerke for kepyng of ye bells & for gresse	xijd
Item for expenses at ye bysshepp is visytacon	iijs vjd
Item paid for oyle for the lampe	vjd
Item payd for ryddyng a bowt ye churche wall	xiiijd
Item paid to Bastyan for makyng of the burds yn ye church howse	viijs viijd
Item paid for glew	viijd
Item paid for mete & drynke ^for his man & hym^	vjs vd
Item for straw for glewyng of the burds	vjd
Item for makyng [makeng crossed out] of ye churche hayge, mete, drynke & hyre	ijs viijd
Item paid to Bastyan for junyng of a burd	ijd
Item paid for makyng of thys accompt	vjd
Item paid hawyn of kays	jd

Summa lvjs xjd ob
Remanet to the wardens ^xiiijd^ [xvd ob xxijd ob crossed out]

f.44

[f.44v]

***Compet Johannis Beys et Edwardi Horetopp gardianos Alt' Crucis ecclesie Sancti Andrie de Stratton facta Dominica post festum Purificacionis Beate Marie Virginis ^anno domini^ Xpi millessimo* ccccc xlvij *et anno regni Edwardi sexti dei gracia Anglie, Francie & Hibernie regis, defensoris fidei et in terris ecclesie Anglicane et Hibernice supremi capitis primo* [5 February 1548]**

Receptes

In primis recevyd of John Jule & John Antony generall recevers	ixs viijd
Item received of Margaret Martyn to regester hyr husbond ys name a pone the comen bedroll	iijs iiijd
Item received for a knyll for Stephyn Daw	iiijd
Item received of Rogger Kyndysman for a knyll	iiijd
Item received of Rychard Curry for a knyll	iiijd
Item received of Wylliam Baron for ij knyllys	iiijd
Item received of Thomas Rose for a knyll	iiijd
Item received of John Rowland junior for a knyll	iiijd
Item received of Richard Call for hys servant a knyll	iiijd
Item received of Johan Hutton to regester hyr husbond the Yrysh man ys name a pone the comen bedroll	iijs iiijd
Item received of John Trevelyan to regester John Curbone ys name apone ye comen bedroll	iijs iiijd
Item received of the same John Trevelyan for hys knyll	vjd
Item received of John Trevelyan for regestryng of Wylliam Tunnyng, Elyn hys wife & ther chyldryn a pone ye bedroll	xs
Item [payd crossed out] ^received^ for knyllys for ij chyldryn	xijd
Item received of Wylliam Baron for to regester iij namys a pone the comen bedroll	xs
Item received of Johan Coper to regester Edward Draper ys name a pone the come[n] bedroll & ^for his grave^	vjs viijd
Item received of Johan Olyver junior to regester hyr husbond ys name & hyr name a pone the comen bedroll	vjs viijd

f.45

Item received of Xrispian Bear to sett here husbond & hyr a pone the bedroll	vjs viijd
Item received of John Beys for a dobelett & a schurte of the gyfte of John Ede	xs
Item received of Johan Wade for a knyll	iiijd
Item received of Rychard Wryng for a knyll	iiijd
Item received of John Jule, tayler for a knyll	iiijd
Item received of Thomas Tayler for ij knyllys	viijd
Item received of Wylliam Lange for a knyll for Wylliam Hamat	iiijd
Item received of the same Wylliam Lang to regester hys name & hys wyffe & hys chyldryn	xs
Item received of Wylliam Lang to regester Wylliam Hamet ys a pone ye bederoll	iijs iiijd
Item received of Thomas Bray to regester hys name & hys wyf & chyldryn	xs
Item received of my Lady Chamond for John Harry to regester hys name iijs iiijd	
Item received of Johan Wade to regester Ame Sowdon a pone ye comen bedroll	iijs iiijd
+Item received for regestryng of Wylliam Hore ys name yt was received for a cote[117]	viijs xd
Item received for a schurt yt John Puddener for to regester his name	iijs iiijd
Item received for Agnes Sampson to regester hyr name	iijs iiijd
Item received for a cote yt Tege Kelly gave for to regester his name	vjs jd

[117] *a* in margin.

Item received of Wylliam Hore at Upton for ij knyllys	viijd
Item received of John Bear for a knyll	iiijd
Item received of Thomas Rose for a knyll for Myzhell Rose	iiijd
Item received of ^Thomas^ Hekett for a knyll	iiijd
Item received of John Trevelyan for a knyll	iiijd
Item received Wylliam Rodde for iij knyllys	xijd
Item received of Wylliam Sparke for iiij knyllys	xvj[ij crossed out]d
[Item received for Thomas & his wife & hys to regester ther names	xs crossed out]
Item received for Wylliam Coper ys goune	xs
Item received for John Lyell to regester hys name a pone ye bedroll	iijs iiijd
Item received for Elyn Clyston to regester hyr apone the bederoll	iijs iiijd
Item received for Rogger Puddener ys schurt	iijs iiijd

[f.45v]

Item received of Thomas Olvere for a knyll	iiijd
Item received of Thomas Bray for his servant Margery Crymp	iijs iiijd
Item received for a knyll for Wylliam Bond	iiijd
Item received of Wylliam Call to regester Wylliam Morgan & Johan his wyff & a pone ye bedroll	vjs viijd
Item received of Nycholas Symon for a knyll	iiijd
+Item received for standyng agenst the church howse	vjs viijd
Item received of the scolemaster[118] for the same howse	iiijd
Item received for a serpels	iiijd
Item received of Water Rose for a crocke for hys syster Alys Batyn ys gyft	iiijs
Ryceived of Nycholas Yoe for a knyll	iiijd
+Item received for Thomas Hore	xs
+Item received of Stephyn Daw for a cote	vjs viijd
+Item received [of crossed out] ^for^ Wylliam Bond	iijs
Item received for owr ale bruyng	xxjs viijd
+Item received of Wylliam Yeo for a knyll	iiijd
+Item received of Wylliam Tremyll	iiijd
+Item received of Thomas Bray for ij knyllys	viijd
+Item of Servys for ij knyllys	xijd
+Item received for a knyll for John Hor	iiijd

[xvs jd crossed out]

Summa [ixli xiiijs xjd xvs vijd crossed out]

Summa – xli xviijs iijd

f.46

Expenses

[**Recetes** crossed out] *In primis* payd for tylyng of the churche for lyme & zond	viijs jd
Item for frythyng of the churche heyge for frythe mete & drynke	xvjd
Item paid to Wylliam Moyse for mendyng of colers of ye bellys	iijd
Item for expenses to the archedecon ys visitacon	xvijd
Item paid for ix pound of wex agenst Ester	vs ijd
Item paid for candels	ijd
Item paid for sope for ye hole yer to wasshe ye church clothyng	ijs ijd
Item paid for ij pound of frankencens	vjd
Item paid for oyle for the lampe	vjd ob
Item paid to John Mocke for scowryng of the chandelers	vd
Item paid for makyng of the tapers	iijd
Item paid for mendyng of ye serples	vjd

118 School in church house.

Item paid to Nycholas Judd for mendyng of a claper xxd
Item paid sylkyn poynts for the best cope jd
Item paid for tymber for a bell whevell iijs
Item paid to Nycholas Gyst for yre warke viijd
Item paid to Rychard Call for makyng a crosse canell for a bell viijd
Item paid for a bell coler xviijd
Item paid for a bell rope xvijd
Item paid for a manuell buck xxijd
Item paid for mendyng of the churche pekys vjd ob
Item paid for ij belropys ijs vijd
Item paid for ij new bell colers ijs viijd
Item paid to Master Vicar for the bedroll vs iij[d]
Item paid for a new bear xijd
Item paid for wex yt was bozft mor y^an^ the parysh gave for to make tapers xxd
Item paid for mendyng of ij clapers iijs iiijd

[f.46v]
Item paid to poremen[119] at the comondement of the viij men ijs
Item paid for taking downe of [Seynt crossed out] ye image of Seynt Georg iiijd
Item paid for mendyng of the northe style ijd
Item paid to Thomas Hekytt for the clock ijs
Item paid to Wylliam Moyse for kepyng of the bellys ijs
Item paid for locks, gemes, naylys for the kyngs cofer iijs iiijd
Item for makyng of the pulpytt xxxiijs iiijd
Item for irestuff for the same iiijs vd
Item to Cholwyll for tymber xvjd
for fettyng of the same tymber iijd
Item for expenses for John Mares & John Beys to ryde to Master Robert Langdon for the church woode iiijs viijd
Item to John Cholwyll for ye kepyng of ye bellys xvjd
Item for gresse for the bellys iiijd
Item for a locke for ye stypell dore vjd
Item payd for bords for the pulpytt xvjd
Item paid at the kyngs vysitacon [^for taking of invitor^] iiijs xjd
Item paid at ye kyngs visitors for expenses vjs viijd
Item for makyng of kyngs cofer & the fettyng xxd
Item paid for a cord for ye Lent clothe jd
Item paid for ij barels of lyme iijs viijd
Item paid for [the hewyng crossed out] more stonys iiijs
Item paid for wryting of namys & for other wrytyng the parysh xijd
Item makyng of thys accompte xijd
Item paid for ryngyng of ye kyngs[120] knyll vd
Item for a compulsior, other charges abowt Master Vicar[121] xxviijs

Summa vijli [xvjs vjd crossed out] xvijs [iijd crossed out] ^vd^
Remanyth [xxxixs jd crossed out xxxvijs x crossed out]
Remanyth [iijli xd crossed out] lixs

119 Poor relief starts?
120 For Henry VIII.
121 Compulsion to serve; see Introduction.

f.47

[f.47v]

Compet Ricardus Wryng & Johannis Cobeldyck gardianos Alt' Crucis ecclesie Sancti Andrie de Stratton facta Dominica post festum Purificacionis Beate Marie Virginis anno Xpi millessimo **ccccc xlviij** ***et anno regni Edwardi sexti dei gracia Anglie, Francie & Hibernie regis, defensor fidei et in terra ecclesie Anglicane et Hibernice supremi capitis secundo*** **[3 February 1549]**

Recepts

In primis recevyd of John Rose senior & George Mayor generall recevers the yer past	xs
Item received of the scolemaster for peces of felvet	ijs
Item received of the same scolemaster for occupying of the churche howse	vd
Item received of Nycholas Symon for a kertell	vjs vd
Item received of Walter Rose for occupyng of ye churchehowse	ijd
Item received of Thomas Arundell armiger for ij peces of felvott	vijs viijd
Item received of Tybott Holman for occupyng of ye church howse	ijd
Item received of John Marys for wyghtyng yn the church howse	viijd
+Item for standyngs agenst ye churchehow for ye hole yer	vs
Item received for owr ale bruyng	xxvijs
Item received of John Cobeldyck for ij barels yt cam with lyme	viijd
Item received for a knyll of Edward Horetop	iiijd
Summa recepts iijli vijd	

f.48

Expenses

Memorandum payd for taking downe of ye horse of ye image of Seynt Georg & of ij standyngs mor	viijd
Item payd for fettyng of ij baryls of lyme at Botryaux Castell[122] which lym J. Beys & Edward Horetop payd for ye lyme	xviijd
Item paid for sope for ye hole yer	ijs
Item paid for ij pownd of frankence	viijd
Item paid for expenses abowt the feoffers lands yn Master Rychard Chamo[n]d ys company & other of ye paryshe	xjd
Item paid to John Avery for helyng of the churche howse mete drynk & wages	ijs
Item paid for ij zemys of zande	ijd
Item paid to Rychard Call for mendyng of a locke	jd
Item paid to Rychard Curry for ij pownde & *dimidia* of wex	xxd
Item paid to John Trevelian for makyng of tapers	ijd
Item paid to John Mocke for scowryng of ye cences	jd
Item paid to John Cobeldyck for a trusse of russhes	iiijd
Item paid to John Rowland junior for lether & thongs for ye belcolers	vjd
Item paid to Rychard Call for makyng of a twyste & mendyng of a loke	xijd
Item paid for stuff for church harnys when ye besynys was be west[123]	vjd
Item paid to Wyllyam Lang for helyng stonys	xd
Item paid to John Avery for mendyng of ye church howse	xijd
Item paid to James Colman for ij crests	iiijd
Item paid for a belrop	xviijd
Item paid for scowryng of ij per of harnys	xxijd
Item paid for expenses at ye vysitacon at Lanceston	ijs vjd
Item paid for paper at ye muster	ob

[122] Boscastle.

[123] Helston rebellion, 1548. See Introduction for this and other entries.

Item paid for Master Vicar for ye bedroll vs
Item paid for threde ob
Item for mendyng of the church clothys & lacyng ijd ob

[f.48v]
Item paid for mendyng of a chalys ijs xd
Item paid to John Mocke for schերyng of ye church hegge ijd
Item paid to Roger Yeo for a bock of ye pystels & godspels viijd
Item paid for the rode takyng downe viijd
Item paid for ye ij pycktors of ye northe syde & sowthe syde vjd
Item paid for iij belcolers vjs jd
Item paid to Rychard Curry for rydyng to Buclond[124] for the chalys & other stuff Master John Grendfyld demaunded xvjd
Item paid to John Mocke for makyng of a hole yn ye kyngs cofer ob
Item paid to a masyn to make the northe wyndow of ye church vjs viijd
Item paid to Rychard Call for yre warke of the same wyndow vjs iiijd
Item paid to Wylliam Moyse for kepyng of ye bellys xxd
Item paid to the same Wylliam for mendyng of the colers ijd
Item paid for gresse for ye same ijd
Item paid to John Avery for mendyng of ye churche iiijd
Item paid to a man to serve hym ijd
Item paid to ye same John Avery for mendyng of ye churche another tyme viijd
Item payd for lathe naylys iijd
Item paid to John Cholwyll for his fee for to se to ye bellys xvjd
Item to Thomas Hykytt for ye clock ijs
Item paid to John Beys for polys xijd
Item paid for makyng of ys accompt[125] viijd

Summa lixs iijd

Remanet to ye church xvjd

f.49

***Compet Wylliami Rodde & Nycholai Gyste gardianos ecclesie Sancti Andrie de Stratton facta Dominica post festum Purificacionis Beate Marie anno Xpi millimo* ccccc xlix *et anno regni Edwardi sexti dei gracia Anglie, Francie & Hibernie regis defensor fidei et in terris ecclesie Anglicane et Hibernice supremi capitis tercio* [9 February 1550]**

Receptes

Memorandum of John Marys & Nycholas Judd stocke wardens xiijs
Item of Thomas Clerke for a knyll iiijd
+Item received of John Beys for a knyll for John Bryant ys wyff iiijd[126]
Item received for viij clothys yt coveryd images vjs
Item received for standyngs a genst the church howse vs iiijd
Item received of John Marys for wyztyng a genst ye church howse viijd
Item received for owr ale bruyng xxs iiijd

Summa [xxvs vijd crossed out] ^xlvs viijd^ [xlvs xd viiij crossed out]

Expenses

In primis payde for makyng of ye kyngs inventory for the church good & for paper vijd
Item for lacyng for ye comunyan bock ijd
Item paid at ye vysitacon at Launceston yn expenses iijs iiijd

[124] Buckland Abbey.

[125] Space for two entries above.

[126] Not paid.

Item paid for a corde & paper jd
Item paid for taking downe of ye rode & ye pagents yn ye rodeloft ^& setting up the rode agen[127]^ xd
Item payd for a staff for a holborne & for a peke for ye same vjd
Item paid for mendyng of iij per of harnys iiijd
Item paid for a quitancs for ye pardon[128] at Launceston iiijd
Item paid for makyng of a per of indentures of ye harnys sen to Lanston vjd
Item paid to a glasyer for glasyng ye churche wyndow xiijs vjd
Item paid to Wylliam Rodd for a mare which ye parysshe was content to pay for ye mare yf he had not hys mare agen xxs
Item he wente to Launceston to have his mare & [he] cowde not have hyr, hys expenses & labor was viijd
Item paid to Thomas Hykytt for ye clock ijs

[f.49v]
Item payd to Wylliam Moyse for kepyng of ye bellys viijd
Item paid to John Trevelyan for iij new bocks notyd for matens & evensong & matens yn Yngglyssh[129] xvjd
Item paid for wassheng of ye churche clothys & for sope xvjd
Item paid for makyng of ys accompt vjd

Summa xlvijs
Remaynyth to ye xvjd

f.50
The cowmpts of William Hore & Nycolas Bawnde wardens of the pariche churche of Saynt Andro of Stratton made the Sunday after the feste of the Puryfycacon of Owr Lady the Virgyn in the yer of owr lorde God 1551[130] & in the 5th yer & rayne of owr soverayne lorde Edwarde the 6th by the grace of God of Ynglond, Fraunc & Yerlond, kynge, defender of the fathe & in the church of Ynglond & Yerlond supreme hed [8 February 1551]

In primis recceived of John Antony for the Lent clothe vs viijd
Item recceived of Nycolas Yeo for the great sepulcre clothe iiijs
ressevyd of the same Nycolas for iiij old payented clothes viijd
recceived of Roger Yeo for ij blew clothes xvijd
recceived of John Maryes for iij old clothes xxjd
recceived of Nycolas Symon for ij clothes viijd
recceived of Nycolas Towyll for a [rode crossed out] rowde clathe iijs iiijd
recceived of John Rowlande for a clathe xiiijd
recceived of Nycolas Symon for clothes xiiijd
recceived of John Antony for old clothes xd
recceived of Jorge Maior for a yeold clathe iijd
recceived for stoannes of the awters iiijs iiijd
recceived of John Trevelyan is executors xijd
recceived of John Maryes for wightyn yn the churche howes viijd
recceived of standens by the churchehows wall iiijs iiijd
recceived for alemony with owr bruinge xiijs iiijd

Som of the hole ressett more xliiijs vijd

[127] Rood set up again during the 1549 rebellion.
[128] 1549 rebellion.
[129] The Prayer Book.
[130] Year correct.

[f.50v]

Expenses

Memorandum payd Tomas Heckett for a c of stone	vd
payd a helyer for helynge of the churche	xviijd
paid for nayles for the churche	vd
paid for meate & drynck for ye helyer for iiij dayes & halfe	xiijd
paid a man to serve hem & for hes meat & dryncke	iiijd
paid John Wolfe for lathes	viijd
paid for expenses to the archdecan is vyzitacon at Lonston	ijs viijd
paid for a busshall of lyme & sonde	xvjd
paid Thomas Clarcke for mendynge of the belcoler	ijd
paid Johan Beys	iiijd
paid at the kyngs vyzitacon	iijs iiijd
paid for lyme & mendynge of a serples	ijd
paid for makyng of a per of endentors of the churche gwds	xijd
paid for a bell coller	ijs iiijd
paid [for crossed out] ^for^ the clarcke of Wicke[131] is dener	iiijd
paid for drawynge downe of the awters	ijs iiijd
paid for owr expenses when we apperyd befor my lorde [the crossed out]	iijs
paid for iiij busshalls of lyme & caryge home of yt	ijs vjd
paid for sowynge of the curtayne	jd ob
paid for whittlymynge of the churche	iiijs iiijd
paid for owr expenses at the vyzitacon at Wicke	xd
paid for lyme for the churche	iiijd
paid for mendyng of the churche & lyme for the same	ijs ijd
[paid John Mocke for hes labare	xvjd crossed out]
Paid Wylliam Moyes for kyepinge of the bell	viijd
Paid for wassheng of the church clothes & for soppe	xd
Paid for makyng S of thes accowmpte	vjd

Som of the expenses more xxxvs ob
so ther remaneth cler to the churche [ixs vjd ob crossed out] xs xd ob
the whiche mony Nycolas Bawnd hathe ressevyd in parte of payement for hes horse
whiche he loste in thes besynes & the viij men wer agred that the sayd Nycolas
showld have xxvs for hem & [hathe resseved at ij p crossed out]
& ther rest to hem for hes horse vs vd ob

f.51

The cowmpts of John Cowertys & Water Symon wardens of the Hey Crose of Stratton made the Sonday after [f crossed out] the feaste of the Puryfycasyon of Owr Ladye in the year of owr lord God 1552 & in the 6th year and rayne of owr soverayne lorde Edward the 6th by the grace of God of Ynglond, Fraunc & Yearlond, kynge, defender of the faythe & in the church of Ynglond & Yearlond in yearthe supreme hed [7 February 1552]

Imprimis reccevyd of the stockewardens	xs viijd
recceived for alemony	xxiijs
thes was ressevyd befor the vall.[132] whe mo	xxixs viijd
paid of thes same mony befor the vall.	
Item imprimis for mendynge of the ledds of the churche	vjs iiijd
Item paid at vysytasyon for iij men	ijs iiijd

[131] Week St Mary.

[132] Re-valuation of coinage after Henrician debasements, see MacCulloch, *The Boy King*, p.55. See also 1561.

Item paid at owr goynge to Wicke for the clappers[133] xijd

Soma mo ixs viijd

so ther remayned of that mony whiche we ressevyd beffor the vall. xxs which is now but xs of suche mony as we have ressevyd sens the vall.

In primis reccevyd of John Marres for hes mothers grawe iijs iiijd
reccevyd of the same John for a chamber in the churche howse iijs iiijd
reccevyd of the same John Marres for wighten in the churche howse viijd
reccevyd for standyngs agen the churchehows wall iijs iiijd

Soma mo xs viijd

Expensys syns the vall.

Item paid at the laste vysytasyon ijs iiijd
Item paid for iij busshells of lyme & fettynge the same iiijs
Item paid the helyer for helyng apon the churche xxd
Item paid for hes meage & dryncke iiij dayes xxd
Item paid a man to serve hem & for hes table xxd
Item paid for soppe & wasshenge of the churche clothes viijd

[f.51v]

Expenses

Item paid for a creste for the churche iijd
Item paid for helyng stones xiiijd
Item for lathes jd
Item for clathe to macke a racchet for the clarcke & for makyng of hem ijs vjd
Item for mendyng of the churchestyles iiijd
Item paid Mocke for kepynge of the bell vjd
Item for makynge of thes accownte vjd

Soma mo xvijs iiijd

So ther remaynethe clear to the churche all things allowed – iijs iiijd

f.52

***Anno domini* 1553**

The cowmpts of Rycharde Call & Rychard Hore wardens of the churche of Sent Andro of Stratton made the xx^vj^ day of February yn the yere of owre lord God 1553 and in the seventhe yere and rayne of owr soverane lorde Edward the vj[th] by the grase of God of Ynglond, Fraunc' and Yearlond, kyng, defender of fayth and yn the church of Yenglong & Yearlond in the yearth supreme hedd [26 February 1553]

Inprimys

recevyd of the stocke wardyns iijs iiijd
recevyd for ale mony xxxijs jd ob
received of Nycholas Judde for brasse iijli iijs vijd
received of Rychard Call for a basyn and old yre iiijs ijd
received of Thomas Jewell for a vyare pan iiijd
received of John Marres for wythtyn yn ye chwrche howse viijd
received of Symon Holman for a chamber & ^ye^ chwrche howse iiijs
+received for standyngs a gaynst the chwrche howse viijs

Summa vli xvjs ijd ob

Expensys Item payd for a boke xiiijd
Item payd for the communion boke iiijs iiijd

[133] See Introduction.

Item for mendyng of the challys xvjd
Item to John Avery for a halfe a hondryd of helyng stone xvjd
Item for a vij busshulls and a halfe of lyme iijs ixd
Item payd to [g crossed out] John Avery for ij days worke uppon the chwrche and chwrche howse xxd
Item payd to John Dromant and a man to serve hem yn ye churche howse kechyng for mendyng of a guttor vd
Item payd for a kee to ye kechyn dore and a twyste to the chwrche style viijd quarter
Item payd for wasshyng of ye chwrche clothys iiijd
Item payd for ^communion^ bred of Johan Call ijd
Item payd to Ysbell Judde for wyne xxd
Item payd to John Marrys and Thomas Taylar iijli vjs viijd

[f.52v]
Item payd to the visitation for v men ys expences iijs vjd
Item payd for the expensys of iiij men to go Lestwythyell[134] before the kyngs comyssioners iiijs [illeg. crossed out] xd ob
Item payd to Mocke for kepyng of the bell vjd
Item for makyng of thys accownte vjd
Sum mor iiijli xijs [v crossed out] xd ob
So ther remaynyth [d crossed out] cle[a crossed out]re to the churche xxiijs xd ob quarter[135]

f.53
The cowmpts of Roger Yeo and Edward Jule wardenys of the church of Sent Andro of Strotto[n] made the ix daye of February yn the yer of owr lord God m ccccc liij and yn ye fyrst yer & raynye of owr nobyll quene herr grasse raynyg quene Marie by the grasse of God quene of Englond & Fraunce and Irelond, defender of ye fayth and yn ye churche of Eynglond & Ireland in the yerth, the supreme hed [9 February 1554]

In primis
Item so resevy[d] of ye last wardenys *anno* presedent xxiijs xd ob
[Item resevyd of the stocke wardenys *anno* presedent ixs jd crossed out]
Item resevyd for ale mony xxvs [vjd? crossed out] vd
Item resevyd of ye parson of [Pol crossed out] Plo[m]tre[136] gevyn un to ye church xxs
+Item resevyd for ye standyngs a genys ye church walle viijs
Item resevyd of John Mares for wythyng yn ye church hosse viijd
Item resevyd of Symon Holman for ye church howsse & ye chamber iiijs
Item ye resevy of T. Jule for ^ye^ grette bell for a knyll iiijd
The summe total resetet cumyth to iiijli xijs iijd ob

Item for lowences
Item ye payd un to ye glaser for ye glasyn of ye wyndays xxiijs iiijd
Item for iij men rydyng un to ye vycytacon at Lanstone ijs vd
Item for iij men rydyng un to Lastetheyll to ^delyver^ ye church goodds[137] vs xd
Item for a new sofyll xviijd
Item for iiij newe bell ropyes viijs
Item ye payd to ij men to ryde att Lanstone to ye vycytors ijs iiijd
Item ye payd to John Cholwyll for mendyng of ye bells for hes dener iiijd

[134] Lostwithiel.
[135] ^By me Thomas Gyst^ different hand
[136] Plymptree, Devon. See John Lyll in 'Notes on People' in this volume.
[137] Snell, *Edwardian Inventories*, p.50.

Item ye payd to N. Gyst & Rychard Call for ryngs of yron for ye bells	viijd
Item ye payd un to T. Hyckyt for ye kypyng of ye clocke	ijs

[f.53v]

Item for ye mendyng of church stele to T. Clerke	iiijd
Item ye payd un to John Avery for ye mendyne of church	iijs iiijd
Item for lazth nelys	jd
Item for helyng stonys	vijd
Item for ye ryngyn of kyngs knylle	iiijd
Item ye payd for ye parson of Plo[m]tre ys knylle	vjd
Item ye payd for ij newe bells colers	ijs
Item ye payd to Rychard Call for ij rengs for ye colers	iijd
Item ye payd un to Rychard for mendeng of ye church	iiijd
Item ye payd un to Wyllyam Rodde & to N. Gyst for pese of clozth of [Gli crossed out] gold yt whasse lefte yn yr hands	xvjd
Item ye payd un to John Rowland for a cherge for ye canepy	xiiijd
Item ye payd to N Calle for trowsse of [Ryc crossed out] russys	iijd
Item ye payd un Rychard Call for crocks ye whas straned[138] of Wyllyam Balechyd	vijd
Item ye payd for gresse for ye bells	iijd
Item ye payd for vli of wex & alfe	iijs viijd
Item ye payd att Ester for wyne forth un tell ^Sent^ John daye[139]	iijs iiijd
Item ye payd for ye makyng of ye tapers	ijd
Item ye payd for ye wassyng of ye church c[l crossed out]lozthys	iiijd
Item ye payd for ye kypyng of ye bells	vjd
Item ye payd un to Master Jull for ye c[i]nyng bred	ixd
Item ye payd for ye makyng of ye c[ou]nt	vjd
Item ye payd for jli of wexe & a alfe a gynnys Candylmass[140]	xijd
the summe of ye expenses cumeth to iijli viijs	
Et sic remanet de claro att *ecclecia Sancti Andree de Strottoniae* [?]	xxiiijs iijd ob

f.54

The compts made by Thomas Julle & John Jude whardyns of ^the^ church [est crossed out] of Straton yn ^the^ yere of owr lord m cccccliiij [1555]

Receptes

Item recevyd of the hold whardyns	xxiiijs iijd ob
Item recevyd for hale mony	xxvjs
Item recevyd for ^the^ churches hosse whall	viijs viijd ob
Item recevyd of the scolmaster for the churche hose	xijd
Item recevyd of Symon Holmone for the heye churche ^hose^	iiijs
Item recevyd of John Marys for wythyng yn the churche hosse	viijd
Item recevyd of Nycholas Jude for iij core[141] & ij ponds of the holde bells clapars	vs ijd
Item recevyd of Wyllyam Barrane & Nycholas Symone stoke whardyns	xxjs viijd
Item recevyd of Nycholas Hore for the gret bell	iiijd
Item recevyd of Robart Nelle for the pyte of Joane Blacall yn the churche	iijs iiijd
Item recevyd of Tocar for a knele for the grete bell	iiijd
Item recevyd of John Pery for the grete bell	iiijd
Item recevyd of Thomas Julle for a whold hayse	xd

[138] Distrained.

[139] 24 June.

[140] 2 February or Purification of the Blessed Virgin Mary, the day when accounts were drawn up.

[141] Transcribed as 'score' by Rose-Troup, *The Western Rebellion*, p.376, and 62lbs may be meant.

Item John Jud recevyd whan he rede to London[142] iijli vjs viijd
Summa viijli xiijs iiijd

[f.54v]

Expenses

Item paid for iij ponde & a quarter of wexe iijs
Item paid for a half a ponde of franceks sens iijd
Item paid for corde to hang the sepulcar jd
Item paid for mendyn of the bords yn the churche hose viijd
Item paid for a prosessynall & a whold manuell vijs
Item paid to Wyllyam Whore for the fetyng of them at Exsater iiijs xd
Item paid to Thomas Clarke for makyng of ij taperes & cundels ijd
Item paid for wykeyerne ob
Item paid for expenses at the vysytatyon ijs vd ob
Item paid for a emanuell to Jamis the Coke[143] iiijs iiijd
Item paid to Nycholas Jud for bollyng of ij claperys vijs
Item paid to Richard Call for a basyn of latyn ijs vjd
Item paid for makyng of a clapare to the leche bell jd
Item paid for mendyng of the lede ijs iiijd
Item paid to Richard Curre for a pyex ijs viijd
Item paid to Roger Youe for ij ponde & halfe of wyexe ijs
Item paid for wykeyerene & makyng ijd
Item paid for ij busuls of lyme xiijd
Item paid to Cholwyll for a bell stoke vjs viijd
Item paid to Roger Youe for wyexe for to make the taperys ij tyms iiijs viijd
Item paid to Wyllyam Martynng for redyn of the kechyng iiijd
Item paid to a mason for mendyng of the gutter iijd

f.55

Item paid to Bastyng for a banar stafe ijd
Item paid to Wyllyam Juelle for a hondart of helyng ^stone^ vd
Item paid at a nothere tyme for mendyn of the lede ijs viijd
Item paid for a hally water bockyte vjs viijd
Item paid to Nycholas Jude for makyng of ij ^newe^ bell claperys wyche dyde wyzh lx & xj ponde xxiijs viijd
Item paid to John Avere for iiij days helyn & ij penard lath iijs iiijd
Item paid to the belluter for mendyng of the grete bell & for v ponds of metell xs
Item paid to Thomas Talar for helyn stone viijd
Item paid to Richard Curre for tymber for to make possys for the bords of the churche hosse vjd
Item paid to Thomas Juelle for a bell collar ijs viijd
Item paid to Nycholas Yerrell for helpyn the bellyter viijd
Item paid to Nycholas Gyst for nales iiijd
Item paid to Roger Yowe for helyng stone iiijd
Item paid to Loke at the syys at Lanstone for hys feys ijs vjd
Item paid for grese for the bells vjd
Item paid for wyssyng of churche clothys iiijd
Item paid to Thomas Clarke yn parte of pament for the kepyng of the bells viijd
Item paid to Nycholas Jude for vj ponde of tyne to mende the gret bell iijs
Item for yare worke a boute the gret bell payd to Nycholas Jude vj[d?]

[142] Chantry case. See Introduction.
[143] Occupational name treated as surname.

[f.55v]

Item paid for the lone of a horse to ryde to London vjs viijd
Item paid to Master Wyllyams owr councell vjs viijd
Item paid to Vyncyng Calmady owr turny iijs iiijd
Item paid to Master Browne aturny of the exchekere iijs iiijd
Item paid for the scharchyng of Master Leye offys for to have a copy of owr charche to make owr ple by xxd
Item for the expenses of John Jude & hys horse for v wykes lackeing a daye iiijli iijs
The sum of the expenses comyt to ixli xvjs vjd
So ther doth remen to be payd to Thomas Juell & John Judde xxiijs ijd

The comptes mad by Rychard Servis and Nycolas Hore wardens of the churche of Saynt Androw in the yere of our lord god m ccccc.l.v. [1556]

Item made of the alle mony xxvs ixd ob
Item recevyd of Wylyam Baron & John Courtys for a trey xs iiijd
Item recevyd of Wyliam Balachat for stondyng in the church house xvjd
Item recevid of Robert the Voler for a bott vijd
Item recevid of John Marys for wyght in the church house viijd

f.56

Item recevyd of Nycholas Giste for the gret bell iiijd
Item recevide of Rogger Yeo for the gret bell iiijd
Item recevid of Nicholas Hore for the gret bell iiijd
Item recevid of Thomas Martyng for the gret bell iiijd
Item recevid for stondyn a gaynst the churche ^hose^ walle ixs
Item recevid of the [skollmas crossed out] scollmaster for the hyer churche house ijs
Item recevid of Thomas Jule for a rope iiijd
Item recevyd of Marcks for the hyer churche hose ijs vjd
^Item recevid for the mote of the tre vijd^
^Item recevid of Nicholas Bonde for the grete bell iiijd^
the hole some of the resetes liiijs viiijd ob

Expensys

Item payde to the plomer for mendyn of the lides vs vjd
Item paide for owde for mollte the lydes vjd
Item payde for brede & drincke & one to serve him iiijd
Item payd to John Giste for a bocke ijs viijd
Item payd to the carpenture Oullocott xxd
Item paide for brede & dryncke for the carpenture iiijd
Item paide to Nicholas Gyste for mendyn of the peckys vjd
Item payde for wyer for the clocke vd
Item payd to Richard Caulle for a rynge of iron for the bell iijd
Item paide to the same man for the kechyn dore for a hapes ijd
Item paide for mendin of the best searpler ijd
Item paide for frankyng sense jd
Item paide for a bell rop ijs
Item paide for beryng of bords jd
Item paide for ij ponde of weckes ijs
Item paide to Thomas Hecchatt for kepyn of the clocke ijs
Item paide to Thomas Clarke for kepyn of the beles viijd
Item paide for lathes iijd
Item paide for the making of the weckes jd
Item payd for two bell colers ijs xd

[f.56v]

Item paid for two ropes for the clocke	ijs
Item paid for a man for mend the bourds in the churche house	xiiijd
Item paide for sope	iiijd
Item paide for a halfe a pound of grese	jd ob
Item paid for a bell rop	ijs iiijd
Item paide for vj men for there expences at the visitacyon	iijs xd
Item paid for fellynge of the tre	xvjd
Item payd for the heler & for lime & one to serve him	iijs iiijd
Item paid for mending of the vesstments	ijd
Item paid for a pere of chandlers	iiijs viijd
Item paid for a yerd of dowlas for mende the vesstments	viijd
Item payd for lasin	jd ob
Item paid for [gap left] lynclath for mend the vestments	ijd
Item for sope	iiijd
Item payd for lathe neles	iiijd
Item paide to Hekett for lime	iijs vjd
Item payde to John Giste for bourding in the churche	xd
Item payd for candeles at Crysmas for the quiere	iijd
Item paide to Nicholas Gyste for nailes for bourd the church	vd ob
Item payd to John Avery for helynge of the churche	iiijs ijd
Item payd to one to serve him	xvjd
Item payd for the makyng of thys count	vjd

The hole some of the expenses comthe to – liiijs vd ob
it remenyght to be paid to the church – iiijd
Item the bords of the tre remenygh to the church – xxij
& the reste bestode a bout the church

f.57

This ys the counte of John Shorte & Roberte Bonde wardens of the Highe Crosse store of the church of Strotton made the Sondaye nexte after the Puryfycon of Owr Blessid Laydy in the therde & iiijth yeres of the raygne of owr soveraigne lorde & laydy Philipp and Mary by the grace of God kinge & quene of Englonde, Spayne, Fraunce bothe Cicelles etc. [7 February 1557]

In primis recevid of ye wardens the yare paste	iiijd
Item recevid of Thomas Taylar & Richarde Hore stocke wardens	vjs
Item recevid of Roger Yowe for Alsen Gistes knyll	iiijd
Item recevid of Nycholas Bonde for a knyll	iiijd
Item recevid of John Antony for Master Callmadys knylle	viijd
Item recevid of the same stocke wardens	xiiijs
Item recevid of Master Kemethorne for helynge uppon ye chauncell[144]	xiiijd
Item recevid of William Balhachette for ye cherche howse	xvjd
Item recevid of the clarke for his chamber one quarter	iiijd
Item recevid of Nycholas Yowe & John Curtis stocke wardens	vs
Item recevid of John Marres for wyzghtynge in ye cherche howse	viijd
+Item recevid for the stondinge agaynst ye cherche howse wall this hole yere	xjs jd
Item made of ther ale this yere	xxxvs iiijd ob
The sume of all the recetes this yere	iijli xvjs vijd ob

[144] John Kempthorne and Thomas Arundell held the great tithes from 1537 onwards and so were responsible for chancel maintenance.

The expensis for this hole yere

Fyrste delivered to the glasyar one halfe boysholl of lyme vijd
Item paid for ij semys of wode for ye same glasyar vijd
Item for a Lent corde a penye jd
Item for vj men charges goynge at the byshopps visitacton vjs
Item paid to Nycholas Giste for makynge of the bolle of the therde bells claper & for ij bokylls vs iiijd
Item paid for lether to make ij bell colers & for ye mendinge of a nother ijs
Item paid for makinge of the same & for suyngs vjd
Item payd for ij pownde of waxe to make ye pascall ta[per] [blotched] ijs iijd

[f.57v]

Item paid to Nycholas Giste for nayls & iij wagges for ye bells iiijd
Item to Roger Yowe for a pownde of frankyn sens vjd
Item paid for sope to whasshe ye churche clothing vd
Item for makyng of the pascall taper jd
Item paid to Roger Yowe for the clothe to cover ye rode ijs viijd
Item for the makyng of the same jd
Item for makyng of the churche pekes vjd
Item paid to Nycholas Giste for a spange for the grete bell whele ijd
Item paid for a newe bell rope ijs iiijd
Item paid to Edwarde Hortoppe for ye holy water bokytte in the cherche porche xixd
Item for ij menys charges at the vysytacon ijs
Item paid for a quarter of lyme brought frome Saynte Damnacke[145] iiijs viijd
Item paid to John Curtis for a hafe a thowsant of helynge stonys iijs
Item paid to John Dromont for ij days for makynge uppe the highe auter for his wages & mete & drinke xvijd
Item paid for ij men to serve hem and a horse to fette morter and for yer mete & drinke & thir wages xvd
Item paid to John Dromond for ye mendinge of ye cherchehowse wyndowse ijd
Item for cc of lathe nales iiijd
Item for lether to mend one belle coler ijd
Item paid to Richarde Cory for one hundred of latthes viijd
Item paid to John Averye for vij dayes worke uppon the chorche for mete, drinke & his wages vs xd
Item paid for one to serve hem ijs iiijd
Item paid to John Avery for iij bushells and halfe of lyme iiijs viijd
Item paid to the same John Avery for viij days worke and halfe daye for his wages & mete & drynke helynge uppon the cherche vijs jd
Item paid for one to serve hem for his wages & mete & drynke ijs xd
Item paid for the beddemans rochette xvijd
and for the makynge of ye same & mendinge of anoyer iiijd
Item for Robats Cholwylls fee to mende ye bells xxd
Item paid to Nycholas Giste for nales & ij plates iijd

f.58

Item paid for lyme for the glasyar jd
Item paid for sope to whasshe ye cherch clothinge iiijd
Item paid to Thomas Clarke to kepe the bells viijd
Item paid for gresse for the bells ijd
Item paid for candells at Christemas for ye quire ijd
Item paid for ij new crests for ye cherche vd

[145] St Dominick.

Item paid for the makynge of a bell claper	vs
Item paid to Thomas Hekitte for ij stapys of yron	jd
Item paid for a lantrane for ye chirche	xiijd
Item for makyng of this accownt	iiijd

The hole sume of the expensis ys thes yere paste iijli xiiijs vd ob
And so remaynythe clare to the churche all thinge alowid this yere ijs ijd
Item ther dowthe remayne in the cherchehowse of small bords & xviij and one halfe borde & iiij planks & ij halfe planks[146]

[f.58v]

Here foloyth the a cownte of Wyllyam Yeo & John Pere wardyns yn the yere of owr lorde god 1557 m ccccc lvij [1558]

Item fyrste recevyd of the wardyns paste yn mone	ijs ijd
recevyd of Nycolas Yeo & John Cortys stoke wardyns	vs
recevyd for Jolowys knell	iijs iiijd
recevyd of Peter Quycke for the grete bell ^ij knyls^	viijd
recevyd of Rychard Vevyn for a knyll	iiijd
recevyd for Rafe Yngerys pyt	iijs iiijd
recevyd for Margeryt Taylers pyt	iijs iiijd
recevyd of the clarke for hys chamber	xvjd
recevyd of Wyllyam Bawthachyt for the cherche howce	xvjd
recevyd of John Morrys for wyghtyn yn the chorche howce	viijd
+recevyd for stondyng a gaynst the chorche howce ys yere	xjs vjd
recevyd for owr drynke thys yere	lijs vd ob
Som iiijli vs vd ob	

f.59

+The expensys for thys hole yere

Item fyrste for ij bell rowps	vjs vd
payd Thomas Clarke for gressyn of the bells	viijd
payd for drynke at the rynggyn of Jolows knyll	ijd
for ij li & *dimidia* of wex to make the pascall taper	ijs viijd ob
for makyn of the same	jd ob
for *dimidia* a li of frankynsence	iijd ob
payd for thred	jd
for the eyers[147] at the awters end	viijd
payd for the waggys for the bells	ijd
for ij quarter of lyme	vijs viijd
for a m of hellyn stone	vjs
for lether to make ij collers	ijs
for makyng of the same	iiijd
payd the plomer for mendyn of the leds	vs iiijd
payd for owde & for servyn of the plomer	iiijd
payd the heller for xij days worke xd the day	xs
payd for lathe nales	vijd ob
payd for lathys	jd ob
payd for servyn of the heller	iiijs ixd
payd for sonde	iijd
for mendyn of the chorche dore keye	vd
for pavyn under the chorche howce ovys	xiiijd

[146] Jottings.
[147] For hanging curtains.

payd Chowllwyll for hys fye	xxd
for yare worke yn mendyn of the bells	vjd
for makyn of the este stele	viijd
for beryn of the stoffe unto hym	iiijd
for ij awter towyls	xd
for a clothe for the deske	xvjd ob
for makyn of the same	ijd
for wasshyn of the chorche clothys thys yere	xijd

[f.59v]

Item payd more for candyls to serve Cressemas day yn the mornyn	ijd
payd for gresse for bells	iiijd
Item payd for mendyn of ij [clappers crossed out] clappers	iiijs
for makyn of thys a cownt	vjd

Sum of the chargys iijli xxijd

So there remenythe clere to the chorch xxiijs vijd ob

Item there was for gotyn to be alowyd of thys a cownte for expensys of fowre men goyn to the vysytasion iijs viijd[148]

f.60

Jesus

Here folloyeth the a cownte be twyne Jamys Call & Thomas O[lyver] wardyns yn the yere of owr lord god 1558 [1559][149]

Item fyrste recevyd of the wardyns past	ob
Item recevyd of Elzabethe Uglow of Marryncherche[150]	vjs viijd
Item recevyd of Rafe Bell to wards the chorche	xijd
Item recevyd of Nycolas Wyll for Bryants pyt & the gret bell	iijs viijd
Item recevyd for Ebotte Taylers pyt	iijs iiijd
Item recevyd of Roier Yeo for the grete bell ^for hys chylde^	iiijd
Item recevyd of Peter Quycke for Rycharde Cowkys knyll	iiijd
Item recevyd for Ebott Cleverdun the grete bell	iiijd
Item recevyd of John Cowrtys for weyng yn the chorche hows	viijd
Item recevyd of the clarke for hys chowmber	xvjd
Item recevyd of Ball Hatchyt for the chorche howse	xvjd
Item for lij fowte of bowrde	ijs vjd
+Item recevyd for stondyng a gaynst the chorche hows wall	xs jd ob
Item recevyd for owr drynke thys yere	ls jd ob
The hole sum ys	vli xxd ob

[Item lente to Nycolas Geste thre c of hellyn stones & iij & iiij lathys[?]

Item lente Peter Yeo ^xx^iiij[151] helyn stone

Item lente all so unto Thomas Olyver afore said ^xx^iiij crossed out] hellyn stone

[f.60v]

The expenses for thys yere paste 1558[–59][152]

Item payd the veker of Powghhyll[153] for ijli & a quarter of wexe to make the pascall taper xjd the li	ijs ob

[148] xxijs ijd and accounting table.

[149] Account faded and hard to read.

[150] Marhamchurch.

[151] Four score, eighty.

[152] See appendix 2.2 for the draft version.

[153] John Cawse.

more *dimidia* a li for the same vjd
payd Thomas Whete for makyng iijd
Item for viij yerds & dimidia of holond to make the Lent clothe at xd ye yerde vijs jd
Item for ryngs & lasyn for the same iiijd
Item for makyng iiijd
Item for a [new crossed out] nyew ymnor ijs
Item for a poynsyn to put lyme ynto xxd
Item for pentyn of Synt Androw iijs iiijd
Item for a yerde & dimidia of canvas vijd the yerde xd ob
Item for makyng of the pallme crosse vjd
Item for ijli & dimidia of lede for the same ijd ob
Item payd Nycolas Gyste for mendyn of the therde bell clapper vs
Item payd Thomas Clarke for makyn of a nyew coller & mendyn of ye owlde ixd
Item payd Nycolas Giste for a pyn for the same ob
Item thre yerds & dimidia of dowlys for a nawter clothe viijd ob ye yerde ijs vd ob
Item payd Bastyn & hys boye for makyng of wyndows & mendyng of fowrms yn the
chowrche howce a days worke & mete & drynke xiiijd
Item payd Rycharde Call for jemys & nayls for the same xvjd
Item payd for ij possys for the a fore sayd fowrms ijd
Item payd for threde to sow the albys unto a syewte of vestements ob
Item payd for wode which servyd Ester yeve jd
Item payd for candyls to put uppon the banner staffe jd
Item payd for makyn of a hole water spryngyll jd

f.61

+ **1558[–59]**

Item for poynts yn makyn of the sepullker jd
Item for a li of frankyn sense vijd
Item payd for fyve men at the vysytatyon iiijs viijd
Item payd for loke for the vonte vjd
Item for *dimidia* a li of wexe to helpe macke the tapers be fore ye rowde vjd
Item for weke yerne ob
Item for makyng of the thre tapers ijd
Item payd John Shorte for ^a^ bull neke to macke ij nyew coffers ijs iiijd
Item payd Thomas Clarke for makyng of the same viijd
Item for a nyew bell rowpe ijs iiijd
Item for heddyn & glewyng of thre sheve of errows iijd
Item for a dosen of heddys to the same iijd
Item payd Buttycke for mendyn of the halle water bockkyt viijd
Item payd for Bryants dener when he came to have mayd ye chorche stile iijd
Item for xxviij yerds of dowleys to macke iiij [new crossed out] nyew serplesys at
viijd ob the yerde xixs xd
Item for makyng of the same iiijs vjd
Item for makyng of thre racchyts vd
Item for mendyng of the banner of sylke jd
Item for makyng of the chownsyll dowre keye iiijd
Item payd John Geyste of Powghhyll for makyng of the chowrche stele for wone
daye & mete & drynke xd
Item for a nyew pece for the same yeate iiijd
Item payd Nycolas Geyste for a tweste & xij nayls for the same yeate ixd
Item for a hapsse & a stape to the same jd
Item payd Nycolas Geyste for ij pyns for ij bell collers ijd
Item payd John Avere for vj days worke xd ye daye vs
Item for sonde & servynge of heym ijs

Item for a c of lathys vijd
Item for thre c of lathe naylys iijd the c ixd
Item payd for ryddyn of the kechyn & gutter a man wone hole daye mete & drynke vjd
Item delyveryd Thomas Whyte thre li dimidia of wexe to make tapers agaynst Cresmas be fore the rowde at xijd the li iijs vjd
Item for makyng of the same[154] iijd

[f.61v]

1558[–59] +

Item payd Jone Clarke for mendyn of the owlde serplesys ijd ob
Item payd for a banckyt to the bell fownder & to wother yt laboryd a bowte ye bell xd
Item payd for pavyng of the kecheng a man wone daye mete & drynk xd
Item payd for servyng of the paver with stoneys & yerthe iiijd
Item payd for ryngyng of the olde Uglows knyll of [marynge crossed out] of Marryncherche vjd
Item for candylls Crecemas daye yn the mornyng ijd
Item payd John Rowlonde for makyng of a nyew coller for the grete bell & for mendyn of the owlde ijs vjd
Item payd Rycharde Call for makyng of a pyn for the same jd
Item payd for Nycolas Gyste for makyng of wadies & tweysts a bowte the grete bell xvijd
Item payd for *dimidia* a quere of paper for thys bocke ijd ob
Item payd Thomas Clarke for gressyn of the bells viijd
Item for gresse for the same & a bowte the grete bell viijd
Item for thre li of sowpe the [wche crossed out] which we have occupyyd thys yere xviijd
Item for makyng of thys a cownte vjd

The hole sum of the charies[155] ys iiijli xiijs xd ob
so there remenythe clere unto the chewrche vijs xd

f.62

The acownte of [He crossed out] John Averye and Wyllyam Wyll wardens in the yeare of our lorde god 1559 [1560]

Recepe

In primis recevid of Thomas Oliver & James Call wardens past vijs xd
Item recevid of Wyllyam Breye xviijd
Item recevid of Petherike Twigges for the gret bell iiijd
Item recevid of the stokwardens at iij sunder tymes xxxs
Item recevid of Anne Daw for the great bell iiijd
[Item recevid of illeg. words the churche xijd? crossed out]
Item recevid of Wyllyam Pryst at Morstawe[156] [th crossed out] towards the churche xxd
Item recevid of Elezabet Trypplet for the great bell iiijd
Item recevid of John Cortys & Edmond Rygyll for weynge in the church house viijd
Item recevid of Jewes ^Jepcyons^ for the churche howse ijs vjd
Item recevid of Alsen Wheer for Ser Water Julls knyll iiijd
+Item recevid for stonding agaynst the churche howse wall xs jd
Item recevid of the clerk for his chamber xvjd
Item recevid for our drynke the yere ls

The hole summe ys – vli vjs xjd
Item lent to the aforsayd John Averye a bushill of lyme

[154] + 1559 below.
[155] Charges.
[156] Morwenstow.

[f.62v]

Item payd for iiijli of wexe for the pascall taper xijd the li	iiijs
Item payd for ijli & halfe to barne befor the rode xijd the li	ijs vjd
^Item payd for maken of the same	vjd ob^
Item payd for a cord to draw the Lent clothe	ijd
[Item payd for wod crossed out]	
Item payd unto Symon Holman for iij cases of aros	xviijd
Item payd unto Wyllyam Hedden for mendyng of the therd bell claper	xs ijd
Item payd unto Rychard Call for mendyng of thre lokes	vijd
Item payd unto Peter Quike for a alder tree	[jd crossed out] ob
Item payd for setten of the same	jd
Item payd for ijli of sope	xjd ob
Item payd unto John Bale for reideng of the keching	jd
Item payd unto Wyllyam Hedden for a newe showle	xixd
Item payd for a new beer	xijd
Item payd for a half a pond of wexe more	vjd
Item payd for weke yerne	ob
Item payd unto Wyllyam Hedden for neles	ob
Item payd unto John Dromet to make ij holes in the churchehouse to make fast the wyndos	jd
Item payd for maken fose bordes & formes in the churche house	iijd
Item payd for wod a Ester yeve	jd
Item payd unto Thomas Oliver for a li of frankensence	vjd
Item for poynts & pyns yn maken of the sepulker	jd
Item expenses at the boshipes vicitation	iijs xd
Item payd to John Megar for tornyng of the gret bell met & drynk for they that were with him	xiijd
Item payd to the aforsayd John Avery for a days worke & on to serve him met & drynk	xiiijd
Item payd for lathe neles	jd
Item payd for a quarter of lyme	iiijs
Item payd to the aforsayd Thomas Oliver for ij presessinall books	vjd
Item payd to the glacier for mendeng of the glase wyndows	ixs
Item payd to the aforsayd glacier for menden of the church house wyndowe	xvjd
Item expenses for John Jude to bryng a comuning book from Exceter	xvjd
Item payd to Jone Yeooe for bred & wyne for the comuning	vjd
Item payd unto Rychard Call for the raze that berethe the deske	vjd
Item payd for book of iniuncion	vd
Item expenses at the boshypes vicitation for vj men at Bodman	xvijs ixd ^ob^
Item payd unto Basten Laurence for maken of the tabell[157]	iijs

f.63

Item payd to the aforsayd John Averye for vj days work and one to serve hem, met & drynk & sond	vjs
Item payd unto the aforsayd Wyllyam Heddon for lathe neles	iiijd
Item payd unto Master Mauris for maken of the ferst inventarye	xijd
Item payd unto John Averye for maken of the last inventary[158]	xviijd
Item payd for parcment for the same	iijd
Item payd to the veker of Poghhill[159] for a copye for the same	iijd
Item payd for leing in of the aforsayd inventary at Bodman	vjd
Item payd for mendeng of the same	iiijd

[157] Communion table.

[158] See appendix 3.1.

[159] John Cowffe: www.kcl.uk/artshums/depts/history/research/proj/clergy.aspx (accessed 2 February 2017).

^Item payd to Wyllyam Wyll for care of the inventary at Bodman	xd^
Item expenses at the same tyme	xijd ob
Item payd unto the aforsayd Wyllyam Wyll for a sauter booke	xxd
Item payd for a quart of wyne agaynst Christmas	vd
Item payd for mending of the serpells	jd
Item payd unto Water Bettick for ix li & a half of mettill viij[d] the li	vjs iiijd
Item payd to the aforsayd Bettick for leing of the same	iijs viijd
Item payd a man to serve him, met & drynk & wod for the fee	xxd
Item payd to the aforsayd John Averye for ij days worke, met & drynk & one to serve hem & for sond	[v crossed out] ijs vjd
Item payd to the aforsayd John Dromet for maken of the sepulker	ijd
Item payd unto Rychard Wrynge for keping of the bells	ijs
Item payd to the aforsayd Wryng for mendeng of the litell bell coler	jd
Item payd for grese for the bells	vjd
Item payd to John Rolond for a bellcoler	ijs
Item payd for makyng of this acownt	vjd

The hole sum of the charies ys vli ijs xjd ob

So ther dothe remeyne cleyre to the churche iij[s] xjd ob

[f.63v]

Jhesus

Hyr followyth the a cownt of Thomas Juell marchant and Crystofer Braye wardens yn the yer of our lord God *anno* m^d^ ccccc lx+ [1561]

Recetts

Item recevyd of the last wardens	iijs xjd ob
Item recevyd of ye Jepsyons one nyzth yn the church howse	iiijd
Item recevyd of ye stoke wardens be for Ester	xs
Item recevyd of Sir John Arundell[160] for ye church howsse	vjs viijd
Item recevyd for our all thys yer	liijs vd ob

Thys mony was recevyd be for the valle wyche ys iijli xiiijs vd

Item paid of the same mony be fore vall.[161]

Item paid for wyn ye fyrst wyk yn Lent	vd
Item paid for v yerdes of lasson for ye Bybell	jd
Item paid for wyne a gayne Ester	xviijd
Item paid for comunyon brede	xd
Item paid for a cope[162] a gayne Ester	iiijd
Item paid to John Avere for iij dayes & hallffe ys worke met & hyer & one to serffe hem	iijs viijd
Item paid to Rychard Call for lathe nayells	jd
Item paid for a tresse for ye orgaynys	jd
Item paid for iiij men ys expences att ye vycytacyon	iijs viijd
Item paid to Thomas Ollver for menden of the hogs heds to put lyme yn hytt	jd
Item paid for gresse for the bells	iijd
Item paid for wyne a gayne [Ester crossed out] Wytt Sondaye	iiijd
Item paid for makyn clen of the harnes to Watter Betyke	vs xd

f.64

Item paid to Wyllyam Heddon for mende of ye great bell claper	ijs

160 For a funeral wake?

161 Vall. – re-valuation of coinage? See 1552, pp.93–94.

162 Wooden communion cup? Appendix 3.3.

Item paid for a comunyon boke	iijs viijd
Item paid for a quarter of lyme	iiijs
Item paid for poynts for harnes	jd
Item paid for pychs & vernessen of the ij bylls	jd
Item paid for ij bowe stryngs	jd
Item paid for iij lether gyrdells	vjd
Item paid to Dromont for wassen of the rowde loft & menden ij holles yn the church	jd
Summa xxvijs viijd	

So ther remaynethe of that mony wyche wye recevyd be fore the vall.– xlvjs ixd, the lost ther of ys – xvs iiijd ob [wych crossed out] ys nowe but xxxjs iiijd ob

Hyer followith of schuge mony as wye have receivyd synnys the vall.

Item recevyd for Sir John Arundell ys ^grave^	iijs iiijd
Item recevyd for wyghtyn yn the church howesse	viijd
Item recevyd of the clarke for hys chamber	xvjd
Item recevyd for standen a gaynst ye church howse wall	xs
Item recevyd of Roger Yoe for a knyll	iiijd
Item recevyd of Wyllyam Rode for a knyll	iiijd
Item recevyd of Thomas Phellype for a knyll	iiijd
Item recevyd of ye Yeryshe man for a knyll for hys mother	iiijd
Summa xvjs viijd[163]	

[f.64v]

Expencys synnys the vall

Item paid for ij [h crossed out] hundred of lathes	xiiijd
Item paid for wyne	jd ob
Item paid to Crystofer Braye ys expences to make awnsur for the church lands	ixd
Item paid for iiij men ys expencys & ye ij wardens att the bysshopes vycytacyon	ijs iijd
Item paid to ther clarke for makyn of a byll	viijd
Item paid to them for recevyng of the byll	vjd
Item paid to the somner	ijd
Item paid to Watter Betyke for menden of the ledes	iijs
Item paid to one to serffe hem met [& hyer crossed out] & wode	vjd
Item paid for wyne	ijd
Item paid to the glassyer for menden of ye church wyndowes	vs
Item paid to Thomas Hekytt for menden of ye stepell dore loke	iiijd
Item paid to John Rowland for menden of iij bell collers & fenden of stwffe	iijs
Item paid for wyne [a gayst Crysemas crossed out]	vijd ob
Item paid to Wryng for kyepen of the bells	ijs
Item paid to John Cotten for menden of ye pyke ex	vjd
Item paid to Wyllyam Barren for a man & ij horsys a for none met & hyer to carre upe ye stonys	vijd ob
Item paid to Thomas Juell for ij horssys & a man mett & hyer a daye & hallffe	xxd
Item paid for wassen of ye church clothys	xxd
Item paid for makyn of the a cownt	vjd
Item paid for a bell coller to John Roweland	ijs iijd
Summa xxvjs vjd ob	

And so ther remayneth cler unto the church xxijs

[163] Repeated at the bottom of the page.

f.65

Heer folowethe the acounte of Nycolas Sonder & Wyllyam Braye wardens in the yeare of our lord God *anno* m ccccc lxj [1562]

The recetes

In primis recevyd of the laste wardens	xxijs
Item recevyd of the stock wardens	xlvjs
Item received of the Ejepcyons[164] for the churchehouse	iiijd
Item received of ^John Bedner^ the old clarke for a half a years rent for his chamber	viijd
+Item received for standing a gaynst the churchehouse wall	xs
Item received for old bellropes	xxijd
Item received of Nycolas Hore for the great bell	iiijd
Item received of John Cleverdon for the great bell	iiijd
Item received for our ale thys yair	ls
Item received of John Pooth for hys knylle	iiijd
Item received of John Marys for weghtyng in the churchouse	viijd
The holl somm comethe to	vjli xijs vjd

[f.65v]

expences

In primys payd for bread & wyne a gaynst Ester	iijs
Item payd for a neell for the therd bell	ob
Item expenses for iiij men at the boyshypes visitacion	iijs
Item payd for a bellrope	ijs vjd
Item payd for wyne at another tym	vjd
Item expenses for iiij men at the boyshypes vicitation	ijs vjd
Item s [*sic*] payd for maken of a byll & for a iniouncion	viijd
Item payd for leyng in of the same byll	xijd
Item payd for the comaundementes & a calender	ijs
Item payd for mendyng of a bokell for the bellcoler	jd
Item payd for wyne	vjd
Item paid to Rychard Wrynge for kepyng of bells	ijs
Item paid for gress for the bells	iiijd
Item paid for a tonng & for mendyng of a coler for the bell	jd
Item paid to John Lamerton for ij men ther meat ij dayes when they begann the wall for the yeat	xvjd
Item paid for ther heer	xvjd
Item paid for vyllynge of the tree	vjd
Item paid for mendyng of the ^chymlye^ in the clarkes chamber	iiijd
Item paid to the masons for maken of the wall	xxs viijd
Item paid for mendynge churchstell j daye & j to serve him, met	xijd
Item paid to Thomas Hortope for drayng of the stones	viijs viijd
Item paid to John More hys horse & hys boye one daye	vjd
Item paid to Rychard Hore for ij horses ij dayes	ij s iiijd

f.66

Item payd Wyllyam Braye iiij dayes & a halfe with iij hor[ses]	vjs ^vjd^
Item paid for ij dayes caryn with one horse to care gret	xxd
Item paid to John Avery ij dayes work upon the church one to [serve hym ijs crossed out] serve hym, meat & wages	ijs viijd
Item for lathe nells	ijd
Item for a peecke of lym	iiijd

[164] This is the last reference to gypsies.

Item paid to Lamerton for John Megar & ij men ther dener when they cam to se the work ixd
Item paid to John Megar for iiij dayes work ijs
Item paid to John Ratenbery for iiij dayes work xxd
Item paid to John Heman for iiij dayes worke xvjd
Item paid to Megar sonne for iiij days work xijd
Item paid [th crossed out] to John Hedyn & Megar sonne a half a daye iiijd
Item paid to John Roland meat & drynk for the carpenter had vijs ^iiijd^
Item paid to John Roland for the tember for yeat xxvjs
Item paid for iijd of basterd nell & ijd of bord neell vd
Item paid to John Avery vj dayes work & one to serve him, met & her viijs
Item paid to Nycolas Bound for iij verdells of lym ijs
Item paid to Thomas Olyver for a m & ijc ^of lath nells^ ijs
Item paid to Wyllyam Yeoo for ccc of lathes ijs
Item paid for beren of the stones iiijd
Item paid to Thomas Clarke for redyng of the yeat vjd
Item paid for a half a peke of lym ijd
Item paid for ij fleells for the wynd beerds viijd
Item paid for vij crestes & a halfe xvd
Item paid for candellyght ijd
Item paid for s a cott clothe for Wyllyam Juell ijs iiijd

[f.66v]
Item payd for [illeg. word crossed out] sope [of the illeg. word crossed out] viijd
Item payd for sand iijd
Item paid to Master Vicar for [illeg. words crossed out] ^maken of indentures^ vjd
Item paid for makyng of thys acounte vjd
The sum of expens comethe to vjli viijs iiijd ob
So ther remenethe cleer to the churche iiijs xjd ob
+ Item boro of Wyllyam Yeoo m cccccc xxx stones
Item of thes sume before ys iiij bayse testers & of other corant mony ijs ivd[165]

f.67
Hyer followythe the a cownt of Justynyan Juell and Nycolas Pere wardenes yn the yer of our lord God *anno* m^d^ ccccc lxij [1563]

Recettes

Item recevyd furst of ye stoke wardens vjs viijd
Item recevyd a nother tym of them vjs viijd
Item recevyd mor another tyme xvs
Item recevyd for ye old claper of the greatt bell iiijs viijd
Item recevyd a nother tyme of the stoke wardens xxs
Item received [of Wyll crossed out] for Wyllyam Barren ^ys^ grawe iijs iiijd
Item received of John Antony for the ^old^ church stell iiijs
Item received of Reger Yeo for a knyll iiijd
Item received of Robart Steven for a knyll iiijd
Item received of Thomas Juell for a knyll iiijd
Item received for ye old Thomas Tayler ys grawe[166]
Item received of John Lane for a knyll iiijd

[165] Sketch of a dragon here.
[166] Sum left blank.

Item received for [for crossed out] the standen a gaynst the ponyon of Wyllyam Yoe ys schope with owtt ye church stell[167] ijd
Item received of Wyllyam Balhachytt for standens yn ye church howsse xvjd
Item received for wyzrten yn the church howsse viijd
+Item received for standen a gaynst ye church howsse wall xs
Item received for our alle thys yer liijs xd
Summa of the recetes ys vjli vijs viijd

[f.67v]

The expences for thys holle yer

Item paid for drynk for ye cloke maker when he came to se the cloke ijd
Item paid for vj yerds of wyer for ye cloke vjd
Item paid for a *dimidia* c of lathe neyells jd
Item paid for drynke for ye viij men when they paid the cloke maker vijd
Item paid for ij c of howesselen bred xiijd
Item paid for wyn ijd
Item paid for a li of sope ixd
Item paid to John Avere & to hys sone for a days ys worke, mett & hyer xvjd
Item paid ^to^ one to serff them, mett & hyer viijd
Item paid to John Avere for lym xd
Item paid to Rychard Call for menden of ij loks vjd
Item paid for wyne a gaynst Ester ijs iiijd
Item paid for iiij men ys expences att the bysshopes vycytacyon iiijs jd
Item paid to John Magar & hys ij men iij dayes for makyn of ye church stell & menden of ye stepell wyndowe iiijs
Item paid for jemys & nayells for the church yette & nayells for the [church crossed out] stepell wyndowes vs iiijd
Item paid to John Avere for iij bordes for ye tower wyndows iijs iiijd
Item paid to Master Vycar for iij bordes more xviijd
Item paid to one to serff hem, mett & hyer vjd
Item paid for [me crossed out] neyells to mend ye bells iiijd
Item paid for makyn clene of the church harnes iiijs
Item paid for nayells & bokyells for ye [hs crossed out] harnes iiijd
Item paid for a quarter [of lyme crossed out] & hallffe of lyme vs ixd
Item paid for a quart of wyne iiijd
Item paid to John Avere for a [a li^illeg.^] of lede xd

f.68

Item paid for gresse for the bells iiijd
Item paid to Thomas Juell for mette & drynke for John Megar & ij men iij dayes iiijs vjd
Item paid to John Avere for a hallff bussell & *dimidia* pecke of lyme xd
Item paid to Thomas Olyver for iiij yerds of wyer iiijd
Item paid to Master Offycall to schow our regester boke att the vycytacyon vjd
Item paid to Master Vicar for takyn owtt of ye names vjd
Item paid for a bell rope ijs vjd
Item paid for menden of a bell coller xijd
Item paid to a mynyster to helpe playe & syng iiijd
Item paid to Wyllyam [Hedden crossed out] Heddon for a newe claper for the greatt bell xxjs iiijd
Item paid hem for menden of ye thurd bell claper iiijs
Item paid for ij m^*dimidia*^ & a quarter of hellen stone xvs iiijd
Item paid to Watter Beatyk for menden of the ledes & ixli & hallff of mettell ixs vjd

[167] See 1583 plans, figures 7–8, pp.218–219.

Item paid for wode & one to serff hem, mett & hyer	xd
Item paid to one to serff hem a nother tym	ijd
Item paid for wyne	vd
Item paid to John Avere & to hys son for iiij dayes worke, mett & hyer	vs iiijd
Item paid to a man to serff them mett & hyer ij dayes	xijd
Item paid to Basten for menden of ye organys	vjd
Item paid to John Cotton for makyn of a nowe kye & nayells for the stepell dower	vd
Item paid for wyne	vjd
Item paid to Wryng for kyepyn of the bells	ijs

[f.68v]

Item paid to John Rowland for a bell coller	ijs ijd
Item paid for menden of a olde coller	vjd
Item paid for a quart of wyne	vjd
Item paid to John Lene & Thomas Marten for makyn of ye church yerd hegg iiij dayes mett & hyer	vs viijd
[Item for wyne crossed out]	
Item paid for a wyell for a bell coller	jd
Item paid for a seme of sond	ijd
Item paid for wassen of the church clothes	viijd
Item for beren home of the hellen stone to Wyllyam Yoes	iiijd
Item paid to the quer man to helpe the quer	xijd
Item paid for wyn	vjd
Item paid for makyn of thys a cownt	vjd
Item paid to Wyllyam Yoe for the lone of ij tressells [for Wyllyam crossed out] att the fer tym	ijd

Summa vjli iijs viijd

and so remayneth cler unto the church iiijs

Item Master Chamon[d] oweth us iijli & hallff of lede

f.69

Hyer folowyth the a cownt of Andro Saungyn and Nycolas Call wardens yn the yer of our lord God *anno* m^d^ ccccc lxiij [1564]

Reccettes

Item recevyd fyrste of ye stoke wardens	vjs viijd
Item recevyd of Thomas Snowe for a knyll	iiijd
Item recevyd of the stoke wardens a nother tyme	xxs
Item recevyd of Roger Yoe for Thomas Tayler ys grave	iijs iiijd
Item recevyd of ye stoke wardnes another tyme	xs
Item recevyd of them another tyme	xs
Item recevyd another tym	vjs viijd
Item recevyd of John Braye for a knyll	iiijd
Item recevyd of Justynyan Juell for a knyll	iiijd
Item recevyd of Bedlyme for hys mother ys knyll	iiijd
Item recevyd of Wyllyam Yoe for Mystrys Hauger ys knyll	iiijd
Item recevyd of heme for her grave	iijs iiijd
Item recevyd of Nycolas Perre for hys father ys grave	iijs iiijd
Item recevyd of Jone Cortes for musterd sede	viijd
Item recevyd of John Marys for wyrtyn yn ye church howsse	viijd
Item recevyd of Mystrys Poyell for her husband ys knyll	xijd
Item recevyd of Balhachet for standen yn ye church howsse	xvjd
+Item recevyd [of crossed out] for standen a gaynst ye church howsse wall	xijs

Item recevyd for our alle thys yer iijli vjs viijd

And so the holl sum of recettes ys – vijli vijs iiijd

[f.69v]

The expencys of thys yer

Item paid to John Avere & to hys sone for vj dayes helyng, mett & hyer viijs
Item paid to John Avere for a *dimidia* bussell of lyme viijd
Item paid to hem for lath nayells iijd
Item paid to the glassyer for glassen of ye church wyndows & ye church howsse & a glasse over ye rodlofft xxiiijs vjd
Item paid hem more for a glasse for the cloke iiijd
Item paid for a pek of lyme a bowtt ye wyndowes iiijd
Item paid for wode for hem ijd
Item paid for drynke when wye paid hem hys mony viijd
Item paid for a newe bottell of tyne xijd
Item paid for ij hundred of howeslen bred xijd
Item paid for a quart & hallff of wyne vjd
Item paid for a li & quarter of sope xijd
Item paid to Basten for removen of a sege yn to the north yeld xvjd
Item paid to John Cotten for makyn of a newe kye & menden of ye loke for ye kyechyn dower iiijd
Item paid to John Antony for ij twyst for the church howsse dowers xvijd
Item paid to John Cottell for wagges & nayells for ye church yett xijd
Item paid to John Megar & to hys ij men on daye xijd
Item paid for ther mett & drynk ijs ijd
Item paid to John Anttony for tember for to mend the church howesse douers & tabell bordes & formes ijs viijd
Item paid for a pake of russes a gayenst Ester viijd
Item paid to John Avere for setten of a glasse over ye organs iijd
Item paid for ij semes of sond iijd
Item paid for wyn a gaynst Ester iijs
Item paid for v men ys expences att ye bisshop ys vycytacyon & for makyn & deleveren yn our byll vs jd
Item paid for a quarter of lyme iijs viijd
Item paid for a quarter & *dimidia* [of crossed out] more of lym vs ijd
Item paid for our expences att ye arsdecans vycytacyon & makyn of our byll & layn yn ijs viijd

f.70

Item paid ther for the Peter ys quarter for the holle parysh[168] viijd
Item paid for a newe bell rope ijs iiijd
Item paid to John Marres for makyn of awnsur for ye rodlofft xijd
Item paid for iij newe bokes iiijs
Item paid for wyn iiijd
Item paid for viij yerdes of howeland for a serpells xvs
Item paid for makyn ther of ijs vjd
Item paid to John Maygar ys iij men for ij dayes work ijs vjd
Item paid for the mett ij dayes & the wardens one daye iijs iiijd
Item paid to John Megar & to hys men iiij dayes, mett & hyer iijs iiijd
Item paid to ij men ij dayes, mett & hyer to helpe them xijd

[168] A former papal tax banned in 1534 but reinstituted by Elizabeth I.

Item paid to the parson of Myllton[169] for our estatt ijs iiijd
Item paid for our expences that tyme viijd
Item paid to Rychard Wryng for kypen of ye bells ijs
Item paid to John Avere & to hys son for one daye ys work, mett & hyer xvjd
Item paid to John Rowland for a newe bell coller ijs iijd
Item paid to John Cottell for menden of ij loks & nayells for the setts & platts & nayells for ye bell whyells xixd
Item paid to Petter Quyk & John Cleverdon for songs for the church yt thaye bowff att Bodman xvjd
Item paid to Basten for removen a bake ye sege xd
Item paid to Master Vycar for makyn of a per yn dentures for crystenyng weddens & buryeng vjd
Item paid to Thomas Olyver for wyer for ye cloke ijd
Item paid for a pak of russes a gaynst Crystemas viijd
Item paid to John Megar for keypen of the bells for ij yeres ijs viijd
Item paid to Ballhachat for a creste iiijd
Item paid for wyne iiijd
Item paid for iiij yerds of cloth for the tabell vs [iiijd crossed out] ^viijd^
Item paid for iiij queres of paper to make bokes for the church xvjd
Item paid for therd and the makyn of them ijd

[f.70v]
Item paid for gresse for the bells iiijd
Item paid to Wyllyam Heddon for menden of a claper ijd
Item paid for makyn of thys a cownt vjd
Item paid to Rychard Call for menden of a pekexs iiijd
The sum of alowans ys vjli xs iijd
and so remayneth cler to the church xvjs [ixd crossed out] xd
Item lend to Thomas Juell a hallff bussell of lyme

Here[170] folowethe the accompte of Symon Holman and Robert Nele wardens yn the yere of our lorde God 1564 made the iiijth daye of Februari anno Elizabethe 7 [4 February 1565]

The recepts

In primis recevid of the stock wardens vjs viijd
Item recevid for Master Poyle vjs viijd
Item recevid for our ale liiijs vijd ob quarter
Item received of Wylliam Wyll for Sir Richerd Wyll ^to ye churche^ xijd
Item received for Margery Short ^to the churche^ iijs iiijd
Item received for Marget Gyst ^to the churche^ iiijd
Item received for Johane Baron ^to the churche^ iijs iiijd
Item received of Nycolas Bond for his childe to ye churche iiijd
+Item for standyngs at the churche house wall xs iiijd
Item received of Wylliam Ballhachett for the churche house xijd
Item received of Master Marris for wyghting in the church house viijd
Sum iiijli viijs iijd ob quarter

[169] Milton Damerell, Devon? William Rolle: www.kcl.uk/artshums/depts/history/research/proj/clergy.aspx (accessed 2 February 2017).
[170] Illuminated initial H with two men's heads and foliage.

f.71

1564
The expences

In primis payde for wyne agaynst Easter	ijs iiijd
Item paid for communion bred	xd
Item paid to Nycholas Call for a packe of russhes agaynst Ester	viijd
Item paid for a newe pyckaxe bysydes the olde stuffe	xviijd
Item paid at the visitacion at Launceston for expences & for making of our byll & putting in the same & for Peters farthings	viijs vd
Item paid for wyer for the clocke	xijd
Item paid for wyne	iiijd
Item paid to John Averye & his man for hayling one daye	xvjd
Item paid to Thomas Clarke for mending the easte style of the churche yerd & for covering of Margerye Shorts pytt	iiijd
Item paid to Nycholas Bond for lone of his horse when Master Marris & John Jud rode to Exeter	xxjd
Item paid to Wylliam Wyll for lone of his horse the same tyme	xviijd
Item paid to John Averye & his man for one dayes helyng more & for lathe neles	xviijd
Item paid for taking downe the s[ea crossed out]ylyng[171] & a beame of the roode lofft	ixd
Item paid for a c of comunion bred	vd
Item paid for wyne	iiijd
Item paid to Rycherd Wryng for keping of the bells	ijs
Item paid to Bastyn for settyng forthe of the seate for the quyre	vjd
Item paid to John Averye & his man for one dayes helyng more	xiiijd
Item paid for a pack of russhes agaynst Christmas	viijd
Item paid to Thomas Clarke for covering of Johane Barons pytt	ijd
Item paid for gresse for the bells	iiijd
Item paid for sope	vd
Item paid at the chepter courte at Launceston	xviijd

[f.71v]

Item payde for wyne	ijd
Item paid for one dayes hayling more to John Averye & his man	xiiijd
Item paid for iij seames of sond	iiijd
Item paid for making of this accompte	vjd
Sum of ye expences xxxjs xjd	

So ther remaynethe clere by this accompt to the churche lvjs iiijd ob quarter

Item there remaynethe with Thomas Jule [illeg. word crossed out] showmaker a halfe busshell of lyme. Item more londe to Roger Yeo a halfe busshell of lyme

f.72

Hyer folowyth the a compte of Robart Sander and Crystoffer Hore wardens yn the yer of our lord God anno m^d^ ccccc lxv [1566]

Reccetts

Item recevyd of the stoke wardens	vjs viijd
Item received a nother tym when wye went att the vycytacyon att Lewnston	vjs viijd
Item received another tym to paye ye plummer	xs
Item received another tyme	vjs viijd
Item received of one Jeffere for hys sone ys knyll	iiijd
Item received of Thomas Juell for a knyll	iiijd
Item received another tyme of ye stoke wardens	xxs

[171] The ceilure survives at Poughill.

Item received for wyrthyn yn the church howsse viijd
Item received of Roweland for stonys that wer a bowtt the kyll xd
Item received of Wyllyam Balhachett for the church howsse viijd
Item received of Thomas Hekytt & Wyllyam Bray vjs viijd
Item received of Rycherd Mark for [drw crossed out] drwyn[172] of woll yn the churche howsse iiijd
Item recevyd for standen a gaynst ye church howesse wall xiijs iiijd
Item recevyd for our alle thys yere liij[s] [viijd crossed out] ob
and so the holl sum of recetts ys vjli vjs [viijd crossed out] ob

[f.72v]

Expences

Item paid to John Lane & Myzhell Hoper for ryden & makyn ye heyges be hynd the church howsse iiijd
Item paid to Symon Hollman for a c of lathes ixd
Item paid for lath nayells jd
Item paid to John Averye for helyng a pon the churche & the church howess ij dayes, mett & hyer xxd
Item paid on to serffe hem ij dayes, mett & hyer viijd
Item paid for lath nayells another tyme jd
Item paid for howselen bred xjd
Item paid for wyn be fore Ester & a gaynst Ester ijs
Item paid for menden of the formes and bordes yn the church howss iiijd
Item paid to a man when the bell was delevered to the bell founder & to tarre ther tyll [hytt crossed out] ^he^ was mylltt, mett & hyer viijd
Item paid for drynke to them that bor the [byll crossed out] bell to the pytt iijd
Item paid for our expences iij men & Master Vycar att the vycytatyon vjs vjd
Item paid for Peter hys quarter viijd
Item paid for maken of our byll & lyen yn viijd
Item paid for a *dimidia* li of sope iiijd
Item paid for drynke to them yt ded drawe the bell from the pytt & when he was hung upe viijd
Item paid to John Rowland for a newe bell coller ijs vjd
Item paid to hem for menden of a nother coller xd

f.73

Item paid to Master Vycar for wryttyng of the ynvetore for weden, crystene and buryen[173] vjd
Item paid to John Megar for hys fyes ye last yer xvjd
Item paid to hem for one daye ys work a bowtt the bells & hawssyn of the beme yt bar the hede viijd
Item paid to one to helpe hem iijd
Item paid for ther mett & drynk for them both xijd
Item paid to John Cottell for ij lytell stapes abowtt the bells jd ob
Item paid to the plumer for menden of the leds yn the tower & a pone the church xlljs
Item paid to one to serff hem mett & hyer ij dayes & hallff xvjd
Item paid for wode for heme xd
Item paid for nayells to nayell uppe the leds ijd
Item paid to Nycolas Sander for a newe stapell and menden of the claper for the thurd bell & brasses & nayells for the same vs iiijd
Item paid for newe songs for the church ijs

[172] Drawing or teasing of wool?
[173] 3s 4d at Tewkesbury. See Litzenberger, *Tewkesbury Churchwardens' Accounts*, p.11.

Item paid for our expences att the ^bushepps ys^ vycytacyon for iij of us & Master Vycar iijs [viijd crossed out] viijd
Item paid for a in jongsyon xijd
Item paid for a nother lyttell boke ijd
Item paid for makyn of our byll iiijd
Item paid for lyen yn & to the somner viijd
Item paid for ioyn att ij devers tymes vijd
Item paid to Rycard Wryng for kyepen of the bells ijs
Item paid for a *dimidia* quarter of lyme ijs viijd
Item paid to Roger Yoe for ij hundrd of helyng ston xxd

[f.73v]
Item paid to hem for iij hundrd of lath nayells vjd
Item paid to Symon Hollman for iij hundrd & xx of lath hayells vjd ob
Item paid to John Avere for a m^d^ & *dimidia* of helyng pynnys ixd
Item paid to John Avere for vij dayes worke, mett & hyer vjs vd
Item paid to hys son for iiij dayes worke more, mett & hyer iijs
Item paid to one to serff them ^vij dayes^, mett & hyer ijs xjd
Item paid to John More for ij senys of sond iijd
Item paidto John Megar for takyn down of the rowde lofft, mett & hyer vijd
Item paid to one to helpe hem mett & hyer iijd
Item paid to John Megar & to hys man for one dayes work for makyn of the tower wyndowe & menden of a nother & menden of the bells & makyn of a newe dower a pon the ledes mett & hyer xxjd
Item paid for nayells for the same & ij lyttell stapes for the dower ixd
Item paid for russes for the chawnsell a gaynst Crystemas vjd
Item paid for sope iiijd
Item paid to the Yeryshman for menden of the clark ys chamber iiijd
Item paid for v boyes a gaynst Crystemas to helpe the qwyer xxd
Item paid to Thomas Olyver for wyer for the clok ijd
Item paid for wyn vjd
Item paid for a *dimidia* quarter of lyme ijs iiijd
Item paid for a *dimidia* hundrd of lathes vd

f.74
Item paid for a hundrd of lath nayells ijd
Item paid for a hallff bussell of lyme vjd
Item paid to Master Vycar for ^hallfe^ a newe boke vs
Item paid to John Corye for a *dimidia* bussell of lyme yt was sent to the bryg viiijd
Item paid for gresse for the bells iiijd
Item paid to John Megar for hys fyes thys yer xvjd
Item paid for paper jd
Item paid to John Avere for ij dayes work mett & hyr xxijd
Item paid to one to serffe hem mett & hyr ^ij dayes^ xd
Item paid for a lok & a kye for the dower apon ye leds iijd
Item paid for wyn jd
Item paid for makyn of thys a cownt vjd [vijd crossed out]
The sum of our expences ys vjli iijs ixd
and so remayneth cler to the church [xxiijd ob crossed out] ijs iijd ob

[f.74v]

anno domini 1566 [1567]

Here folloyth the a cownte of Thomas Badcoke & Peter Hallet wardins

Item fyrste the resetys as after folloyth

Item recevid of Thomas Heckyt stocke wardyn vijs
Item recevid of Wylliam Bre xiijs iiijd
Item recevid of John Antone for ayer which we sowlde iijs iiijd
Item recevid more of Wylliam Bre yn mone vjs viijd
Item recevid more of Thomas Hekyt iiijs
Item recevid of Wylliam Braie more yn mone xiijs iiijd
Item recevid more of William Bre yn mone vjs viijd
Item recevid of Master Marris for wyghtin yn ye churche howse viijd
Item recevid of Water Brode for kepin of hys ware yn ye cherche howse xijd
+Item recevid for standins a gaynste ye cherche howce wall xiijs
Item recevid for owre aele ys eer xlijis vd ob quarter
Some ^of the recetes ys^ vli xiiis vd ob quarter

f.75

+ Here folleyth the chargys of thys yere 1566 [1567]

Item fyrst for howselin bred a gaynste Ester xijd
Item payd for wyne at sondry tymes a gaysnte Ester iiijs ijd
Item payd for fetchyn of the same at Howllsewere[174] vjd
Item payd for lime which was fet to Beddefowrde & for carrin of ye same vs viijd
Item payd to John Avere for iiij dayes worke xjd ye daye iijs viijd
Item payd for fetchyn of sonde for ye heller iiijd
Item payd for servyn the heller iiij days viijd ye day ijs viijd
Item for a c of lathys ixd
Item payd Simon Hollman for *dimidia* m of lathe nayles xjd
Item payd John Megar for mendin of ye cherche howse wall viijd
Item for carrin of stonis & servin of hym iiijd
Item payd Wyllyam Yeo for the same stonys iiijd
Item payd Bastyn for makyn of setys for chyldrin vjd
Item payd for rowshys a gaynste Ester vd
Item payd for a li of soppe vjd
Item payd for wasshyn at sondre tymes vijd
Item for owre chargys at ye fyrste visitasion vijs iiijd
Item payd Peters ferthyng at ye same visitasion xvjd
Item payd for wyer for the clocke jd
Item payd at a nother chapter corte chargys & expensis ijs viijd
Item payd the veker for wretin ys yndenters owte of ye regester bocke vjd
Item payd more unto John Avere for iij days worke, xjd the daye ijs ixd
Item for servin the heller iij days viijd ye day ijs
Item payd Thomas Jule showmaker for *dimidia* m of hellin stone iijs
Item payd Bastin for makyn of a new sege iiij days & *dimidia*
makyn xd ye daye iijs xd
^Item payd for nayls for the same jd^
Item payd at a nother chapter cowrte chargys & expensys iiijs

[f.75v]

Item payd for iiij crests ijd ob ye pece xd
Item payd for j c & *dimidia* of lathys, ixd ye c xiijd ob

[174] Holsworthy, Devon.

Item payd unto John Avere more for iiij days worke, xjd ye day iijs viijd
Item payd for servin of hym iiij days, viijd ye daye ijs viijd
Item payd more for j m of lathe nayls xxd
Item payd unto ye ermerer for dressin of the harnis iiijs
Item payd for bockyls [for crossed out] & lether for the same harnis viijd
Item payd more for wyne for ye [cherche crossed out] ^chorche^ vd
Item payd more unto John Avere for ij days & *dimidia* worke ijs iijd
Item payd for servin of hym ij days & *dimidia* viijd ye date xxd
Item payd for carrin of ij semys of sond vjd
Item payd for mendin of ij bell clappers vjs viijd
Item payd yn ridin at Lonston be fore the [comision crossed out] ^comischeners^ yn chargys for ij men iiijs viijd
Item payd Water Bytticke for mendin of the leddis iijs
Item payd Choppe for makin of mettis to serve ^before^ ye comewnion tabel xijd
Item payd more for wyne xd
Item more yn expensis at a nother chapter corte at Saint Mare Weke[175] xvjd
Item payd more for wyne ijd
Item payd John Lane for mendin of ye cherche ladder ijd
Item payd John Cottin for hache nayles for ye heller jd
Item payd Richarde Call for wone jeme & yn nayles for the cherche yeate xd

f.76

+ anno.....

Item payd John Meger ^& his man^ for makin of a sege yn the north ele & for nother worcke yn ye tower & yn ye cherche & ye cherche yeate for ij days & *dimidia* worcke at xxijd ye daye iiijs vijd
Item for iij planckes of Thomas Badcocke for the same sege at xvd the pece iijs ixd
Item payd more for a bell rope ijs iiijd
Item payd Rycharde Wrynge for kepin of the bells ijs
Item for gresse for the same vjd
Item payd John Meger for hys fie xvjd
Item payd for Martin Drin[?] for helpin of the quer xijd
Item payd more for wyne jd ob
Item payd John Cottin for a new locke for the clocke howse dore & a stape for the same vijd
Item for makin of this a cownt viijd
Som ^of ye expensis ys vli vs vijd
so ther remenyth clere un to ye chorche vijs xd ob quarter

[f.76v]

Here followithe the acounte of Harrye Higence and Petter Quike, Hie Crosse wardens in ye yeare of our lorde God *anno* m cccc lxvij [1568]

Resettes

Primis received of ye stokewardes vjs viijd
Item more of ye stokewardins vjs viijd
Item more of ye stokewardens vjs viijd
Item more of ye stokewards xxijs vjd
Item more of ye stokewardens iijs iiijd
Item more of ye stokewardens xiijs iiijd
+Item more received by ye cherche howse wall xiijs

[175] Week St Mary.

Item more received of Master Morys for weghting in ye cherche howse viijd
Item more received of Watter Hedyn for kepyng of his wares in ye cherch heowse xijd
Item more received for our alle xxxviijs
[this is ther charge is bocke recevd [?] of Thomas Gist crossed out]
And so ye holle some of resets ys vli xjs xd[176]

f.77

Expences

Primis for syngin bread xd
Item more for wyne jd
[Item more for a halfe bushell of whete..... xvjd crossed out]
Item more payd for wyne viijd
Item more for a pond of sope vjd
Item more for wyne ijs viijd
Item more to George Meagor for ryshes agenste Ester vjd
Item more for our expences at ye vysytation ^at Lanson^ vs
Item more for Petters farthings viijd
Item more to John Heden for mendinge of ye formes & spering of ye cherche house ijd
Item more for wyne iiijd
Item more for mendyng of the botry loke to John Cotton v[j]d
Item more for our expencis at ye sessyans at Bodman ijs xd
Item more for a rope for ye pease of ^ye^ cloke ijs vd
Item more to Rychard Call for mending of ye ^cherche pekys^ vjd
^Item more for ye expencis at Bodman before ye quines comysyners for ye cherche land iiijs jd^
Item more for a bell rope xxiijd
Item more to Boshell for lokyng upon ye lyds jd ob
Item more for a quere of paper for the sygyne bockes [of crossed out] ^for^ ye cherche iiijd
Item more to John Corye for mendynge of ye lyds vjd
Item more to John Lane for mending of ye est cherche styll & castyng of ye drang by the northesyde of ye cherche iiijd
Item more to Symond Homan for a peke of lyme iiijd
Item more for owde for ye glasyer iiijd
Item more payd to ye glasyer for newe glace xxijs vjd
Item more to John Roweland for two bell collers iijs iiijd
Item more to Watter Betteke for mendynge of ye leds iijs
Item [s crossed out] more for owd & [*dimidia* crossed out] bred & drinke & tendance of him xd
Item more to Rychard Wrynge for kepynge of ye bells ijs
Item more to Nycollas Sander for mendyng of ye cherch showlle viijd
Item more for grese for ye bells at sondry times vjd
Item more for our expences at ye [at crossed out] vycitacion at Lanson vjd
Item more payd to ye glasyer for mending of ye cherche wyndowes xiijs
Item more to Master Morys for going to Lanson [fo crossed out] before ye comyssyners viijs
Item more the same ^time^ to Wylliam Te hella viijd

[f.77v]

Item more to Bastian for mendyng of [the cherche crossed out] ^a seedge^ ijd
Item more to Thomas Olyver for a c of lathes for ye cherche ixd
Item more to Thomas Olyver for iij c ^& halfe^ of lathe naylls vijd
Item more for wyne vjd
Item more for syngyn brede jd

[176] Sketch of a bearded face.

Item more payd to ye hellyer & his man for iij dayes	ijs
Item more to John Cotton for ye heller & his man for iij dayes tabell	ijs
Item more to Moke for servyng of ye hellyer iij dayes	xviijd
Item more to Nycollas Bound for two boshells of lyme of Strotten myssyer[177]	iijs iiijd
Item more ^our expences^ at iij sondry cortes at Lanson agene John Oglowe[178]	iijs vjd
Item more to Master Vycar for wrytinge of ye reiester bocke	vjd
Item more we borid a boshill of lyme of John Cotten[179]	
Item more to Julle of Bowd ^for^ fetynge of a seme of sand for ye cherche	jd
Item more for makyne of ys aconte	viijd

The some of our expences ys iiijli ixs vd ob
and soe remaynes clere to the cherche xxijs iiijd ob

f.78

Hyer folowyth the a count of John Bray and John Cottell wardens yn the yer of our lord God anno m^d^ ccccc lx viij [1569][180]

Item recevyd of the stoke wardens	vjs viijd
Item recevyd a nother tyme	vjs viijd
Item recevyd for Nycolas Wyll ys grawe	iijs iiijd
Item recevyd of Nycolas Hor for hys chyld ys knyll	iiijd
Item received of Crystoffer Hor for hys chyld ys knyll	iiijd
Item received of John Corre for hys servant knyll	iiijd
Item received of John Howge for hys servant knyll	iiijd
Item received of John Mares for wyrrten yn the church howsse	viijd
Item received for Roger Yoe ys grawe	iijs iiijd
[Item received ^of Nycolas^ for Thomas Olyver ys graves grawe & hys wyff	vjs vj ^viijd^ crossed out]
+Item received for the church howsse wall	xxijs iijd
Item received of Nycolas Olyver for ij graves	vjs viijd
Item received of the stoke wardens	ixls
Item received for our all thys yer	ls iijd

And so the holle sum of the recettes ys vijli xs

[f.78v]

expences

Item paid to John Roweland for mendin of ij bell collers	ijs
Item paid to Roger Yoe for a c & hallff of howesslyng bred	xijd
Item paid to Mystrys Yoe for wyn	vjd
Item paid for a bottell of wyn yt came from Lanston	vjd
Item paid to Mystrys Yoe another tym for wyn	viijd
Item paid for a bockell for the bell coller	ijd
Item paid for gresse for the bells	iijd
Item paid to Elsabeth Olyver for wyne	xvd
Item paid for iiij men ys expences att the vycytacyon att Lawnston	iiijs vd
Item paid for makyn of our byll & lyen yn	xijd
Item paid for Peters fardens	viijd
Item paid for wyn to Mystrys ^Yeo^ another tym	xijd
Item paid to Crystofer Tremell for setten upe the bordes yn the church howesse	vd
Item paid for nayells the same tym	jd

[177] Larger local measure?
[178] Probably concerning Hele mill.
[179] Sum blank.
[180] SSS at the end of the date.

Item paid for hys mett & drynk iijd
Item paid for [our expences crossed out] iiij men^y^s expences att the busshupe ys vycytacyon iiijs vd
Item for makyn of out bylls & lyen yn them xvjd
Item paid to Thomas Olyver for wyer for ye cloke iijd
Item paid to Robart Nells boys for fetten of the church dower kye [att Stawe[181] crossed out] jd

f.79
Item paid for menden of the vestments ijd
Item paid for wyne vjd
Item paid for ij newe bell ropes iiijs viijd
Item paid to Rycard Wryng for kyepen of the bells ijs
Item paid to one to carre the regester boke att Lawnston xijd
Item paid for perusyn of the same boke vjd
Item paid to Marten Clyfton ye same tym iijd
Item paid to Nycolas Call for russes viijd
Item paid to Thomas Juell for sope viijd
Item paid to Symon Hollman for howssele bred jd
Item paid to John Yoe for howesselyng bred ijd
Item paid for gresse for the bells jd
Item paid to Marten Clyffton for a yn jwngsyon bok xvjd
Item paid to Myrstrys Yoe for wyn xijd
Item paid for makyn of the church pyk ex vjd
Item paid to Master Vycar for wrytten of the regester bok vjd
Item paid for Samson ys denar f when he barganed for the tower iiijd
Item gave hem yn e[r]ne[s]t for the tower iiijd
Item paid to hem for poynten of the tower xlviijs iiijd
Item paid for xxiiij busshells of lym xs
Item paid for caryag of the same lym ijs vjd

[f.79v]
Item paid for fetten of viij semes of gravell att Hollmans Myll ijs
Item paid to John Cottell one bussell of lyme yt was borrowid ye last yer[182]
Item paid for makyn of thys a cownt viijd
The sum of our expences ys – iiijli xviijs [vjd crossed out]
and so ther remyenyth cler to the church – ljs [vjd crossed out] ixls
Item lend to Thomas Whyte a hallffe hundred of helyn stone & xx cc[183] John Antony

f.80
Hyre folowyth the a counte of John Barne and Willyam Pirse wardens yn the yere of our lord God anno M^d^ ccccc lx ix [1570]

Item resevyd of the stoke wardnes vjs viijd
Item resevyd of John Hewe to be beryed in the cherche & his knyll vjs viijd
Item resevyd of John Wade for hys child js knyll iiijd
Item resevyd of John Rolond ys grave iijs iiijd
Item resevyd of Thomas [Bet crossed out] Bere ys child knyll iiijd
Item resevyd of John Hecket for ys chillds knyll iiijd
Item resevyd of John Treweke for ys chilld knyll iiijd

[181] Stowe, Kilkhampton.
[182] Sum blank.
[183] Two hundred score?

Item resevyd of John Jude beyng stoke wardens	xiijs iiijd
Item resevyd of Thomas Jule cordyner for his wyfe ^grave^	iijs iiijd
Item resevyd for Margaret Symon hys grave	iijs iiijd
Item resevyd of Thomas Call for his chilld knyll	iiijd
Item resevyd of John Barne ^for^ his chilld knyll	iiijd
Item resevyd of Master Marys for wetyng in the church house	viijd
Item resevyd for our alle this yere	lvjs
+Item resevyd for the pentes for this yere	xlvs
with a xis iiijd remenes for the pentys[184]	
[Et crossed out] and so the hole some ys of resetes ys	vijli iiijd

[f.80v]

expences

Item payd for paper	ijd
Item payde to the boyes that soune	ixd
Item payd to Herry Hore for makyng of cherche yerd wall for v dayes worke met & her	iiijs
Item payd to Willyam Perse for servyng and redyng of the f same worke	xijd
Item payd to the penters for by colers	iiijs
Item payd to Thomas Jule wife marchant ii yerdes clatch	xviijd
Item payd for chalke & scrydos and wode for the same ^werkes^	vjd
Item payd to Edward the scorer of the hernys	iijs vjd
Item payd to Cimond Holman for a halfe pond of sope	iiijd
Item payd to Mystrys Yoe for wine	viijd
Item payd for a botell of wine fro[m crossed out] Lanston	xijd
Item payd to John Auger for ij yeres fes	ijs viijd
Item payd to Cymond Holman for hoslen bred a ganse E^ste^tor	xid
Item payd to Willyam Rode for packe of roches	viijd
Item payd for ij botiles of wine	xvd
Item payd for ij barelles of leme	iiijs xd
Item payd for iiij men at the vicytacyon	iiijs
Item payd for our bill & the leyng of him	xijd
Item payd for Peters ferthings	viijd
Item payd to Mystrys Yeo for wine	xvid
Item payd for John Meger met & drynk wen he ded mend the beles	iiijd
a and one to helpe him a monse the belles	iijd
Item payd to Peter Pryer for bryng home of the lyme	viijd
Item payd for hoslen brede	iijd
Item payd to John Corye for the caryng of ^the^ Bebell to Exceter[185] and home a gayne	xd
Item payd John Cottell for jere for the cloke	xxd
Item payd John Cottell for neles for the belles & a stape for the churche house dore	iiijd

f.81

Item payd for towe strynes for ij bowes[186]	ijd
Item payd towe dosen of pontes for the hernes	iiijd
Item payd to v men that ded where the hernes at Jacobstow	xd
Item payd for a halfe pond of sope & [li crossed out] therd	vjd
Item payd ^for^ a rope for the cloke	xvid
Item payd for a bell rope	ijs vjd
Item payd for lether & for bokeles & for dresen of one pere of hernes	ijs

184 Sloping roof added to the church house to protect market stalls.

185 Exeter, Devon.

186 See Douch, *Cornwall Muster Roll 1569*, pp.131–2 for this and other entries.

Item payd to Nycolas Hore for brynge home of lode helen stones & for mete and drynke viiis xd
Item payd to v men that ded wh[e]re the churche hernes Jacobstowe to the morstryng xd
Item payd [for crossed out] for wyer for the cloke vjd
Item payd for a bowe for the chrche iiijs
Item payd to Mystrys Yeo [^for^ crossed out] wyne at sondre tymes xij[s erased]d
Item payd for caryng of the hernes to the last moster iiijd
Item payd for caryng of *m^l^* helen stones to Willyam ^Wormonton^ xijd
Item payd to Mystrys Yeo for wine vjd
Item payd to Rycherd Wryng for kepyng of the beles ijs
Item payd for t[w]o cc of lates for Master Chamond xijd
Item payd to the boshepe vycitacytacion for & in juncyon and a bill of artekell xijd
Item payd for iiij men for there dener xxd
Item payd for leyng in of our bill iiijd
Item payd for a bell coler to Rycherd Wryng ijs
Item payd to John Avery for iii dayes worke[s crossed out] mete & hire ijs vjd
Item payd to Willyam Pirse for servyng the heler xviijd
Item payd to Master [Vyker crossed out] Vyker for wrytyng of the regester bok vjd

[f.81v]
Item py^a^id for a seme of sande jd
Item payd to Willyam Perse & Jencen Chope for the makyng of ^the^ cherche yeard heddgs for iiij dayes worke mete & here ijs
Item payd for grese for the belles [v crossed out]jd
Item payd [th crossed out] to John Antony for a planke xd
Item payd to John ^Antony^ for a yend of a [parr of crossed out] planke for make a polle for the cloke[187] iijd
Item for makeng of this a counte viijd
the some of our expenses ys iiijli viij d
[so remenes crossed out]
so remethe to the I church ^clere^ iij li
[illeg. word crossed out] lakyng iiijd
wyth a xis iiijd that ys owed

f.82

1570 [1571]

Here[188] folowythe the accompte of John Cory & John Wade churche wardens in the yere of our lorde God m ccccc lxx made the 19th daye of Februarye *anno* Elizabethe *regine decimo tertio* [19 February 1571]

In primis recevyd of the stockewardens vjs viijd
Item received of William Grove for his childes knell iiijd
Item received for ij lytell stones solde to John Short iiijd
Item received of Thomas Jule showemaker for his datters knyll iiijd
Item received [for crossed out] of Mistris Yeo for her housbands grave iijs iiijd
Item received of Nicholas Jud for his servants knell iiijd
Item received of Lewse [Sharsell crossed out] ^Sawnder^ for his childs knill iiijd
Item received of the stocke wardens [att ij tymes crossed out] ^when we bought the comunion cup^ iiijli
Item received for the chalys xxxvijs

187 See appendix 3.2, p. 216.
188 Initial decorated.

Item received for [f crossed out] cherubyms[189] sold xxd
Item received for ij peces of olde bockes sold xijd
Item received for an ernest to the sale of the rood laught iiijd
Item received of Wylliam Wyll for his mother in lawes grave & for his wifes grave vjs viijd
Item received of John Rad for his wifes grave iijs iiijd
Item received of Wylliam Heddon for ij knylls viijd
Item received of Thomas Jule merchante for his daughters knyll iiijd
Item received of John Hamet for his daughters knyll iiijd
Item received of Wylliam Braye for his daughters knell iiijd
Item received of Richard Walkye for his dafftes knyll iiijd
Item received of Master Marrys for wyghtyng in the churche house viijd
Item received for owr ale thes yere xlvs ob
+Item received for standings at the churche house xxxvs iijd
bysydes [ijs crossed out] that Brocke oweth us 2s 6d which shalbe payd when we maye gete yt
Item received of the stocke wardens agayne xls
Item received of Trymells wife for the knyll of Barbors childe iiijd
Some of the receptes xiijli vs ob

[f.82v]

The expences this yere /1570/[1571]

In primis paid to Thomas Clarke for mendyng of a sege jd
Item payde for rydyng of the churche house & mendyng of the formes iiijd
Item paid for bred & wyne which the olde wardens left to paye iijd
Item paid for comunion bred against Ester ixd
Item payde for wyne agaynst Easter iijs viijd
Item payd to the plumber fo[r] mendyng of the leads of the churche & the towre & for his sawdrye vijs
Item paid for a plate of led of vli & *dimidia* xjd
Item paid for woode vd
Item paid for neles that were occupyed aboute the leds & in the sege ijd
Item paid for the statute of rebellion xijd
Item paid for rushes agaynst Easter viijd
Item de[livered]? to Rycherd Wryng in gresse for the bells vjd
Item paid for sope to washe the churche clothing xjd
Item paid to Nicholas Oliver of Sent Tyves[190] for a song of *Te Deum* xijd
Item for mendyng of John Judes' Bybell which he lonyd to the churche when the other was to bynd iiijd
Item paid to the boyes at Easter for syngyng in the quyre viijd
Item paid at the visitacion for the dynner of the wardens & sydemen iijs
Item paid for the byll & Peters farthings & for the baylyes fees xxd
Item paid for wyne the Sonndaye after Trynytye Sonndaye[191] iiijd
Item [p crossed out] for [f crossed out] communion bred jd
Item paid for iijli of flox to stuff the cusshin for the comunion tabell vjd
Item for makyng of the same cusshyn iijd
Item paid to Rycherd Wryng for a bell coler ijs
Item paid to the boyes at Whyt Sonndaye for syngyng viijd
Item paid for mendyng of the regyster bocke jd
Item paid to Master Marrys for cariyng of the regyster bocke to Lanceston to the chepter courte iiijd

189 Roof angels.
190 St Ives.
191 28 May.

Item paid for viij bushells of lyme iiijs
Item paid for a thowsand of hellyng stones iiijs viijd

f.83
Item payde for the fettyng home of the ^hellinge^ stones from Bede viijd
Item paid to Davye Walkye for the rydyng the fowndacion of the wall byhend the churchehouse iijd
Item paid to Knight for the makyng of the stone worke of the same wall viijs
Item paid to Thomas Clarke, Davye Walkye & Michaell Hooper for makyng of the cobworke of the same wall iijs iiijd
Item for strawe to make the morter xijd
Item paid for comunion bred again vd
Item spent at the chepter the iiijth of August xiijd
Item paid for the comunion cup[192] iijli xixs
Item paid for a newe comunion bocke & a psalter in the same vjs
Item paid for glassing of the churche wyndows vijs iiijd
Item paid to Nicholas Mocke for scowring of the harnIes iijs ijd
Item paid for leathers for the same harnyes ijd
Item paid for oyle, buckells & neles for the same harnies vd
Item paid for a sawser to put the comunion bred on iiijd
Item paid to Mistrys Yeo for wyne fet at dyvers tymes before All Hallon daye[193] xijd
Item paid to Richerd Wryng for keping of the bells ijs
Item paid to Richard Perye for ij seames of sand iijd
Item paid for ij c of lathe neles & a *dimidia* c of long lathes ixd
Item paid [for crossed out] to the glasyer for mendyng of one wyndowe agayne yn the churche xd
Item paid to John Averye for ix dayes helyng & meate & drynke vijs vjd
Item paid for one to serve the helier ix dayes, meate & drynke, & for makyng of morter iiijs
Item paid to John Cottell for newe makyng of ij barres of iron for the churche house wyndowes iijd
Item paid for neles for the bells jd
Item paid for a keye & neles & other things aboute the organs iiijd
Item paid to John Cottell for neles & spuks aboute the quyre iiijd[194]

[f.83v]
Item paid more for hatche neles jd
Item paid to Christofer Trymell for meate drynke & wages to make the quyre xd
Item paid to the glasier for mendyng the olde wyndowe of the church house & for newe glassyng of the other wyndowes xviijs
Item for seale wax for the feoffement jd
Item paid for russhes for the chancell at Christmas iiijd
Item paid to vij boyes at Christmas for syngyng xvd
Item paid to Nicholas Oliver for help serving of the quyre xijd
Item paid to John Cottell for newe sharping & mendyng for the pyckaxe viijd
Item paid for a nele for the bell coler jd
Item paid to Knight the mason for walling of holes in the churche xiiijd
Item paid to Richard Pery for carryng of morter ijd
Item to a man to make the lyme iiijd
Item paid for rydyng of the gutter & the stones yn the backesyde of the churche house ijd

[192] Made by John Jons of Exeter.
[193] 1 November.
[194] 6li [6 crossed out] s d 9/8: marginal entry.

Item paid to John Mabyn for mendyng of the organs & for ij li of led which he caste to make faste the barres of the churche house wyndowes xijd
Item paid to Mystrys Yeo for wyne fet at divers tymes[195] xvijd
Item paid to Master Vycar for keping of the regester bocke vjd
Item for bering of the planching of the rood laft in to the churche house ijd
Item paid to John Maggar for his fee for the bells xvjd
Item paid to Richard Wryng for mendyng a bell coler ijd
Item paid to John Yeo for synging bred jd
Item paid for makyng of this accompte viijd
Item paid to John Baron for that caunty dyd abate of the rent of the churche house the laste yere vd
Some of the expences ixli xvs [iiij crossed out] xd
So remenythe clere to the churche iijli ixs ijd ob
[Item Symon Holman hath a lytell tabell borde crossed out][196]
Thomas Whyte hathe a *dimidia* c of helyng stones & John Anthony hathe xx heling stones as apperythe before in anno 1568
John Jud hathe a peke of lyme as John Baron sayde
John Braye hathe a peke of lyme " " " "

f.84

1571 [1572]

Here followethe the accounte of Nicollas Oblin and Nicollas Will churche wardenes in the yere of our lorde god m ccccc lxxj made the [xx crossed out] ^iiiith^ of Februari *anno* Elizabeth *regine* xiiij [4 February 1572][197]

[Receitts [?] crossed out]

In primus receved of the stock wardens vjs viijd
Item received of Lewes Saunder for vj bords xviijd
Item received of John Corye for two knills viijd
Item received of the stockwardens xiijs iiijd
Item received for John Menard knills xijd
Item received of Richerd Hore for his wifes grave iijs iiijd
Item received of Roberte Sander stock warden xxs
Item received of Master Mores for stofe sold to the chorche yewes[198] iijs
Item received of William Orchard xvjd
Item received of Nicollas Will xd
Item received of Robert Sander xviijd
Item received of Andro Sangen ijs viijd
Item received of Richard Mark xviijd
Item received of Richard Kall xvjd
Item received of John Corye vijs xd
Item received of Richard Yeo ijs vjd
Item received for the water bukett and for yere ware solde to John Koke iiijs ijd
Item received of John Baren for John Judges grave iijs iiijd
Item received of John Tremeell for hes childe knile iiijd
Item received our alle this yeare xlv[ij crossed out]s viijd
Item received for the pentis this yeare xxxvs ijd
Item received of Master Mores & for wighten in the chorche hose viijd
Som of the recetes is vijli xixs iiijd

195 [28s 8d, 29s 6d crossed out], 29s 6d: marginal entries.
196 Appendix 3.2.
197 Extremely difficult and blotchy script.
198 Use. This and following entries probably relate to sale of church goods.

[f.84v]

The expences this yere 1571 [1572]

Item paid Herye Yeare for makinge the stoneworke of the walls & redenge of the same	iijs iiijd
Item paid Nicollas Person & William Smalle for makinge the klob of the same walle & strow for the same	iijs vjd
Item paid Knyghte for hellen ^of^ the same walle & lathes	ijs iijd
Item paid Tomas Takell for xx kiefe for the same wall	vs
Item for ij semes of sande	iiijd
Item paid Tomas Brok for redinge the drange	iiijd
Item paid Nicollas Mock for skowrynge the hernes	iijs vd
Item paid for owle for the same hernes	iiijd
Item paid John Yeo for neles & grett bockelles	vijd
Item paid for letther for the same	ijd
Item paid John? Colwell for nelles to hange the hernes to	ijd
Item paid Knighte for mendinge the ledes & for his sodre	xxijd
Item for ord for the same	ijd
Item paid Knighte for hellen the cheche hose met & drink	xviijd
Item paid for ^lathe^ neles & lathes for the same	iijd
Item paid Knighte for mendinge the tower ledes & for his sodre	xviijd
^Item paid John Yeo for rossin for the same	jd^
Item paid for ord for the same	ijd
Item paid Simon Holman for howslen bred agenst Ester	ixd
Item paid Nicollas Kall for russhes	xiiijd
Item paid the sengen boyes a geft of	xijd
Item paid for wine a genste Ester & a genst Whit Sundaye	viijs iiijd
Item paid for sope to wash the chorche clothinge	xijd
Item paid for owre expenses to the fi[r]ste vesetacion	ijs iiijd
Item paid for makinge of one boll & pelores & fechinges[199] and the belles fyes	xxd
Item paid Pett[er] Streck for setting up of the bord in the chorche hose	vd
Item for his meat & drink	iiijd
Item paid the singen boyes	viijd
Item paid for xx bosshulls of lime	xs
Item paid John Yeo for a bell rope	ijs iiijd

f.85

Item paid for ^our^ expenses to the busshepes vesettacion	iijs xd
Item paid for the in juncksion	xxd
Item paid one bylle and leyenge the same	xijd
Item paid for wine	ijs
Item paid Walter Rose for makinge ^clene^ the chorche hose	jd
Item paid Wringe for a bell koller	ijs viijd
Item paid for wine to Tomas Mocke	ijd
Item paid William Heden for a new showll	xviijd
Item paid Wringe for kepenge of the belles	ijs
Item paid for borden of segeȝ for the viij men, mette & drinck and nelles for the same	xviijd
Item paid for a newe sheete[200] for Tomas Wite to helpe the quere	ijs iiijd
Item paid for makinge the same	ijd
Item paid Robart Shorte for singen att Chrismas	xijd

[199] Meaning of first part unclear, but connected to bells.

[200] Sheet of music?

Item paid for wine fett at Lanson ijs
Item paid for ix quere of paper to make v singen bookes iijs
Item paid John Corye for bendinge of the same books & for olld xvjd
Item paid for a besson to putt the communen ^kop^ yn xd
Item paid Richard Oblin for xiij des ^hallen^ [mete crossed out] & drink xjd the day xjs xjd
Item paid Petter Toker for xiij des, mete & drink xd the day xs xd
Item paid for a man to sarve them ^xiij des^, mete & drink viijd the day viijs viijd
Item paid for ij bushilles of lyme xijd
Item paid Tomas Takell for a *dimidia* dosen of kiefe xvjd
Item paid for iij semes of sand vjd
Item paid for a m of latthe neles xxd
Item paid for a c of latthes ixd
Item paid John Yeo for hosslen bred iiijd
Item paid for wine xjd
Item paid Knighte for mendinge ^ye close[?]^ be Richard Kalle xijd
Item paid Robarte Sonder for the huge att, ix des iijs vjd
Item paid for iij yeards of cherse to make the childe linnen clothyeng and thred for make the same[201] ijs iijd

[f.85v]
Item paid Tamsen [illeg. word][202] for making of the same iiijd
Item paid Old Basten for kepenin the cheld one daye & a nighte iiijd
Item paid for chanvas to make the childe apurnes & makinge of the same vijd
Item paid for a pettikote xxd
Item paid Walter Rose for kepenge of the child one daie and a [night] ijd
Item paid for a pere of hossen ijd
Item paid for a pere of shose iiijd
Item paid Walter Rose for xxvj wekes kepenge of the cheld xvs ijd
Item paid Master Vekar for [kepeng crossed out] writtenge the regester bock vjd
Item paid for gryse for the belles vjd
Item paid for our expenses when we wente be fore the comyesinors ijs viijd
Item paid for [our bill crossed out] makinge of our bill iiijd
Item for making of this a konte viijd
Som of expenses this year is vijli xs iijd
So remeneth there to the chorche ixs jd
Item lond William Orchard iij bords
Item londe Tomas Austyle xxx hellen stones and a *dimidia* a c as apearethe be fore

f.86

Here[203] folowethe the accompt of Thomas Beare & Rycherd Marks churche wardens in the yere of our lorde God 1572 made the viijth daye of Februarye anno Elizabeth regine xv [8 February 1573]

The receytes

In primis recevyd of the stocke wardens vjs viijd
Item recevyd of Symon Holman ^for^ an olde ladder of the clocke house ijd
Item recevid of the hatter for his chelds knill for the greate bell iiijd
Item recevyd of John Perye for his childs knell iiijd
Item recevyd for William Grove & his mothers burialls in the churche vjs viijd
Item received of John Marks for a knill iiijd

[201] Pauper child left in parish?
[202] Some letters are clear but do not make a word or surname.
[203] Initial H with Renaissance helmeted man and greyhound chasing hare (see Plate 1).

Item received of Walter Yeo for a basket	vd
Item received of Edward Dunne for ij cruets	iiijd
Item received of Richerd Pryst for a cofer	vs
Item received of John Yeo merc[er] for a chest	vjs viijd
Item received of John Cory for a corporas case	vijs xjd
Item received of Symon Holman for ij candell sticks	xixd
Item received of Master Marrys for woden angells	iiijd
Item received for Thomas Hycketts grave	iijs iiijd
Item received of William Heddon for a bason	iijs
Item received of Richerd Jule constabell for led	vd
Item received for wyghtyng in the churche house	viijd
Item received of Nicholas Wyll for putting of things in the kyching of the churche house	vjd
Item received more of Richerd Jule constabell for led	ixd
Item received for William Yeo of Hobbacocks knill	iiijd
Item received of Nicholas Hore for his childs knill	iiijd
Item received of Roger Jefferye for his childes knill	iiijd
Item received of Rafe Baylye for his sonnes knill	viijd
Item received of the stocke wardens at one tyme	xxs
Item received of them at one other tyme	xxs
Item received of them more	liijs iiijd
+Item received for the standings of the churche house	xxxjs
Item received for the ale	ls ijd
Some of all the receyts	xjli xixd

[f.86v]

Here folowethe the expences this yere 1572 [1573]

In primis payde for makyng clene of the butterye of the churche howse & for settyng up of the hayling stones	ijd
Item payd for sope to washe the churche clothing	vd
Item payde for ^xixli of^ led at one tyme to Marke Payne which Mabyn had to bestowe aboute the clocke	ijs iiijd
Item payde for wyne at ij divers tymes	xijd
Item paid to John Cory for viij li of led which John Mabyn had also for the clocke	xijd[204]
Item paid for a bottell to kepe wyne there in	jd
Item paid for comunion bred	jd
Item paid for mending of the surples & for clothe for the same	vd
Item paid for wyne before Easter	iijs
Item paid to John Cottell for mendyng of the clapper of the greate bell & for nayles	xxvjd
Item paid for gresse for the bells	jd
Item paid for meate & dryncke for John Maygar & his man for ryghtyng of things aboute the bells	vijd
Item payde for sope agayne for the churche clothing	vd
Item payde for wyne	vjd
Item payde for comunion bred	vijd
Item to John Mayger at an other tyme when he mendyd things aboute the bells for his wages ^& his man^	xijd
Item the same tyme for theire meate & drynke	viijd
Item payde to John Maygar for hys fee	xvjd
Item payde to William Heddon for mending of the second bell claper	ijs iiijd
Item paid to Richard Wryng for a bell coler	xxd
Item paid for wyne	iijd
Item paid to Marke Payne for a clothe of led	xijs iiijd

[204] 'Mabin had 9li of the churche led': marginal entry

Item paid more fore wyne xijd
Item paid for wyne agayne vjd
Item paid for russhes agaynst Ester to William Rad vijd
Item paid for a lytell met[205] for Master Vicar to knele on ijd
Item paid to Richerd Wryng for a bell coler iijs
Item paid for a loke for the hyer churche house dore vjd
Item paid to iij boyes for synging in the quyre vjd
Item paid for two bell colers iiijs iiijd
Item paid for scowring the swerd & dagger which appoyntyd to the sawldiers ijd
Item paid for nayels jd
Item payd for wine vjd
Item payde for a barell of lyme ijs vjd
Item payd for carying home of the same lyme ijd

f.87
Item payde to Thomas Whyte the yonger for singing ijd
Item payd for mending of the churche house dore & for a newe keye xvjd
Item payd ^to Davye^ for makyng clene of the lower churche howse ijd
Item paid for wine jd
Item payde for a bell rope ijs iiijd
Item paid to Walter Rose for sweping of the gutters of the churche jd
Item payde for meate & drincke for certen of the viij men & the plumber [& when crossed out] when theye were aboute to make a bargayne for mending of the leds xijd
Item payde to John Thorne for carryng of letter to the plumber iiijd
Item payde to John Ching baker for ij semes of woode ^to melt the sawder^ xijd
Item payde to the plumber when he came to se the worke iiijs
Item payde for three horses for caryng of the led to Stawe xijd
Item payd to Bryant the juner for mending the tymber under the leddes & for neles for the same worke vd
Item payde for ij bell ropes more iiijs viijd
Item paid for the plumer jd
Item paid to a man for meate, dryncke & wages foure dayes to attend to the plumber ijs viijd
Item payde to the plumber for the mending of the ledds & the newe clothes in all lvs iiijd
Item payde to Symon Holman for *dimidia* hundred of lathes & for a c of lathe neles vijd
Item payde to John Averye for hayling the churche iijs iiijd
Item paid for a man to serve hym meate, drinke & wages iiij dayes ijs viijd
Item paid for wyne ijd
Item paid for the expences ^& charges^ of iiij men yt dyd ryde to Lanceston before the comissioners vjs iiijd
Item paid to John Cottell for mending of the churche pickaxe vjd
Item payde for carying up of tymber ^in to the tower^ to un hang the bells upon for unhangyng of them xxijd
Item paid to John Yeo for a pece of tymber to mend the bell stocks xvjd
Item paid to John Tom for newe arrowes & for fethering of the olde xxjd
Item paid for a bowe string jd
Item payde to Nicholas Mocke for scowring of the harnyes xxd
Item payde to William Heddon for iron stuffe for the bells vjs xjd
Item payde to Symon Holman for cariyng of ij bell brasses [for crossed out] to Lestwythell & for the castyng of the same vs xd
Item payde to Robert Cholwyll for newe hangyng & stocking of ij bells xvjs
Item payde for bred & wyne iijd
Item payde to John Cottell for mendeng of the second bell clapper ijs iiijd

[205] William Martyn's communion mat.

[f.87v]
Item paid for a nele for the bell coler jd
Item paid for gresse for the bells vd
Item paid to Richard Wryng for mending of a bell coler viijd
Item paid for wyne iijd
Item paid to the boyes for syngyng iijd
Item paid to John Yeo for carryyng of the harnyes to the mowster viijd
Item paid for bred & wyne agayne iijd
Item paid to Richard Wryng for keping of the bells ijs
Item payde to Richard Wryng for mending of an other bell coler xijd
Item payde for makyng of a newe dext & a newe covering for the fonte xvjd
Item paid for wyne iiijd
Item paid for comunen bred jd
Item paid to Thomas Whyte for singyng vjd
Item paid for wyne vjd
Item paid ^to Wylliam Cooke^ for the fettyng of the same wyne at Holsworthye ^beneght^ ijd
Item paid John Averye to hayle the churche, j daye meate, drink & wages xd
Item paid for a man to serve hym, meate, drenk & wages viijd
Item paid for lathe neles ijd
Item paid for wyne ijd
Item paid to John Cotell for iron to mend John Shortes sege iiijd
Item bestowed aboute the poore woman yt was brought from Lancells in bred & drinke & for cariyng of her backe agayne vd
Item paid for the wardens & the syde men at the vesetacion in expences ijs xd
Item paid for Peter farthengs & the fees of the courte xxjd
^Item paid for mending of a clapper & for a keye & neles & other worke to the bells xiijd^
Item paid for makyng [of the crossed out] & kepyng of thes accompte viijd
Item paid to Master Vicar for keping of the register bocke vjd

Some of the expences ixli vijs [illeg.d crossed out] xjd
so remenithe clere xxxiijs iij d
+ + there remenithe in William Swepers hand for rent of his standing iijs
+ + there remenithe in the hands of [blank] Perde of Welcomb[206] iijs iiijd
+ + there remenythe to the next wardens a newe bell coler
[+ & a newe bell roppe crossed out] & xxjli *dimidia* of led [& saide crossed out] remenithe as apperyth by the old accounte in William Archers custodye iij bords & with Thomas Whyte xxx hayling stones

f.88

Hyer folowyth the accompt of Rychard Walkye & John Hore church wardens yn the yer of our lord God m^dl^ ccccc lxxiij made the xv daye of Febrwary [15 February 1574]

The recettes

In primis recevyd of the stoke wardens vjs viijd
Item recevyd of John Cottell for a lytell led ijd
Item recevyd of the stoke wardens another tym xiijs iiijd
Item recevyd of Wyllyam Heddon for the old yer of ye greatt bell claper xvd
Item recevyd of ye stoke wardens another tym iijs iiijd
Item recevyd of Thomas Badcok the peces of the rode lofft vjs
Item recevyd for wygtyn yn ye church howsse viijd

[206] Welcombe, Devon.

Item recevyd of Nycolas Wyll & John Kyetto for ye kyechyn yn ye church howsse viijd
Item received of Roger Gyst for a knyll iiijd
Item received of Rychard Chyng for a knyll iiijd
Item received for Nycollas Jwd ys grawe iijs iiijd
+Item recevyd for the standens under the pentis xxxijs iijd
Item recevyd for our alle iijli
Item recevyd of Thomas Takell for ye botte xviijd
Item recevyd of John Rod for hys father ys grawff iijs iiijd
Item recevyd of Payed for hys standen iijs
Item recevyd of Sweper for ye laste yer iijs
The holle sum of the recettes ys vjli xixs ijd

[f.88v]

Hyr folowyth the expences

In primis paid to Wyllyam Lighe for makyn of the yn dentures the last yer ijd
Item paid for sope viijd
Item paid for a c of comunyon bred vjd
Item paid for ij croks of yron to hang ye bayer iijd
Item paid for a boke of prayer vjd
Item paid for wyne xiiijd
Item paid to John Corye for a [c crossed out]cxij of comunyon bred viijd
Item paid for menden of a per of serpells & cloth for Master Vycar iiijd
Item paid to ij men to take down ye rowdlofte mett & hyer xd
Item paid for wyne be for Pall[m] Sondaye xviijd
Item paid for ij men ys expenses att Lawnston be for Ester xiijd
Item paid for a pak of russes a gaynst Ester viijd
Item paid for wyn a gaynst Ester ijs jd
Item paid to Wylliam Heddon for the newe makyn of the greatt bell claper iiijs
Item paid for iiij men ys expences & Master Vycar att Synt Mary Wyk att the arsdecon ys vycytacyon vs jd
Item paid for makyn of our byll iiijd
Item paid for pute yn of our byll iiijd
Item paid to Peters j quarter viijd
Item paid to the sumner iiijd
Item paid for makyn clene of the church howsse ijd
Item paid to Nycolas Mok for makyn clene of the church harnes ijs ijd
Item paid for lether bokells & nayells for ye same iijd
Item paid for poynts for same ijd
Item paid for carre of ye same harnes to Synt Mary Wyke vjd[207]

f.89

Item paid for wyne a gaynst Whytt Sonday vd
Item paid for cloth & menden of ye clarks serpells iijd
Item paid for ij men ys expences att Lawnston att the busshype ys ycytacyon xvd
Item paid to John Megar for menden of the third bell mett & hyer xijd
Item paid for iiij men ys expences to Camellford att ye quene ys vycytacyon iijs iijd
Item paid for our byll yt tyme vjd
Item paid for wyne in sondre tymes ijd
Item paid for iiij men ys expences hyer att home to make ye byll for ye awnsur of ye artyklys xvd
Item paid for makyn of the byll & the hyer of a horsse to ryde to Camell ford vjd

[207] xxiiijs vd running total at the bottom of the page.

Item paid for ij men ys expences att Camell ford to lye yn the present ments xijd
Item paid for a [hallff crossed out] quarter of lyme vjs
Item paid for a lok for the cloke vjd
Item paid to Robart Sander for hys expences att Lawnston att the quen ys vycytacyion vjd
Item paid to one that gawe us warnyng to aper yer iiijd
Item paid for a c of lath nayells ijd
Item paid for a ^hallff^ c of lathes iiijd
Item paid to Robart the hyellyar for vj dayes work att xd ye daye, mett & hyer vs
Item paid to one to serve hem vj dayes, mett & hyer iijs
Item paid for nayells to mend the ladder ob
Item paid for iij semes of sond vjd
Item paid to Rychard Wryng for kypen of the bells ijs viijd
Item paid for iiij yerds of howeland for the communyon tabell att xxd the yerd vjs viijd
Item paid for the makyn ther of jd[208]

[f.89v]
Item paid for wyne a gaynst Allhallen daye vijd
Item paid to ye hellyar for one dayes work, mett & hyer xd
Item paid to one to serff hem, mett & hyer vjd
Item paid for wyne a gaynst Crystemas viijd
Item paid for russes a ganst Crystemas vjd
Item paid for a bell rope iijs
Item paid for iiij bowsells of lyme att Bodcastell iiijs
Item paid to Thomas Call for carre of hytt ijs
Item paid for nayells to mend the bell whyell jd
Item paid to the glassyer for glassen of the wyndowes xiiijs vjd
Item paid for wode ijd
Item paid to one to helpe hem ij dayes, mett & hyer viijd
Item paid for a per of jemys for ye church yerd yett viijd
Item paid for bords & poy^n^ells for the standens under ye pentis a gaynst the fer viijd
Item paid to Thomas Phelyps for a owe for ye bell jd
Item paid for gresse for the bells vjd
Item paid to Symon Hollman for tember for the church stell, mett & hyer xvjd
Item paid for lath nayells iiijd
Item paid for a c of lathes viijd
Item paid for comunyon bred jd
Item paid for wyn iijd
Item paid for a bussell of lyme xijd
Item paid for a M^d^ & hallff of hellen ston, mett & hyer ixs
Item paid to John Avere for iiij dayes work [work crossed out] att xd ye day, mett & hyer iijs iiijd
Item paid to one to serffe hem iiij dayes att vjd the daye, mett & hyr ijs[209]

f.90
Item paid to John Avere for iiij dayes & a hallff more att xd the day, mett & hyer iijs ixd
Item paid to one to serve hem iiij dayes & *dimidia*, mett & hyer ijs iijd
Item paid to Master Vycar for kyepen of the regester boke vjd
Item paid to Thomas Marten for the lone of a lader ijd
Item paid for makyn of thys a cownt viijd
Item paid to Nycolas Olyver & [p crossed out] to ij boyes to helpe the quer xviijd
Item paid for ij crests vjd

[208] xxxvs iijd ob, running total at the bottom of the page.
[209] xlvijs vd, running total at the bottom of the page.

Item paid for a [st crossed out] seffe ^to sefft^ for the lyme	ijd

The holl sum of [alowens crossed out] expences ys vli xvjs viijd ob

So ther remayneth cler xxijs vd ob

Item ther remayneth yn Wyllyam Sweper ys hand for rent iijs[210]

[f.90v]

f.91

Here folowythe the accompt of Water Yeo & Wyllyam Mejher churche wardyns yn the yere of our lorde God /1574 / made the xvjth daye of February *anno Elizabethe Regine* xvij [16 February 1575][211]

The receptes

Inprimis recevyd of the stockewardynes	vjs viijd
Item recevyd of the stockewardynes at	xs
Item recevyd of the stockewardynes	viijs
Item recevyd of John Bedlyme for a bussyll	iiijd
Item recevyd for a hundryd & foure score stones ^for the shammylis^[212]	xijd
Item re^ce^vyd of Wylliam Pearse for a knyll	iiijd
Item recevyd of Edwarde Dune for a knyll	iiijd
Item recevyd of Nycholas Hortope for a knyll	iiijd
Item recevyd [of crossed out] for Rychard Call grave	iijs iiijd
Item recevyd for Jone Rodes grave	iijs iiijd
Item recevyd for lyme for the shammyles	iijd
Item recevyd for [the crossed out] wrtynge yn the churche house	viijd
Item recevyd for the kechyng	viijd
[Item recevyd for Edmunt Regyles grave	xijd crossed out]
& Edmant Regyle hath gevyn to the churche	xijd
Item recevyd of Robert Jude for a knyle	iiijd
Item recevyd for our ale	iijli xvs iijd ob
+Item recevyd under the pentys	xxxvjs xijd
Item recevyd of Thomas Takyle for the butterye	xvjd

Sum totall of the receptes vijli xs jd ob

[f.91v]

f.92

Here folowythe the expensys thys ere /1574/[1575]

Imprimys payd for foure men there expensys at the vysytatcyon	ijs xjd
Item payd for makynge of a bylle	vjd
Item payd for laynge yn of the same byll	viijd
Item payde for a bocke of prayers	xijd
Item payde for wyne	xiijd
Item payde unto Nycholas Mocke for makynge clene of the churche harnys	ijs iiijd
Item payde for neales	ijd
Item payde gres for the harnys	jd
Item payde for strapis & neales for the same harnys	jd ob
Item payde for twyne for the harnys	ob
Item payde for wyne	xijd
Item ^more^ payde for wyne	xijd

210 ^ho:^ [vijd iiijd viijs crossed out] xd ixs vj.

211 Richard Yeo possibly the scribe, with capital R like an S.

212 Butcher's shambles.

Item payde unto Jhon Megar for mendynge of the stocke beles vd
Item payde for wyne xvd
Item payde unto Davye Mabyn for floxe for toe stofe the cosshynes[213] ijd
Item payde for wyne xviijd [altered from xvd]
Item payde unto Nycholas Saunder for neales ijd
Item payde unto Richard Wrynge for a coller iijs iiijd
Item payde [unto crossed out] for oure expensys at the visytatyon xxijd
Item payde for a [bylle crossed out] makynge of a byle iiijd

[f.92v]
Item payde for laynge yn of the same byle viijd
Item payde for Peters farthynge viijd
Item payde for hanginge oute of the artycles xijd
Item payde unto Jhon Megars man for one dayes worke, meeate & heare viijd
Item payde for carryinge of foure zeames of stones from Beude viijd
Item payde unto Jhon Megirs man for towe dayes, meate & heare xvjd
Item payde unto Thomas Call for mendynge of the churche eate iiijd
Item payde unto Water Yeo for iiij yerds & a quarter of crese for a shroude for the bedman darsessyd ^yn viijd^ ijs xd
Item payde unto Nycholas Mocke for to carrye the mouster arrous unto Ponstocke[214] to be newe fetheryd jd
Item payde unto John Tome for the fetheryng of ij dosin of arroes xijd
Item payde for foure newe arroes iiijd
Item payde for moster heades for the arroes vd
Item payde for wyne ijd
Item payde unto Thomas Call for newe sherpyncke of the pekys iiijd
Item more payde for wyne ijd

f.93
Item payde for a bocke callyd my Lorde Jules bocke[215] xiijs iiijd
Item payde for carrydge of the same bocke & exspensys vjd
Item payde for comunyon brede vd
Item payde for wyne jd
Item payde for sope vd
Item payde unto Wyllyam Hedin for mendynge of the bele claper xiiijli of jare iiijs vijd
Item payde for wyne iijd
Item payde ^unto^ Wrynge for mendynge of a bele ^coller^ [claper crossed out] xijd
Item ^payde^ for wyne jd
Item payde for wyne jd
Item payde unto Roucke the paver for pavynge yn the churche porche vjd
Item payde unto Water Rose for berynge stones unto the paver jd
Item payde unto Knyght for mendynge yn the churche house iijd
Item ^payde^ for towe quear of paver for ^toe make^ [makyng crossed out] of a newe regester bocke viijd
Item payde for comonyon brede vd
Item payde unto Wyllyam Orcharde clarcke for wretynge of the newe regester bocke iijs iiijd
Item payde for sope vd

[213] Appendix 3.3.
[214] Poundstock.
[215] Bishop Jewel's *Apology*. See Duffy, *Voices of Morebath*, p.179.

[f.93v]

Item payde for a quarte of wyne vijd
Item delyver unto ^the stocke wardyns^ [Jhon Corye crossed out] at one tyme xxs
Item payde for comunyon brede jd
Item payde for towe crestis for the churche vjd
Item spente at the chapter courte & showynge of the ^regester^ bocke xvjd ob
[Item payde for communion brede jd crossed out]
Item payde for a tynnyng bottyll xvjd
Item payde unto Wrynge for kepynge of the beles ijs viijd
Item payde unto Robert Saunders for a pere of showes for Wyllyam Trymbyll xixd
Item payde unto Jhon Corye for one weacks table for towe men ^one day^ meate & drynke for towe zawe the elmes iiijs iiijd
Item payde unto the same towe men for there hear one weacke yn vd a daye vs
Item payde for neales for mendin the seges jd
Item payde unto one for towe bear the bourdes & possys yn to the churche house ijd
Item payde unto Water Rose & Nycholas Mocke for levyle the chaunsyll[216] ijd
Item payde for grese for the beles vjd
Item payde for a bele rope iijs

f.94

Item payde unto Wrynge for mendynge of a bele coller vjd
Item payde for wyne agaynst Chrysmas ixd
Item payde for towe packs of russhys xiiijd
Item payde for one zeame of sande jd
Item payde for carrynge of ^certyn^ [the crossed out] lyme from the brydge jd
Item payde unto Knyght for iiij dayes worke yn ixd a daye iijs
Item payde unto Nycholas Mocke for fyve dayes & halfe to serve the masyns yn vjd a daye ijs ixd
Item payde unto Symyn Holman for a hundryd of lathes viijd
Item payde unto Colman for a hundryd of lathes vjd
Item payde unto Symyn Holman for towe hundryd of lathe neales iiijd
Item payde unto Wyllyam Yeo for foure hundryd of lathe nearles viijd
Item payde unto Jhon Cottyll for a barryle of lyme iijs ijd
Item payde for a zeame of zande jd
Item payde for wyne jd
Item payde unto Jhon Averye for vij dayis worcke, meate & her, yn xd a daye vs xd

[f.94v]

Item payde unto Nycholas Mocke for one dayes worcke, meate & here vjd
Item payde for wyne jd
Item payde for wyne iijd
Item payde unto Master Vycar for kepynge of the regester bocke vjd
Item payde for paper to put yn thys bocke jd
Item payde for makyng of thys accompt viijd
So the hole sum of exspensys ys vjli jd ob
So there remaynthe clear xxxs
[Sum totall amonthe unto vjli jd ob crossed out]
Item we have borowyd of Marckes Payne one hundryd xx of large ^helyn^ stones

[216] Remove the chancel step.

f.95

1575 [1576]

Here folowithe the accompt of John Saunder and Marke Payne chruche wardines in the yeare of our lorde God 1575 made the vj daye of February *anno* Elizabethe *regine xviij* [6 February 1576]

The recetes

Inprimis receved of the stocke wardines	vjs viijd
Item received of the stocke wardines	xs
Item received of the stocke wardines	vjs
Item received of the stocke wardines	xs
Item received of the stocke wardines	xs
Item received of Anes Olyvers knill	iiijd
Item received of Jone Hores knill	xijd
Item received of the stocke wardines	vjs viijd
Item received of John Jule for his childes knill	iiijd
Item received of Nycolas Will for his childes knill	iiijd
Item received of Edward Dobell for his childes knill	iiijd
Item received of John Pere for his dafteres knill	iiijd
Item received of Thomas Jule for his childes knill	iiijd
Item received for William Groves grave	iijs iiijd
Item received for the kecinge	viijd
Item received for witting in the chruche house	viijd
Item received for the buttere	xvjd
Item received for our ale	iijli ijs vd ob
+Item received for stonding under the pentis	xxxijs vjd ob
Sum totals am[oun]t to vijli xiijs iiijd[217]	

[f.95v]

f.96

expencis

Inprimis payed for wine	id
Item paid for paper for this bocke	ijd
Item paid for wine	iiijd
Item paid for comenyen bred	viijd
Item paid for viij yeardes of holand at xvd the yeard to make the serpeles	xs
Item paid for iiij yearde and halfe of holand at xvjd the yeard to make a table clothe	iiijs viijd
Item paid for threde	iiijd
Item paid for sope	vd
Item paid for wine	xiiijd
Item paid for ij bareles of lime	vjs
Item paid for comynen bred	iiijd
Item paid for wine	xiiijd
Item paid for russhess	viijd
Item paid for mendinge of the porche	ijd
Item paid for wine	vijd
Item paid for comyning bred	iiijd
Item paid to John Meger for his fees	xvjd
Item paid to John Meger for mending of the beles	viijd
Item paid for ij plates and neles for the beles	xiiijd

[217] Penmanship, doodle after total.

Item paid for making of the serpeles xxd
Item paid for wine ijs iiijd
Item paid for bourdes for mende the bell whele iiijd
Item paid for gres for the beles vjd
Item paid for wine xijd
Item paid for neles for the beles iijd
Item paid for wine jd
Item paid for iiij men ther expencis at the vecitacion ijs xd
Item paid for our articeles xijd
Item paid for sande jd
Item paid to Lake for working uppon the chruche house ij daies for mete and heare xxijd
Item paid for wine jd
Item paid for sand jd
Item paid to Water Rose for working a boute the chruche viijd

[f.96v]
Item payed for wasshinge of the chruche[218] vjs viijd
Item paid for a seve to sefte lyme in iiijd
Item paid for the lone of 3 panes for pute lime in xijd
Item paid for sand jd
Item paid for a barel and halfe of lyme iiijs vjd
Item paid to Nycolas Mocke for 1 dayes worke iiijd
Item paid for wine iiijd
Item paid for neles that we had when the chruche was wasshed jd
Item paid to Master Morys when he rode to Lanston for the cathecheseme bockes and for the proclymacion xijd
Item paid for wine iijd
Item paid to Perys for making of the segges iijs ijd
Item paid for neles for the same segges iiijd
Item paid for wine ijd
Item paid for a trece for the orgones jd
Item paid for mending of the chruche pecis iiijd
Item paid for plates and neles for the beles vjd
Item paid for a bell rope iijs
Item paid for wine ijd
Item paid to Harry the plomer for mending the ledes ijs xd
Item paid for owed and one to sarve him vjd
Item paid for wine jd
Item paid for tounges for the beles colers ijd
Item paid for wine iiijd
Item paid for mending of the chruche stile iiijd ob
Item paid for leing of the tile jd
Item paid for wine vijd
Item paid for wine xvd
Item paid to Rychard Wryng for keping of the beles ijs viijd
Item paid for sope iiijd
Item paid to Master Moris when he rode to Lanstoyn with mony for Colomford haven[219] xijd
Item paid to Nycolas [to crossed out] Mocke for sarving of the helyer:
4 dayes for mete and heare ijs
Item paid for lathes and neles iijd

[218] Whitewashing church.

[219] Colyton near Axmouth, Devon. See Osborne, *The Church Wardens' Accounts of St Michael's Church, Chagford*, p.236.

Item paid to John Avery for 4 dayes worke for mete and heare	ijs iiijd
Item paid for our expencis when we weare at Bodmon be fore the comissyners	vijs iiijd
Item paid for our othe	iiijd

f.97

Item payed for our bill	iiijd
Item paid for leing in of the same bill	viijd
Item paid to Rychard Wring for ij bell colers	viijs
Item paid to Rychard Wryng for mending of the bell collers	xvjd
Item paid to Rychard Orchard for russes	viijd
Item paid for comening bred	jd
Item paid for wine	xiiijd
Item paid for comenyon bred	ijd
Item paid to William Hedden for mending of the bell claper	ijs xd
Item paid to Master Morys for a halfe busshell of lime	vijd
Item paid for mending of the serpeles	ijd
Item paid to Nycolas Mocke for scoryng of the harnes	ijs
Item paid for neles and lether for the same harnes	iijd
Item paid for oule for the harnes	jd
Item paid for wine and for fetting of the same	xd
Item paid for mending of the helyng	ijd
Item delyveres to the poure in mete and drink that was lefte uppon our handes as muche as came	vs viijd
Item for making of this accounte	viijd
Item I have lede oute 146 [longe hellien crossed out] of longe hellion stones the price	iijs 4[d]

[So the whole some of crossed out] expenses is -vli xviijs [ixd ob crossed out]
[so restethe cleare xxxiiijs vijd ob crossed out]

Item payd for kepinge of the register boocke	vjd

So the whole some amount to – vli xixs iijd ob So restethe cleare xxxiiijs ob

[f.97v]

Here folowyth the accounte of John Yeo and John Hodge churche wardyns in the yere of our lorde God 1576 made the xjth day of February *anno* Elyzabeth *Regine* 19th [11 February 1577]

Inprimis a recevyd of the stocke wardyns	vjs viijd
received agayn of the stocke wardyns	xls
received for Mystres An Callmade yes grave	iijs iiijd
received of Andro Sangwyn for his sonnes grave	iijs iiijd
received of John Barne for his dafters knell	iiijd
received for Mystres An Calmady is knylle	iiijd
received for John Sanguyn and Mary Sanguyn is knylles	viijd
received of Rycherd Chyng for his chylds knylle	iiijd
received of Nycholas Sander for Phyllyppis dafters knylle	iiijd
received of John Bole and John Moore for a knylle	iiijd
received of John Pryst for his brothers knylle	iiijd
received of the stocke wardyns	vjs viijd
received agayne of the stocke wardyns	vijs
received of Wylliam Bray and Thomas Badcok stocke wardyns this yre	vs ijd
received of Nycholas Wyll for his mothers grave	iijs iiijd
received of the stocke wardyns	vs
[received for the standyngs under the pentyce xxxs xjd xxxs,xxxjs iiijd ob crossed out]	
received for the churche ale	iijli xs vjd

+received for the standyngs under the pentyce	xxxs ob
So the whole som of receptes is	9^li^ 3^s^.9^d^.ob

f.98

Expences

Item payd for mendyng of the bell coller	xvjd
Item payd for mendyng of the lytyll bell whyll	ijd
Item payd for wyne	jd
payd for russhes	xvjd
payd for wyne	iijd
Item payd for wyne	xiiijd
payd for synging bred	xd
Item payd for mendyng of the kytchyng dore of the churche howse	ijd
Item that we layd out when we were at the vycitation for the two wardyns & one syde man	v[j crossed out]s jd
payd to Water Rose for wurke	ijd
Item payd to John Corry for ij peces of tymber for ye speryng	vs
payd to Symon Holman, Megers man, for iiij days worke	xxd
payd to Humfry Arthure for iiij days warke	xvjd
Item payd to Harry Eare for hewyng of the more stone	vjd
Item payd to Robart Sawnder for a pece of tymber	xvjd
payd to John Anthony for a dore durnes, loke, kee & jemes to the churche howse	xjs vjd
payd to Nycholas Mocke for warke	iiijd
Item payd to the juner for worke when Meger was workyng abowte the speryng of the churche howse ^meate & wages^	ijs vjd
+Item payd to Thomas Jule marchant for a pece of tymber	iijs vjd
Item payd to Thomas [Badcokke crossed out] Calle for neales & sherpyn of the workemens hamers	xvd
payd to Bande the mason for ij days worke	xijd
Item payd to Meger & his man for iiij days worke	iijs iiijd
payd to Nycholas Mocke for rydyng of the churche howse	jd
Item payd to Nycholas Mocke for tendyng of the workemen when thay were a bowt the pentyce when we gatheryd corne	vd
Item payd to John Meger & his iij men for vj days for ther meat & drynke	vjs
Item for meat & drynk ij days for Band the mason	viijd
payd for wyne	vjd
payd for wyne	xiiijd
Item for wyne	xiiijd
Item payd for wyne	xijd
Item payd for wyne	ijs viijd
Item payd to Richerd Wryng for kepyng of the bells	ijs viijd
Item payd to Rycherd Wryng for makyng of a new bell coller & the mendyng of [a crossed out] ^ij^ olde colers	iiijs iiijd
Item payd to Wylliam Hedon for mendyng of ^the^ great bell claper ij plates & ij neales	vij[s] viijd
Item payd for russhes for the chancell at ij sondry tymes	iiijd
Item payd when we were at the vyzytacion for vj men & the pristes charges	vjs iiijd

[f.98v]

Item payd to John Yeo marchant for the cover of ye communion cup[220]	xvijs vjd

220 See 1570–71 account for the cup, p.125.

payd for a thowsand of helyng stones	iijs xjd
payd for a barryll of lyme	xxijd
Item payd for a bell rope	ijs ixd
Item payd for wyne	iijd
Item payd for wyne at ij sondry tymes	iijd
payd for wyne	jd
Item more for wyne	jd
Item payd for wyne	iijd
payd for wyne	ijd
payd for wyne	iijd
Item payd for wyne	xijd
Item payd for comunion bred	ijd
payd for wyne	ijd
Item payd for wyne	vjd
Item payd for wyne	iijd
Item payd to Thomas Jule merchante for a ladder that the other wardyns brake	xijd
Item for wyne	vjd
payd for comunion bred	ijd
payd for wyne	iijd
Item payd for wyne	xiijd
Item payd for wyne	jd
Item payd for wyne	iijd
Item payd to the synggen scholers	iiijd
Item payd to the comyssyeners for the dyschargyng of the hatts[221]	vijs
payd to Sir Wylliam Palmer for the bryngyng home our dyscharg for ye same	ijs
Item payd to George the penter for drayng of the x comondements	vs vjd
Item for meat & drynke for hym ^iiij days^	xvjd
Item payd to the junor for mendyng of the stondyng	iijd
Item payd for neales for same stondyng	jd ob
Item to Wylliam [D crossed out] Hydon for a showle	ijs
Item payd to Wylliam Smale in his syckenes	ijs
Item payd for paper for make this accompt	jd
Item payd to Nycholas Wyll for thre bordys to drae the commondements	iijs
Item payd to Thomas Lake for fowre days worke to heale the churche for his meate & wages	iijs iiijd
payd for lath neales	ijd
Item payd for servyng of the helyar one day	vjd
payd to Thomas Call for neales	vd
Item payd to Thomas Call for a buckyll & [neylys crossed out] kee	vjd
Item for comunion bred	jd
payd for wyne	jd

f.99

Item payd to the churche of Bath[222]	vs ijd
Item payd for wyne	vjd
Item payd for kepyng of the regester booke	vjd
Item payd for sope ij sondry tymes	xd
payd for gresse for the bells	vjd
Item to John Meger for his fee for ye bells for this yere & the last yer	ijs viijd
Item for makyng of this accompt	viijd

[221] CRO, P216/25/224.

[222] Bath, Somerset.

The som of expences 7^li^ 5^s^ 9^d^ ob

So there remeaneth in our hands 38s

[illeg. words thousand of helyng stones crossed out]

[f.99v]

Here folowythe the acount of John Rode & John Averye the yongar church wardins in the year of our lord God 1577 [1578]

In primis recevyd of the stoke wardens vjs viijd
Item recevyd of the stock wardens 20s
Item recevyd of John Shortte for hys wyfes grave 3s 4d
Item recevyd of the stok wardens 10s
Item recevyd of the stok wardens 50s
Item recevyd of Wyllyam Wyll for a chylds knyll 4d
Item recevyd for standyng under the pentyse thys year 31s 4d
Item recevyd for our ale thys year 3li xd ob

The hooll sum of the recettes comethe to – 9li 22d ob

f.100

Expences

Item fyrst payd for comunione bread 4d
payd for wyne 1d
payd for wyne 3d
payd for wyne 18d
payd for russhes agaynst Ester 16d
payd for wyne 4d
payd for wyne 18d
payd for wyne agaynst Ester 2s 9d
payd to John Avere the elder for 8 days worke & a hallfe to heall the churche for meat & wages ten pence a daye 7s 1d
payd for lathe neeles for the same 4d
payd for one to serve him 8 days & hallfe meatt & wages 7 pence a daye 5s
payd for 2 seames of sand 4d
payd for 5 stoanes to John Yeoo jd[223]
payd for a boyshyll of lyme 16d
payd for grese for the bells 2d
payd for one pound of lead to cast a staape in the tower dore 2d
payd to Nycolas Mocke for scowerynge of the churche harnys 2s
payd for oylle for the same 2d
payd for lether & neeles for the same 2d
payd for grese for belles 1d
payd to Nycolas Mocke for scowerynge of towe moryngs 6d
payd for expences of one warden & 2 syde men at the archdecons vycitacion [6d]
payd for 3 quarters of canvas to lynne them[224] 6d
payd for halfe a pounde of wolle for the same & for thryd 4d
payd for lether & bockells for the same 2d
payd for mendyng of the churche pyckys 6d
payd for makyn faste of boordes & formes in the churche house 2d
payd for neelles for the same 1d
payd for wyne 3d
payd for 6 busshylles of lyme 2s 9d

[223] Late use of Roman numerals.

[224] This refers to the morions.

payd to Nycolas Mocke for makynge cleyn of [a crossed out] a costhell	10d
payd for oylle for the same	1d
payd for makyng clyen of a swerd & settyng on a peer of hyllts	6d
payd to Nycolas Saunder for the same hyllts	16d
payd for a new skabrydge for a daggar	6d
payd for wyne	2d
payd to Nycolas Mocke for maken clyen of tow morians & a swerd	4d
payd for oylle for the same	1d[?]

[f.100v]

payd for wyne	12d
payd for comunion bread	2d
payd for wyne	6d
payd to Rychard Wryng for kyepyng of the belles	2s 8d
payd for wyne	3s 2d
payd for mendyng the paafmentt in the churche porche	2d
payd for a newe keye for the stoockes	2d
payd for wyne	6d
payd for sharppyng of pickys	1d
payd to John Megar his fees for kyepyng of the bells	16d
payd to the glasiar for mendyng the church wyndows	3li 6d
payd for woode for the glaciar	12d
payd to John Avery the elder for 17 dayes worke to mend the churche for meat & wages ten pence a day	14s 2d
payd for one to serve hyam 6 dayes for meat & wages 7 pence a day	3s 6d
payd to Simon Hollman for one hondred of lathes	9d
payd for one creste	3d
payd to Simon Hollman for one hondred of lathe neeles	2d
payd to John Yeoo for 5 hondred of lathe neeles	10d
payd for one boyshyll of lyme	14d
payd for one boyshyll & 3 pecke of lyme	2s 4d
payd to Rychard Wryng for one newe bell coller	4s
payd the same Rychard Wryng for mendyng an old coller	20d
payd for wyne agaynst Chrystmas	12d
payd for expences for one warden & 3 syde men at the byshipes vycitacion ^& for the charges of the cortte^	9s 3d
payd to Roger Pearse for mendyng the churche yeatte	2d
payd for comunion bread	1d
payd to John Avery the elder for 5 days worke & a hallfe to mende the clarkes chamber, meat & wages, ten pence a day	4s 7d
payd for 3 hondred of lathes	2s
payd for 5 hondred lathe neelles	10d
payd to Water Yeoe for 20 stonnes	3d
payd to Nycolas Mocke for skoweryng of the church harnys	2s
payd for oyle for the same	1d
payd laythes & neelles for the same	2d
payd for for a boyshyll & a hallfe of lyme	2s 6d
payd for 4 seemes of sand	8d
payd for a bowestrynge	1d

f.101

payd for wyne	3d
payd for soope	12d
payd for a barell of lyme	2s 4d

payd for carydg of the sam for Buyd	4d
payd for 3 seemes of sand	6d
payd for a ^silke^ laase for a tyche bockes	1d ob
payd to Thomas Calle for makyng a new cock to a calyver & for mendyng of a flaske	8d
payd to Sir Wyllyam Palmer for keypyng the regester booke	6d
payd for a horse to cary the churche armoure to Camellford at the last moster	12d
payd for makyng of this acountte	8d
The hoolle sum of our exspences for this year comethe to	8li 8s 3d ob
so remaynethe cleer to the churche	13s 7d

[f.101v–2]

[f 102v–104v][225]

f.105[226]

[225] Appendices 2.2–2.3 and 3.1–3.3.
[226] In June 1884, Ex.

Part 2

General Receivers' Account Book 1: 1531, 1534–49

f.1

Liber Compet General Receptor Sci Andrie de Stratton[1]

f.2

***Competus Johannis Trevelan et Nicholai Wyll generalium receptorum ecclesie Sci Andrie factus Dominica post festum Sci Dionisij anno domini millessimo* ccccc xxxij *& anno regni regis Henrici octavi* xxiij [15 October 1531]**[2]

Recept

In primis received of Thomas Taylour junior & Thomas Bray recevers the last yere past xxvjli xvs

Item received of Isbell Judd & Johan Chyng, Owr Lady Maydens xxd

Item received of Wylliam Trebarfor for to sett hym a pone ye bedroll iijs iiijd

Item received of Nycholas Judd for ye remaynaunt of his accompt of ye Trinite store xxs vijd ob

Item received of John Schort & Rychard Chyng, Hycrosswardens xls vjd ob

Item received of Robert Regyll & Walter Bryant wardens of Sent Armyll xxvjs ijd ob

Item received of Master Vicar of Stratton for ye church wode xiijs iiijd

Item received of the Sextens xijd ob

Item received of John Uglow & John Sangwen wardens of Owr Lady Holmadon xxs vjd

Item received of Robert Uglow junior & John Marten wardens of Sent George xxvijs vd ob

Summa xxxiiijli ixs viijd ob

[f.2v][3]

f.3

***Competus Williami Gyst & Johanni[s] Jule receptorum factus Dominica post festum Sancti Luce Evangeliste anno domini millessimo* ccccc xxxiiij *et anno regni Henrici* viij xxvj [25 October 1534]**

Recetes

Memorandum received of Rychard Ronell & Wylliam Baron last recevers iijli vjs ijd ob

Item received of the gyzfte of Sir John Chamond knyzth xxvjs viijd

Item received of John Udy junior & John Daymond wardens of Sent Armell iiijli vijs ixd

Item received of Alhalwen yeld xxvjs viijd

Item received of Sent Androw is yeld by the hands of Thomas Marys xxvjs viijd

Item received of Owr Lady yeld by ye honds of Nycholas Judd xxvjs viijd

Item received of Crysts yeld by the honds of Nycholas Yeo xls

Item received of Sent Thomas yeld by the honds of Nycholas Wyll xiijs iiijd

Item received of Sent George is store by the hands of Wylliam Sparke xxs ixd

Item received of John Beare for hys fyne[4] xxvjs viijd

Item received of Rychard Jule & John Hogge wardens of Sent Armell iijli [xlvjs viijd crossed out]

Item received of Thomas Coke alias Grendon & Edward Horetop wardens of Owr Lady Holmadon xxs iijd

Item received of Robert Regull, Sexten ijs ijd

Item received of John Jule & Thomas Heket, Hye Crosse wardens liiijs viijd

1 BL, Add MS 32244

2 1530–31; High Cross wardens and regnal year are correct for 15 October 1531. The heading roughly translates as 'The account of John Trevelan and Nicholas Will general receivers of the church of St Andrew made the Sunday next after the feast of St Denis the year of our lord 1532 and the 23rd year of the reign of Henry VIII'.

3 Blank.

4 Hele. See CRO, P216/25/83.

Item received of Owr Lady Maydens, Elzabeth ^Bette^ & Johan Call xixs
Summa xxvli xvijs [jd crossed out] ^vd^ ob

[f.3v]

Expenses

Memorandum payd to John Payne & W. Sparke, Hyecros wardens xs
Item payd to the organ maker xxvjs viijd
Item paid for vj lode of more stone xiiijs
Item payd to the masyn Rowclyff yn parte of payment of hys bargyn xxs
Item payd to John Dawe the kerver[5] yn parte of payment of hys bargyn xiijli vjs viijd
Item paid for makyng of thys accompte iiijd
Item paid for paper to make a compt ^bock^ ijd
Item paid to the organ make[r] for to mend the organs whan nede requiryth xijd
Summa xvjli xviijs xd
Remanet cler viijli [vs crossed out] ^xviijs^ vijd ob

Memorandum that Wylliam Gyst & John Jule payd the iij^de^ day of November ^the yer a forsayd^ to Thomas Coke alias Grendon & to Nycholas Symon of Bowrwode the sayd sum of viijli xviijs vijd ob of debeth beyng yn present John Trevelan & Thomas Hykytt & John Hore *sic solut quietus est*

f.4

***Competus Thome Coke alias Grendon et Nicholai Symon de Bowrwod receptorum generalium ^ecclesie^ Sancti Andrie de Stratton anno domini millessimo* ccccc xxxv *et anno regni regis Henrici octaui vicesimo septimo* [1535]**

Recept

In primis recevyd of Wylliam Gyst & John Jule recevers the yere last past viijli xviijs vijd
Item received of Thomas Tayler junior for a heryott[6] for the deth of Wylliam Uglow xiiijd
Item received of the same Thomas Taylour for the remaynaunt of his accompt of the Trinite warden vs ijd
Item received for Alhalwyn yeld by the honds of Wylliam Gyst xs
Item received for Seynt Androw ys yeld by ye hands of John Pery xxs
Item received for Owr Lady yeld by the honds of John Rose xxs
Item received for Crysts yeld by the hands of Wylliam Grove xxs
Item received for Seynt Thomas yeld by the hands of Wylliam Call xs
Item received of John Payne & W. Spark, Hyecross wardens ixs ixd
Item received of John Ede of the towne & John Bhare wardens of Sent George xxjs ijd
Item received of Alson Jule & Johan Bette, Owr Lady Maydens xvjs
Item received of Alson Puddener for rent yt was be hynd to pay vjs
Item received of J. Greby which was callyd Robynhode & of hys felows xijs iiijd
Item received of Thomas Wade & Edmund Regell wardens of Sent Armell iijli xs [vijd crossed out] ^viijd^
Item received of George Hacke & Wylliam Lang wardens of Owr Lady Holmadon xxiijs vd
Item received of John Rowland & Wylliam Besshepp, Sextens xxijd ob
Item received of Master Vycar for the wode xxxxvjs viijd
Summa xxiijli xvs vijd

[f.4v]

Memorandum payd to John Daw the kerver yn parte of payment for the makyng of the redeloft xiijli vjs viijd

[5] See appendix 1.
[6] Hele, see CRO, P216/25/83.

Item paid to John Rowclyff yn parte of payment of all hys bargyn wy^th^yn the church iijli xiijs iiijd
Item paid to the same Rowclyff for helyng of church xxxvjs viijd
Item paid to John Payne & John Pery for viij busshels of lyme iijs iiijd
Item paid to them for caryeg of the same lyme ijs ijd
Item paid for bred & drynke for them yt caryed home the more stone frow Efford[7] yt made ye new pyler iijd
Item paid to Rowclyff is servant for pynnyng of the olde pylers vjd
Item paid to John Jule crowder[8] for beryng of the olde stuff of the rodeloft to a howse of Wylliam Gysts iiijd
Item paid to Nycholas Heddon for yrewarke of the new wyndow of the northe church & the old stuff was alowed ixs viijd
Item paid to Nycholas Heddon for lyme & caryeg xijd
Item paid for mete & drynke for them yt caryed the more stone frow Efford yt made the new wyndow vjd
Item paid to the mason yt made the wall over the wold pylers for ij days jurney mete & drynke & wages xijd
Item paid to John Daymond for servyng of hym ij days mete & drynk viijd
Item paid to the plummer for the leds makyng ye furst tyme vjs viijd
Item paid to John Daymond for drayng up stonys with yn the church & for gaderyng of stonys withowt ye church for the mason xxd
Item paid to John Rede & to Robert Bary for ix busshels of lyme & caryeg of the same frow Bedeforth vs
Item payd to John Daw yn parte of payment for settyng of the northe rowff vjs viijd
Item paid to the same John Daw for settyng of the seges vjs viijd
Item paid for iij ^m^ of helyng stone & iij quarters iiijs jd
Item for caryng of the same stone & for mete & drynke when yer came ixs vijd

f.5
Item paid to Robert Hayne for a days warke to make wall over the wyndow yn the northe syde ^met & drynk^ vjd
Item paid to John Crowder for hys wages, mete & drynke to serve hym iiijd
Item paid for lede & for the caryeg frow Lancestone iiijs ijd
Item paid to the plumer now last for the makyng of the led vs iiijd
Item paid to Master Vycar for a quarter of lyme iijs iiijd
Item paid to Nycholas Uglow for xx crests iijs iiijd
Item paid for the makyng of ys accompte[9] viijd

Summa xxijli xiiijs jd
Remaynet cler xxjs vjd ob

Memorandum that Thomas Coke alias Grendon & Nicholas Symon of Bowrwode hath payd to Wylliam Byshepp & John Payne xxjs vjd ob a forsayd & so they be quite

[f.5v]
***Competus Willelmi Bysshepp et Johannis Payne generalium receptorum ecclesie Sancti Andrie de Stratton anno domini millessimo* ccccc xxxvj *anno regni regis Henrici* viij, xx[viij] [1536]**

Memorandum recevyd of Thomas Coke alias Grendon & Nycholas Symon of Bowrwod general recevers the last yere past xxjs vjd ob
Item received of John Udy, Trinite warden viijs iiijd ob

[7] The original name for Bude.
[8] Fiddle player. A Tudor fiddler of c.1535 is depcited on a bench end at Altarnun.
[9] Space above.

Item received of Alhalwyn yeld by the hands of Wylliam Lang xiijs iiijd
Item received of Nycholas Symon of Bowrwode for Sent Andrew ys yeld xls
Item received of John Cawetham, Owr Lady yeld xls
Item received of John Udy for Crysts yeld xls
Item received of Nycholas Wyll for Sent Thomas yeld xiijs iiijd
Item received of Sir Nycholas Gyste for the bell mony vs ijd
Item received of John Lange & Wylliam Moyse for Sent Georges store xxvijs viijd ob
Item received of John Rowland junior & John Pery junior wardens of Sent Armell is store vjli
Item received of Wylliam Gelberd for a geft to ye rodeloft iiijd
Item received of John Mares & of hys company yt playd Robyn Hoode xxxvijs ^viijd^
Item received for Robert Uglow ys gyft to ye church & for his grave xiiijs iijd
Item received of John Roland senior & John Cobeldyck wardens of Owr Lady Holmadon xxs xd
Item received of Th[10]

Summa xxli ijs iijd ob

f.6

Expenses

Memorandum payd to John Dow for yt he was he hynd to pay of the northe roff xiijs iiijd
Item paid to John Mayow & other of ye iiij men of Kylkhamton[11] for centerns to schett ye archys viijd
Item paid to John Mock for makyng of ye same cynters xd ob
Item paid to Wyilliam Call & Wylliam Olyver, Hyecroswardens vijs vjd
Item paid to John Daw yn parte of payment for ye rodeloft xiijli xiijs iiijd
Item paid to Thomas Taylor junior for viij ^ml^ of lathe nayle vjs [vj crossed out] viijd
Item for makyng of ys accompte iiijd

Summa xvli ijs viijd
Remaynythe clere iiijli [xv crossed out] xixs vijd

[f.6v]

***Competus Johannis Rose & Thome Bray generalium receptorum ecclesie Sancti Andrie de Stratton factus Dominica post festum Sancti Martini anno domini millessimo* ccccc xxxviij[12] [18 November 1537]**

Recetes

In primis recevyd of Wylliam Besshepp & John Payne generall recevers the yere past iiijli xixs vijd
Item recevyd of Allhalwyn yeld by ye hands of John Mock xiijs iiijd
Item received of Sent Androw ys yeld by the hands of John Pery xiijs iiijd
Item received of Owr Lady yeld by ye hands of Wylliam Bysshep xxs
Item received of Crysts yeld by ye honds of Wylliam Grove xiijs iiijd
Item received of Sent Thomas yeld xs
Item received of Wylliam Olyver & Wylliam Call, Hyecrosswardens xljs ijd
Item received of John Hore for the rescull of ye ledd viijd
Item received of John Uglow & John Wade wardens of Sent George xiiijs iijd
Item received of Esbell Bray & Agnes Grendon, Owr Lady Maydens iiijs viijd

10 Rest is blank.
11 Kilkhampton.
12 Wrong year written by mistake, so the dating is a year earlier for this account and the next.

Item received of Sent Armell ys wardens Thomas Hekytt junior & Wylliam Hore iijli ijs ^iiijd^
Item received of Wylliam Morgan & George Mayor [war crossed out], Sextens iiijs jd
Item received of Wylliam Rodd & John[13] wardens of Owr Lady Holmadon xvs
Item received of Robyn Hode & hys men iijli xd
Item received of John Trevelan, Trinite warden xxijs vjd
Summa xixli xvjs jd

f.7

Expenses

Memorandum payd to the organ maker for iiij yeres iiijs
Item payd to John Cholwyll for hys promys for kepyng of the bellys xvjd
Item paid to the same John for turnyng of a bell ijs viijd
Item payd for mendyng of the bell yt was brokyn yn parte of payment of hys bargyn vjs viijd
Item paid to John Martyn for helpyng of hym vjd
Item paid to Nycholas Mock to helpe hym ijd
Item paid to Thomas Hekytt senior for naylys vjs viijd
Item paid to Thomas Hekytt junior for a lock for a cofer vd
Item paid to John Daw yn parte of payment for ye rodelofte xvijli vjs viijd
Item paid for makyng of thys accompte vjd
Summa xviijli ixs vijd
Remanent de claro xxvjs vjd

Memorandum [that crossed out] John Rose & Thomas Bray hat hath payd ye sayd debett to Thomas Taylour junior & to Wylliam Grow| *quietus est*

[f.7v]

***Competus Thome Thaylour junior et Willelmi Grove generalium receptorum ecclesie Sancti Andrie de Stratton factus Dominica ante festum Omnium Sanctorum anno domini millessimo* ccccc xxxix *& anno regni regis Henrici* viij, xxx [27 October 1538]**

Recetes

In primis recevyd of John Rose & Thomas Bray generall recevers the yere past xxvjs vjd
Item received of John Bhare, Trinite warden vijs jd
Item received of Alhalwyn yeld by the honds of John Buys xs
Item received of Sent Androw is yeld by ye honds of Wylliam Moyse xxvjs viijd
Item received of Thomas Hekytt for Owr Lady yeld[14] xxvjs viijd
Item received of Crysts yeld by ye honds of Nycholas Yeo xxvjs viijd
Item received of Sent Thomas yeld xvs viijd
Item received of Nycholas Symon & John Lang, Hyecrosswardens xlijs ijd
Item received of Robert Regell & Rychard Jule wardens of Sent George xiiijs vijd
Item received of Nycholas Symon of Bowrwode for ye olde rodeloft iijs
Item received of John Carwetham for the same old rodelofte iijs iiijd
Item received of John Rose for the olde story of ye rodeloft vijs vjd
Item received of Walter Rose & Wylliam Bond wardens of Sent Armell ys store iiijli iijs jd ob
Item received of Thomas Taylour & Wylliam Call wardens of Sent George xxxiijs iiijd
Item received of Tomsyn Pery & Johan, ye servant of Wylliam Gyst, Owr Lady Maydens vs vjd
Item received of John Marys & Wylliam Morgan wardens of Owr Lady Holmadon xxijs

[13] Surname omitted.

[14] This entry and the next had been reversed, as indicated by *b* and *a* in margin.

Item received of John Buys & Robert Bond, Sextens iijs vjd
[Item for makyng of ys acompte xjd crossed out]
Summa xvijli xvijs iijd ob

f.8

Expenses

Memorandum payd to John Canne for makyng of the dore for the rodeloft xxd
Item paid to John Dromand & to Robert Hayne for makyng of the vyce for ye rodeloft ixs iiijd
Item paid to John Puddener for quary stone xvd
Item paid to the belluter for mendyng of ye bellys xiijs iiijd
Item paid for caryng of ^ij^ lode of morestone for the wyndows yn the rodeloft vs vd
Item paid to Thomas Hekytt for naylys for ye rode loft xs
Item paid to the masyn for drawyng of ye morestone & for makyng of the wyndows yn the rodeloft xvjs viijd
Item paid to the vestment maker xs[15]
Item paid to John Daw ys yere for the rodelofte xiiijli xiijs iiijd
Item paid for makyng a compt vjd
Summa xviijli xviijd
Remaynet to Thomas Taylor & W. Grove iiijs ij ob

[f.8v]

***Competus Thome Bryant et Willelmi Lang generalium receptorum ecclesie Sancti Andrye de Stratton factus ante festum Omnium Sanctorum anno domini mi^l^lessimo* ccccc xxxix[16] *et anno regni regis Henrici* viij, xxxj [late October 1539]**

Recetes

Memorandum recevyd of All Halwyn yeld by the hands of Thomas Wade xxs
Item received of Sent Androw ys yeld by the hands of Rychard Currye xvjs
Item received of Owr Lady yeld by the honds of Thomas Hekytt xls
Item received of Crysts yeld by the hands of John Mayor xxs
Item received of Wylliam Lang, Trinite wardyn xjs iiijd
Item received of Wylliam Moyse & John Mayor, Hyecrosse wardens xliiijs jd ob
Item received of Johan Call & Cheryte Trevelan, Owr Lady Maydens xxiiijs
Item received of Thomas Hore & John Olyver wardens of Sent Armell ixli vijs ijd ob
Item received of Thomas Wade & George Maior, Owr Lady Holmadon ys wardens xxiiijs ijd ob
Item received of John Wade & John Antony, Sextens ijs xjd ob
Item received of Thomas Hekyd for Rowclyff, the masyn ijs
Summa xixli xs viijd

Expenses

Memorandum payd to John Daw for the rodeloft xijli iijs iiijd
Item payd to Thomas Hekyt for yre warke for the rodeloft xlvs iiijd
Item paid to Nycholas Kyng for fettyng of a image to thauton[17] iiijd
Item paid to Wylliam Byshep & Thomas Taylor yn parte of pament that they lent to the church iijli vjs viijd
Item payd to John Payne for mony he lent to ye church vijs vjd
Item payd to John Rose for mony he lent to ye church vijs vjd
Item payd for a c of lathys vd

[15] Space left below.
[16] Duplicate date to the last account, but this is correct.
[17] *The altar* or an unidentified place name.

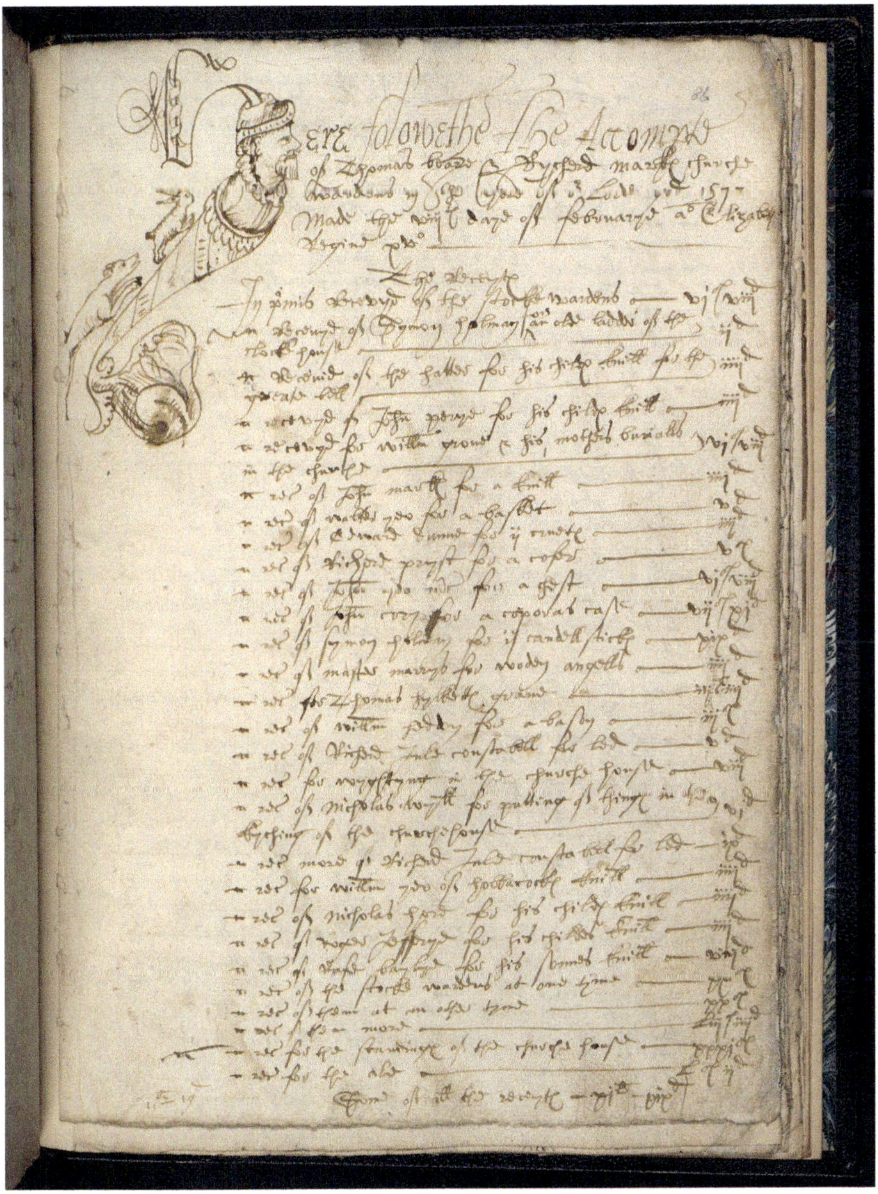

Plate 1 Churchwardens' account, 1572, with illuminated initial. (© The British Library Board, BL, Add MS 32243, f.86r)

Plate 2a St Andrew's church north side. (Photograph by Alexis Jordan, by kind permission of Stratton PCC)

Plate 2b St Andrew's church interior looking east. (By kind permission of Stratton PCC)

Plate 3 St Christopher, early fourteenth century, recycled as general receivers' book 1 back cover. (© The British Library Board, BL, Add MS 32244)

Plate 4a St Armel, from an early sixteenth-century screen, Torbryan, Devon. (By kind permission of The Churches Conservation Trust)

Plate 4b South side-chapel and rood screens, Wolborough, Devon. (By kind permission of Wolborough PCC)

Item payd to John Trevelyan for *dimidia* bosshell of lyme & makyng a quitans be twene Daw & the parysh vjd
Item payd to Rychard Curry for naylys ixd
Item payd for makyng of ye accompt vjd
^Item payd to Master Thomas Arundell^ xvijs viijd
Summa ^xixli ixs viijd^ [xvij li xijs xd crossed out]
Remanet to the church [xvijs xd crossed out] ijd
Solutus quietus est

f.9

***Competus Wyllelmi Moys & Johannis Lang generalium receptorum ecclesie Sancti Andrye de Stratton factus post festum Omnium Sanctorum anno domini millessimo cccccmo xxxx et anno regni Henrici viij xxxij* [November 1540]**

[Rec crossed out] **Recet** memorandum recevyd of Wylliam Barne, trenite wardyn xxvijs jd

[f.9v]

***Competus [Willelmi crossed out] ^Johannis^ Lange, Willelmi Moyse factus Dominica post festum Omnium Sanctorum generalium receptorum anno ^domini^ millessimo* ccccc xl [7 November 1540]**

Recetes

Memorandum recevyd of Thomas Bryant & Wylliam Lang recevers ye yeer past ijd
Item received of Wylliam Baron, Trinite warden xxvijs jd
Item received of John Rowland senior for Alhalwyn yeld vjs viijd
Item received of Nycholas Symon for Sent Androw ys yeld vijs vjd
Item received of Thomas Hekyt senior for Owr Lady yelde xs
Item received of Nycolas Judd a pone a rekenyng of yre yt bozst of ye parysh iiijd^ob^
Item received of John Pery & Rychard Wryng wardens of Sent George xxvijs vd
Item received of Agathe Yeo & Cherite Coke, Owr Lady Maydens xvs vjd
Item received of Walter Symon & Thomas Glawen wardens of Sent Armell iiijli xiijs ixd
Item received of John Wyll & John Maior, Owr Lady Holmadons wardens xxvjs ijd
Item received of Rychard Curry & John Hore junior, Sextens iiijs xd
Item received of Alson Dyer for a kertyll vijs
Item received of John Ede yn towne & Wylliam Grove, Hyecrossewardens xxxijs ixd
Item received of John Carwetham for olde stoff of the rodeloff iijs iiijd
Summa xiijli ijs vjd ob

f.10

Expenses

Memorandum payd to Thomas Tayler junior for mony ye parysh awyd hym xvijs vjd ob
Item paid to the same Thomas for yt Master Vicar lent liijs iiijd
Item paid to Thomas Nicolson & Nicholas Symon for costage to the assies at Launceston for Treburtell[18] iijs iiijd
Item paid to the same Thomas & Nycholas Judd for to dystrayne yer ijs
Item paid for beryng of a letter frow Sir John Chamond to Penhele[19] viijd
Item paid to John Kymthorne is dener for his goodys to ye paryshe iijd
Item paid for kepyng of a mare to Thomas Nycolson xiiijd
Item paid more for ye same mare viijd
Item paid to the same Thomas to go to the sessions viijd

[18] Treburtle, Tresmeer. See CRO, P216/25/178–83 and the jottings on the back cover of these accounts.
[19] Penheale, Egloskerry.

Item paid to Pozwyll churche for Sir Nycholas Gyst ys gyft yer we shuld pay for ye chalys yt he gave to the churche vjs viijd
Item paid to them yt brozst the chalys viijd
Item paid to Thomas Nycolson for a precept & for servyng ye same xvjd
Item paid to Wylliam Bysshepp & to Thomas Tayler the last pament of xli yt was borryd iiijli
Item paid to Nycholas Symon & to Thomas Nycolson for expenses to the lawcurte at Lanceston ijs
Item paid to John Hore for costage at Marhamchurch to speke John Harry iiijd
Item paid to John Payne for expenses for iiij men to ryde to Treburtyll xd
Item paid to John Trevelian for makyng of a new bedroll ijs
Item paid to the organ maker yt he was behynde to pay iiijs
Item paid to Master Thomas Arundell xxs
Item paid to Nycholas Wyll for yt the priste dyd sue for ye bucks vd
Item paid to Rychard Curry for the overplus of his a compt iiijd
Item paid for makyng of ys accompt vjd

Summa ixli xviijs viijd ob
Remanet clar iijli iijs xd

[f.10v]

***Competus Thome Hyket senior et Johannis Bear generalium receptorum ecclesie Sancti Andrie de Stratton factus a[sic] Dominica ante festum Sancti Andrie appostoli anno domini millessimo* ccccc xlj [27 November 1541]**

Recetes

Memorandum received of John Lang & Wylliam Moyse generall receivers the laste yere paste iijli iijs iiijd
Item received of Nycholas Yeo & Wylliam Lange, Hyecrosswardens ye last yere past xxjs jd
Item received of Wylliam Rodd & Wylliam Morgan, Seynt George ys wardens xviijs iiijd
Item received of Johan Lang & Johan Cradock, Owr Lady Maydens vjd
Item received of Wylliam Coper & Wylliam Bray, Seynt Armell ys wardens iijli viijs viijd
Item received of John Wade & Thomas Rose, Owr Lady Holmadon ys wardens xxvs vijd
Item received of Wylliam Grove, Trinite wardyn ixs viijd
Item received of John Rowland junior & John Cobeldyck, Sextens iiijs vjd

Summa xli xjs viijd

Compet Willelmi Gyst generalis Receptoris[20]

f.11

Expenses

Memorandum for John Marys & Thomas Nycolson & Gery expenses to Bodman sessions for Treburtyll landds & to John Cympthorne for makyng of a byll & obligacon vijs iijd
Item for John Marys & Thomas Nycollson expenses for takyng of possession for the feoffers at Treburthyll ijs
Item payd to John Rose & Nycholas Wyll for yer expenses to ryde to Lanceston for besynys for Treburtyll vjd ob
Item paid to John Kympthorne for wrytyng of the award that was made bytwene John & ye parysh & for wrytyng of a relece ijs viijd
Item for a quarte a wyne iijd
Item paid for expenses whan ye warde was made iijs vjd

[20] Bottom of the page, upside-down.

Item paid for Master Thomas Arundell ys dener & other other cumpany of ye parysh yt came with hym xijd ob
Item paid for John Cympthorne & John Marys ys expenses & labour to Phylipp for to se evydens[21] xiijd
Item paid to John Trevelyan for wrytyng of ye feoffement xvjd
Item for wex jd
Item for expenses to Launceston assies for Treburthyll ijs viijd
Item paid to John Harry for the award yt was made Master Carnesow & Thomas Arundell[22] xvjs
Item for expenses at Treburthell at the selyng of the relese xiiijd
Item paid to John Mares for hys expenses to ryde to Exeter to the kings collectors for the chauncell[23] vjs vjd
Item to the same John for hys labour xxd
Item for Kympthorne ys expenses xijd
Item for bocksys to sex[24] evydens yn xijd
Item for the caryng of the bocks jd

[f.11v]
Item for mendyng of ye clock ijs
Item for expenses for makyng of the acompt for to over laber & drynkyng iiijd
Item for the copyng of the dede that John Phyllipp hathe in hys cowpartener[?] with the churche iiijd
Item for makyng of ys accompte vjd

Summa liijs

Remanet cler to the churche vijli xviijs iiijd

f.12

[*Competus Nicholai Yeo & Mathei Rose generalium Receptorum ecclesie Sancti Andrie de Stratton facta Dominica p[ost] festum Omnium Sanctorum anno domini Millessimo ccccc xlij & anno regni Henrici VIII xxxiiij* [1542]]

Recept *In primis* received off

f.12v

***Competus Nycholai Yeo & Mathei Rose generalium receptorum ecclesie Sancti Andrie de Stratton anno domini millessimo* ccccc xlij *& anno regni Henrici* viij, xxxiiij [5 November 1542]**

Recepts

In primis recevyd of Thomas Heckytt & John Bear recevers the yere past vijli xvjijs iiijd
Item received of John Marys & John Rose, Hye Crosse wardens xxviijs vijd ob
Item received of John Beys & Wylliam Hore, Sent Georg ys wardens xvijs
Item received of Alson Wyll & Richard[a] Squans, Owr Lady Maydens xiijs iiijd
Item received of Rogger Yeo & John Curtys, Sent Armell ys wardens liijs iiijd
Item received of Wylliam Coper & Edward Jule, Sextens iiiijs vjd
Item received of Rychard Wryng & Rychard Jule, Owr Lady Holmadon wardens xijs

Summa xiijjli [xvs crossed out] ^vijs^ jd ob

21 CRO, P216/25/180.
22 CRO, P216/25/182.
23 See Introduction.
24 Seek.

Expenses

Memorandum payd to Thomas Wade & John Bear of J. Mares & Rose is compt Hycroswardens the last yere before — vjs vijd
Item paid to Rychard Apryce for layng of tyle — vjs iiijd
Item paid to Thomas Hykyt junior for a new cofer — ijs
Item paid to Rychard Aprice for layng of ij rebytts — ijd
Item paid to John Rose for Hugh Corter ys wages — xiiijs
Item paid to John Mock for drawyng downe of Owr Lady chapyll[25] — ijs
Item paid to Mathe Rose for iij bosshels of lyme & for hys labour — ijs iiijd
Item paid for makyng of thys a compt — [vjd viijd crossed out]

Summa xxxiiijs ijd

Remanet clar to the church xijli ^xijs^ xjd ob

f.13

***Competus Johannis Marys et Nycholus Judde generalium receptorum Sancti Andrie ecclesie anno domini millessimo* ccccc xliij *& anno regni Henrici* viij, xxxv [1543]**

Recepts

In primis recevyd of Nycholas Yeo & Matthe Rose generall recevers or stocke wardens the yere past — xijli xijs xjd ob
Item received of John Dromand, Trinite warden — vjs iiijd ob
Item received of Thomas Wade & John Bear, Hyecrossewardens — xvijs xd ob
Item received of Edward Horetopp & James Kyng, Seynt Georg wardens — xvjs iiijd
Item received of John Gyste & Wylliam Chyng, Seynt Armells wardens — xls vd ob
Item received of Mathe Rose & Margaret Martyn for the wode of Robyn Hode is howse — iijs vd
Item received of John Pery junior & John Badlam, Sextens — xvjd
Item received of Johan Olyver for Owr Lady Maydens — xxd

Summa xvijli vd

Expenses

Memorandum payd to John Uglow & John Wade, Hycrosse wardens — vjs vijd
Item paid to John Daw the kerver for a reward of ye paryshe — vjs viijd
Item paid to George Jule for drayng of stonys to the More for the chauncell — vjs viijd
Item paid to Ede for [s crossed out] caryng of ij lode of the same stone — vs
Item paid for the mete & drynke — viijd
Item paid to plommer for mendyng of ye church ledde — xxd
Item paid for naylys yt John Daw had to mend ye fawtes in ye rodeloft[26] — ijd
Item paid to George Jule for [drawry crossed out] drayng of stonys to the Mor agen — iijs iiijd
Item paid to Ede & hys company for caryng of iiij lode of ^more stone^ — xijs
Item paid for ther mete & drynke ye same tyme — xvjd
Item paid to the clerke of the markytt — xxvs
Item paid for caryng of stone from the chapell — xvjd
Item to the masons for makyng of the churche wall — xiijs iiijd
Item paid to the masons for drayng of stone to the More & other [jusyny crossed out] jurneys to the churche wall — vs iiijd
Item paid for makyng of ye a compt — vjd

Summa iiijli ixs viijd

[25] The north chapel in the church.
[26] See appendix 1.

[f.13v]

Expenses for makyng crosse[27] yn the towne

Memorandum paid to Broke ye mason for viij days jurney for makyng of the same crosse ijs viijd
Item paid for vij days jurney more xxijd
Item paid to George Jule for iij days jurney ther xijd
Item paid to Mathe Rose for caryng of grett & makyng of morter viijd
Item paid to the same Mathe & for hys man for serve the masons iij days, mete, drynk & wages xijd
Item paid to the ye same Mathe for iij bosshels of lyme ijs iijd
Item paid to Rychard Foster for caryng of stonys to ye same crosse iiijs viijd
Item paid to George Jule [for caryng o crossed out] for drayng of ye same stonys & other stonys xviijd
Item paid to the same Mathe for v peck of lyme more ixd
Item paid for mete & drynke for fortenyzt & iiij days for the masons ijs viijd

Summa [xviijs crossed out] xixs

Summa totalis expensis ... [v viijli viijs viijd crossed out] vli viijs viijd

Remanet cler to the church xjli xjs [xjd crossed out] ixd

f.14

***Competus Johannis Ede & Richardi Currye generalium receptorum ecclesie Sancti Andrie de Stratton factus Dominica post festum Omnium Sanctorum anno domini millessimo* ccccc xliiij *et anno regni Henrici octavi* xxxv [2 November 1544]**

Recept

In primis recevyd of John Marrys & Nycholas Jude generall recevers the ye[re] past xjli xjs ixd
Item received of Mayor, Trynite warden xs ijd ob
Item received of John Marrys for Seynt Androw ys yeld vjs viijd
Item received of Thomas Hyckyt for Owr Lady yeld vjs viijd
Item received of John Wade & John Uglow, Hyecrosse wardens xs iiijd
Item received of John Rowland junior & Robert Bond, Seynt George is wardens xx^iiijs^[ijs crossed out]
Item received of Cawnter & Johan Morgan, Owr Lady Maydens xijs v[ij crossed out]d
Item received of Walter Symon & Rychard Servys, Sextens ixd
Item received of John Judd & John Bryant, Seynt Armell ys wardens xxxiijs ^iiijd^
Item received of John Kympthorne of the kyngs grace is mony yn parte of payment for byldyng of the chancell ^vli^[xx crossed out] vjs viijd
Item received of Wylliam Payne & Edward Jule, Seynt George ys wardens thys yere xxvjs viiijd

Summa [xixli crossed out] ^xx iijli [i crossed out] ^ ixs vjd ob

[f.14v]

Expenses

In primis paid to Rychard Walshe for a lampe xijs
Item paid to George [Maior], John Antony, Hycrosse wardens vjs viijd
Item paid to Thomas Clerke for makyng of the wache howse[28] ixd
Item paid to Thomas Wade for [mete crossed out] ^bred^ & drynke for Sir John Chamond ys knylles vjs xd
Item delyvered to John Avery for harnys xxxiiijs
Item paid to the tyler for tylyng of ye churche iiijli xvjs iijd

[27] *Y* changed to *o*. Market cross.

[28] Also 1570.

Item paid to Stawfor & George Jule for takyng downe of ye chancele	viijd
Item paid to Stawford & the same George for the makyng of the chancell yn parte of payment	xxxiijs iiijd
Item paid to the same Stawfor & George	xxs
Item paid more to ye same Stawford & George	xxvjs viijd
Item paid to ye same Stawford & George Jule	xiijs iiijd
Item paid to Stawford & George	xs
Item paid to John Badlam to rede abowt ye chancell	viijd
Item paid to Nycolas Mock for redyng abowt ye chancell	viijd
Item paid to the plummer	xs [iiijs crossed out] iiijd
Item paid for a dosyn of tresys to bynd ye scaffetts	vjd
Item paid to Byttyck to serve ye masens	xvjd
Item paid for ij busshells of lyme to[29]	xvjd
Item for caryng of zonde	iiijd
Item paid to Edward Horetop for caryng stonys frow ye chapel[30]	xvs iiijd
Item paid to Ede of Oterram[31] for caryng of ij lode of more stone	viijs
Item paid the same tyme for mete & drynke for them	vijd
Item paid to Byttyck for rydyng a bowt the chauncell	xvjd
Item to ye same Byttyck for syftyng of erthe & redyng	xiiijd
Item to ye same Byttyck for v days	[xxiijd crossed out] xxijd
Item paid to ye same Byttyck for iiij days work	xviijd
Item paid to the plummer yn parte of payment	ijs
Item paid to a helyer & to hys man for mete & drynk one day	xiijd
Item paid to John Pery for caryng of stonys	ijs viijd
Item paid to John Cholwyll yn parte of payment for ye chauncell	iiijli

f.15

Item paid to Nycholas Gyst for ij busshels of lyme	xvjd
Item paid to Walter Rose & Robert Hyghadon for drayng of sronys[32]	xijd
Item paid to Byttyck for iij days warke	xijd
Item paid [paid crossed out] to Edmund Mabyn for caryng of vj c of ledd frow Hartlond[33]	xijd
Item paid to the plummer for castyng of ye ledd	xijs jd
Item paid the helyer for iiij days warke	xvjd
Item for mete & drynke for hym	xd
Item paid for lathe nayle	jd
Item paid for viij busshels of lyme to Lord of Sent Damnek[34]	vjs ixd
Item paid to Robert Hyghadon for iiij days warke	xvjd
Item paid ij ^m^ of helyng stone to[35][Call crossed out] Cullo	iiijs vjd
Item paid to the lymer for x busshells of lyme	iiijs
Item paid to John Holman of Hartelond for vj ^c^ of led	xxxjs
Item paid to Hyghadon for iiij days wark	xvjd
Item for makyng of ys acompt	vjd

Summa ^xxiij^ [xix crossed out] li vijs viijd ob

Remaynyth to ye church iijs ob

[29] Space left.

[30] The Lady chapel.

[31] Otterham.

[32] Stones.

[33] Hartland Abbey, Devon?

[34] St Dominick. Oliver Padel suggested Richard Lord identification.

[35] Space for Christian name.

[f.15v]

***Competus Johnannis Payne, ^Willelmi Sperk^ generalium receptorum ecclesie Sancti Andrie de Stratton factus Dominica post festum Omnium sanctorum anno domini millessimo* ccccc xlv *et anno regni Henrici octavi dei gracia Anglie, Francie & Hibernie regis, defensoris fidei et in terra ecclesie Anglicane et Hibernie supremi caput tricesimo septimo* [8 November 1545]**

Recepts

^Recevyd of Rychard Curre & John Ede recevers ye yere past	iijs ob^
In primis recevyd of John Trevelian for Allhalwyn yelde	xs
Item received of Mathe Rose for Seynt Androw ys yeld	xiijs
Item received of Thomas Hekytt for Owr Lady yeld	xxvjs viijd
Item received of Crysts yeld	xiijs iiijd
Item received of Seynt Thomas the Appostoli ys yeld[36]	xs
Item received of Wylliam Coper, Trinite warden	xiijs xd ob
Item received of Thomas Arundell esquier[37] for ye chancell	xvjs viijd
Item received of George Mayar & John Antony, Hyecroswardens	vs iijd ob
Item received of Wylliam Payne & Edward Jule besydes yt they before paid to Rychard Currye & John Ede for Owr Lady & Seynt George wardens[38]	iiijd
Item received of Mawt Lang & Mary Symon, Owr Lady Maydens	iijs viijd
Item received of John Rose junior & Wylliam Wyll, ^Sent Armels wardens^	iijli viijs ijd

Summa rec ixli xiiijs ijd

f.16

Expenses

Memorandum payd to George Jule for ij days & *dimidia* for workyng apone the northe punyon & a pone ye gutter mete, drynke & wages	xiiijd
Item paid to John Mower for a day & halfe for ryddyng of ye chancell & zeftyn of grete	iijd ob
Item paid to Stephyn Glanfyld for a days warke there, mete, drynke & wages	iijd
Item paid to John Bryant yn parte of payment for ^zayng of^ the treys	iijs iiijd
Item paid to John Mowr for rowtyng of a tre	iiijd
Item paid to John Avery yn parte of payment for helyng of ye chancel	vjs
Item paid to the same John for ij days & half a pone ye northe churche	xvjd
Item paid to Rychard Call iiij^m^ lathe naylys & halfe ^m^ & ij c	vijs
Item paid to John Bryant more yn parte of payment for zayng	iijs iiijd
Item paid [for v^c^ of lathes to Thomas Hekytt ijs jd crossed out]	
Item paid to John Avery for more for helyng of the chancell	vjs
Item paid to Thomas Hekytt viij^c^ of helyng stonys	ijs viijd
Item paid to the plumer for [s crossed out] mendyng of the olde ledd	xijd
Item payd to John Mocke for cuttyng of ye lower yends of the ^[thers crossed out] treys^ mete & wages	vijd
Item paid to Thomas Clerke for rowtyng of treys	xd
Item paid to Thomas Hewett the glasyer[39]	xxxiijs
Item paid to Nycolas Judde for [space] yre warke of the chauncell wyndow	xxvjs viijd
Item paid to John Cholwyll for parte of payment for ye chauncell rowfe	xxs
Item paid to Bownde & hys brother for zayng	iiijs
Item paid for makyng of the bekyn at Launcels	viijd

36 Was the original dedication to Becket?

37 Space left for John Kempthorne's name?

38 St George and Our Lady Holmadon's amalgamation.

39 Mattingly, 'Who Made the St Neot Windows?', pp.227–32.

Item paid more to Bownde & hys brother for zayng iijs
Item paid to John Mayor & W Sparke for makyng of the alers vs [xxd crossed out]
Item to Thomas Arunder[40] esquier iiij^c^ lathys xxd
Item paid to Nycholas Judde more for yre warke for ye chauncell wyndows ixs xd ob
Item paid to John Rose senior for Cholwyll v[j crossed out]s viijd
Item paid to Nycholas Wyll for Cholwyll vjs viijd
Item paid to George Jule for pargettyng of the chauncell viijs
Item paid to Basterd for lycens to cary morestone over ye More[41] xd
Item paid to Nycholas Mocke for zayng of the bottome of ye elmys vjd
Item paid to ye same Nycolas to serve the masons, mete ^ dryng iiijd
Item paid ^to^ Wylliam Baron for a m of helyng stone iijs xjd
Item paid to the tyler for tyle lefte viijs
Item paid for the makyng of this acompte vjd

[f.16v]

Summa expenses viijli xijs vd
So *remanet de clar ecclesie* xxjs viijd

***Competus Thome Taylor senior & Johannis Wade generaliium receptorum factus Dominica post festum Omnium Sanctorum anno Christi m^i^llessimo* ccccc xlvj *et anno regni regis Henrici* viij *dei gracia Anglie, Francie & Hibernie regis, defensoris fidei & in terra ecclesie Anglicane et Hibernie supremi caput, tricesimo octavo* [7 November 1546]**

Recepts

Memorandum received of John Payne & Wylliam Sparke generall recevers the yere past xxjs viijd
Item received of John Hore, Trinite warden xxxiiijs vd
Item received of John Trevelian for All Halwyn yeld vjs viijd
Item received of Rychard Currye for Seynt Androw ys yeld vijs
Item received of John Rose for Owr Lady yeld vijs
Item received of Wylliam Rodde for Crysts yeld vjs viijd
Item received of John Hore for Seynt Thomas yeld vjs viijd
Item received of Raphe Auger & Rychard Curry [for crossed out], Hyecroswardens xs viijd ^ob^
Item received of Water Symon & Rychard Servys wardens of Owr Lady & Seynt George xxiijs ijd ob
Item received of Nycholas Pery & Thomas Tayler junior wardens of Seynt Armell iijli iiijs ijd
Item received of Master John Brode & Thomas Hore, Sextens ijs vjd ob
Item received [of Rychard crossed out] of Nycholas Judd & Rychard Curye for plate of sylver[42] vjli ijs iijd

Summa xvjli iijs ob

f.17

Expenses delyuered to Rychard Chamond armiger for goyng yn the kyngs grace ys besynes iiijli
Item payd to the sawdyrs xxs
Item paid to Thomas Hekyd for ij swerds & ij dagers vs iiijd
Item paid to John Rowland junior & Rychard Jule, Hye Crosse wardens xs

[40] Arundell.

[41] For Rowtor, Bodmin Moor quarry licence, see CRO, P167/5/1, f.42.

[42] Church plate, 1548.

Item paid to John Trevelyan for makyng of wrytyn	ijs viijd
Item paid to Thomas Hyckytt for the l dole[43]	xxxviijs
Item paid for ij yerds of crymsyn velfotte	xx^iiijs^ iiijd
Item paid to the vestement maker for makyng of ye vestment	vjli
Item paid for makyng of the bargayne	iiijd
Item paid for makyng of ys accompt	vjd
Item paid to Master Vicar for Seynt Armell meneday[44]	xijd
Summa xvli ijs ijd	
Remanet cler to the church xxs xd ob	

[f.17v]

***Competus Johannis Jule & Johannis Antony generalium receptorum factus primo die mensis Januarij anno domini m^l^ ccccc xlvij et anno regni regis Edwardi dei gracia Anglie, Francie & Hibernie regis, defensoris fidei & in terra ecclesie Anglicane et Hibernie supremi caput, primo* [1 January 1548]**[45]

Recepts

In primis recevyd of Thomas Tayler & John Wade recevers the last yere past	xxs xd ob
Item received of Raphe Auger for Alhalwyn yeld	vjs viijd
Item received of Wylliam Merman & John Cobeldick, Owr Lady & Seynt George ys wardens	xxijs xd
Item received of Seynt Androw ys yeld	vjs viijd
Item received of Owr Lady yelde	vjs viijd
^Item received for Crysts yelde	vjs viijd^
Item received of Seynt Thomas ys yeld	vjs viijd
Item received of Thomas Lang & Androw Sangwen, Sent Armell ys wardens	lvs
Item received of Wylliam Payne & Robert Barry, Sextens	iijs xd
Item received of John Rose for the vycar for costage	iijs [ijd crossed out] ^iiijd^
Item received of John Hore for a pownd of wex	[xijd crossed out] vijd
Item for old wex	[vjd crossed out] vd
^Item received of John Marys	iiijd[46]^
Summa vijli iid ob [*summa* vjli xiijs ob crossed out]	

Expenses

Memorandum payd to John Olyver, Trinite warden	iijs [ixd crossed out] ob
Item paid to the brodyer	vjs viijd
Item paid to John Marys & Raphe Auger for the xvth dole	xxxvs viijd
Item paid [mor crossed out] to John[47] Beys, Hycrose warden	ixs viijd
[+Item paid to Raphe Auger for that he was to pay of ye xv dole iiijs crossed out]	
Item paid to John Coke ys wife	viijd
Item to Bodyscastyll men & for to make a hawne	vs
Item paid for makyng of ys accompt	vjd

[*Summa* liijs iijd ob *Remanet cler* iiijli ^ixd^ to ye church crossed out]

Summa iijli xijd ^iiijd^ ob

Remanet iijli xixs iiijd

iiijli xiiijd [ob crossed out] & remanet iijli xixs viijd

[43] Fifty dole tax. Entries at bottom of page 160 appears to relate to a Stratton troop fighting in France.

[44] 16 August.

[45] This account should have been made in autumn 1547.

[46] Marginal entry: vijli vjd ob.

[47] Space left.

f.18
[blank page]

[f.18v]
***Competus Johannis Rose senior generalis receptoris & George Mayor sociise suis de parochia de Stratton factus Dominica ante festum Sancti Andrie appostoli Anno domini mi^l^lessimo* ccccc xlviij *et anno regni regis Edwardi sexti dei gracia Anglie, Fraunce & Hibernie regis, defensoris fidei & in terra ecclesie Anglicane et Hibernie supremi caput, secondo* [25 November 1548]**

Recepts

In primis recevyd of John Beys & Edward Horetopp [general recevers crossed out], ^Hye Crosse wardens^ the yere past lixs
Item received of John Jule & John Antony generall recevers the yere past iijli xixs iiijd
Item received of John Brode & Nycholas Gyst, Owr Lady & Seynt George ys wardens xviijs ob
Item received of Thomas Tayler for yt Sir Wylliam Martyn servyd ^for^ the vicar & others yt he recevyd xxvjs iiijd
Item received of Margaret Chyng & Alson Petheck, Owr Lady Maydens xvijs
Item received of Rychard Olyver & John Grove wardens of Seynt Armell xxxjs jd ob
Item received of Wylliam Hore & John Lamerton, Sextens iiijd
Summa xjli xjs ijd

f.19
Expenses

In primis paid to Rychard Wryng & John Cobeldyck, Hye Crosse wardens xs
Item payd to Sir Wylliam Martyn of the mony yt we had of ye vycar yt he servyd for hym vs
Item paid to John Marys & Thomas Tayler to go to Seynt Marywyke to ye kyngs vysitors lvs
Item delyvered to Wylliam Grove & Stephyn Daw for the besynys yt was yn the weste parte[48] xs
Item paid for bred to them xvjd
Item paid for chese yt they had with them xjd ob
Item paid to Master Thomas Arundell by the honds of Wylliam Yeo to pay them yt went west at ys besynys xxxjs iiijd
Item paid to Wylliam Fote for the parysshe gyfte for the kay of [Botryaux castell crossed out] Tyndagell vjs viiijd
Item paid to Master Vicar for ij grayle bucks xvjs viijd
Item paid for caryng frow Peryn to Bodman[49] viijd
Item paid to John Uglow for caryng of them frow Bodman xd
Item paid to Master Vicar for halfe parte of a bock callyd Erasmus vjs
Item paid for makyng of ys accompte vjd
Summa vijli iiijs xjd ob
Remanet iiijli vjs ijd ob
Solut John Marys & Nycholas Judd
quietus est

[f.19v]
The accont of John Marys, Nycholas Judde stokewardens yn the thurde yere of our soveryng lorde Edwarde the sexthe by grace of God of Inglonde, France & Irelond kyng, defender of the faythe & yn yerthe the supreme hede bothe of the church of Inglond & also of Irelond [1549]

48 Helston rebellion 1548: see Introduction.
49 Penryn to Bodmin.

[Item payd for horssemett whan we rode with Master Schereffe ijs vjd crossed out]
Item payd unto the
Item recevyed off Thomas Heckett for that he recevyed of the parysche xxviijs vd
Item recevyed off Rychard Wryng & John Cobeldeke, Hycrossewardyns xvjd
Item recevyed off Rychard Core for halfe the pecktors ijs viijd
Item recevyed off John Davy for that he was send with the parische ijd

Summa xxxijs vijd

Item payd for the mett off x horsses when the compeny ded ryde wt Master Schereffe to serve the kynges mageste ijs vjd
Item payd unto John Marys for that he dede serve with company ijs v[iijd]
Item payd to Rychard Core ijs viijd
Item payd to Rychard Call ijs viijd
Item payd to John Jude ijs viijd
Item payd to Thomas Martyn ijs viijd
Item payd to John Davy ijs viijd
Item payd to Rychard Olyver ijs viijd
Item payd to Roger Meyo ijs viijd
Item payd to Robert Yeo ijs viijd
Item payd to Nycholas Bond ijs viijd

f.20
Item payd unto John Moke for makyng off the gaylles[50] iiijd
Item payd unto Thomas Clarke for helpyng them upe ijd
Item for makyng off the a comt vjd

Summa expences xxxxs ijd

soe remenethe – ijs vd wyche ys deleveryed un to Wylliam Yeo xd parte off payment of ijs viijd[51]

[50] Gallows. Rose-Troup, *The Western Rebellion*, p.356, fn.1 comes to the same conclusion, but did not make the Mourton link.

[51] Notes on the back cover (see frontispiece and plate 3) regarding a 1540 Treburtle court case. References to John Robyn, Launceston and Robert R… v. John Geeke etc. See, CRO, P216/25/185 for court case.

Part 3

General Receivers' Account Book 2: 1557–81

[f.1]
Liber compotatis gardianorum numerosorum parochiarum Stratoniensi pertinens[1]

Factus in anno[2] ***saluti nostrae millesimo quingentesimo [septuagesimo sexto*** **crossed out]** ***quinquagesimo septimo***

[ff.1v–2v]

[f.3]
The a cownt of Nycholas Yoe & John Lamerton stokewardyns yn the yere of our lorde God *m^l^* ccccc lvij & ynthe fowrethe & the fythe yere of our sovyreign lorde & lade Phelep & Mare by the grace of God kyng & quene of Ingland, Spane, both Cicelles, Fraunce, Jherusalem & Ireland deffenders of the fayth etc [1557]

The recettes

Inprimis recevyed of Thomas Taylor syneor & Rychard Hore stokewardyns the last yere	xlvs jd
Item recevyed of Rychard ^Hore^ for a hole yeres rente for hes tenement that he holedethe yn Hele[3]	
Item recevyed of the same Rychard for the pastoure of [the wood]	
Item recevyed of John Ude for a hole yeres rente ^yn Sto[neland]^[4]	
Item recevyed of John Judde for a hole yeres rente ^for two [medows][5]^	
Item recevyed of Wyllyam Sperke for a hole yeres rent[6]	
Item recevyed of John Dobell for a hole yeres rente in Mel[lock][7]	
Item recevyed of Nycholas Yoe for a hole yeres rente[8]	
Item recevyed of John Langdon for a hole yeres rente in Exnet[her][9]	
Item recevyed of the thurde parte of Hele mell	
Item recevyed for the Glybe[10]	

Sum – vijli xvs vd

[f.3v]

Expences

In primis deleveryed unto John Braye & Wylliam Martyn, Sextons[11] the last yere	ijs viijd
Item payd for a quere of paper to make thes boke	iiijd
Item payd for parchement to cover thes boke[12]	jd

1 CRO, P216/25/208. The original is faded and water-damaged, so the headings are copied twice in later-sixteenth-century and nineteenth-century-hands. The nineteenth-century hand concludes: 'This Book was begun AD 1557 and was ended AD 1582 and contains the Stockwardens' Accounts during that time' signed GBK. This account is in poorer condition than the other two, with a lot of fading and many damaged or even detached edges of pages, and sums missing or incomplete. Folio numbers have had to be assigned. There are a number of blank pages starting with ff.1v–2v.

2 Corrected from *anor*?

3 Hele or Pont-Hele was ex-chantry land which lay in the south of Stratton, with a mill and a wood. See parish map (Figure 1) and Goulding, *Blanchminster Records*, for the history of this and the other church lands listed below.

4 Stoneland alias Pope's Place near the Strand, Bude.

5 Parish meadows.

6 For Treburtle, Tresmeer parish.

7 Millook, Poundstock parish.

8 For the church house.

9 Exe, Week St Mary.

10 Glebe land.

11 Only the Sextons and the High Cross store definitely survived the 1548 dissolution of guilds and chantries.

12 Part of a late 15th or early 16th century Antiphoner or Breviary used by Benedictine monks, see cover image.

Item payd for parchemente to make a rentall ijd
Item geven unto the belefowneder to paye for hes dener vjd
Item payd unto the glasear for hes fee iijs iiijd
Item payd unto Wyllyam Payne for the makyng of a feythement of the churche howse xvjd
Item payd unto Wyllyam Hore & Thomas Hortope for drawing of stonys to make the heght awter xviijd
Item payd unto Robat Bonde & to John Schurt, Heghtcrosewardyns [the] last yere to paye for the mendyng of the thurd belle ys claper vs
Item payd unto John Maryes & Nycholas Judde & there other men for there expences & att two sondrye tymes whan thay dede sette the subsyde iiijs
Item payd unto Thomas Heckett for a loke & a keye & a pere of gemys for the boxe that the sacrament ys yn xijd
Item deleveryd unto Wylliam Yoe & John Pere junier for there expences att the vysytations vs
Item payd unto the constabells for the quitanse of the kyngs & quenes yn payment of the last subsyde vjd
Item payd unto John Mares for the lorddes of Benemy[13] ys heght rentts for Stone lond & Helles warde[?] vjs xd
Item payd unto Thomas Heckett for a sence iijs iiijd
Item payd for heght rents for Mellok ijs vijd
Item payd unto John Ley att Lonston[?][14] for the heght rentts of Treburtell suit & for servyse xiijd ob
Item payd unto John Antony for tember for the boxe to poutte the sacrament yn vijd
Item deleveryd unto [p crossed out] Wylliam Feremoth to delever unto Annys
Gere wedow towardds the makyng of a hagh att Treburtell iijs iiijd
Item payd unto John Sangwyn & John Jule for metyng of grownde & Treburtell xijd
Item payd of the makyng of thes a cownt xd

expences – xlvs ob remaynethe to the chirche clere – vli xs vd

[f.4]

The accowont of Thomas Heckett & Wylliam Sperke stokewardyns yn the yere of our lorde God M^l^ ccccc lviij & yndeth yn the furst yere of the rayne of [quene crossed out] Elezabyth by the grace of God, quene of Ynglond, France & Irelond deffender of the faythe [1558][15]

Recetes

In primis recevyed of Nycholas Yeo & John Lamerton wardyns the yere past vli xs vd
Item recevyed of Jacob Call & Thomas Olyver, Sextons the yere past jd ob
Item recevyd of Martyn Powyele for a geft to the grett belle xijd[16]
Item recevyed of hes wyff for a geft to the bell xd
Item recevyed of Rychard Hore for a hole yeres rent yn Pont Hele xxxs viijd
Item recevyed of the same Rychard for the payesture of the woode vijd
Item recevyed of John Ude for a hole yeres rente for Stone Lands xijs
Item recevyed of John Judde for a hole yeres rente for ij medowys
Item recevyed of Wylliam Sperke for a hole yeres rent yn Treburtell
Item recevyed of Wylliam Dowbell for a hole yeres rente for Melloke
Item recevyed of Nycholas Yeo for a hole yeres rentt
Item recevyed of John Langdon for a hole yeres rentte for Exenether
Item recevyed of Thomas Uglow for the thurde parte of Helemell

13 Binhamy.
14 Launceston?
15 '1558 1 Eliz' added in nineteenth-century hand in the margin.
16 Sums from here are on a detached fragment of paper.

Item recevyed for the Glybe

Summa Recettes – xjli ijs viijd ob

Expences

Item payd to the lordds of Benemye for hyzghe rentt for Hele, Stoneland & Exnythyr
Item payd for the heygh rentts of Melloke ijs vijd
Item payd for the heygh rentts of Treburtell & for sute xiijd ob
Item payd for a smoke clothe & for the makyng for powre Johane[17] xixd
Item payd for brede & drenke for the powre un Newars yevyn[18] & other charge ordenarii att that tyme vs vjd
Item payd unto Wylliam Payne & to Nycholas Symon to pay for the dener whan t[hey] ware with Master Underdon & to aske cownesell appone sertyn wretyngs vjd
Item payd unto Masterr Underdon for drowyng uppe the wrettyng viijd
Item payd for expences whan that counsell was askett of Master Chamo[nd] & Master Underdon att Wylliam Yeo ys howse
Item payd for waxe for seleng of the wretyng
Item payd unto Elen Bole for wascheng of powre Johane ys clothyng
Item payd unto Matthe the clokemaker
Item payd for the wedyng of the woodde

[f.4v]

Item payd unto the constabells & to fowre other men that ratyfyed the subsydy iiijs
Item payd for the quitance vjd
Item payd unto Rychard Wreng for two days worke att the brege[19] with hes horse xixd
Item payd unto John Davy & to John Ude & Thomas Martyn for hes horse one day xixd
Item payd unto Elen Bole att a nother tyme for wascheng of powre Johane vjd
Item payd unto the forbor for clensyng of the churche harnys vjs
Item gave by the avyse of the viij men to the clarke of Hartlond[20] xijd
Item deleveryed unto John Whyt the beleffownder att the begenyng of hes worke[21] xs iiijd
Item payd unto Jose Mowre for the carege of xx^ti^ lode of cleye & for the make of the haulls yn the grownd to sette the posses for the bellfonder ys howse xiiijd
Item payd unto John Gest & to hes man for setting uppe of the tember of the howse for the bellfowndder & for mett & wages xijd
Item payd unto Jacobe Croseman for thackyng of the howse mett & wages viijd
Item payd for naylls ijd
Item payd unto Jacob Croseman for stonys & the caryge home xd
Item payd unto John Uglow for to trusse of strowe to thecke the howse xvjd
Item payd unto Robat Bawys for one das worke mett & wages vd
Item payd unto John Cobeldeke for carege of stonys fyve days [with to horse crossed out] iiijs ijd
Item payd for hes mett & drynke that fyve days xxd
Item payd unto John Davy for drawyng of stonys iiijd
Item payd unto John Whyt for taking downe of the bell & for drenke xiijd
Item payd unto John Cobeldeke for xiiij pownd of brasse iiijs viijd
Item payd unto Walter Beteke for xv pownd of brasse vs
Item payd unto Thomas Wyer for iij pownd a quarter of brasse xiijd
Item payd unto Alsyn Carlyne for fyve poownd of brasse xxd
Item payd unto John Buschell for [lxxx crossed out] lxxxiiij pownd of brasse xxviijs

17 Poor relief.
18 New Year's Eve.
19 Town bridge?
20 Hartland, Devon to the north of Stratton.
21 Possibly a Bristol bellfounder.

Item a lowyed John Judde yn hes rent for sertyne lyme wyche was unpayed for whan the brege was vettyd ijs iiijd
Item payd for Walter Wolffe ys mett & drenke a halffe a day ijd
Item payd for the makyng of a newe rewell vs
Item payd for two pownd of waxe to sett apone ye rewell ijs
Item payd for wekes & for the makyng of the waxe iijd ob
Item payd unto John Buschall for xxxiij^ti^ pownd of brasse more xjs
Item payd for a horse to care the the brasse iiijd
Item payd unto Martyne Powyll for xxiiij pownd of brasse xs iiijd
Item payd unto Thomas Taylor for xlij pownd of brasse iiijd
Item payd unto Wylliam Heddyne for the stapell of the bell wyche ys x pownd ijs jd
Item payd unto John Whyt for wyzghtyng of [of crossed out] the bell ijs [ijs crossed out]
Item payd for naylls to hang uppe the harnys ijd
Item deleveryed John Whyte ye mony vs
Item payd unto Wylliam Baron for xliiij pownd of mettell xiiijs viijd
Item payd unto John Rosse for xxxvj^ti^ pownd of mettell xijs
Item payd unto Rychard Call for xxij pownd of mettell & one pownd he geve vijs viijd
Item payd unto Wylliam Rodde for xij pownd of brace iijs viijd
Item payd for the faketts makyng vjs
Item payd for wyzghtyng of the brace vjd

[f.5]

Item payd unto John Averye for viij pownd & halffe of mettell ijs xd
Item payd unto John Whytt for hongyng upe of the bell vs
Item payd unto John Whyt & the man ys soper whan the bell was taken upe viijd
Item payd for expences att sondreye tymys the belfounder & sertyn of the viij men xixd
Item payd for a seme of woode to mellte the metell vjd
Item payd unto John Lamerton for sertyn woode att the same tyme iiijd
Item payd unto Rychard Call for naylls to truse the grett bell iijd
Item payd unto Wylliam Jule for xx lode of claye xijd
Item payd for v bellroppes xs
Item payd for a new claper for the bell xijs
Item payd for mendyng of the brases of the bell ijd
Item payd for candells ijd
Item payd for thes a cownt xijd

Summa – xjli [vijs xd ob crossed out] xs ijd ob
so remaynyth to Thomas Hecket & Wylliam Sperk – vijs vjd [vs ijd crossed out]

[f.5v]

The accountt of Nycholas Symon & John Rowlond stoke wardens in the yere of our lorde God *m^lli^* ccccc lix & yn furst yere & rayne of our soueryng lade Elezabeth by the grace of God quene of Inglond, France & Irelond deffender of the fayth etc [1559]

Recettes

Item *in primis* recevyed of Rychard Hore for a hole yeres rentt yn Pontte Hele xxxs viijd
Item recevyed of John Udye for a hole yeres rentt yn Stone Londe xijs
Item recevyed of Rychard Hore for the pasture of the woode vijd
Item recevyed of John Judde for a hole yeres rentt for two medowys xvjs
Item recevyed of Wylliam Sperke for a hole yeres rentt yn Treburtell ixs
Item recevyed of Wylliam Dobell for a hole yeres rentt yn Melloke xxs
Item recevyed of John Longdon for a hole yeres rentt yn Exenether xijs
Item recevyed of Nycholas Yeo for a hole yeres rentt[22] viijs

[22] Church house annual rent.

Item recevyed of Thomas Uglowe for the thurde parte of Hele mell ijs
Item recevyed for the Glybe jd
Item recevyed of Rogger Yeo of the harnys[23] monye xxvs
Item recevyed of Thomas Hekett & Wylliam Sperke wardyns the yere past ccx li *dimidia* of bell metell
Item recevyed of Nycholas Judde for two honderede ^of the same metell^ after iiijd the pownd iijli vjs vjd
Item recevyed of the same Nycholas for xli & a halfe wych was corse mettell after ijd ^ye pownd^ xxjd
Item recevyed of John Maryes & Thomas Whyt for ^cc^ [the crossed out] faketts att Hele woode ijs vjd

Summa – xli vjs iijd

Item payd to the lordds of Benemye & Strotton for hygh rentt for Ponte yn Hele, Stone Land, Exnether vjs xd
Item payd for the high rentts of Melloke ijs vijd
Item payd for the hygh rentts of Treburtell & for sute xiijd ob
Item payd unto Thomas Heckett & Wylliam Sperke for that they hade leyed owte more than thay hade receved the yere past vijs vjd
Item payd unto John Whyt the bellfownder xxvs
Item payd unto Nycholas Judde for the same John Whyt iiijli
Item payd unto Thomas the bellfounder ys servant for a rewarde for hes payns iijs iiijd
Item payd unto Margett Crempe for the kepeng of powre Johane xijd
Item payd unto Rysse Phelepppe for hes howse att the furst tyme vjd [xijd vjd crossed out]
Item payd unto Ryce Phelypp for [att crossed out] att a nother time xijd
Item payd unto Thomas Heckett for the mendyng of the cloke xiijs iiijd
Item delyveryd unto John Averye & to Wylliam Well the churche wardyns att thre sundry tymys xxxxs
Item payd unto the constabells for that lacked of ther sume of ther bell the yere past and for ther quettance ijs
Item payd unto Ryce Phelypp att Medesomer last for powre Johane ys howse xijd
Item payd unto John Baron & to John Hewe for the careg home of tember wyche made the howse to cast the bell yn iiijd
Item payd for expences for the constabells & fowre other men whan thay appered before the commyschyners & for the subsydy at to sundry tymes iiijs vijd
[f.6]
Item payd unto Margret Crempe att a nothyr tyme xijd
Item payd unto John Gest for a carped for the tabell[24] vjs viijd
Item for expences appone the offychall to speke to the quenys maieste ys vyseters for us ijd
Item payd unto Thomas Whyt & to Robat Nele, Sextyns the yere past xiijd ob
[Item payd for the making of thes acount viijd crossed out]
Item payd for the aquitanse for the subside vjd
^Item payd for the making of thes accounts^ *Summa* ^viijd^

summa – ixli xs iijd
so remaynythe clere – xvjs

[f.6v]
The a cownt of Wylliam Yeo & Rychard Jule stoke wardance in the yere of our lorde God *m^lli^* ccccc lx & yn therde yere & rane of our soveryng lade Elezabeth by the grace of God quene of Inglond, France & Irelond deffender of the fayth etc [1560]

[23] Parish armour.
[24] Communion table carpet. See appendix 3.2.

Recettes

In primis recevyed of Nycholas Symon & John Rowlond wardance the yere past	xvjs
Item recevyed of the Sextonse the yere paste	iijs xd
Item recevyed of Rychard Hore for the hole yeres rentte yn Pontte Hele	xxxs viijd
Item recevyed of the same Rychard for the pasture of the woodde	vijd
Item recevyed of John Ude for a hole yeres rentte for Stone Londe	xijs
Item recevyed of John Judde for the rentts of two medowys	xvjs
Item recevyed of Wylliam Sparke for a hole yeres rentte yn Treburtell	ixs
Item recevyed of Wylliam Dobell for a hole yeres rentte yn Melloke	xxs
Item recevyed of John Langdon for a hole yeres rentte yn Exnether	xijs
Item recevyed of Nycholas Yeo for a hole yeres rentte	viijs
Item recevyed of Thomas Uglowe for the thurde parte of Helemell	ijs
Item recevyed for the Glybe	jd
Summa – vjli xs ijd	
Item payd unto Wylliam Payne for the makyng of dyvers wretyngs the yere past	ijs
Item payd for a schrowde cloth for John Davye	ijs vjd
Item payd for sertyn mercymentts of Treburtell more then was before peyd	vjd
Item payd unto J. [J[crossed out] Maryes to ryde to Lanston[25] for the discharge there of	viijd
Item payd for vj men ys dener att the furst callyng for the subsidy	ijs jd
Item payd for the dener att the daye of s[er]tyffycats	ijs vjd
Item deleveryd unto the churche wardens before Ester	xs
Item payd unto the constabells for the quytanse for the subsyde	vjd
Item payd for expences for the viij men whan thay ware yn besenys for the parysch att dyvers tymys	xd
Item payd unto John Maryes for hes costs & payne to ryde to Weke to make unswere before the schereffe for the churche londe	viijd
Item pay unto the same John to ryde to Lonstone to make unswere before the quenes recever for the church landds	xxjd
Item payd for the makyng of thre schertts wyche was geven to the powre	vjd

[f.7]

expences

Item payd unto the same John for hyghe rentts for the lordds of Benemy	vjd[26]
Item payd for hyghe rentts for Treburtell	xiijd
Item payd for hyghe rentts of Mellocke	ijs [vijd]
Item destrybyte to the powre yn money & brede	vjs [viijd]
Item payd unto John Ude for thes yere for yeverye weke iiijd sume	xvijs iiijd
Item payd for the makyng of thes a cownte	vjd

Summa – lixs vjd ob

Remaynyth – iijli xs vijd ob

in wyche sume ys lost by the falle of the mony – ixs vijd

so remaneth clere iijli xiijd ob

[f.7v]

The accontt of John Maryes and Wylliam Baron stoke wardens in the yere of our lorde God *m^lli^* ccccc lx[ii crossed out]j & yn the fowrthe yere & rayne of our soueryng lady Elezbeth by the grace of God quene of Inglond, France & Irelond deffender of the fayth etc [1561]

In primis recevyed of the wardance the yere past Wylliam Yeo & Rychard Jule	iijli xiijd ^ob^

[25] Launceston, as also Lonstone.

[26] Should be vjs viijd. Edge torn.

Item recevyed of Rychard Hore for one hole yeres recete yn Ponte Hele xxxs viijd
Item recevyed of the same Rychard for the pasture of the woodde vijd
Item recevyed of John Ude for one hole yeres rentt xijs
Item recevyed of John Judde for two medowys one hole yere rent xvjs
Item recevyed of Wylliam Sperke for one hole yeres rentt for Treburtell ixs
Item recevyed of Wylliam Dobell for one hole yeres rentt for Melloke xxs
Item recevyed of John Langdon for one hole yeres rentt for Exnether xijs
Item recevyed of Nycholas Yeo for one hole yeres rentt viijs
Item recevyed of Thomas Uglowe for the thurde parte rentt for Helemell ijs
Item recevyed of Stephen Smale for Glybe[27] jd

Summa – viijli xjs iiijd ob

[f.8]

expenses

Item payd for the change of xij base testrons wyche we recevyed of the wardyns
Item payd unto John Ude alias Jenken for thes yere xvijs jd
Item payd for a schrowde for Annys Mowre xviijd
Item deleveryed unto Margett Skekerd yn her seckenes iijd
Item payd for the expences of John Meger whan he gave hes advyse yn makynge upe of our churchestyle jd ob
Item payd for a smoke clothe for Alsyn Martyne xxiijd ob
Item delyveryed unto our newe clarke[28] att Whytsondaye att hes foruste comyng ijs
Item payd unto Vensent Calmade for the newe makyng of our recoverye xxjs
Item deleveryed unto Margett Crempe yn her sekenys & nessecite ijs
Item payd unto the surgen that coute her iijd
Item payd unto Rychard Call for the makyng of two newe keys & reppynge of the lokes & the mendyng of other lokes
Item payd for expenses for John Meger & the mason whan thay we[nt] to see the worke [illeg. word] tember[?] xjd[?]
Item deleveryed unto Wylliam Braye & to Nycholas Sander wardens xxviijs
Item deleveryed unto them att a nother tyme xviijs
Item payd for hyghe rentts to the lordds of Benemye [for T crossed out] vjs xd
Item payd for the hyghe rentt of Treburtell xiijd ob
Item payd for the hyghe rentt of Melloke ijs vd
Item to be deleyveryed unto the powre of the parysch vjs viijd
Item for the makyng of thes a cownte vjd

Summa expences vli xs[?]

remaynyth of clere of these sute xls
Item there yevyn for Cristemas [?]. x
[whare of there is [illeg. word] crossed out]
Item yn to for [illeg. word] crossed out] crownys [?] the lost
Item t[w]o schelyngs [illeg. word] yeres past
the hole yere

[f.8v]

[f.9]

The account of John Rose thellder & John Jud stocke wardens in the yere of our lorde God [156 crossed out] m ccccc lxij *anno quinto* Elizabethe etc [1562]

Receptes

In primis recevid of the olde wardens John Marrys & Wylliam Baron lixs jd ob

[27] Space left above.
[28] William Archer or Orchard.

Item more received of Christofer Hore in parte of payment of vli vjs viijd for a fyne[29]	liijs iiijd
Item received of Richerd Hore for a hole yeres rent yn Pont Hele	xxxs viijd
Item received of the same Richard for ye pasture of Hele woode	vijd
Item received of John Udy for a hole yeres rent	xijs
Item received of John Jud for a hole yere rent	xvjs
Item received of Wylliam Sparke for a hole yeres rent of Treburtell	ixs
Item received of John Dobell for a hole yeres rent of Mellooke	xxs
Item received of John Langdon for Exnether ^for a hole yeres rent^	xijs
Item received of Nycholas Yeo for a hole yeres rent	viijs
Item received of Thomas Uglo for a hole yeres rent for ye third parte of Hele myll	ijs
Item received of Stiven Smale for the Glebe	jd
Item received of Wylliam Braye & Nicholas Saunder, Hye Crosse wardens the yere past	ijs
Item more of ye same wardens iiij base shillings	

Summa total of the recepts – xjli vs iijd ob

Expences

In primis delivered to Emmet Pethycke this yere at certen tymes	xviijd
Item paid for a newe gowne for the same Emmet Pethicke	vjs
Item delivered to Wylliam Wescot on Candellmas daye in his syknes	vs
Item paid to the clocke maker for the newe makyng of the clock	xxjs
Item more delivered to the Hyecros wardens at dyvers tymes	xlviijs iiijd
Item paid to John Marrys for hye rent for the lordes of Benami & Stratton	vijs xd
Item paid for hye rent for Treburtell	xiijd ob
Item paid for hye rent for Mellooke	ijs vjd
Item paid [f crossed out] to Jenkyn for this hole yere	xvijs iiijd
Item to be delivered to the poure folke of ys parisshe	vjs viijd
Item for making of this accompte	vjd

Som of ye expences – vli xvjs xd ob

So remaynethe clere to ye churche – vli viijs vd & iiij base testers

[f.9v]

The acownt of Nycholas Well and John Schurt stoke wardyns yn the yere of our lorde God m ccccc lxiij anno Elizabeth *regena* sexto [1563]

In primis resevyed of John Rosse siner John Judde wardynse the yere past	iiij base testons	vli viijs vd
Item resevyed of Rychard Hoore for a hole yeres rente yn Pont Hele		xxxs viijd
Item resevyed of John Udy for a hole yeres rente yn Stone land		xijs
Item resevyed of the same Richard Hoore for the pasture of the woode		vijd
Item resevyed of John Judde for a hole yeres rente		xvjs
Item resevyed of Nycholas Yeo for a hole yeres rentt		viijs
Item resevyed of Wylliam Sperke for a hole yeres rent yn Treburtell		ixs
Item resevyed for a hole yeres rent of Mellocke		xxs
Item resevyed of John Langdon for a hole yeres rent yn Exnether		xijs
Item resevyed of Thomas Uglowe for the thurd part of Hele mell		ijs
Item resevyed of Stephen Smale for the Glybe		jd
Item resevyed of Crestoffor Hoore yn parte of hes fyene		xlvjs viijd
Item resevyed of Thomas Beare yn full payment of hes fyene[30]		xiijs iiijd
Item resevyed of Justyne Jule & Nycholas Perye, Hyecrosewardyns		iiijs

[29] Christine Hore is named as tenant of Ponte alias Hele in 1563, CRO, P216/25/85.

[30] Reversionary lease of Ponte alias Hele etc. See CRO, P216/25/85.

Item resevyed of Nicholas Judde for a geffte towardds the makyng of the brege iijs iiijd
Summa of the hole resetts – xiiijli vjs jd, iiij base testers

[f.10]

Expenses

Item payd unto the lordds of Benemye for hygh rentts vjs xd
Item payd for the hygh rentts of Mellocke ijs vijd
Item payd for the hygh rentts of Treburtell xiijd [ob]
Item payd unto John Udy alias Jenkyn for thes hole yere xvijs iiijd
Item payd unto Rychard Servys towardds the relyffe of hes chelederne frome the xxiiij^ti^ day of Januarij untell the xxvij^ti^ day of June vijs viijd
Item payd to John Judde & Roger Yeo, Thomas Jule, Thomas Ronall ijs vjd
Item deleveryed unto a powre man wyche hade the quenys browde sele xijd
Item deleveryed unto Androwe Sangwyn & to Nycholas Call churche wardyns vjs viijd
Item payd unto John Mabyn for mendyng & kepyng of the cloke vs
Item payd to Androwe Sangwyn & to Nycholas Call att a nother tyme xxxs
Item deleveryd unto the same Androwe & Nycholas Call att a nother tyme vjs viijd
Item gave to Morse whan he came to take the work of the brege xijd
Item payd for the constabells & fowre other men ys expences to Botruxcastell[31]
& ells whare that ratyfyed the subsyde iiijs viijd
Item payd for the aquittans for the payment there of vjd
Item payd to Morse att a nother tyme vijs
Item payd unto Morse a nother tyme xx[d]?
Item payd to the same masin for makyn [of crossed out] of the lytell brege[32] for mette & wages xvjd
Item payd for a blanket for Emet Pedoke iiijs
Item payd for careng of mourestonys xjs v[j]d
Item payd to Morse att Weke fere[33] vs iiijd
Item payd to vj men for fellyng[34] of the weste syd of the brege, mette, drenke & wages iijs
Item payd to iiij men more, mett, drenke & wages ijs
Item payd to iij wemen yn the same worke, mette & wages js vjd?
Item payd for [t crossed out] iij horsses one halffe day vjd
Item payd for two horses a nother halfe day iiijd
Item payd to ij men fellyng of the same, [horses?], mett ^wages^ vj[d]
Item payd to ij men to serve the mason att the lytell brege, mett ^wages^ xijd
Item payd for the makyng of thes accownte viijd
Summa expences – vijli xjs iijd ob
remayneth clere – vjli xiiijs ixd ob & iiij base testers etc

[f.10v]

The accompte of Nycholas Jud & James Call stockewardens yn the yere of our lorde God m ccccc lxiiij anno Elzabethe septimo [1564]

In primis recevid of Nycholas Wyll & John Short stockewardens the laste yere vjli xiiijs ixd ob & iiij base testons
Item resevyd of Rychard Hore for a whole yeres rente in [Stone land crossed out] Pont Hele xxxs viijd

[31] Boscastle.

[32] 'Little bridge' and 'bridge' refer to Stratton's former clapper bridge near Bridge Cottages and much rebuilt town bridge at Bridge Street.

[33] Week St Mary fair was held on 8 September. See Gazetteer of Markets and Fairs to 1516, www.history.ac.uk/cmh/gaz/cornwall.html (accessed 16 January 2006).

[34] Unclear if filling or felling trees is meant here and below.

Item more of the same Richard Hoore for ye pasture of ye woode vijd
Item recevid of John Udy for a yeres rent in Stone land xijs
Item recevid of John Jud for a yeres rent for ij medowes xvjs
Item recevid of Nycholas Yeo for a yeres rent viijs
Item recevid of Wylliam Sparke for a yeres rent in Treburtell ixs
Item recevid for a yeres rent for Mellooke xxs
Item recevid of John Langdon for a yeres rent for Ex nether xijs
Item recevid of Thomas Uglo for a yeres rent of ye third parte of Hele mill ijs
Item recevid of Steven Smale for the Glebe jd
Item recevid of Nycholas Call & Andrewe Sangyn, Hye Cross wardens the laste yerexvjs xd
The some of all thes recepts – xiijli xjd ob & iiij base testons
[f.11]

The Expences

In primis payde unto John Short for expences that he layde oute when theye were at Botrescastell before the comissioners for ye subsyde ijs
Item payde to Wylliam Hore for drawing of stone for the brydge ii[js]?
Item payde to Whortop for drawyng of stone the same tyme vj[d]
Item payde to Master John Reskarocke for a gyft to help Mussell home oute of Fraunce vjs viijd
Item more delivered unto Ede Smale the xvj^th^ daye of Januarye she lying sycke xijd
Item more delivered to the olde Bole at the comandement of ye parisshe to geate him a testimonial ijs
Item paid ^at Bodman^ for the pryckyng of the procession in iiij parts ijs[35]
Item delivered to Robert Nele & Symon Hollman, Hye Crosse wardens vjs viijd
Item paid for a smock clothe for Emet Pethick js
Item paid to John Mabyn for keeping of the clocke vs
Item paid to John Short for yt he was overe rekened in his accompt as it dothe appere by the accomte of Nicholas Call & Andrewe Sangwyn Hye Crosse wardens xi[s or d]
Item paid for expences for the constabells & ij other men when theye were before the comissioners for the subsyde & for a quytans j[s]
Item paid for a pere of shows for Emet Pethicke xd
Item paid for exepences for John Marris & John Jud when theye were at the chepter courte at Lanceston for the roode lafte ijs vd
Item paid to the clarke for keeping of the clocke j quarter of a yere xvjd
Item paid to the clark also for wyer for the clocke ijd
Item paid to an organ player for looking upon the organs xijd
Item paid for expences for John Marris & John Jud at an other chepter courte which was holden on Lamas daye ijs vijd
Item delivered to Johane Kytowe to warde the buldyng of a newe house upon the churche lands iijs iiijd
Item delivered to John Corye & Christofer Hore towards the newe cawse[36] vijs iiijd
Item paid for ij bocke yt is a parafrace of Eurasmus & a psalter viijs[?]
Item paid to John Marris & John Jud for expences & makyng ye bylls ^& for other charges^ when they were at Hunington[37] with my lord bishop for the roode lofte xviijs viijd

[f.11v]
Item paid to John Marris & John Jud for theire dynner at a chepter courte holden at Sent Marye Weke xijd
Item paid to the lordes of Bynamye & Stratton for hye rents vjs xd

35 Adding music to a processional book.

36 Causeway at Bude?

37 Honiton, Devon.

Item paid for ye hye rent of Treburtell xiijd ob
Item paid for the hye rent of Mellooke ijs vijd
Item delivered to Whyte the bell fownder at the comandement of the parisshe for a gyft vs
Item paid to Rycherd Cory for stones for the bridge & for drawyng of the same stones vjs
Item paid to Master Anderdon to be a cownsell with us aboute our churche lands [& crossed out] vs
Item we have taken up of this accounte to distribute amongst the poure peple yt be not sufficientlye relived with the gathering of the parisshe vjs viijd
Item for makyng & keeping of this accompte viijd

Sum of ye expences – vjli xiiijd ob
so remenithe clere – vijli ixd & foure base testons[38]

[f.12]

The accownt of John Maryes & Nycholas Sau[nder] stoke wardyns yn the yere of our lorde God M^ll^ ccccc [ccccc crossed out] lxv *anno* Elezabeth regina [sextyns crossed out] *octavo* [1565]

In primis resevyd of Nycholas Jude & *Jacobus* Call stokewardyns the yere past ^vijli ixd, iiij base testons^
Item resevyd of the Hyzght Crose wardyns the yere past lvjs iiijd ob
Item resevyd of Rychard Hoore for one hole yerres rentt xxxs viijd
Item of the same Richard for the pasture of ye woode vijd
Item resevyd of Thomas Jule cordener[39] for one hole yerres rentt ^for Stone land^ xijs
Item resevyd of John Jude for a yerres rent for two meedes xvjs
Item of the same John for a yerres rent for Mellocke xxs
Item resevyd of Nycholas Yeo for a yeres rent viijs
Item resevyd of Wylliam Sparke for a yerys rent yn Treburtell ixs
Item resevyd of John Longdon for a yerys rent yn Exnether xijs
Item resevyd of Thomas Uglowe for a yerys rent for Hele mell ijs
Item resevyd of Stephen Smale for the Glybe jd
Item resevyd for iij basse testers passelle of our resett vjd
Item resevyd of John Jude for the fine of Mellok[40] iiijli iijs iiijd
[Sume of the hole Resetts – xvli vijs xjd ob quarter crossed out]
Item resevyd for John Udy ys herett[41] iijd
Summe – xixli [vijs crossed out] xjd ob quarter

Expences

Item delveryed unto Hyzghcrosse wardens vjs viijd
Item payd to John Mabyn for kyepyng of the cloke iiijs iijd
Item payd to a powre man wych hade the quenys browdesele xijd
Item payd for chargges yn the fee courte att John Evyn sute ij[s?]
Item payd to a nother powre man owte of Brewton[42] xijd
Item delveryed unto the Heyzghcrosse wardyns att a nother tyme xs
Item payd to a nother powreman wych burned hes howse vjd
Item delveryed unto the Hyezghcrosse wardans att a nother tyme vjs viijd[?]

[38] Accounting marks occur here and elsewhere in the accounts.
[39] Shoemaker. See CRO, P216/25/33 for his 1556 reversionary lease.
[40] CRO, P216/25/22.
[41] Stone land, CRO, P216/25/33.
[42] Bruton, Somerset.

Item payd for the hyere of a horse & expences att Schere[43] att the sute of John Evyn iiijs ixd
Item payd to Rychard Perye for carege of stons to make a kell[44] iiijd

[f.12v]
Item payd for expences att Exceter & home for John Marryes [ad crossed out] & Wylliam Rode whan the chuche ^wardyns^ & the hole parysch was excomunycatt[45] xiiijs^vjd^
Item payd for the revacachyon yn wretyng & the sele vjs iiijd
Item payd for wyne & goodchere for the buschuppe ys servants ijs viijd
Item deleveryd unto the Hyezghcrosse wardans att a nother tyme vjs viijd
Item payd to John Whytt for castyng of the belle vjli
Item payde for brede & drenke for men to helppe upe the belle off ^the grownd^ iiijd
Item payd for a quarter of lyme for the brege iiijs
Item payd John Meger for v days worke, mett & wages vs
Item payd to Bonde the mason for vj days worke, mette & wages vjs
Item payd to Bonde ys man for iij days worke, mette & wages ijs
Item payd to John Cole to serve the masonce, mette & wages viijd
Item payd to Michall Howper for serve the masons viijd
Item payd to Hortoppe for drayng stons xijd
Item payd for hye rent for Treburtell xiijd ob
Item payd for hye rent for Mellocke ijs vijd
Item payd for hyezgh rentt for Ponte Hele ijs
Item payd for hyzght rent for Stone land iijs iijd
Item for the church howse iijd
Item payd for hyzght rentt for Exenether xvjd
[Item we have retayned to deseburse to the powre vjs viijd crossed out]
Item payd to Nycholas Bond for one croke of xixli & halffe for the bell vjs^vjd^
Item payd to the same Nycholas for a nother croke of xijli iiijs
Item payd to Richard Wreng for a croke wych wayed xli iijs iiijd
Item payd to Justyne Jule for a croke waying xiiijli & a quarter iiijs vd
Item payd to John Rowlond for a croke wayng xli iijs iiijd
Item deleveryed to the Hyecrose wardyns att a nother tyme xxs
Item to be destrybyt unto the powre vjs viijd
Item for the makyng of thes a cownt viijd
Sume of the hole expences – xiijli [iiijs iijd ^xd^ob crossed out]^ixs vjd ob^
remaynethe clere – vjli [vjs vd quarter crossed out]^xxjd quarter^

[f.13]
The a cownt of Thomas ^Hekkett^& Wylliam Brey general resevers in the yere of our lord God m^lli^ ccccc lxvj yn the nenthe yere of quene Elez[abeth] [1566]

Resetts
In primis resevyed of John Marryes & Nycholas Sander wardanse the yere past vjli xxjd
Item resevyed of ^Robert Sander Crestoffor Hoore^ the Hyecrosse wardynse the yere past ijs ii[jd]
Item resevyed of Rychard Hoore for a yerers rentt yn Punt Hele xxxs viijd
Item resevyed of the same Rychard for the pastowre of the wood vijd
Item resevyed of Thomas Jule corver for a yerrs rent yn Stone land xijs

[43] Shire court?
[44] Kiln.
[45] For refusing to take down the rood loft. Kilmington parishioners in East Devon were also excommunicated in 1561–62; see Cornish, *Kilmington Church Wardens' Accounts*, p.15.

Item resevyed of John Jude for a yerrs rentt for two meedes xvjs
Item of the same John for a yerrs yn Mellocke xxs
Item resevyed of Nycholas Yeo for a yerrs rentt viijs
Item resevyed of Wylliam Sperke for a yerrs rent yn Treburtell ixs
Item resevyed of John Langdon for a yerrs rent yn Exe nether xijs
Item resevyed of Thomas Uglowe for a yerrs rent for Hele mell ijs
Item resevyd of Stephen Smale for the Glebe jd

Summe – xjli xiiijs iiijd ob

[f.13v]

Expences

Item payd to Robat ^Sander^ & to Crestoffor Hoore, Hyecrose wardynse the yere past vjs^ vijd^
Item payd to Thomas Badcoke & to Peter Halett, Hyecrosse wardyns vijs
Item deleveryed more att sondrye tymes to Thomas Badcocke & to Peter Halett xliiijs
Item payd to the clarke of the market for a bocke of a syse of the statuttes for wyzghtes & mesures xijs
Item payd to the relyffe of a powre chelde fownd att Jacobstowe xijd
Item deleveryed att two sondrye tymys to proprietors of lazar howses xvjd
Item deleveryed unto the lame Helhen att Warpestowe[46] xijd
Item payd to Roger Yeo for a schorede clothe for Robat Bawse ijs^viijd^
Item deleveryed unto Wylliam Sperke & John Baron supervyserys for the hyeways for makyngs of the cawse vs vid
Item payd to John Mabye for kyepeng of the cloke the yere past vs[?]
Item payd to Wylliam Payne for brasse for the bell xs
Item payd to two powre men att a nother tyme xvjd
Item payd to Wylliam Warmenton [x crossed out] lxvij^li^ of brasse xxijs iiijd
Item payd for the glassing of one wendowe yn the clarke ys chamber xxd
Item payd for the careg of a [bav crossed out] lame bawe[47] to Marhamchurch xijd
Item payd for hye rentts to the lordds of Benemy for Stone land iijs iijd
Item payd to the same lordds for hye rentts for Ponte yn Hele ijs
Item payd to the same lordds for the hye rentts of Exnether xvjd
Item payd for the hye rentt of Treburtell xiijd ob
Item payd for the hye rentts of Melloke ijs vijd
Item payd for the hye rentts of the churche howse iijd
Item payd for mendeng of the cawse by Heckett ys gardyne vjd
Item to the powre vjs viijd
Item for the makyng of thes accownt viijd

Summa expences – vijli [iiijd crossed out] ^xd^ ob
remayneth clere – iiijli xiij[j crossed out]s vjd

[f.14]

The a count of Nicolas Yeoo & John Avery generall recevers in the year of our lord God m ccccc lxvij in the x year of Elizabethe our quyne [1567]

In primis recevid of Thomas Hikette & Wylliam Braye being general receverse the year past iiijli xiijs vjd
Item recevyd of Wyllyam Warmentonne gevinn to the bell xijd
Item receyd of Thomas Badcock & Peter Halett, Hyecroswardens in the year past vijs xd ob quarter
Item received of Rychard Hoore for a years rent in Pont Heell xxxs viijd
Item received of the same Rychard for the pasture of the woode vijd

46 Warbstow.
47 Lame boy?

Item received of John Jude for a yearse rent for two medowys	xvjs
Item received of the same John for a yearse rent in Mellocke	xxs
Item received of Thomas Jule corver for a yearse rent in Stonland	[x]ij[s]
Item recevyd of Nycolas Yeo for a yearse rentt	v[iijs]
Item received of Wyllyam Sperke for a yearse rentt yn Treburtell	ixs
Item received of John Langdon for a yearse rentt yn Exenyther	xijs
Item received of Thomas Uglowe for a yearse rent for Hele mell	ijs
Item received of Stevyn Smaelle for the Glyebe	jd

The hoolle sum of recettes comethe to xli xijs viijd ob quarter

[f.14v]

Expenses

Item for expences at Camellford for ij constabells & ij other men for the queyns supsidye	ijs iiijd
Item payd for ther horsmeett	ixd
Item foor ther expences at Stratton at the satyfykett	xvjd
Item payd for makyn of ther byll	iiijd
Item deleverd to a poore man	vjd
Item gevenn to a cownseller	xs
Item payd for a blankete for Margaret Skeycarde	iijs
Item deleverd to a poore doum man	iiijd
Item deleverd to Peter Quyk & Harry Heygeynes, Hyecroswardens this year	vjs^viijd^
Item payd for a quittnes for the supsyde	vjd
Item deleverd to another poore man	iiijd
Item deleverd to Peter Quyke & Harrye Heygynes at sondry tymes	lijs vjd
Item deleverd to the clarke of the market	iijs vd
Item payd for wyeghtes	ijs iiijd
Item payd to Roger Yeoo for iij yeardes & a halfe of canvase to make a sheytt for Joonne Mooke	ijs iiijd
Item payd to the clarke for kypyne of the clooke	vs
Item deleverd to another poore man	iiijd
Item deleverd to a poore man of Lanstoune	viijd
Item payd for beryng a lame woman at Mara[m]churche	xvjd
Item payd for hye rentt of Stouneland	iijs iijd
Item payd for hye rentt of the churche howse	iijd
Item payd for hye rentt for Treburtell	xiijd ob
Item payd for hye rentt of Exenether	xvjd
Item payd for hye rentt of Pontheell	ijs
Item payd for hye rentt of Mellowke	ijs vijd
Item to the poore	vjs viijd
Item payd for makyng of thys acompte	viijd

Sum of expences – vli xjs xd ob quarter

remenethe clere – vli xd quarter

[f.15]

The accompte of Wylliam Yeo & Nycholas Call generall recevors yn the yere of our lorde God 1568 made the xixth daye of December anno Elizabethe regine x[j] as folowethe [19 December 1568]

In primis recevyd of Nycholas Yeo & John Averye recevers in the yere past	vli x[d quarter]
Item recevyd of Henrye Hyggyns & Peter Quycke, Hyecrosse wardens	xxijs iiijd
Item recevyd of Wylliam Rad for the first payment of the woode	xxxs
Item received of Rycherd Hore for one yeres rent yn Pont Hele	xxxs viijd
Item received of the same Rycherd Hore for the pasture of ye woode	vijd
Item received of John Jud for j yeres rent of ij medowys	xvjs
Item received of ye same John Jud for j yeres rent of Mellooke	xxs

Item received of Thomas Jule cordiner for j yeres rent in Stone land xijs
Item received of Nycolas Yeo for j yeres rent viijs
Item received of Wyllyam Sparke for j yeres rent yn Treburtell ixs
Item received of John Langdon for j yeres rent yn Ex nether xijs
Item received of Thomas Uglowe for one yeres rent for Hele myll ijs
Item received of Steven Smale for the Glebe jd
Sum of the receptes xiijli iijs vjd quarter[48]
[f.15v]

The expenses for the yere as folowethe

In primis paid for iiij mens dynner when theye were abowte the subsydye for the laste payment xvjd
Item for makyng of the byll of subsyde iiijd
Item for the acquyttance vjd
Item delivered to John Cotten & John Braye, Hyecrosse wardens vjs viijd
Item delivered to the same wardens also when theye went to the visitacion vjs viijd
Item delivered to the same wardens to ye poynting of the towre xlixs
Item delivered to a poore man with one legge viijd
Item paid to Roger Yeo for a shrowde for Robert Baylye the taylder ijs viijd ob
Item paid to the clarke for keeping of the clocke vs
Item delivered to Thomas Hycket towards the pentyse xxiiijs jd
Item delivered to poore men at an other tyme iiijd
Item paid to Roger Yeo for a shert for the olde Bole ijs iiijd ob
Item delivered to a poore man at an other tyme xijd
Item delivered to an other poore man viijd
Item paid for hye rent of [Treburtell crossed out] ^Ex nether, Stone land, Pont Hele & ye churche howse^ vjs xd
Item paid for hye rent of Treburtell to John Alye xiijd ob
Item paid for ye hye rent of Mellooke ijs vijd
Item delivered to the poore people at ij tymes in the churche xd
Item delivered to the red Roberts wife xijd
Item delivered to Margerye Ketowe vjd
Item delivered to John Marrys & John Jud for theyre charges when theye were before the comissioners at Launceston vs
Item delivered to Thomas Hycket at an other tyme xls
Item delivered to Thomas Hycket xxvjs viijd
Item delivered to Thomas Hycket xiijs iiijd
Item delivered to Thomas Hycket xxs
Item paid to Roger Yeo [more crossed out] for a blanket for Margerye Ketowe iiijs viijd
Item to be distributed to the poore vjs viijd
Item paid for makyng of this accompte viijd
Some– xjli xjs ijd ob
So remaynithe clere by this accompte– xxxijs iiijd quarter

[f.16]

The accompte of John Jud & Rycherd Call generall recevers yn the yere of our lorde God 1569 made the xviijth daye of December *anno* Elizabethe regine xij as folowethe [18 December 1569]

In primis receved of Wylliam Yeo & Nicholas Call recevers for the laste yere xxxijs iiijd quarter
Item recevyd of John Braye & John Cottel,^Hye Crosse^ wardens xlixs

[48] 13. 3.6.quarter in margin. First use of Arabic numerals in Stratton accounts? See also date on p.180.

Item received of Robert Sawnder & others for Helewoode iijli ixs
Item received of Rycherd Hore for j yeres rent in Pont Hele xxxs viijd
Item received of Rycherd Hore for the pasture of the woode vijd
Item received of John Jud for one yeres rent of ij medowes xvjs
Item received of John Jud for one yeres rent of Mellooke xxs
Item received of Thomas Jule cordener for one yeres rent in Ston land xijs
Item received of Nycolas Yeo for one yeres rent viijs
Item received of Wyllyam Sparke for one yeres rent in Treburtell ixs
Item received of John Langdon for one yeres rent in Exnether xijs
Item received of Jone Uglowe for one yeres rent of Hele myll ijs
Item received of Steven Smale for the Glebe jd

Sum of the receptes – xiijli viijd

[f.16v]

The expenses for this yere

In primis paid to Thomas Hycket aboute the pentyce xxiiijs
Item paid more to Thomas Hycket for the same ijs iiijd
Item paid more to John Marrys for the charging forthe of a man when theye went in to Irland ^as yt apperythe by a byll^ there of made xxiiijs iijd
Item paid to Anthonye Arthure & an other man for theyre charges forthe & back to Bodman when theye were before the comissioners iijs iiijd
Item delivered to John Baron & Wylliam Perse, Hycrose wardens at severall tymes xxs
Item delivered to Roberts wife for keping of Marget Kete one halfe yere iijs iiijd
Item paid to John Cottell for the bull ryng xd
Item paid to John Marrys for rydyng to Camellforde & at an other tyme to Lanceston before the comissioners for his charges iiijs iijd
Item paid for charges of John Marrys, Nicholas Yeo, John Jud, John Short when theye dyd rate the parisshe for harnis[49] xvd
Item paid to Master Chamonds clarke for ij bocks concerning the harnys & the mooster ijs
Item paid to John Corye for makyng of a byll according to the statute to laye before the comissioners vjd
Item paid to Nicholas Jud & John Cory for charges theye layde out in counsels fees & for the discharging of the clarke of the market xviijs vjd
Item paid towarde Brydge rule[50] brydge more then the constabells gatheryd iiijs xjd
Item paid for the newe bendyng of the Beble xs
Item paid to the clark for keeping of the clocke vs
Item paid to Wylliam Heddon for makyng of a bell clapper iiijs iiijd
Item paid to Mabyn for mendyng of the clocke iiijs iiijd
Item paid ^to Nicholas Oliver^ for a shrowde for Jone Aferys ijs viijd
Item paid to ij poore men that gatheryd to ^ij^ hospitals xxd
Item paid to Ede Smale at the comandement of the viij men at divers tymes ijs
Item paid [for crossed out] to John Marrys for hye rent vjs xd
Item paid for hye rent of Treburtell to John Alye xiijd ob
Item paid for hye rent of Mellooke ijs vijd
Item paid for a shrowde for ye old Cole to John Yeo iijs ob
Item paid to John Yeo for a shrowde for an Ieryshechylde that dyed in Nicholas Bonds house xviijd
Item reserved to be distributyd amongst the poore vjs viijd

[f.17]

Item paid for makyng of this accompte viijd

Sum of the hole expenses [vi crossed out] viijli xxiijd
so remenythe clere – iiijli xviijs ixd

[49] Douch, *Cornwall Muster Roll 1569*.

[50] Bridgerule, Devon.

1570

The accompte of Nycholas Jud & Christofer Braye generall recevers in the yere of our lorde God 1570 made the xvijth daye of December yn the xiijth yere of Quyne Elizabethe etc

In primis recevyd of John Jud & Richerd Call recevers for the yere past iiijli xviijs ixd
Item recevyd of John Baron & Wylliam Perse churche wardens the last yere ixs viijd
Item recevyd of Rycherd Hore for one yeres rent in Pont Hele xxxs viijd
Item received of Rycherd Hore for the pasture of the woode vijd
Item received of John Jud for one yeres rent of ij medowes xvjs
Item received of John Jud for one yeres rent of Mellhooke xxs
Item received of Thomas Jule cordener for one yeres rent in Stone land xijs
Item received of Nycolas Yeo for one yeres rent viijs
Item received of William Sparke for one yeres rent in Treburtell ixs
Item received of John Langdon for j yeres rent in Ex nether xijs
Item received of Jone Uglowe for one yeres rent of Hele myll ijs
Item received of Steven Smale for the glebe jd
Item received of Thomas Hyckyt towards the newe butts xijd
Sum of the hole recetes – xiijli ixs ixd

[f.17v]

The expences for this yere

In primis [recevy crossed out] deliveryd to v boyes for syngyng in the quyre at Christmas xvd
Item paid for a smocke for a poore mayde which the tynker left here xijd
Item paid to a mayde to attend her whyle she laye sycke iiijd
Item paid for a shrowde for the same mayde xvjd
Item delivered to ij poore men that came oute of Irland with a pasporte xijd
Item delivered to Margery Kytow in bred when she laye sycke iijd
Item delivered to a lame boye which came oute of Camellford with a pasporte viijd
Item paid to Davye Walkye to carye a precept from the Justyce to Master John Kympthorne iiijd
Item paid for a brekefaste for John Marrys, Nicholas Jud, Nicholas Yeo, John Jud & Wylliam Braye when theye were at Master Prideaux his courte or hall[51] Mondaye for maters of the churche howse xiiijd
Item sent to Wylliam Marten when he was in the gayle for the parishes gyft iijs iiijd
Item delivered to Rycherd Oliver one of the collectors for the poore to help relyve Margerye Ketowe yn her sycknes xijd
Item delivered to John Cory & John Wade churche wardens vjs viijd
Item delivered to Roberts wife for house rome & keeping of Margerye Ketow for Our Ladye daye quarter xxd
Item delivered to a poore man of Salteasshe[52] the xvjth daye of Aprill that came with a testimonial to the churche xijd
Item paid to John Mabyn for keeping of the clocke vjs viijd
Item delivered to ij poore men in the churche the vjth daye of Maye viijd
Item paid to Thomas Whyte for standing of the butts iijs iiijd
Item paid to John Short for meate & dryncke that he had deliveryd to Alse Cooke yn her syckenes viijd
Item delivered to Bedlyme & his sone in theyre sycknes at severall tymes ijs iijd
Item delivered to iiij men coming oute of Irland with a pasporte iiijd
Item sent to Nycholas Oliver of Sent Tyes[53] to help hym in his sickenes vjs viijd

[51] Prideaux Place, Padstow.
[52] Saltash.
[53] St Ives.

Item paid for expences at Camellforde for John Jud & Walter Yeo when they were before the quynes commissioners xxd
Item paid for wrytting of certen articles the same tyme xvjd
Item delivered to John Cory one of the churche wardnes when the communion cup was bought iiijli
Item paid for hyghe rent to the lords of Bynamy & Stratton vjs xd
Item delivered to poore Thomas wyfe to paye for hes leche craft & to departe awaye iijs iiijd

[f.18]
Item paid for expences for John Marrys, Nicholas Yeo, William Braye & John Jud at the chapter courte at Lanceston the Frydaye after Sent Lukes daye[54] aboute the rood lofft iij[s]
Item paid to Nicholas Hortop for makyng of the watche house[55] iij[s]
Item delivered to a man of Anthonye[56] which had taken lost by surtye ship as apperyd here by his testimoniall xijd
Item paid for hyghe rent of Mellhooke ijs [vijd]
Item paid to Wylliam Rad for taking downe of the organs ijs
Item more to Wylliam Rad for a pece of a borde to set the organes upon viijd
Item paid for hyghe rent of Treburtell xiijd ob
Item paid to John Cory for makyng of the feoffement of Stone Land & Mellhooke[57] viijd
Item paid for paper to put in this bocke jd
Item delivered to the churche wardens at an other tyme xls
Item we have taken up of this accompt to distribute amongst the poore vjs viijd
Item paid for makyng of thes accompte viijd

Some of the expences – ixli xviijs vd ob
so remaynithe clere by this accompte – iijli xj[s iii]j[d]

[f.18v]

1571

The accompte of Wylliam Braye & Symon Holman generall recevers yn the yere of our lorde God 1571 made the xvjth daye of December yn the xiiijth yere of the reigne of our sovereign ladye quyne Elizabethe etc [18 December 1571]

In primis recevyd of Nycholas Jud & Christofer Braye recevers for the yere past iijli xjs iiijd ob
Item received of John Cory & John Wade churche wardens the last yere iijli ixs
Item received of John Jud for woode & tymber that he had in Melloke vjs viijd
Item received of Rycherd Hore for one yeres rent in Pont Hele xxxs viijd
Item received of Rycherd Hore for the pasture of the woode vijd
Item received of John Jud for one yeres rent of ij medowes xvjs
Item received of John Jud for one yeres rent of Mellooke xxs
Item received of Thomas Jule cordener for j yeres rent in Stoneland xijs
Item received of Nycolas Yeo for j yeres rent viijs
Item received of William Sparke for one yeres rent in Treburtell ixs
Item received of John Langdon for one yeres rent in Exnyther xijs
Item received of Jone Uglowe for j yeres rent of Hele myll ijs
Item received of Steven Smale for the Glebe jd

54 20 October 1570.
55 Replacing the 1543–44 one on Beacon Hill at Efford?
56 Antony, near Saltash.
57 CRO, 216/25/22.

Item received of John Marris for certen church stuffe solde to Misterys Marye Arundell xxs
Some of the recetes – xiijli xvijs iijd ob

The expences for this yere 1571

In primis paid to Thomas Whyte for j halfe yere for standing of the buttes xxd
Item delivered to ij poore mariners viijd
Item paid to John Yeo for iiij yerds & a halfe of linclothe to make Alse Cooks shrowd iijs
Item paid for iiij yerds of linclothe for Marget Skyberds shrewde ijs xd
Item paid for iiij yerds of linclothe to shrewde a poore woman that dyed in Sent Marye[58] ijs viijd
[Item paid for] a shrewde for the childe ixd
Item paid for other charges aboute the same poore woman vjd
[Item paid for] weke & a halfe for the keping of the same woman ixd
[Item paid for] syngyng boyes iiijd
Item paid to Wylliam Payne for makyng of the feoffement of Hele[59] ijs iiijd
[Item paid] to Nicholas Oliver & Nicholas Wyll churchewardens vjs viijd

[f.19]

more of the same expences

Item paid for a shrewde for Jone Mocke iijs
Item paid to John Mabyn for kepyng of the clocke vjs v[iijd]
Item delivered to Knights wife when he laye sycke ijd
Item delivered to Master Marris to paye Marten Hortops charges when he went to Bodman for a sawdier xvjd
Item delivered to the churche wardens at an other tyme xiijs
Item delivered to a poore man of Weke[60] xxd
Item paid for a gowne for Jenkyn makyng & all iiijs
Item delivered to a poore man of Sent Penicke[61] vjd
Item paid to Thomas Whyte for the other halfe yere for the buttes[62] [xxd]
Item paid for a shrewde for an other poore chylde xijd
Item paid for a shrewde for Jone Jeffryes chylde xijd
Item paid for a shrewde for a poore woman that dyed in the churche house ijs vd
Item delivered to Richerd Oliver to paye the paver xxd
Item delivered to Jone Moore xijd
Item delivered to a poore Brytton[63] xijd
Item delivered to a poore man that had burnt his house vjd
Item Wylliam Braye spent when he was ryding towards Lestwythell vjd
Item paid to ^Master Marris for^ the foure raters when theye ratyd the subsedye iijs
Item paid to John Lye of Lanceston for the hye rent of Treburtell xiijd ob
Item paid for hye rent to the lords of Bynamye & Stratton vjs [xd]
Item delivered to a poore man of Sent Leonards[64] vjd
Item delivered to a poore man that gatheryd to Sent Laurence[65] xijd
Item delivered to a poore man that had bene a sawldier in Irland iiijd
Item paid for a pasporte to send three beggars to Shrewseberye[66] iiijd

58 Week St Mary?
59 CRO, P216/25/79.
60 Week St Mary.
61 St Pinnock.
62 There is a hole where the sum should be so it is assumed to be same as above.
63 A Breton.
64 Launceston hospital.
65 Bodmin hospital.
66 Shrewsbury.

Item paid for the hye rent of Mellooke ijs vijd
Item paid for an acquittance for the subsedy xijd
Item paid for j iiij yeres hye rent that was byhend to paye ^for Mellooke^ before the makyng of John Juds leasse[67] xs iiijd
Item delivered to a poore man that gatheryd to the house of Tengmethe[68] viijd
Item we have taken up of this accompt to distribute amongste the poore vjs viijd
Item paid for makyng of this accompte viijd

Some of the expences – iiijli xviijs vj[d ob]
So there remenithe clere by thes accompte – v[ii]jli xviijs ixd[69]

[f.19v]

1572

The accompt of John Braye & Robart Saunder generall reseavers in the yere of our lorde God 1572 made the xxjth daye of December in the xvth yere of the Reigne of our soverayne ladye Quene Elizabethe etc [21 December 1572]

[In pri]mis receved of Wylliam Braye & Symon Holman reseavers the ^yere^ past viijli xviijs ixd
Item reseavyd of Nycholas Wyll & Nycolas Olyver hye churche wardens the last yere ixs jd
Item received of Thomas Beare[70] for a yeres rent of Ponthele xxxs viijd
Item received of Thomas Beare for the pasture of the woode vijd
Item received of Elyzabethe Jude[71] for one yeres rent of Melloke xx[x crossed out]s
Item received of the same Elyzabeth Judd for one yeres rent of ij medowes xvjs
Item received of Nycolas Yeo for one yeres rent viijs
Item received of Thomas Jule cordener for one yeres rent of Stoneland xijs
Item received of Avys Sparke for one yeres rent in Treburtell ixs
Item received of John Langdon for one yeres rent of Exnyther xijs
Item received of Crystover Hore for one yeres rent of Hele myll ijs
Item received of ^Steven Smale^ for the Glebe jd
Item received of Rychard Hore[72] for a heryot for his wife xxxxijs iiijd
Item received of Elyzabethe Judd for a heryot for John Judd for Melloke vs
Item received of Elyzabethe Judd for a heryot for John Jude for the medowes iijs iiijd
Item received of Wyllyam Rad for the rodloft vli vjs viijd
Item more of Wyllyam Rad for that was behind to paye of Hele wood xxjs
Item received of Rychard Jule for that he had left in his hand of the monye that was gathered of the paryshe for the brudge viijs

Some of the recetes – xxiijli vs vjd[73]

[f.20]

The accompt of Nycolas Hore & Thomas Juell generall recevers yn the yere of our lord God 1573 made the [ ] daye of Desember in the xvjth yere of the raynege of our soverayne lade Quyne Elyzabeth etc [December 1573]

Item yn *primis* recevyd of John Bray & Robart Saunder recevers the last yere iijli xs xd
Item recevyd of Thomas Bayer for a yeres rent yn Pont Hyell xxxs viijd

67 CRO, P216/25/26 (1563).
68 Teignmouth, Devon, was a Magdalen house: Hanham, *Churchwardens' Accounts of Ashburton*, p.178.
69 Marginal notes: 4li 18s 6d ob, 8li 18s 9d.
70 CRO, P216/25/85 (1563).
71 CRO, p216/25/121 (1556).
72 Hele.
73 Expenses missing.

Item for the pawstur of the woode vijd
Item recevyd of Ellsabeth Jud for one yeres rent in Melhoke xxs
Item received of the same Ellsabeth the ij medowes for one holle yere xvjs
Item received of Nycolas Yoe for one yeres rent viijs
Item received of Thomas Juell cordener for one yeres rent in Stone land xijs
Item received of Avys Sparke for one yeres rent in Trebertell ixs
Item received of John Langdon for one yeres rent in Exnether xijs
Item received of Chrystofer Hore for one yeres rent of Hell myll ijs
Item received of Steven Small for the Glebe jd
Item received of Thomas Bayer & Rychard Marks church wardens the last yere ^xxxiijs^viijd
Item received of Wyllyam Rode for lyme yt was Water Y[e]o lyft to the bridge xijd

The some of the recettes – xli xiiijs xd

[f.20v]

The expences for thys yere

[Item] *yn primis* paid to Wyllyam Rode the same daye xlviijs
Item paid to Rychard Walky & John Hore church wardens vjs viijd
Item paid to Robart Sander for a per of schowys for Thomas Clarke xviijd
Item paid to Thomas Whytt for one yeres rent for the botts vs
Item paid to John Corre for makyn of ij passe ports iiijd
Item paid to Antony Gad to bring them to Marhamchurch to the constabell ijd
Item paid to the church wardens a gaynst Ester vjs viijd
Item paid to [illeg. word crossed out] Rycherd Hor for one yeres rent for Ellnar Bolle vs iiijd
Item paid to John Mabyn for kyepen of the cloke vjs viijd
Item paid to the church wardens a nother tyme vjs viijd
Item paid for lyme for the bridge vjs
Item paid to the church wardens a nother tyme iijs iiijd
Item paid to Master Underdon for drawyn of a passe port for Jone Morton vjd
Item paid to John Corre for makyn of the same iijd
Item paid to John Adam Chynge ys man, for a dayes work & half to ye bryge ^mett & hyre^ xijd
Item paid to Watter Chyng for a *dimidia* a dayes to the bryge mett & hyre iiijd
Item paid to Terell the massen for ij dayes worke to helpe me & stope ye watter mett & hyre xiiijd
Item paid to Wylliam Rod to bring John Rode to Synt Lenerds att Lawnston xls

[f.21]

Item paid for hye rent of Mell Howk ijs [vijd]
Item paid for hye rent to the lords of Bename & Stratton vjs x[d]
Item paid for hye rent of Trebertell ixd ob
Item paid to Nycolas Olyver & Thomas Juell for tember a bowt the cloke vjs viijd
Item paid to John Gybs for paven of lx yerds & iij att the bryge att a jd the yerd vs iijd
Item paid to Edward Knyzht for workyn to the bryge, mett & drynke & mony xvs jd
Item paid to Wyllyam Rode for worke a bowtt the bryge vijs viijd
Item paid to Robart Sander for a ^nother^ per schowys for Thomas Clarke xviijd
Item paid to iiij men to bere Jone Morton from Orchard to Borro[74] viijd
Item paid to Peter Halett a jd for that he leyd owtt for Exnether jd
Item paid to Thomas Juell cordenar for hys expences att the sessyons att Bodman viijd
Item wye have taken upe of thys a cownt [vj crossed out] to dystrybyt amongst the power vjs viijd
Item paid for maken of thys a cownt viijd

The holl sum of the expences – ixli xiiijs viijd ob
and so restett clere of thys a cownt – xxs jd ob

[74] Launcells, not Week St Mary, to Stratton, see p.131.

[f.21v]

The accompte of John Cory & John Rad generall recevers in the yere of our lorde God 1574 [& crossed out] made the xixth daye of December in the xvijth yere of the reigne of our soveragne ladye quyne Elizabethe [19 December 1574]

The receytes

In primis recevyd of Nycholas Hore & Thomas Jule recevers the yere past xxs jd ob
Item received of Elizabethe Jud for j yeres rent of Mellowke xxs
Item received more of the same Elizabethe for ye rent of ij medowes xvjs
Item received of Nycolas Yeo for j yeres rent viijs
Item received of Thomas Jule cordener for j yeres rent xijs
Item received of Thomas Beare for j yeres rent xxxs viijd
Item received more fore the pasture of the woode vijd
Item received of Agnes Sparke for the rent of Treburtell ixs
Item received of John Langdon for j yeres rent of Ex nether xijs
Item received of Cristofer Hore for the rent of the myll ijs
Item received of John Short for the glebe jd
Item received of the churche wardens of the laste yere xxijs vd ob
Item received of Robert Jud to ylyde?[75] up Ex nether xxs
Item received of John Cory for fyshe taken in the bridge poole vjd
Item received of Nicholas Yeo for a lyme barell viijd
Item received of Walter Yeo ^ye churchewarden^to by harnys xxs
Item received of John Moore for the [tree crossed out] oke yt was bi the churche house xjxd
Some of the recetes is – ixli xvs viijd

[Memorandum we lende to Thomas Badcocke a moore stone contening iij foote & a *dimidia* in lengthe & in brede x inches 1 square & viij inches the other which was a steare of the churche house in price of ijs iiijd or to yelde the lyke stone agayne at the parishe pleasure. Paid in the 8th November costs crossed out]

[f.22]

The expences

In primis paid for paper ijd
Item paid for neales for the roodlafte vjd
Item paid for setting up of the [so crossed out] peces to stop the holes xd
Item for making of a pasporte for a poore man ijd
Item paid for a wryte for Robert Jud[76] vs
Item paid for a special warrant ijs viijd
Item paid for expences for a man & a horse to ryde to the sheriffe xiiijd
Item paid for his labor yt rode xiiijd
Item paid to the bayelyes to arest Robert Jud xxd
Item paid to Thomas Whyte for the rent of the butts for iij partes of the yere which endyd at Lamas iijs ixd
Item paid to the clarke for pricking of one order of songe in the church bocks for servece vs
Item paid to Richerd Hore for Mother Boles rent at Christmas xvjd
Item paid to John Cobelldycke senior for worke aboute the brydge the laste yere xxd
Item paid to William Rad for worke yt he had doune a boute the brydge more then he was paid for iijs ijd
Item delivered to the newe wardens vjs viijd
Item delivered to Garde in his sicknes xijd
Item delivered to Chopes wife in her sicknes iiijd
Item delivered to Lewse Sharsell when he went to Sent Lawrens xxs

75 Yield up.

76 Exe tenancy?

Item delivered to Walter Rose in his sicknes viijd
Item paid to Robert Sawnder yt he had delivered to a poore man when I was lack viijd
Item delivered to a poore man yt had a testimonial undere the seales of me lorde Admirall & of the towne of Lestithell[77] vjd
Item delivered to Gaye of Lesaunt[78] that burnt his howse xijd
Item paid for wyer for the clocke ob
Item delivered to the wardens to send to Bodman for Bishop Juells[79] bocke xiijs viijd
Item delivered to the wardens when theye went to the Archedekens visitacion vijs iijd
Item delivered to a poore man the weke after Ester vjd
Item delivered to Thomas Clarke in his sickenes xijd
Item paid for fetting home viij lode of stones & for sand to mend the wall of the churche howse kychin xvjd
Item paid to John Maygar for ij dayes walling of the same xijd
Item for his meate & drincke viijd
Item for a boye to serve hym meate, drinke & wages ij dayes viijd
Item for v posses of tymber & a pece to make pinnes for the bords & benches of the churche house viijd
Item paid for a halfe busshell of lyme viijd
Item paid to Peter Hallet for worke aboute the bridge the laste yere vjs iijd
Item paid for Mother Boles rent at Ester xvjd
Item paid to Thomas Jule cordener for riding of the roble of the churche house wall[80]

[f.22v]
[Item paid] to Davy Mabyn for keping the clocke halfe the laste yere ijs vjd
Item paid for Roodmas[81] rent for Mother Bole ixd

Item paid for charges aboute the bridge as folowethe
Item paid to John Hamet for ij dayes worke & a halfe, meat, drinke & wages xviijd
Item paid to Raynburne Lucas for *dimidia* a dayes, worke, meate & drinke iiijd
Item paid to Nicholas Bond for a dayes carriage with his ^ij^ horses xiiijd
Item paid more to Nicholas Bond for a dayes work & *dimidia*, meate & drincke xijd
Item paid to Robert Sawnder for a dayes carriage with ij horses ^but^ bisydes yt he gave a halfe dayes labour xijd
Item paid to Nicholas Yeo for a daye & *dimidia*, meate, drinke & wages ixd
Item paid to James Call for his mans labor [a daye & crossed out] ^a^ *dimidia* daye ^& better^met & drink iiijd
Item paid to Peter Hallet for j daye & for his sonne almoste ij dayes ^& for meat & drink^ xviijd
Item paid to John Rad for ij dayes worke & for bering in of his bords ^& mete & drenk^ xiiijd
Item paid to John Hygens for a dayes labour, meate & drenk vijd
Item paid to Raynburne Lucas for ij dayes wages vjd
Item paid to John Corye for his mans labour, meate, drinke & wages, ij dayes & halfe xvjd
Item paid to Jone Call for bord & drynke yt Ma^y^gar & the masons had ijd
Item paid for meate & drinke for John Mayger, John Bond & [John crossed out] ^Ed[ward]^ Knight j daye xd
Item paid to John Mayegar for his wages j daye & halfe & for coming first to vewe the stones xvjd

77 Lostwithiel.
78 Lezant.
79 John Jewel, Bishop of Salisbury's *Apology*. See Duffy, *Voices of Morebath*, p.179.
80 Sum missing. 4li 12s 4d ob running total at the bottom of the page.
81 14 September.

Item paid to John Bond for a halfe dayes worke	iijd
Item paid to John Bond & his sonne for j dayes worke, meat, drink & wages	xviijd
Item paid to Knight for his wages ij dayes	xjd
Item paid to John Yeo for lyme	vs
Item paid to Nicholas Yeo for fetting of iij barrels of lyme from Bede	iiijd
Item paid for sand	iiijd
Item for hellyng slatts to pinne the walle	ijd
Item paid to Androwe Yeo for a dayes worke, meate & drink	vjd
Item for [iiij labo crossed out] John Corye labour ij dayes [& bede crossed out] meate & drinke	xijd
Item for meate & drinke for Knight & Raynburne Lucas j daye	viijd
Item paid to Master Marris for a barell of lyme	ijs vjd
Item paid to Thomsyn Hele for Mother Boles rent at Lamas	ixd
Item paid to iij poore mariners yt had mi lorde of Bedfords[82] licens	iiijd
Item paid to Marye Jule for worke about the bridge the laste yere	xiiijd
Item paid for lyme to mend the wynd barge of the churche house	iijd
Item paid to John Wade & John Jule for drawing of ^36 semes of^ stones for the bridge ^& for cariag of the sand up over cliffe	vijs viijd
Item paid for a costilet full furnished	xxxs
Item paid for a morian	vs [iiijd crossed out]
Item for fettyng of the same from Exeter	ijs
Item for mending of certen hurts in the same harness	jd
[Item paid for] writing of a supplication for Chub	iiijd
[Item paid Thom]as Cater for Helland bridge	vs[83]

[f.23]

Item delivered to a sawldier which came from Holland	
Item for writting of the bocke of covenants for taking of under tenants	vj[s]?
Item paid to the clarke for keping of the clocke this yere	v[js viijd]
Item paid to John Frenshe for hye rent of Mellouke	ijs vjd
Item paid to Master Lye for hye rent of Treburtell	xiijs ob
Item paid to Master Marris for hye rent of Hele	ijs
Item for Stone land	iiijs iijd
Item for the churche house	iijd
Item for Ex nether hye rent	xvjd
Item paid for bering of stones from the crosse[84] in to the churche house	ijd
Item for a pecke & halfe of lyme & somewhat better yt was occupied at the crosse	xvijd
Item for a horse j daye to carye roobell & morter	iiijd
Item paid to Thomas Bole for a dayes worke	iijd
Item paid for Mother Boles rent at All Halloutyde	ixd
Item paid for makyng of this accompte	viijd

Some of the expences – ixli xiiijs ijd

Whereas there hathe bene usyd to take up vjs viijd to distribute amonst the poore we have but xviijd left & ^of^ that we have taken up xijd to distribute amongst the poore & so remain in the stocke - vjd[85]

[82] Sir John Russell knight of Tavistock.

[83] 4li 2s [1 crossed out] 6d running total.

[84] Iconoclasm?

[85] Marginal notations: 19li 3s ob, 9li 19s 2d corrected to 9li 14s 2d.

[f.23v]

The accompte of John Marryes & John Antonye generall recevers yn the yere of our lorde God 1.5.7.5. & made the xviijth daye of Dessember yn the xviijth yere of our soueryng ladye [q crossed out] quene Elizabeth etc [18 December 1575]

The recettes

In primis resevyed of John Corye & John Roode wardyns the ^last^ yere	vjd
Item resevyd of Elezabeth Jude for j yerers rentt for [Treb crossed out] Mellocke	xxs
Item resevyd more of the same Elezabeth for [q crossed out] ij medowys	xvjs
Item resevyd of Nycolas Yeo for j yerres rentt	viijs
Item resevyd of Thomas Jule cordener for j yerres rentt	xijs
Item resevyd of Thomas Beare for j yerres rentt	xxxs viijd
Item resevyd more of the same Thomas for the pasture of the woode	vijd
Item resevyd of Amys Sparke for Treburtell	ixs
Item resevyd of John Longdon for j yerres rentt of Exnether	xijs
Item resevyd of Crestofer Hoore for the rentt of the mell	ijs
Item resevyd of John Schurte for the Glebe	jd
Item resevyd of Water Yeo & Wylliam Mager church wardynes the yere past	xxxs
Item recevyd of John Yeo merchant for the fyne of Exnether yn parte of payment of a more some	viijli
& so remaynethe vjli to pay att Mychalmas next	

Some of the resettes ys – xvli xd

[f.24]

Expences

Item payde a man wages two days to serve the mason abowte the peler	
Item payd for thre men two days for mette & wages	ij[s]
Item payd to Bande & to hes sone for ij days for mette & wages	
Item deleveryed unto Marke Payne & John Sander, Haycrosewardyns	vjs viijd
Item deleveryed unto the procter of Sent Maris of Exceter[86]	vjd
Item paid to Antonye Garde & to balance for careg of a prisoner to Lanston	iijs
Item deleveryed unto the Hyecrosewardyns att a nother tyme	x[s]
Item payd for Elener Bole ys yerres rentt the yere endede att Alsentts daye	
Item deleveryed unto the Hyecrosewardans to by lyme	vjs
Item deleveryed unto Margett Comen a genst Ester	viijd
Item deleveryed unto the Hyecrosewardyns att ij sondrye tymys	xxs
Item deleveryed unto Elener Bole yn her seckenes	xijd
Item deleveryed to the procter of Totnes	viijd
Item deleveryd Wylliam Whale to depart ^frome^ the parysche	js
Item deleveryd unto the wederrs of the woode	xvjd
Item deleveryed unto the procter of the howse of Sent Lenardes	viijd
Item payd for a schroude for Edward Knyzght	ijs viijd
Item payd to Roba[r]t Sander for tember to make iij barrawys	xd
Item payd to Nycolas Sander for tember to make ij other barrowys	iiij[d]
Item payd to John Yeo for tember to make the barres of the barores	
Item payd to Perese to make the barrowys	x[d]?
Item deleveryd unto the procter of the howse of Sent Caterens of Exceter[87]	
Item deleveryd unto Thomas Beare for the wedyng of the woode	
Item deleveryd unto a powre man that was robbed att see	
Item deleveryd to Conce of Jacobestowe howye[88] howse was burned	vjd

[86] St Mary Magdalen's hospital. See Cresswell, *Churches of Exeter*, p.20.

[87] St Katherine's almshouse. See Cresswell, *Churches of Exeter*, pp.90-1.

[88] Whose?

Item payd to the clarke for the kepyng of the [th crossed out] cloke vs
Item payd to John Roode for a mowrestone for the brege iijs
Item payd to Johane Leppe balance to seke Johane Parterege iijd
Item payd to John Mowre for kepyng of Johane Parterege ys chelde iiij wekes and thre days & for her mette & loggyn one [y crossed out] nyzght iijs iiijd
Item payd to Bonde the mason for workyn att the brege xvjd
Item payde to John Mowre & to John Prine to secke Johane Parterege these expences iiij s
Item deveyeryed unto the ryngers the day of the quenes majestyes ix[d][89]
Item payd for a buschell ^& halffe^ of lyme of Strotton mesure[90] for the brege ijs vjd[?]
Item payd to Nycolas Hoore for the carege of a mowerstone to the breg ijs
Item payd for the hye rent for Ponte yn Hele ijs
Item payd for the hye rent for Stone land iijs iijd
Item payd for the hye rentt for the churche howse iijd

[f.24v]
Item payd for the hye rent of Exenether xvjd
Item payd for the hye rent of Treburtell xiijd ob
Item payd for the hye rent of Mellocke ijs vijd
[Item illeg. word for the powre vijs viijd crossed out]
Item payd to Wylliam Hoare for drawyng of stonys for the brege xijd
Item payd to Nycolas Yeo for caryng of the stonys to the brege vjd
Item payd to John Corye to make a passeporte for Johane Parterege ijd
Item payd to John Mowre for kepeng of Johane Parterege one nyzght more iiijd
Item payd to John Yeo & Androw Yeo for working att the brege xijd
Item we have takyn upe for the powre vjs viijd
Item for makyng of thes accounte viijd
Item payd to Jone Parterege to departe the parysche with her chelde vjs viijd
Summa expences – vli xixs [vijd crossed out] ^iijd^ ob
so remaynethe clere – ixli xviijd [ijd crossed out] ob

[f.25]
The account of Nicolas Bond and George Meager generall rec[evers] in the yere of our lord God [157 crossed out] ^1576^ made the xxiij daye of Dessember [in] the xixth yere of the reigne of our souerynge ladye queene Elyzabethe [23 December 1576]

The receyts
In primis recevyd of John Marris and John Antonye recevers the yere pas[t] ixli
Item received of Elizabethe Jud for j yeres rent for Mellooke xxs
Item received of the same Elyzabethe for the rent of ij medows xvjs
Item received of Thomas Beare j yeres rent xxxs viijd
Item received of Thomas Jule cordener for j yeres rent xijs
Item received of Thomas Jule marchant for widynge of Heale woode xd
Item received of Nycolas Yeo for j yeres rent viijs
Item received for a herret for Exnether vjs viijd
Item received of the Highe Crosse waredens xxxvjs ob
Item received of John Langdon for j yeres rent in Exnether xijs
Item received of Thomas Beare for the pasture of the woode vijd
Item received of John Yeo for the last payment of his fyne of Exnether v[jli]
Item received of Annys Sparke j yere rent for Treburtell [ixs]
Item received of Cristover Hore for the rent of the mill [ijs]

89 Sums are on a detached piece.
90 Larger local measure? See BL, Add MS 32243, f.77v.

Item received for the Glybe [jd]

Some of the recetes is – xxiijli vs vijd[91]

[f.25v]

[f.26]

The expence

Item paide for meate & drinke for the poore people in the beginning of the yere at dyvers tymes as by another byll apperethe	xixs ob
Item payde to Water Yeo for clothe to coller iij smockes for iij poore women	ijs ob
Item payde to John Yeo for canves for the same iij smockes	iijs
Item payde for threde for the same	jd
Item payde for makynge the same iij smockes	vjd
Item payde to John Meger for working at the bridge ij dayes	xvjd
Item delivered to the [/Highe/ crossed out] churche waredens	vjs viijd
Item payd to Tamsyn Hele for rent	ixd
Item delivered to the churche waredens at a nother tyme	vjs viijd
Item payde for mendinge of the clocke	xs
Item payde to the clarke for fettynge of the clocke maker	xd[?]
Item payde to a nother clocke maker for mending the clocke	ijs
Item delivered to the churche waredens at a nother tyme	xvs
Item payde to Thomas Call for mending of things about the clocke	xv[d?]
Item payde to John Corye for wyer, oyle & lid for the clocke	
Item delivered to George Holofords wife	
Item delivered to the churche waredens	v [s]
Item delivered to ij poore men with testimonials	xij[d]
Item paid for a shrewde for Towells childe	xixd
Item paid for a shrewde for Annis Buttick	ijs viijd
Item paid to fowre men that went to Camellforde for ratinge the subsidye	ijs xjd
Item paid for counsel concerning the tytell of the churche house[92]	xs
Item paid to John Scott for knowledging of a fine	iijli
Item paid for expences when the viij men agreed with Scot & when the sought counsel	iiijs
Item paid to Colonton haven[93]	xijd
Item paid for making of a feoffement	xvjd
Item paid for drawinge of a fine	xviijd
Item paid for John Scots expences & iiij men more at the syse	xs vd
Item paid to the judge & to his clarke	xs
Item paid to a poore woman for shrewding of the cutler	viijd
Item paid to Nicolas Mocke	vjd
Item delivered to George Hollever in his sycknes	viijd
Item delivered to Thomas White in the tyme of syckenes	ij[d]?
Item delivered to Richard Rose	iij[d]?
Item paid to the clarke for kepinge of the clocke	vs[?]

[f.26v]

[Item paid] to John Corye for v yeards & a quarter & halfe quarter of frice for Joane Beawes to make her a gownde	vs iijd
Item paid to Water Yeo for yearde & halfe of canvas for Jynsen Chope for make him a dowblet	xiiijd
Item delivered to John Moore the elder in his sicknes	ijd
Item paid to Thomas Bole for kepinge William Clarks child: xxxj weeks	xvs vjd

91 23li 5s 7d added.

92 CRO, P216/25/131–2.

93 Axmouth near Colyton, Devon.

Item paid to Master Calmady towards his charges for to bringe downe the fine	xxs
Item paid for a peare of shows for Marget Freer	xijd
Item delivered to Badlimes wife	iijd
Item paid to the ringers on the daye of the queens coronacion	xijd
Item delivered to the church waredens	vs viijd
Item delivered to Chopes wife in the sickenes[94]	iijd
Item delivered to Symon Holman for iij shrewdes	iiijs xd
Item delivered to William [illeg. surname] in the sicknes	xijd
Item delivered to Whale in the sickenis	xijd
Item delivered to Ellin Bole	ijd
Item delivered to Water Jago in the sickenes	vjd
Item paid for a shrowd for Water Jagoe	iijs viijd
Item delivered to Chope in his sicknis	iijd
Item delivered to Nicolas Sawnder & Robarte Nele collectors for the poore at ij tymes	xijs xd
Item paid to Water Yoe for shrewdes & other things for the poore	vjs iijd
Item paid to Richard Jule for that he had delevered to the poore	iiijs
Item delivered to Symon Holman for dyvers shrewdes & other thinges that he had deliveryd to the poore	xxxvjs
Item paid to Symon Holman for a shrewde more	xviijd
Item paid for discharginge of the parishe for wearing of capps[95]	vijs
Item paid for a shrewde for Joane Jyfferye	iijs
Item paid for canvas to line Ellin Boles gowne	vjd
[item paid] to Joane Martyn in the tyme of sicknes	xijd
Item delivered to Thomas Bolt	iiijd
Item paid for expences for the raters of the subsiddys and makinge of the bill	xxd
[Item paid] for the highe rent of Mellooke	ijs vijd
[Item paid] for the highe rent of Pont Hele	ijs
[Item paid] for the hye rent of Stone land	iijs iijd
[Item paid] for the hye rent of the churche house	iijd

[f.27]

Item paid for the hye rent of Exnether	xvjd
Item paid for the hye rent of Treburtell	xiijd ob
Item delivered to Nicolas Sawnder & Robart Neele at a nother tyme	iiijs
Item delivered to the old woman Bole	vjd
Item paid to Whales wife for tending the old woman Bole	iiijd
Item paid to Nicolas Oliver for so much clothe to make William Clarkes childe a sharte	viiid
Item paid to Master Callmadye for the fine & his fees	xvjd
Item paid to John Corrye for yeard & halfe of clothes for make William Clarkes childe a coate	xvd
Item paid to John Yeo for so muche clothe for make William Clarks childe ij [a crossed out] biggins	vjd
Item here wee have taken up to distribute amongst the poore	vjs viijd
Item paid for makynge of this accownt	viijd

Some of the expenses is – xixli xvs vjd
so remenithe clere – iijli xs jd

94 But this was not a high mortality year for the better off.

95 Act for the continuance of the making of caps, Goulding, *Blanchminster Records*, p.97, fn.1.

[f.27v]

The accompte of Wylliam Bray and Thomas Badcokke generall recevers in the yere of our lorde God 1577 made the the [sic] xxijth daye of December in the xxth yere of the reyne of our souerayne ladye quene Elyzabeth [22nd December 1577]

The receytes

In primis recevyd of Nycholas Bonde and George Mayor general recevers the yere past	iijli xijs[96]
Item recevyd of the Hye Crosse wardens	xxxviijs
Item recevyd of John Shortte for parte of his fine[97] for Elyzabeth Judds medowes	iiijli xiijs iiijd
Item recevyd of Elizabethe Judds j yeres rent for Mylloke	xxs
Item recevyd of the Elyzabeth Judde for the rent of ij medowes	xvjs
Item recevyd of Thomas Beare j yeres rent	xxxs viijd
Item recevyd of Thomas Jule cordiner j yeres rent	xijs
Item recevyd of Nycolas Yeo for j yeres rent	viijs
Item recevyd of John Langdon for j yeres rent in Exnether	xijs
Item recevyd Thomas Beare for pasture of the wode	vijd
Item recevyd of Angnes Spark j yere rent for Treburthell	ixs
Item recevyd of Christopher Hore for the rent of the myll	ijs
Item recevyd for the Glybe	jd

Some of the recetes – xvli xiijs viijd

[f.28]

The expenses

Item payd to Rycherd Jule constabull when thay dyd rate the whete	
Item payd to Nycholas Yeo for one that gathered to a poore howse that he layd out	
Item payd to the Hygh Crosse wardens ye last yere	vs ijd
Item payd to Margaryt Fryer for iij quarters rent	iijs
Item payd to Robart Judde for a peare of shouwys for Nycholas Mocke	xviij[d]
Item delyvered to John Avery & John Rodde, Highe Crosse wardyns for this [last crossed out] yere	vjs viijd
Item payd to Wylliam Wyll[98] & Peter Hallyt for sekyng of cowncell a bowte the churche howce	ijs viijd
Item payd to Rycherd Pery for that he had hurttyd his legge	ijs iij[d]
Item payd to John Cory for makyng of ^up^ writyngs for the churche howce ^& Trebertell^[99] & for wax	vs
Item payd to Robart Neale & his felowe for that thay dyd lacke mony for the poore	vj[s viijd]
Item delyvered to a poore sawdiar that came out of Irelond	
Item payd to John Avery & John Rodde, Hygt Crosse wardens	
Item payd for two o [sic] daggers for the sawdyars	v[s]?
Item payd to Rycherd Jule constabull for the sawdyars expences and for shote	ixd[?]
Item payd to one that mended the [c]lokke?	
Item delyvered to Thomas Boole a gaynst Whyt Sonday	iij[s?]
Item payd to the sawdyars in the Whitson wyke	vs[?]
Item payd to ij poore men that wer meamyd in the warres	viijd[?]
Item payd to a man that brent his howse	viijd

[96] Space left below.

[97] CRO, P216/25/122.

[98] CRO, P216/25/135.

[99] CRO, P216/25/134, 199?

Item payd to one ^of^ Tyndagyll[100] that gatheryd to the kee xij[d?]
Item payd to James Jule for a gune v[illeg.]
Item payd to Alys Lane for that she kept Whales wife in her syckenes xvi[ijd]
Item [payd] for drayng of the buttes in the churche yerde xviijd
Item payd to Thomas Call for a calyver xiijs iiijd
Item payd to John Yeo for a sworde & a dagger xs vjd
Item payd to Nycholas Wyll for viij men that were a bo[wte] the kee at Bude vs iiijd
Item payd to Robart Sawnder for a man that mendyd the clokke viijs vjd

[f.28v]
[Item] payd to them that ratyd the subside for yr expence xijd
[Item] payd to iij men for ther expences when thay went to Camyllford ijs vjd
[Item] payd to Nycholas Olyver for ij sworde gurdells iijs iiijd
[Item] payd to Nycholas Oliver for halfe a pownd of gune powder xd
Item payd to John Olyver for a sworde for one of the sawdyars viijs
Item payd to Wylliam Archer for kepyng of the clokke vs
Item payd to the rengers for the quyne iiijs
Item payd to a pore man of the west party that was dekeyd by suertyeshyp vjd
Item delyvered to John Avery & John Rodde the Sonday after Sent Androse Day[101] xs
Item payd for high rent for Hele ijs
Item payd for high rent for Stone Lande iijs iijd
Item payd for high rent for the churche howce iijd
Item payd for high rent for E[x]nether xvjd
Item payd to Symon Holman for a shrowde for Bastyan iijs vjd
Item payd to John Anthony for that he had leyd out for ye poore ijs
Item payd for high rent of Melloke ijs vijd
Item payd to a pore man that gatheryd to a hospytall howce [tow]ards Totnys[102] viijd
Item payd the high rent of Treburthyll xijd ob
Item delyvered to a pore man that went to the bath[103] iiijd
Item payd to the wardyns this yere for glassing of the churche wyndowes ls
where is takyn up of this accompte for to dystrybute to the pore vjs viijd
Item for makyng of this accompte viijd

Summa of the expences – xjli xs vd ob
delyvered to Thomas Badkocke iiijli which he wyll make accompt therefore
so remaynyth by the hands of Wylliam Bray upon his accompt iijs [i crossed out]jd ob

[f.29]
The accompte of Thomas Badcocke for the iiijli he reseved the stocke
In prymis payde to Edwarde Dobell for the makynge of thre gownes [for] Bastyan & one for Wyllyam Tremell & one for Ellyn Bole in viijd a pece[104]
Item for makyng of a gowne & a waste cote for Whales children
Item delyvered to Ellyn Bole vjd
Item delyvered to Thomas Boles wyfe for norsynge of Wyllyam Clarkes child for ix wekes in vjd the weke iiijs vjd
Item payd to Rychard Walkye for makynge of a gowne & a payre of slyves ^for Jone Barne ^ & a cote for Wyllyam Clarkes child ixd
Item delyvered to Jone Mowre iijd

100 Tintagel.
101 1 December 1577.
102 A hospital at Totnes is noted in Orme, *The Church in Devon* (2013), p.92.
103 Possibly Bath in Somerset is meant here.
104 Edge damaged and sums missing.

Item delyvered to Ellyn Bole iijd
Item delyvered to Whales wyfe iijd
Item delyvered to Margeret Fryer to helpe releve her when she was sycke at sondrye tymes xijd
Item delyvered to Whales wyfe at sondrye tymes for the releyfe of Ellyn Bole when she was sycke ijs iiijd
Item payde to Symon Holman for a shrowde for Ellyn Bole iijs vjd
Item payde to Harrye Jule for Margeret Fryres rent for Our Ladye day quarter
Item delyvered to Thomas Bole iiijd
Item delyvered to Hye Croswardens[105] xs
Item delyvered to a man of Tawstocke that had bornde his howse viijd
Item payd to Thomas Call for makyng of lockes vs iiijd
Item payde to Roger Jefferye for the carrynge of artylyrye to Camelforde for the soyldres xijd
Item payde to James Cater for the collecyon for Wade bridge[106] ijs vjd
Item payde to to Nycholas Mocke for scorynge of the harnys & lynynge of the moryon vjd
Item payde to to Nycholas Olyver for canvas & thred for the moryon iijd
Item payde to John Martyn for beryngynge home of the artylyrye frow Camelford xijd
Item payde for the carryng of yt agayen to Camelford ageynst the moster xijd
Item payde to Rychard Jule constabell for a callever, a flaske & a toche box xviijs
Item payde more to Rychard Jule constabell for a swerde viij[s]
Item payde more to Rychard Jule constabell for a nother toche boxe & a flaske viij[d?]
Item payde more to Rychard Jule constabell for a moryon vs iiijd
Item payde more to Rychard Jule constabell for hys expenses at the fyrst moster ijs
Item payde to Harye Jule for Margeret Fryers rent for Mydsommer quarter xijd
Item payde to Alsen Lane for the releve of Whales wife when she was sicke xxd
Item payde to Harrye Jule for Margeret Fryers rent for Myghellmas xixd
The hole some ys – iiijli ijs viijd

[f.29v]

[f.30]
Here[107] folowethe the acount of John Short and Thomas B[Beare or Braye?] generall reseaovers in the yere of our lord God 1578 made the xxjth daye of December in the xxjth yere of the raygnne of our soverayne ladye quene Elyzabethe [21 December 1578]

The[108] receits

In primis reseved of Wyllyam Braye one of the stocke wardens [the yere last] past iijs jd
Item reseved of John Short for his tow last payments for the medowes ixli vjs viijd
so the feofers have taken up of the fine of the medowes which is destybide amongst the poore xxs
Item reseved of John Avery and John Rode churchwardens the yere [p]ast xviijs vijd
Item reseved the xxijth daye of June of the paryshe towards the bell iijli
Item reseved of Nycolas Yeo for one yeres rent viijs
Item reseved of the Elyzabeth Judde for the rent of the medows xvjs
Item reseved of Elyzabethe Judds one yeres rent for Melloke xxs
Item reseved of Thomas Jule cordener for one yeres rent for Stone land [xijs]
Item reseved of Annys Spark for one yeres rent of Treburthell [ixs]

105 Tawstock, Devon.
106 See Langdon, *Wade-Bridge*, pp.39–40.
107 ^Stratton^ later addition before this word.
108 ^*recepta*^.

Item reseved of the tenaunts of Exnether for one yeres rent [xijs]
Item reseved of Thomas Beare for one yeres rent for Pont Hell [xxxs viijd]
Item reseved of Chrystover Hore for one yeres rent of the mylls [ijs]
Item reseved Thomas Beare for the pasture of the woode [vijd]
Item reseved of John Short for the Glebe jd
Sum totalis amount to – xviijli iiijs vijd
[f.30v]

Expencis ys yere

In primis payd to Thomas Bolle the xxiiijth daye of December for the [building]ge up of a bridge going to Heaward[109] viijd
Item payd the xxvijth daye of December to a poor man of Launston that lye in prysone xijd
Item paid to Margeret Freer for Christmas quarters rent xijd
Item payd to a poore man callyd Jagoo the xixth daye of Januarye xijd
Item payd to Rychard Jule constabell for the souldyers cost viijs iiijd
Item payd to Nycolas Will constabell that he had payd to a pore man iiijd
Item payd to Master Morys that was left to paye for making of aquitaunce for the supsydye the yeare past vjd
Item payd to Thomas Badcocke that he had [ly crossed out] layd out more then there some and that he reseved of Wylliam Braye ijs viijd
Item payd to Thomas Call smeythe for making of a spill for the clocke iijs iiijd
Item payd to Wyllyam Smale in his sicknes at sundrye tymes xijd
Item payd to a poore man the viijth daye of February & that dwelled in [the] towne of C[---]cke[110] he had a lycennce to gather vjd
Item payd to John Cobledicke and Richard Yeo the ixth daye of February [church] wardens this yere vjs viijd
Item payd to Richard Jule and Nycolas Wyll constabells the ninthe daye of [Feb] ruarye for the expencis of them that went to Camellford to the moster xiijs iiijd
Item payd the xviijth daye of Februarye to the farmer Colwill for a discharge for a discharge for wearynge of hats ^for^ this paryshe[111] xxd
Item payd to Wyllyam Archer clarke for iiij singing bockes vjs viijd
Item payde to Harye Eare in his sicknes iiijd
Item payde to Nycolas Mocke in his sicknes at sundrye tymes viijd
Item payd to Margeret Freer for Our Ladye daye quarters rent xijd
Item payd to John Cobeldycke and Rychard Yeo churche wardens the viijth daye of Aprill vjs
Item payd to a poorman on the xjth daye of Maye that gathered to the laser house of Pilton[112] vjd
Item payd the same daye to a pore man that was mayhaymd in the wars iiijd
Item payd ^the sam daye^ to a poore man of Bodman [of Bodman crossed out] that had a testimonyall to gather ijd
[Item] payd to a poore man the xviijth daye of Maye that gathered to the [laser] house of Saynt Leonards in Launstonn vjd
[Item payd to] Thomas Bole the xixth day of Maye for making up of ye buts iiijs vjd
[Item payd to] Nycolas Yeo to the same daye for stones and earthe for the [buts] iijs vjd

[f.31]
Item payd to Nycolas Wyll constabell the same daye for carying of the same buts
Item payd to Nycolas Bond the same daye for the clats for the same
Item payd to John Chinge baker for cuttinge of the clates

[109] Hayward, now Howard.
[110] Hole in paper so unclear.
[111] CRO, P216/25/224; Goulding, *Blanchminster Records*, p.97, fn.1.
[112] Pilton near Barnstaple, Devon.

Item payd to John Bedlime for a flake for one of the butts
Item payd to a poreman callyd John Atkyns the viijth daye of June that [had] a paspot iij[d]
Item payd to a pore woman the xvth daye of June that had a testymonyall she came from London viij[d]
Item payd to the sheryfes baylyes the xvijth daye of June for a poste finne for the churche house vjs viij[d]
Item payd to [Nycolas Wyll constabell crossed out] ^John Badlime^ the xxij daye of June for the making up of one of the butts that was fallen downe vjd
Item paid to Nicholas Will constable the xxijth of June for prest men for the souldiers ixs
Item payd to a poore man the xxiiijth daye of June that gathered to the laser house of Saynt Lawrence viijd
Item payd to Margeret Freer for Mysomer quarters rent xijd
Item payd to a pore man the xxth daye of A[u]gust that gathered to the laser house of Exeter iiijd
Item payd to Master Crome the iiijth daye of September for his expencis when he was here to se the artylerye of the par[ish]
Item payd the xiiijth daye of September to Colonton haven[113]
Item payd to a pore mane the xxth daye of September that gathered for a blynd pryst vj[d]
Item delivered to Rychard Yeo one of the church wardens the xxixth of September vijs
Item payd to Margeret Freer for Mychaellmas quarter rent xijd
Item delivered to Rychard the pedler the vth daye of October otherwise he yt is [the crossed out] called Rychard Ellys yt had a testymonyall to gather xijd
Item payd for hie rent for Pount Hele ijs
Item payd for hie rent for Stone laund iijs iiijd
Item payd for hie rent for the churche house iijd
Item payd to Master Morys for hye rent for Exneither xvj[d
Item payd to Master Jacobe the xijth daye of October vjs viijd
Item payd to the traynd soldyers the xijth of October iijs xd
Item payd to Master Anderdon for consell xijd
Item payd to Nycolas Olyver for that he layd out more then he reseved for the hie wayes xijd
Item payd to James Cater the xjth daye of October for that had a licence of my lord of Bedford and of the Justyses of the Shere to gather for a pore man x[ijd]
Item payd to Wyllyam Archer clarke for kepinge of the [clock a] whole yere

[f.31v]
[Item payd] to John Bedlime the xxxjth day of October for makyng up [the] buts that was fallen down vjd
[Item payd] to a pore man the xxxvjth daye of October that had the Quens [broad] seale he gathered to the laser house of Totnes vjd
[Item] payd to John Yeo marchaunt for a shroud for the pore Elyzabethe iijs [vjd]
[Item] payd to Rychard Yeo on of the church wardens the vth daye of November iijs iiijd
Item payd to fouer men for there expencis when the rode to mete the lords of Exneither for the partition of the same ijs iiijd
Item we payd to the ryngers when the did ringe for the [bell crossed out] quene iijs iiijd
Item payd to John Bedlyme the viijth daye of December for Jone Bonnfortunes rent for syxe weekes vjd
Item payd to a poore man of Lantegles the ixth daye of December that had licence of the Justices to gather viijd
Item payd to John Yeo marchaunt for the Bybell xxxjs vjd
Item payd to the suprovisers xxs

113 Second collection.

[which] is taken up of this account to be destribute amongst the [poore] vjs viijd
Item payd for making of this acounte viijd

[f.32]

the acompt for the [v crossed out] bridge

Item payd for one to go after Bond the mason for the bridge
Item payd to Richard Jule constabell for one dayes worke, me[at, drink] and wages
Item payd to Bond the mason & his man for ij dayes worke, meat, dr[ink] & wages iiij[s]
Item payd for a man and a horse to cary stones one daye, for meat & wages x[d?]
Item payd to Nycolas Wyll constabell for ij dayes worke xiiijd
Item payd to John Yeo of Bridge for ij dayes worke, meat, drinke and wages x[viijd?]
Item payd to Andrewe More for ij dayes worke, meat, drinke and wages xviijd
Item payd to Peter Hallet for ij dayes worke, meat, drinke and wages xvjd
Item payd to Robert Vevian for ij dayes worke, meat, drinke and wages xvjd
Item payd to Davye Pengellye for ij dayes worke, meat, drinke and wages xvjd
Item payd to Thomas Hodge for ij dayes worke, meat, drinke and wages xvjd
Item payd for a barell of lime ijs
Item payd for the caryge of the same barell of lyme to the bridg iijd
Item payd [for crossed out] to Wyllyam Hore for stones for the bridg & for one seame of sannd xd
The some of the compt of the [bell crossed out] bridge is – xviijs ixd

The acompt of the bell

Item payd to the bellfounder to paye for his dinner on Trinytie Sonndaye vjd
Item payd to White the [th crossed out] bellfounder for hanging up of the bell & ^for^ that he was well willing to plesure the paryshe and is at anye time when you have nede ijs
Item payd to the belfounder the xxijth daye of June xxxvs
Item payd more to the belfounder the xxvth daye of June viijs vd
Item payd to John Bole for [x crossed out] xijli / and a quarter of mettell iiijs
Item payd to Rychard Jule constabell the xxixth daye of June for fyfty pounds [of bell for the mettell crossed out] of mettell for the bell xvs iii[jd?]
Whereof remaynethe four pounds ^of metell^ to paye fore the wich Rychard Jule hathe geven towards the bell
Item payd to John Yeo marchaunt the iiijth daye of December for lix pounds of mettell for the bell in iiij pence the pound xixs viijd
Item payd to Thomas Jule cordener for [r crossed out] xxix pounds & a halfe of metell for the bell in four pence the pound ixs xd
The of the count of the bell is – vli iiijs ixd
The some of expences amount to – xvli xiij[s] ixd
so ther remaynethe clear – xlvs [ ]d ob

[f.32v]

[f.33]

Heare folowethe the account of Nicholas Yeo & Thomas Juell general recevers in the yeare of our lord God 157[9] made the xviijth daye of December in the xxijth yeare of the raygne of our soveraygne lady quene Elyzabethe etc [18th December 1579]

This recceptes

In primis receved of John Short one of the stocke wardens the yere last past ^xlvs [illeg.]jd^[^xxxixs iijd quarter^ xxixs crossed out]
Item receved of Nicholas Yeo for one years rent viijs

Item receved of the Elyzabeth Judg for j years rent for the medowes xvj[s]
Item receved of Elyzabethe Judge j years rent for Mellocke xx[s]
Item receved of Annes Sparke for j years rent of Treburthell ix[s]
Item receved of the tenaunts of Exnether for j years rent xijs
Item receved of Thomas Beare for j years rent for Pont Hell xxxs viijd
Item receved Thomas Beare for the paster of the wood vijd
Item receved of Christouer Hore for j years rent of the mills ijs
Item receved of Thomas Juell cordinar for j yeare rent for Stone land xijs[?]
Item receved of John Short for the Glybe jd

[The some of recetes amonts to vijli xd crossed out]

The recetes for the bell

Item receved of John ^Cory^ mony that was geven towards the bell vs vjd
Item receved of Thomas Beare for the bell xijd
Item receved of William Well for the bell xijd
Item receved of Richard Call for the bell iiijd
Item receved of Mathy Chope for the bell iijd
[Some of recepts for the crossed out] bell viijs jd
[Some tottall – vijli vjs viijd crossed out]
Item John Yeo ded allowe for making of an indenture the which he gave to wards the bell xvjd
Some tottalles for thes yeare amonts to – viijli iijs iijd ob

[f.33v]

Expences for the yeare 1579

[*Imprimi*]*s* payed for hie rent which the old wardnes have payed for Millocke ijs vijd
Item payed for hie rent for thes yeare for Millocke ijs vijd
Item payed for hie rent for [Treburtell crossed out] Exnuendell[114] xvjd
Item payed for hie rent for Stone land iijs iijd
Item payed for hie rent for Pont Helle ijs
Item payed for hie rent for the churche house iijd
Item payed to a pore man that gathered to the lasser house of Pellton[115] the ij of Maye viijd
Item payed to a pore man that gathered to the house of Pllimton[116] the viij daye of Maye vjd
Item payed to a pore man of Trurowe[117] iiijd
Item payed to Margeret Fearer for Cristmas quarter xijd
Item payed to Margeret Fearer for the other three quarters iijs
Item payed to Johane Willcocke vjd
Item payed to Johane Ketowe iiijd
Item payed to iiij mussisians iiijs
Item payed to Johane Ketowe ijd
Item payed to a man that gathered to the havener of Porquin[118] ijs
Item payed to Master Johnes when he preched ijs viijd
Item payed to ij pore mariners that were robbed upon the see iiijd
Item payed to the churche wardens vjs viijd
Item payed to John Bedlyme for a quarters rent for John Cocke iiijd
Item payed to iij pore maryners that came from Cattya[119] xijd
Item payed to a pore man that gathered to the house of Exeter vjd

[114] Garbled version of Exe.
[115] Pilton, Devon.
[116] Plympton, Devon.
[117] Truro.
[118] Porthquin.
[119] Not identified, possibly Cathay or China?

Item payed to a pore man that gathered to the house of Tadyport[120] vjd
Item payed to John Bedlyme another tyme for rent for John Cocke viijd
Item payed to Brone in his sicknes iiijd
Item payd to the surgent for helling of Broune vs
Item payd to Broune a nother time iijd
Item payd to Richard Prist for vittles for Broune in his sicknes iiijd
Item payd a nother time for bread & drink for Brone iijd
Item payed to Nicholas Mock for tending of Brone in his sicknes viijd
Item payed to iij men that fett home Brone from Launcells iiijd
Item payed to a pore oman that had bornd her house viijd
Item payed to a pore man of Bodman viijd
Item payed to Master Johnes when he preched iijs iiijd
Item payed to the churche wardnes for the trayned soldiers xs
Item lent to Master Johnes by the consent of the viij men xiijs iiijd
Item payed to the prissonnars that laye beyond the sea for th[eir] raunsom xs
Item payed to Nicholas Horttope for caridge of that mony to Bodman xviijd
Item payed to a pore man that borned his house viijd

[f.33A][121]
Item delivered to Harry Juell for Margret Frier ijs vjd
Item delivered to John Badlam xijd
Item delivered to Jesper Badlams wyffe iiijd
Item delivered to Watter Rosse vjd
Item delivered to Jone Keto iijd
Item delivered to Brounes wyffe iijd
Item delivered to Jamys wyffe ^& her mother^ iiijd
Item delivered to Jone Bewes & her mother iiijd
Item delivered to Wyllyam Tremell [iiijd crossed out] vjd
Item delivered to Nycollas Moke iijd
Item delivered to Thom[as] Takells wyffe iijd
Item delivered to Whalls wyffe iiijd
The holle total some ys – vjs viijd
stocke wardens in the yeare of [our] lord [God]
1579 Nycholas Yeow, Thomas [Jule] cord[enar]
[f.34]
Item payed to a pore man that gathered to the lasser housse of Collomton[122] the xxth daye of Maye
Item payed to Nicholas Mocke for a pere of showes
Item payed to John Bedlyme for Johnes Cockes rent
Item payed to Nicholas Will for the soldiers when the[y] went to Bodman
Item payed to Antony Gard to bye powder for the soldiers ijs iiijd[?]
Item payed for the soldiers super when the came from Bodman viij[d]
Item payed to a pore man of Sent Berine[123] that borned his howse viijd
Item payed to Johane Cocke in her sicknes iiij[d?]
Item payed to John Bedlyme for keeping of Johane Cocke wen she laye sicke iiijd
Item payd to Johane Cocke one week when she laye sick vjd
Item payed to one that gathered for the pore house of Sent Martens[124] vjd

[120] Taddiport, Little Torrington, Devon.
[121] Half-page account in a different hand written on one side and stitched in.
[122] Cullompton, Devon.
[123] Very faint, St Burian?
[124] Looe?

Item payed to an Oxford skoller[125] xijd
Item payed to the clarke for keeping of the clocke for one wholle yeare vs
Item payed to Master Cory for the soldiers cott viijs
Item payed to Master Cory for a flaske for the soldiers ijs
Item payed to a pore oman, one Best wife vjd
Item payed to Symon Hollman for a shrod for Walter Rosse is wife iijs iiijd
Item payed to a pore man of Sent Lawrence v[iij]d
[Item payed to ^Master Corye^ for v mens expences to Bodman sessions xixs viijd crossed out]
[Item payed to Master Cory for the reliefe of plaged parishes in the west part xijd crossed out]
[Item payed to Master Cory for a boke of orders for the plage xxd crossed out]
[Item payed to Master Cory for making of the byll & gathering of the mony for the same ijd crossed out]
Item payed for [the crossed out] expenses to the [visitacion crossed out] wardens when the went to the vissytacion vjs viijd
Item payed to a pore man of Bodman vjd
Item payed to Joh[a]n Cocke in her sicknes ixd
Item payed to Tamsson Bedlyme for washing of Johanes Cockes clothes in her sicknes iiijd
Item payed to John Bedlyme for bred, drink & candelleight vjd
Item there is taken up of thes accomt to distrubit a mongest thes pore vjs viijd
Item for making of this accomt viijd
Some tottalles for all the expences for thes yeare amounts to vijli ixd
so there remaynethe chlere to the next stocke wardens – xxijs vjd ob

[f.34v]

Anno 1580[126]

[H]ere folowethe – the accompte of Roberte Sawnder and Wyllyam Will [ge]neral recevers in this present yeare (beinge) the yeare of our lord 1580 made the xviijth daye of December in the xxiijth yeare of the raigne of our soveraigne ladye Queene Elizabethe etc [18 December 1580]

The receiptes

In primis received of Nicholas Yeo and Thomas Juell stockwardens the last yeare xxijs vjd ob
Item received of Elizabethe Judd for one whole yeares rent of Melluck xxs
Item received of the same Elizabethe for one yeares rent of the medowes xvjs
Item received of Nicholas Yeo for one whole yeares rent viijs
Item received of Thomas Juell for one whole yeares rent of Stoneland xijs
Item received of Thomas Beare for one yeares rent for Pontheale xxxs viiid
Item received of the said Thomas for the pasture of the woode vijd
Item received of the tenannts of Exneither for one whole yeares rent xijs
Item received of Brocke[127] one of the tenants of Ex: of the xijd which was left to pay the last yeare vjd
& so theire remayneth yet to pay vjd
Item received of Master Nicholas Greinville for one hole yeares rent of Treburtle ixs
Item received of the constables which they gathered toward the haven of Hastings viijs ijd
Item received of Wylliam Heddon & John Juell churchwardens the yeare last past xxvijs xd ob

[125] Similar payments at Ashburton, see Hanham, *Churchwardens' Accounts of Ashburton*, pp.161, 178, 188.
[126] Different hand.
[127] CRO, P216/25/199.

Item received of John Corye which Master Johnes borrowed of the laste stockwardens xiijs iiijd
Item received of John Prist & Wylliam Yeo which they gave to the poore the laste yeare xijd
Item received of Andrew Sangwine for the two payments of Heale Woode liijs iiijd
Item received of Browne wyffe for a panne which was at gage to the parishe ijs
Item received of Nicholas Wyll, Wylliam Wyll & Robert Sawnder for one whole yeares rent of Heale mills ijs
Item received of John Short for the Gleeb jd

Summe vli viijs iijd

The whole somme of the receipts is – xjli xixs jd

[f.35]

Anno 1580

The Expences

In primis payde for the hyrente of Mellucke for this yeare
Item paid for the hye rente of Exneither
Item paid for the hye rente of Stone Land
Item paid for the hye rente of Pont Heale
Item paid for the hye rente of the church howse
Item delivered to Wylliam Heddon & John Juell churchwardens the laste yeare 15 daye of December xxs
Item delivered to Nicholas Wyll constable the 31 day of December which he gave to a poor man that had a testimonial to gather iiijd
Item delivered to the constables the same tyme for theire charges when the Justice sate here for the Ireland souldiers viijd
Item paid for makinge of a byll the same tyme iiijd
Item paid to Nicholas Wyll which was left to paye for a dagger jd
Item delivered to Nicholas Wyll the 16 of January toward the haven of Hastings[128] ijs vjd
Item delivered to an Ireland souldiour the /24/ of Januarye vjd
Item delivered to a poore man that gathered to St Leonardes of Launceston the last daye of Januarye vjd
Item paid to Margerye Hollman which was left to pay for Harrye Eares shrowd xijd
Item paid more to Margerye Hollman for a shrowd for Margaret Fryer iijs
Item paid to John Badlam which was left to pay (the last yeare) for the attending of Johane Cooke in her first sicknes in September iijs
Item paid to Nicholas Wyll constable the /8/ February for his charges when [the] clark of the market was here to keep him company bicause no other man should have trouble withall ijs
Item paid to Richerd Juell constable for his expenses the same tyme vjd
Item paiud to John Averye for helinge of the churche for one whole yeare the 9 of F[ebruary]
Item delivered to Thomas Call & Thomas Smithe churchwardens this yeare the same tyme vjs viij[d]
Item paid to Nicholas Wyll the /18/ of February which he had delivered to send[d] Ireland souldiours of the county of Gloucester iiijd
Item paid to Sir John[129] of Poughill the /24/ daye of Februarye which he paid at Camelford for this parishe towards the rebuildinge of the towne of Charde[130] ixd
Item paid for his paynes because we would not send thither one of the wardens iiijd
Item paid to John Yeo marchaunt the /6/ of Marche for writting of a supplicacon to my lord byshoppe when the wardens wente to Exon[131] to my lords courte iijd

[128] 'Hastinges' written in margin.
[129] Hodge.
[130] Chard, Somerset.
[131] Exeter.

Item paid to the saide wardens for theire expences the same tyme xs vijd
Item delivered to James Cater the /8/ of Marche whiche we were rated by the Justices of Cornwall to paye to St Tyves[132] vjs viijd
Item delivered to a pore man of Bodmin the 13/ of Marche which had a testimonial to gather vjd
Item paid to another poore man of Bodman called John Crosse the 26 of March which had a testymonyall of some of the Justices to gather vjd
Item delivered to Thomas Call one of the churchwardens this yeare the xxijth daye of Marche v[iijs] iiijd

[f.35v]

Anno 1580
Expences

[Item paid to] a poore man of Symonward which had burnt his howse & had a [test] imoniall to gather the /21/ of Maye vjd
[Item pai]d to Pears the joyner the 23/ of Maye for making of the cooking [st]ole[133] ijs vjd
Item paid to Robert Neale for makynge of the butts vjs viijd
Item delivered to Thomas Smigthe one of the churchewardens this yeare the 26 of Maye vjs viijd
Item paid for the booke of common prayer for the churche the /29/ of June iijs iiijd
Item paid to Pears the ioyner the /7/ of August for taking downe the roodlofte[134] & placing the seates for iij dayes worke & [*dimidia* crossed out] meate & hyre ijs iiijd
Item paid to Richerd Juell Constable the same daye for ij dayes work & *dimidia* about the same xvjd
Item paid to Master Mocke for leying of the tyles & rydding the churche ij days [wo]rke & *dimidia* viijd
Item [pa]yd to Henry Snell to help bere oute the morestones & other things and of a daye iiijd
Item paid to John Kyne for one dayes worke & *dimidia* aboute the same viijd
Item paid to Nicholas Sawnder for nayles to make fast the pues & for one gemie for the hyer seate xiijd ob
Item paid to John Heckett for one gemie more for the same iijd
Item paid for drinke for them that bare out the stones & helpe to remove the pues iijd
Item paid to a poore man that gathered to an house of mayhaymed men at Exeter the 7 of September vjd
Item delivered to James Cater the 27 of September which we were rated by most parte of the Justices of Peace in Cornwall to paye to the restoringe of the old custom called Cornish heare[135] xs
Item delivered to a pore man of Pylton that had a lycence to gather the 2 of October vjd
Item delivered to the churchwardens the /9/ of October xs
Item delivered to a pore man which gathered to the pore howse of Launceston the same day vjd
Item paid to the clarke the 24 of October for kepinge of the clocke for one whole yeare vs
Item paid to John Yeo merc[er] the last day of October when the souldiours wente to Bodmin to be trayned for powder & ledd for them xxjd
Item paid to the souldiours for theire expences the same tyme xs viijd
That is to say for iij dayes wages & for carrying of there armour viijs
& which they payd to the capitayne & the drummer xvjd
for the hanging of a sword girdle – xijd

[132] St Ives.
[133] Cucking stool.
[134] Rood loft demolition completed.
[135] Possibly inheritance custom? See Introduction, p.36.

for a lether to hang one of the flasks –	iijd
& for amending one of theire gun rods –	jd
Item paid to iiij men which went to measure & to parte Exneither for theire expences	xvjd
Item paid to Thomas Call & Thomas Smithe churchwardens this yeare the 5 of November	xiijs iiijd
Item paid to the ringers the /17/ of November	ijs
Item paid to Nicholas Rundell the same daye for a shirte for Mocke	ijs xd
[Item paid] a poore man of Callstocke[136] the /20/ of November which had a [testim]onyall to gather	vjd
[Item paid to] Thomas Call & Thomas Smithe churchwardens this yeare the /24/ of November	viijs

[f.36]

Expences Anno 1580

Item delivered to a poore man of Symonward[137] whiche had burnte h[is house and] had a testimonyall to gather the /28/ of November	
Item paid for this parrishe towards the collection for the h[aven of] Portesmouthe the /13/ of December	
Item paid to a man for his paynes to carry yt to Camelford	
Item we have taken up of this accompt which is distributed am[ongst the] pore	[vjs viijd]
Item paid for making of this accompte	

The whole some of the expences is – ixli[138] iijd ijd

So ther remainethe cleare bye this acc[ompt] to the next stockwardens – ls xd ob

The Accompt ^of ye distribucon^ of that vjs viid which was t[ake]n up of the stocke to be distributed amongst the poore /*ut sequitur*

In primis delivered to John Badlam	vjd
Item delivered to his wyffe	jd
Item delivered to Jasper Badlams wyffe	iijd
Item delivered to Chubbs wyeffe	jd
Item delivered to Davye Walkyes mayden[139]	jd
Item delivered to Walter Rose	iiijd
Item delivered to Tomasine Huddell	iijd
Item delivered to Wylliam Smale	iiijd
Item delivered to Thomas Bole	iiijd
Item delivered to Elizabethe White	ijd
Item delivered to Amy Clarke	ijd
Item delivered to Brownes wyffe	iijd
Item delivered to Nicholas Mocke	iiijd
Item delivered to Isott Whale	iijd
Item delivered to John Moore the yongers wyffe	iijd
Item delivered to Wylliam Tre[mell crossed out]	iijd
Item delivered to Thomasine Heale	iijd
Item delivered to Jane Quecke	iijd
Item delivered to Alice Bastyan	ijd
Item delivered to Johan Ketow	iiijd
Item delivered to Johan Bewes	xvjd

136 Calstock.

137 Old name for St Breward as previous page.

138 The rest of the sum is on a detached piece of paper.

139 Daughter or servant.

Item delivered to Richawrd Perye iijd
Item delivered to Emm Juell iijd

So the whole some amounteth to – vjs viijd

R.S.

W W[140]

[f.36v]

Here folowethe the accounte of Nicholas Hore and Walter Yeo [ge]neral resevers thes present yeare beinge the yeare of our [lord 1581] made the xvjth daye of Desember in the xxiiijth yeare of the raigne of our soveraigne ladye Quene Elizabethe etc [16 December 1581]

The receptes

In primis reseved of Robart Saunder and [Nicholas crossed out] ^Willyam^ Will stocke wardens the last yeare ls xd ob
Item receivd of Nicholas Yeo for one hole yeares rents viijs
Item receivd of Elizabethe Jude for one hole yeares rent of Mellucke xxs
Item received of the same Elizabethe for one yeares rent of medowes xvjs
[Item] received of Thomas Jule for one hole yeares rent of Stoneland xijs
[Item] received of Thomas Bayre for one hole yeares rent for Pounthealle xxxs viiid
[Item] received of the said Thomas Beare for paster of the woode vijd
[Item] received of Master Nicholas Grenville for one hole yeares rent of Treburfull ixs vijd[?]
Item received of Androw Sangwine for one payment of Heale woode xxvjs
Item received of Thomas Smith and Thomas Call wardens the last yeare xjs xjd ob
[Item received] of John Short for the Glebe jd
[Item received rent of Hele mells ijs

The hole somme of the resetes comes to – ixli vijs jd [viijd crossed out] xd

Ch[arge] of the pareshe of Stratton for Portsmouth 12d[141]

John Sumaster

21 Aprilis 1582
Stratton receaved of the wardens there for the collectyon made for the [inhabitauntes?] of Portesmouthe xvjd

by me Gregorie Friggens

[f. 37]

In primis payde for the hy rente of Mellucke ijs v[ijd]
Item payde for the hyrente of Stone Land iijs [iijd]
Item payde for the hirente of Ponnt Healle ijs
Item payde for the hirente of the churche house iij[d]
Item paid for the hirente of Exnether xvj[d]
Item delevered to the stocke warden the last yeare Wylliam Will[142] iii[js?]
Item delivered to a poure man the xviijth daye of Desember
Item delivered to John Averye the second of Januiary for heleng the church
Item payd at Camelfurd at the vesitation for our expences
Item payd to Whites when shee was sicke
Item delivered to John Yeo and Robart Braye churche wardens

140 Initials of Robert Sawnder and William Will.
141 This and the next slip are stitched in.
142 Space above.

Item payd to John Cory when he went to Exnether to mete the gro[und] xxijth daye of Febreary
Item delivered to John Yeo and Robart Braye the xxth day of Janiary
Item payd to a pore mane the xxvth daye of Febreary whiche he had a t[estimonial]
Item [payd crossed out] ^delivered^ to John Yeo and Robart ^Braye^ churche wardens this yeare
Item delivered to John Yeo and Robart Braye churche wardens thes ye[ar] sauders went to Bodmond
Item payd to a poure man that came out of Sumersheere[143] which
Item payd to a pore man that was rubed a pon the saye the xiith
Item payd to a pore man of Helston the xxth daye of Janiary which [had] a toryty vjd
Item payd to a pore man that came out of Erlond[144] the xxvth day of
Item payd to Rager Cincocke [for menden of crossed out] a newe swell and bring and for mendeng of the stape ^of the bulringe^ xd
Item payd for meate and drinke for towe wemen that Sur Richard Grenvell tocke for iij dayes in prison[145] x[d?]
Item payd to three pore men that came from Erlond the xxth day of [ ] viijd
Item payd to a poure mane of Padstowe the xxviij daye of Fe[bruary] vjd
Item payd to a poure mane of Bodmound[146] the xiiijth dayte of Marche vjd
Item payd to a poure mane of Sint Lauers[147] vjd
Item payd for foure [fy crossed out] men at Camellford when the wente before the Justices to rate the supsides and for ther expenses
Item payd to a poure man of Sint Towdy[148]
Item payd to foure men when the did rate the supside

[f.37v]
[Item paid to] foure men at Camellfurd when the layd in ther bill be fore and for ther charges iiijs
[Item paid] a poure man that came out of Erlond that was sicke [with a] pasbote vjd

the xijth daye of August

[Item paid] to a pore [man crossed out] oman that came out of Alternune vjd

The xxth of September

[Item pai]d to a poure mane that gathered for a house of memed sauders viijd
[Item pai]d to a pour man of Tinmothe[149] vjd
[Item pai]d to a poure man that gethred to the Quenes benche[150] vjd
[Item pai]d for a warrant for Thomas Marten and John Pearse for ther goods [before] the Justice xijd
[Item pai]d to a poure man of Plimouth that had a toryti vjd
[Item paid] to the ringers the xvijth daye of Nouember ijs
[Item pai]d to John Cory for [the] bayes that was put upon Sur Richard [d crossed out] deske xd
[Item paid] to ^William Archard, clarke^ the clarke for kipinge of the clocke vs
[Item paid] to tow pore men of Bodmond the viij daye of [Februa]ry xijd

143 Somerset.
144 Ireland.
145 See Rowse, *Richard Grenville*, pp.157–77 for context.
146 Bodmin.
147 St Lawrence's Hospital, Bodmin.
148 St Tudy.
149 Teignmouth, Devon.
150 Westminster law court.

[Item paid] to a poure man the xijth daye of Februeary iiijd
[Item a]lowed William Sweper and John Yeo fro the standen in [illeg.]c[?]age times [iiijs crossed out] iiijs
[Item paid] for lid for the haufe bushel iijd
[Item paid] to a masen for furen of the haufe bushell, for mete and drink xviijd
[Item paid] to the seler for selen of the haufe bushel vjd
[Item paid] [the crossed out] of tow pore men the vjth daye of Nouember viijd
[Item paid] for precepe of the clarke of the market iiijd
[Item paid] for our expences when the clarke of the market was here for vj men ij dayes xs
[Item paid] for a smocke clathe for Jone Cetow ijs
Item payd for a shert for William Trimbell ijs iiijd
Item payd for a shert for Mocke ijs jd
Item payd for iij yeards of graye fries for Nicholas Baye to make hime ^jerkyn and breches^ ijs ixd
Item more gave to Jone Bawyes for to by her a smocke xd
[Item paid for] making of this accompte viijd
Sume totalis ^of the expensis^ with vjs viijd which is apon the otherside for the pawre & ammounts unto vjli [ijs ob crossed out] & xiijd

[f.38]
So heare remenethe to the next sto[ckwardens]
Item we have taken up of this acommpte which is distribed amo[ngst the] poure vj[s viijd]
Item payd for mackinge of this accompte viijd

The accompte of the disribitation of vjs viijd which the was of the stocke to be distributed amongst the poure *ut sequentur*

In primis delevered to Jone Bewes vjd
[Item delivered to Jone Cittow vjd crossed out]
Item delivered to Margit Eles iijd
Item delivered to Jane Quicke iiijd
Item delivered to Wylliam Trimbell iijd
Item delivered to ^Esit^ Whales [wife crossed out] iijd
Item delivered to Richord Pery iijd
Item delivered to Wylliam Smale iiijd
Item delivered to Dave Walke ijd
Item delivered to Tamsen Huddell iijd
Item delivered to Walter Rose iijd
[Item delivered to Nicholas Mocke vjd crossed out]
Item delivered to Chubes wife jd
Item delivered to John Bedlime [ij crossed out] iijd
Item delivered to Jone Bedlime iijd
Item delivered to Esbell Tackell iijd
Item delivered to Thomas Bole ijd
Item delivered to the younge Jone Moure ijd
Item delivered to John Moure ijd
Item delivered to Jesber Bedlime iijd
Item delivered to Ame Clarke iijd
Item delivered to Esbel Whit iijd
Item delivered to Tamsen Heale iijd
Item delivered to [illegible word crossed out] Alse Basten iiijd
Item delivered to the Wauters wife ijd
Item deleviered to Thomas Tremell xijd
So the whole sume is – vjs viijd

[ff.38v–9]

[f.39v]

[Here] folowether the ac[ount] be twyne Nicholas [Hore] & Walter Yeo stocke wardens[151]

the xviijth of Desember	
to William To at Heall and Robart Sander	ls xd
[Item] pead to the stock warden before William [illeg.]	iiijd
[Item] pead to a pour man [that crossed out] the xviijth daye of [D]esember	vjd
[Item] pead to John Averie the taylder the second of Juniary	
xiijth January to Camellfurd at the	
[the]ir diner ^and drink^ xxijd. Item for yor horses	
[Item] pead makyng the bill vjd the hole sum	ijs viijd
horses	iijd
Tamas [ ] and Thomas Smithe warden	xjs xjd ob
[rec]evid Robert Braye	vjs
Item ped the to W[ylliam] Yeo and Robar[t] Bray xxth of Juni[ary?]	vjs viijd
[Item] pead to John Cory the xxijth of Feberay when he thee went to Ex to ^measse^ the ground	xijd
[Item] ped to a pure man the xxvth of Febreary to a pour man that dwelt to Milbrowk[152] t[ha]t had burnd his hou[se] the which had a testimony	iiijs
John Yeo and Robart Braye had xxth of Aprill	xs
John Yeo [and] Robart Braye[?] had the sauders w[ages] to Bodmound	x

[f.40]

[Item] resevd of

Item to John Yeo

Item pead to a pore man that[

[.....] had a testimonys

[f.40v][153]

[Item] that he reseved	xxs
reseved	xxviijs ^iiijd^
reseved	[illeg.] ls[?]
Andro Sangen	iiijli vjs viijd
rent for one rent	ijs vijd
Nicholas Will for the [illeg. words]	
the xiijs iijd and [illeg.] in Helin[?]	xijs
Esbell Jud for	ixs

[151] This is a more detailed, but damaged, draft of the preceding 1581 account, see f.37.

[152] Millbrook.

[153] This may be a partial draft of f.36v. Back inside cover has a face in profile and various jottings in Latin and English including: '*liber quo continet computatio comunis seisio de* Stratton, William Rad hath xld, I have xs jd ob, iijli xvijs' – and other sums including xs iiijd, xxli, xxxiijli, xlli, xiijs iiijd, xvs xijd, xijs ixd, iijs.

Appendices

Appendix 1: Rood loft contract and bond, 29 May 14 July 1531

1.1 Stratton rood loft contract, 29 May 1531 (CRO, P216/25/215)
Thys indenture made the xxix^th^ day of May in the xxiij yere of the reygne of kyygg Henry the viijth. betwene John Chamond knyghth, Rychard Carlyghan clerk,[1] Thomas Mares, John Carwetham, George Awnger, Wylliam Besschepp & John Payne of the parysh of Stratton yn Cornewall yn the name for and yn the behalf of all ye hole parysh of Stratton aforsayd of the one party and John Dawe of Lawhyton of the sayd county of Cornewall & John Pares of North Lew yn ye county of Devon^scher^ of the oder party.

Wyttenyssyth that hytt ys barganyd, promised, covenantyd and fully agreyd betweene the sayd partyes by thys presentts in maner & forme follo[w]yng:

That ys to wete that the sayd John Daw & John Parys shall by the grace of ^God^ make or cawse to be made a rodelofte withyn the parysh church of Stratton forsayd contaynyng iij churches and iij roffes whych as now be ther that ys to wyte over all the bred[2] of the same churches and iij roffes frow ye sowthr wall of the sowth amletory of ye same church unto the north wall of the north amletory there and the same rodloft to be made after the patrone, forme and facyon yn everythyng as the rod loft of Seyntt Kew ys made with a backe behind yn every amletory and all other thynggs as ys att Seyntt Kew as well as thoff everything thereof were here specyally and partycularly resytyd be name.

Also hytt [is] covenantyd and agreyd between the sayd partys that the sayd John Daw & John Pares schall make or cawse to be made yn the back of the sayd mydell rome[3] of the sayd church a crucyfyx with a Mary and John and all other werkemanshepp after the patron, fascyon and workemanshepp yn everythyng as hytt ys above ye crucyfyx yn the bake of the mydyll church of Leskerd[4] Church.

Also hytt is covenantyd and agreid betwyne the sayd partes that the sayd John Daw & John Pares schall make or cawse to be made ij awturs of tymber one bothe endds of the sayd rodelofte that is to weytt one by the sowther wall and a nother by ye northe wall of the sayd church with ij images & tabernacles for them and the same imagys and other worke ther to be, or better, and wroft after the patron and workemanschepp as ys att Seynt Kew aforsayd the one image to be of Seyntt Armell, the other of the Visitacon off Owr Blessyd Lady.[5]

Also hy^tt^ ys covenantyd and agreid betwene the sayd parties that the sayd John Dawe & John Pares schall make or cawse to be made ij interclosys of tymber fro pyler to pyler the one betwene the sowth amletory and the quere of the sayd church and the other betwene ye northe amletory and the sayd quere of the sayd church every of them fro the sayd rodloft upward unto the pylers nex[t] the hy awter and hit to be made with the hyzth of the vawte of the sayd rodloft after the patron & facyon as the interclose between the the amletores yn the parysh churche of Synt Colombe the over.[6]

Also hytt ys covenantyd and a greyd betwene the sayd partyes that the sayd John Daw & John Pares shall make or cawse to be made fyve segys or pewys that ys to weyt iij yn the sowthe amletory whereof one to be by the chauncell dore ther yn the same sowth amletore for

1 Vicar and also rector of Lawhitton.
2 Breadth.
3 Nave.
4 Liskeard.
5 Our Lady Holmadon (holy maiden)?
6 St Columb Major.

a woman and the other ij pewys to be yn the same amletory hard by the sayd interclose and lekewyse the ij other seges to be yn ye north amletore har[d]by the sayd selyng ther.

And also the sayd John Daw & John Pares covenauntyth & grauntyth that they shall sett the dexis of the quere a yen and make or cawce to be made a sufficyant stage for organs yn the sayd northe amletore a hye by ye vawte of the sayd rodloft by the advyce of a organ maker.

Also hytt ys covenantyd and a gred betwene the sayd partyes that the sayd John Dawe & John Pares shall make or cawce to be made ij wyndows yn the myddell roff of the sayd church above the crucyfyx and to seyll the same wyndowys after the fassheon of Seynt Mary Weyke[7] and to provyde & se that ye coples of the sayd church be surely posted and orderyd that the sayd churche take no hurte whyle the same wyndowys be a makynge.

Also the sayd John Dawe and John Pares covenantyd & grawntyth for to reys the wall plate off the northe wall off the sayd church so that hytt may agre with the myddyll roff of the same church and to devyse and make a waye and a goyng by or under the archys of the pylers of the amletores of the sayd church so yt a man may go throw the sayd rodloft from one amletore to a nother.

And also the same John Dawe & John Pares covenantyth and grauntyth to post the same roff, wall plate, archys and pylers so that no hurte be to ye same church during the tyme ye same worke ys a makyng and the posts to be brozt to ye works by ye parysh.

Also the same John Dawe & John Pares covenantyth and grauntyth & promysyth that all the tymber of ye same worke shall be substancyally seysynyd and of one maner of dryyng.[8]

Allso hit ys bargaynyd covenantyd and fully aggreyd betwene the sayd partyes that as well all the costs & charges of all the tymber as of caryage therof nessissary and requysyte for all the sayd worke and every parcell therof and also all other maner of costs & charges what so ever they be belongyng or requysyte for the premysses or any parcell theroff shall be att the only costs & charges of the sayd John Daw & John Pares excepte the ironworke and the mason worke nessesary for the premysses whych shall be to ye coste & charge of ye parysh.

Also ye sayd John Daw & John Pares shall at all tymes duryng the space & tyme of iiij yeres after the sayd worke be fully fynysshd shall at all tymes amend the same rodloft and all other ye premysses at all tymes as nede shall requyre.

And also the sayd John Daw & John Pares covenantyth and grauntyth that they yn all convenient haste & spede shall go abowte the makyng of ye same rodeloft and other ye premysses and to make & fully fynyshe and end the same rodloft and all other ye premyssys withyn the space of vij yeres next and immedyattly insuyng after thys present date.

Also hytt ys covenaunttyd, condycendyd and agreyd betwene ye sayd partyes that for the makying, fynessheng and fulfyllyng of all the same rodloft, crucyfyx with Mary and John, auters, images, interclosyng or spyryng betwene the sayd amletores, pewys, segys, stages for organs, setyng of dextys of ye quere, making of ye sayd wyndowys, posting and reysyng of the wall plates and roffys and the sesynyng of the tymber and for all the caryage of the same tymber and other thyngs nessessary for the same and for all other costs and charges what so ever they be nescyssary or requisyte for the premisses as ys afore rehersyd which be appoyntyd and lymyttyd by ys present indentures to the sayd John Daw & John Pares to do so that hytt be done with yn the tyme & yeres be fore lymyttyd.

The sayd John Chamond, Rychard Carlyghan, Thomas Marys, John Carwetham, George Awnger, Wylliam Besshepp & John Payne shall content & pay or cawse to be contentyd & payd unto ye sayd John Daw & John Pares – xlvjs viijd includyng all premysses to be yn & for every fote of the worke of the bred of the sayd church of Stratton to be metyn apone ye grownd along by the sayd rodloft & no other interclose to be metyn but to go yn the same & for ye same mony frow the north wall of the sayd church unto the sowth wall ther of ye same church all the sayd worke to be encludyd withyn the forsayd xlvjs viijd the fote payable yn forme folwyng that ys to weyt appone the sellyng of ys indenture xx^{ti} markes and the

7 Week St Mary.

8 Timber was normally used soon after felling.

resydu to be payd yerely by suche porcyons as therof as the worke goyth forth. And that as John Chowyll or any workeman woll juge.

In wyttenes wherof the partyes abovesayd interchaunable ^to ys presents^ have sette owre seals the day & yer above sayd.

[Back]
Memorandum that John Dow & John Pares & ther suretes have recevyd of John Trevelan & Nycholas Wyll[9] yn ye behalf of ye hole parysh of Stratton the xvj day of Julij *anno regni regis Henrici* viij, xxiij [16 July 1531]–xiijli vjs viijd yn parte of payment for makyng of a rodeloft new withyn the church of Stratton beyng yn presence of Mr Harry Rayvell, John Rode[?] & Alexander Lang.

Item received of Rychard Ronell & Wylliam Baron a pone Trinite Sonday & of other the xxv^ti yere of ^kyng^ Herry the viij^th^ [8 June 1533] xiijli vjs viijd

Item received of Wylliam Gyste & John Jule yn the fest of ye Concepcon of Owr Lady ^*anno regni regis H* viij, xxv^*th*^ [8 December 1533] vjli xiijs viijd

Item Received of Wylliam Gyste & John Jule yn the fest of Seynte Mathy the apostell *anno regni regis H viij xxvj^th^* [21 September 1534] vjli xiijs iiijd

Item the sayd John Daw received of Thomas Coke alias Grendon & Nycholas Symon of Bowrwode yn the fest of Sent Denys *anno regni regis H* viij, xxvij [9 October 1535] xiijli vjs viijd

Item received of Wylliam Byschep & John Payne general recevers in the fest of Sent Myrhell the Arch[angel] *anno regni regis Henricus octam* xxviij [29 September 1536] xiijli vjs viijd

Item the sayd John Daw received of Thomas Braye & John Roose general recevers in the fest of Sent Myzhell the arch[angel] *anno regni regis Henricus ocatam* xxviiij [29 September 1537] [xiijli vjs viijd crossed out] xvijli vjs viijd

Item the same John Daw hath recevyd of Thomas Taylor & Wylliam Grove ye yere of kyng *Henricus* the viijth xxx [1538–39] xiiijli xiijs iiijd

Memorandum received befor the xth day of November *anno regni regis H octam* xxx cviijli

^H vjli vjs viijd^[10]

1.2 Bond for £200 between John and Richard Daw of Lawhitton, carvers John Parys, carver, Richard Medlond and Thomas Glanfyld, yeomen of Northlew, Devon, Reginald Whyte of Treneglos, John Ley and John Hyll of Egloskerry, John Harry of Tremaine, yeomen, John Kyttowe of Tresmeer, husbandman[11] and for Stratton, John Chamond, knight, Richard Carlyan, clerk, Thomas Marys, John Carwetham, George Aunger, William Byshoppe & John Payne, 14 July 23rd year Henry VIII [1531] (CRO P216/25/216)[12]
The condycon of thys oblygacon ys suche that yf the above bounden John Dowe, John Parys, Richard Dawe, Reynold Whyte, John Ley, John Hyll, Richard Medland, Thomas Glanfyld, John Harry and John Ketowe do well and truly observe, fulfyll, performe and kepe all and singuler covenauntts, appoyntmentts and aggrementts on ther behalff to be observyd and kept whych be comprysed yn a pere of Indenturs made betwene the a bove namyd John Chamond, Richard Carlyghan, Thomas Marys, John Carwetham, George Aunger, Wylliam Byshoppe and John Payne yn the name for and the behalf of the hole paryshe of Stratton of the one partye and the a bove bounden John Dowe, John Parys, Richard Dowe, Reynold Whyte, John Ley, John Hyll, Richard Medland, Thomas Glanfyld, John Harry and Kyttowe ^of thoder partye^who ys date ys the xxix^th^ day of May yn the xxiij^th^ yere of the reygne of king

9 General receivers hereon.

10 Additional sum paid after the last date.

11 Stoate, *Cornwall Subsidies* and *Devon Subsidies* c.1524–44, shows that Kyttowe had £2 of goods, Richard Dawe £3, Hill £8-9, Glanfyld £9, Ley £11 and Medland £14, while Harry and Whyte had £5 and £6 of lands.

12 Summary of Latin bond only given here in translation.

Harry the viij^th^ that then thys oblygacon to be voyde or els to stand yn full vertue, strengh and effecte.

Appendix 2: Draft accounts (BL, Add MS 32243)[13]

2.1 Brewing account, 1559 (f.4)

Jamys Call & Thomas Olyver

Fyrste recevyd ye mone[y]	xxiijs viijd
Recevyd more	xxviijs xd ob
Recevyd for small drynke ye laste brewyng	xviijd sum for drinke
for draffe	xiijd
^Recevyd for the browne mele	ijd^
	lvs ijd ob
charges owte of the same	
there was lefte to pay yn wode of the fyrste brewyng	vd
Jamys was yn wod the laste brewyn	vd
& I was the reste of the wod	xd
payd my mother for chekyng which were for William Westecot	iijd
for wode to roste all the tyme	xijd
for bred which was [^of^ illeg. word crossed out].occupyd of owr one	xiijd
for bakyn of bred & pyys	iiijd
for vj pottyls of syder	ixd
for vyne yefer[?]	jd
for hoppys the laste brewyng	iiijd
for fowre pesys of bacun Trenete Sonday	iiijd
My wyffe ys to pay for a pecke of mele, by hepe & ij boxsys of flowre	viijd
Summa lvjs vjd	

2.2 High Cross account, 1559[14] (f.104v)

pascall tapers	iijd
Thomas Clarke for gresyng	viijd
paid the veker of Poffyll for ijli & quarter wex xjd the lii	ijs [vjd crossed out]
More j *dimidia* li of wexe beryne	vjd
Paid for viij yeards & *dimidia* of holand to make the Lente cloth xd the yerd	vijs jd
for ryngs & lasyn to hange hym upe	iiijd
for makynge of the same	iiijd[15]
for a hymnor	ijs
for a poynshyn to put lyme yne	xxd
for pentyn of Saynt Andrew	iijs iiid
for a yeard & *dimidia* of canvas at vijd the yeard ^for the same^	xd ob
paid for makyn of the Pallm cross	vjd
& *dimidia* of led to caste hym with all	ijd ob
for ^mendyn^ [newe castyn crossed out] of the therd bell clapper	vs
of a pyne for the bell coller	ob
[T]homas Clarke for a new coller	viijd
[ma]kyn of ij collers	jd
& *dimidia* of dowlys ^for a nawter cloth^ viijd ob the yerd	ijs vd ob
[makyn] of the same	ob
for makyn of wyndowys mendyn of bords &	

[13] All three accounts cancelled. The first was added in to earlier accounts and latter two recycled for church inventories.

[14] 1577, 1577, 1575, 3li 9d at the top, and folio torn on the left side. Same scribe as the final version: see f.65.

[15] ^Lorde God^ in later hand.

chorche howes one day ^&^mete & drynk	xd
worke & meate & drynke	iiijd
jem[es] [ne]yls for the same wyndowes	xvjd

2.3 High Cross account, 1575[16] (f.103)

Item Water Yeo hathe recevyd for the monye of next	xiijs
Item ^Water Yeo^ Wylliam ^Majer^ hathe recevyd her	iijs 4d
Item more recevyd	xiijd
Item more rcevyd	iijd
Item recevyd of Sweper	6s
Item recevyd at the fear	xs [jd crossed out] xd
Item more recevyd of Dun for a knyle	4d
Item recevyd of Pearse	4d
Item Water Yeo hath recevyd of Wyllyam Majer ^for the standynges^	xxjs xd[17]

Item recevyd at the feare	xs xd
Item recevyd of fears	6s
Recevyd of the parryshe[18]	
yn monye the sum of	vijs vd
Item more recevyd	ixs ixd
Wylliam Major hathe recevyd	ijd
for standyn	6s[?]
hys form	7s

Appendix 3: Church inventories (BL, Add MS 32243)

f.104

3.1 [1559][19]

Item [a crossed out] two chalys	iiijli iiijs
Item a sute of vestments of damaske	viijs

Item a sute of blake wostyed with tow coppes
Item a pere of vestments of rede velvett[20]
Item a pere of vestments of lekeys gold
Item a pere of vestments of whyte damaske
Item a pere of vestments of blewe satyn
Item a pere of [y crossed out] vestments of yowlow selke
Item thre frontts of selk with [a crossed out] ^the^ pere of cortynes
Item vij pere of serpylls & ^[the ^the^crossed out] iiij^ rachett
Item ^v^iiij auter towlys
Item [vjj crossed out] ^vij^ corporys cases with ^thre kercheffs^ ther kerchers
Item a palle for a herse[21]
Item two crose banners & a stremer of selke
Item two howselyng towells & ij vante clothe
Item a rede front
Item a clothe for the sacrament
Item a pole of ierne?[22]

16 See f.91ff for the final version.
17 Altered from ixs ixd.
18 Upside-down entries.
19 Snell, *Edwardian Inventories*, pp.32–3 suggests a 1549 or earlier date.
20 ^xx m[ar]cs?^ between this and the next entry and sums torn away.
21 ^ale money xlvjs jd ob^ crossed out.
22 Pulley of iron? Snell, *Edwardian Inventories*, p.33 mistranscribes this as 'a pere of sensers'.

Item a cross & a staff of coper gellte
Item a pexce of coper
Item a sence of coper
Item a scheppe
Item a lattyn basyn
Item a pere of candelstycks
A cope of velvette
and a pere of vestesments of the same
Item x peces of velvett and a stole of
Item a lantran & a nyew deskclothe
Item a new ro^w^de clothe
[P fowr new surplesys crossed out] a Lent clothe &^a nyew^ [ij illegible word crossed out]

[f.103v]

3.2 The cownt of the church stuffe [1570–71][23]

Item a chales. A swtt of blak wosterd with ij coppes, but these lakytt a wobe & a nalb
A per of vestements of red vellvett
A per of [lewks crossed out] vestements of lwks gold
A per of vestements of whytt damaske
A per of ^vestements of ^ [yowlle sylke lackyn his wobe crossed out] yollo sylk
ij frunts of yowlo sylke with ij cortens
v per of serpells and iiij rachatts
iiij awter clothes and one towell
A clothe for the pyxke and ij fawnt clothys
v corporis casses// and ij kyerchars.
A pall for the hyersse and a stremer of sylke
A letten basson & a per of candell styks
A skones a [chea crossed out] chesse abell of blwe sylk
A carpett for the tabell[24]

The stuff that be longeth to the churche howesse

Item iiij tabell bordes/ vj long tressells of ellme
Item iiij ellme planks/ ij tressells for syssyers
Item a dressen bord for the kyechyn
Item iij assen planks
Item on assen plank
^ther remyneth with Symon Holman one tabell bourd of vj fout^[25]

[f.102v]

3.3 A true noott of all such thyngs as belongeth to paryshe [1578]

Fyrst towe coupes on of sylver & on of wood
Item tow tabell clothes
Item iiij pear of serpelles
Item on[e] pello for the comunyon tabell
Item on[e] costlett
Item fyve pere of harnys
Item iiij swords & iij dagars
Item ij calyvers wyth iij flaskes & tychbocks
Item iij bowes & iij shewe of aros & towe bylls

23 Snell, *Edwardian Inventories*, p.33 ascribes this to 1553, but a later date is likely. For Chagford ale wardens list 7 January 1570–71, see Osborne, *Church Wardens' Accounts of St Michael's Church Chagford*, p.218.

24 ^14s 1d, 8li 7s 9d^ marginal entries.

25 End of 1570–71 account, BL, Add MS 32243, f.83v.

Item one cootte for a sawdyor
& two murrions

Appendix 4: Church house court case interrogatories and depositions, 19 September 1583 (CRO, P216/25/140).

[f.27][26]

Intergatoryes to be mynistred on the behalfe of John Corrye plentiefe againste againste Nicholas Rundell alias Oliver defendaunte

1 *Imprimis* whether youe knowe the plentiefe & defendaunte & the tenemente called or knowne by the name of the churche house in Stratton yea or not.

2 Item whether [doe crossed out] youe knowe any of the feoffees to whome the said tenement was geven or graunted & to what use or uses the same tenement was geven [or graunted crossed out] & [wh crossed out] how the rentes revennewes, yssues & profittes of the same have bynne ymployed & bestowed by the said feoffees or any of theme or by any others from tyme to tyme.

3 Item whether youe knowe how muche lande the said feoffees have or ought to have [wh crossed out] withoute the said churche house wall and whether youe knowe the bondes therof & by what meanes youe doe know the same.

4 Item whether youe knowe that at faires & merkettes holden & kepte within the towne of Stratton that the churche wardens of the same parishe for the tyme beyinge have let & sett standinges

[f.28]

againste & by the walle of the said churche howse & upon thereunto next adioyninge & withoute & before the place where the [staied crossed out] staire of the said howse did stand & how longe have youe knowne the same & whether that the profit therof hathe bin taken from tyme to tyme to the use of the parishe ye or no.

5 Item whether youe know that the said defendaunte did at any tyme here to fore promyse to doe in everi thinge as the reste of the feoffees of the said tenemente shoulde or would doe for the preservacon of there estate, right, title & intereste of, in & to the same or not.

6 Item [w crossed out] whether youe knowe what keyes of the [premysses crossed out] said tenemente the defendaunte or his assignes hathe and whether hee have taken or had any manner of profitte, comoditie, gayne or advantage by the same howse to his owne [y crossed out] use or not.

[f.29]

7 Item whether youe knowe that the said defendaunte or any others hathe at any tyme or tymes practised or used any waies or meanes to decease[27] or defeate the feoffees or any of them of there right title & intereste of, in or towe the said tenemente or the rentes, revennewes, yssues & profittes therof or of any parte therof by settinge of standinges upon ^any^ parte of the same at faires or markets or have interrupted or disturbed them or any of them in that behalfe & who they be that have so done & [when crossed out] how longe since.

f.1

Deposyons taken at Stratton the xixth daye of September in the xxvth yere of the raigne of our soveraigne ladye Elizabeth the qenes majes^tie^ & that now is etc. taken before us Richard Chamonde esquire [between John Corry plaintiff & Nicholas crossed out]

[26] 'Depositions concerning the church house' on the back, rearranged to make best sense of the case. Interrogatories appear at the end of the bundle of twenty-nine folios.

[27] Disseise.

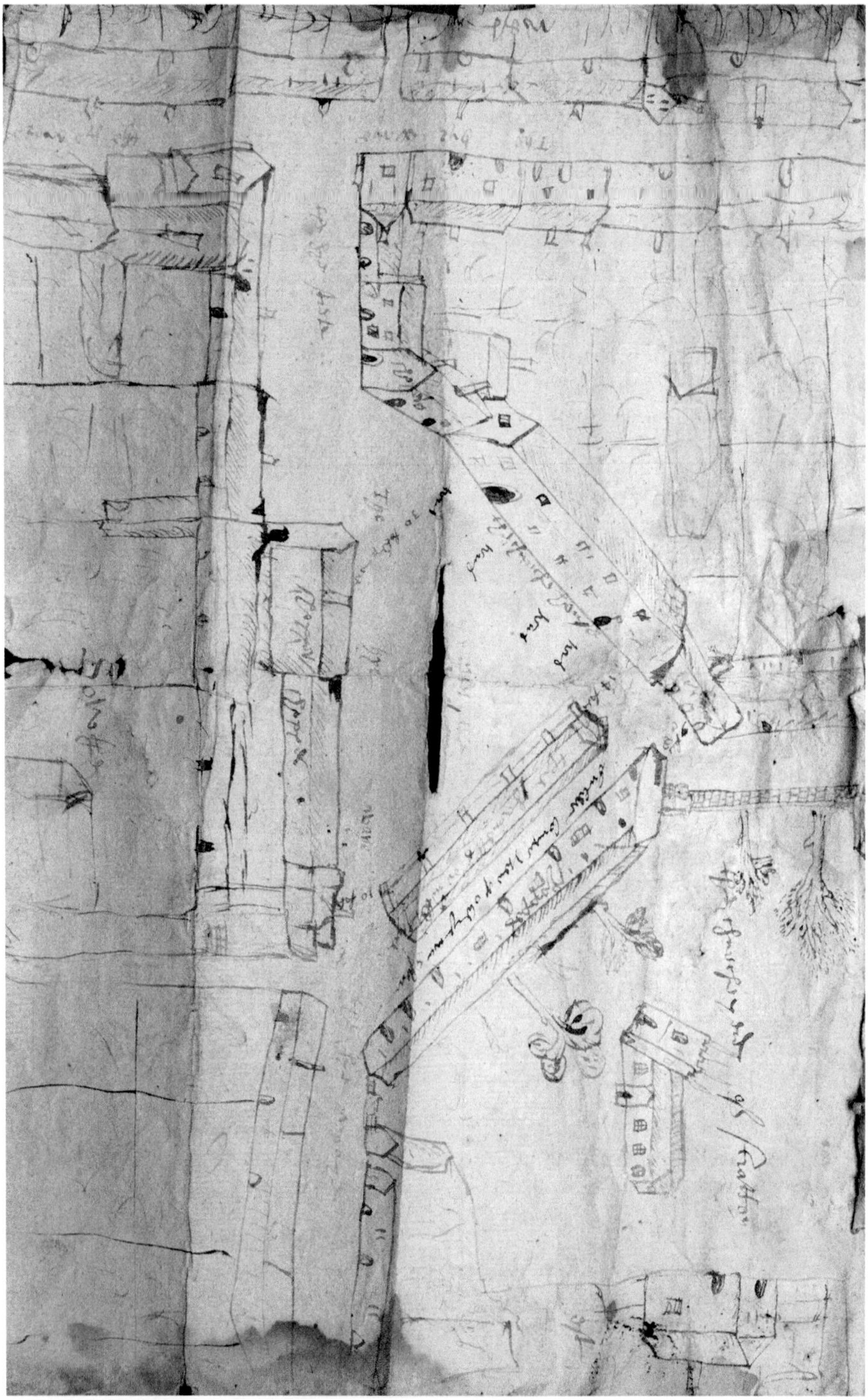

Figure 7 Pictorial plan of church house, the church and the marketplace, 1583. (Reproduced courtesy of Cornwall Record Office, CRO, P216/25/140a)

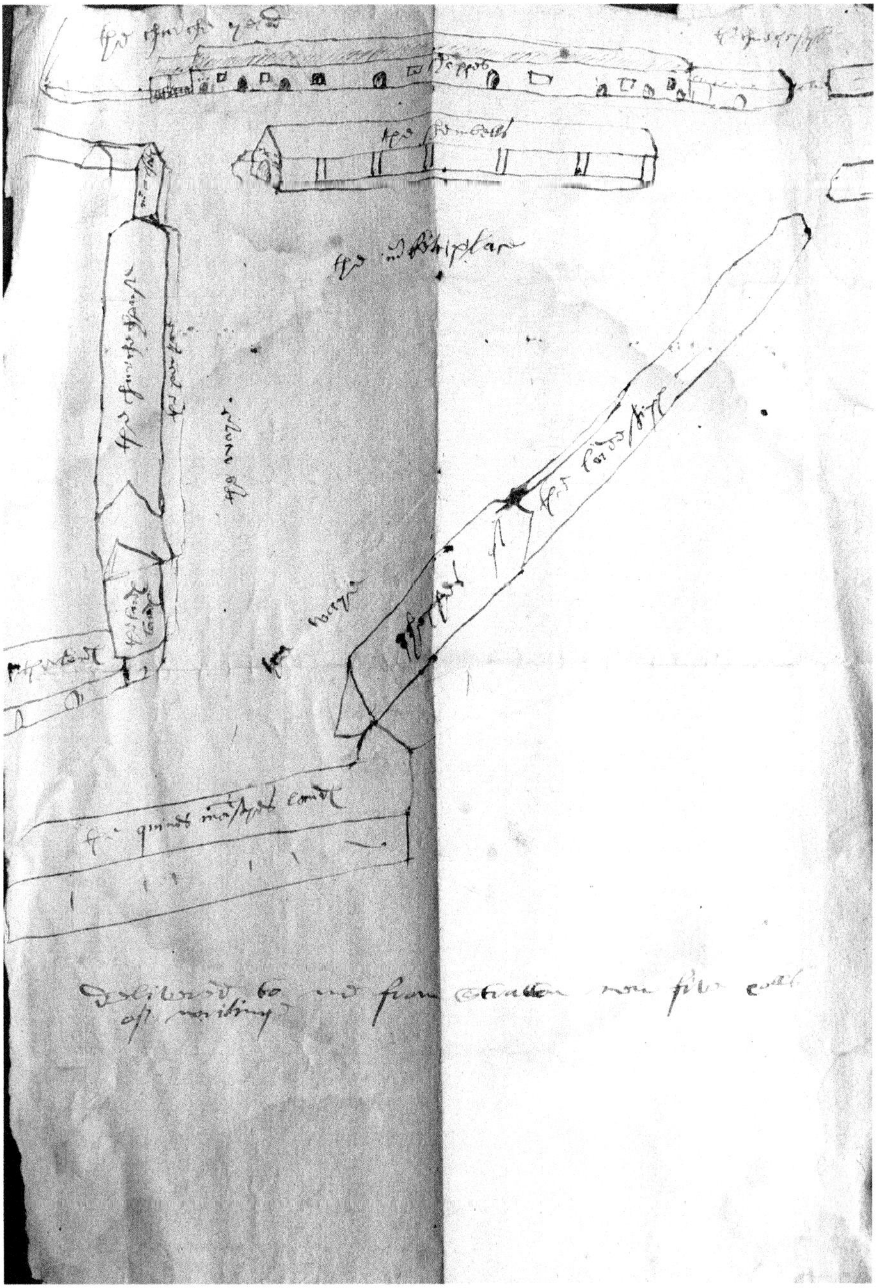

Figure 8 Bird's-eye view of the marketplace and church house, 1583. (Reproduced courtesy of Cornwall Record Office, CRO, P216/25/140b)

John Kempthorne esquier & Degory Tremayne esquire betwene John Corry plaintiff & Nicholas Rundell defendant by vertue of comission to us directed as followeth – etc[28]

^*Ex parte John Cory queren*^

1 *Imprimis* [In the first] **Richard Corrye** of Whalesborrow of thage of threescore & tenne yeres or theraboute s[w]orne & examinyed saieth to the furste intergatorye that he knowethe the partie [f crossed out] plaintiff & defendant & the tenement menconed in the same intergatory.

2 Item to the seconde intergatorye he saith that he knewe that the same tenement was geven to certen feoffees but to whome he doth not certenly remember but as he thinkethe that one William Call[29] was one of the said feoffees but to what use or uses the same tenemente was geven he knowethe not. And also ^he saithe^ ther [was crossed out] were twoe wardens chosen yerelye in the parishe of Stratton named the Highe Cross wardens otherwise called ^the^ church wardens of the sayd parishe that had the yerely collection of the rentes & profites of the said tenemente & churche howse. That is to weet of the profittes of the standinges againste the churche howse wall of the said parishe

f.2

of Stratton & in the churche howse wherof the said wardens had the only lettynge & settynge therof did yerely make accompte & deliver the same to the stocke wardens in like manner yerely chosen to the use of the said parishe who distributed the same to gether with other moneyes also collected to the use of the said [poore crossed out] parishe. That is to weet as well to wardes/ the relieffe of the poore of the said [poore of the said parish crossed out] parishe, reparacon of the churche & other necessary affares & chardges of the parishe aforesaid.

3 Item to the third intergatorye he saethe that he dothe not knowe how muche landes the said feoffees have or ought to have withoute the said churche howese walles but he hath hard by the reporte of old men that the said feoffees should have forten foote withoute the said church howse walles and

f.3[30]

that for the space of fourty & seaven yeres or theraboutes he saieth he hathe knowen divers standynges for merchantes againste the said churche house walle reachinge owte from the walle tenne foote or there aboute beynge sett by the said churche wardens at faires & merkettes.

4 Item to the fowerthe intergatory he saith as before he hathe said in the thirde intergatory, & farthear saiethe that he dothe remember that there was a steare[31] builded oute from the said churche howse reachinge oute into the streate sixe or seaven foote or there aboute to goe [upon crossed out] ^uppe^ into ^the^ upper rome of the said howese and that againste that staire towards the streight the church wardens did sett a standing for a hatter comonlye & that he hathe knowne the same fowrety seaven yeres or there aboute

f.4

and that the profittes thereof hathe bin taken so longe tyme by the said wardens to the use of the parishe as he hathe before deposed.

5 Item to the fyvethe intergatory he can say nothynge.

6 Item to the sixth intergatory he saithe that by reporte the said defendaunte dothe kepe the keyes or some of them of the said churche howese & that he knowethe not what gayne the

[28] Ff.1–21 all signed by Henry Baker and John Dobell.

[29] CRO, P216/25/130 (1556).

[30] ^*Ex parte John Cory queren*^ heading.

[31] Not shown on the 1583 plans, the stair, probably at the higher end, was removed in 1574. See p.188.

said defendaunte hathe of the said howse but that he occupiethe the said howse & putteth in certen stuffe to his owne use.

7 Item to the seaventh intergatory he saith that by reporte he hathe hard that the said defendaunt hath interrupted & disturbed the said [defendaunte crossed out] church wardens to sett or lett the standinges [of the said crossed out] ^agaynst the said^ churche howse walle & to have the

f.5

use of the[m crossed out] said howse as before they have hade & that the said defendaunte hathe disturbed them divers & sondrie tymes by the space of one yere now last paste or there aboute.

1 **William Hore** of Stratton of the age of three score yeres or there aboute sworne & examined saiethe to the firste intergatory as the foresaid Richarde Corrye hathe saiethe to that intergatorye.

2 Item to the seconde intergatorye he saiethe that he did knowe one William Call some tyme of of thold feoffees of the said tenemente & churche howse and that he dothe also knowe divers of the nowe feoffees of the same as namely John Yeo at Tree,[32] John Yeo at Bridge, Thomas Call, smyth, one Hallette & Nicholas Rundell[33] the defendaunte ^and^ that they be feoffees of truste of the same to the use of parishe of Stratton and that the profites therof were gathered by the [hew crossed out]

f.6

hed wardens of the said parishe. And that the same profittes were imployed to the use of the churche that is to weete in relyvinge of the poore of the same parishe, reparacons of the churche, expences of the wardens at visitatons & other necessarye affares of the parishe aforesaid.

3 Item [k crossed out] to the third intergatorye he saiethe that he knewe three bonde stones in the streate of Stratton distante from the church wall, twelve foote or ther aboute oute into the streat of the towne aforesaid of which thone stone was against the [& mideste crossed out] ^myddeste^ of the said churche house, one other by the shamnels end[34] & the third againste the lower ende of the churche howse all which bondestones are now taken away but by whome he knoweth not but he saith he can goe very [never crossed out] near the place with in twoe foote where they were or there aboute.

4 Item to the fowreth intergatory he saieth that he knowethe

f.7

that at faires & markets holden within the said towne that the hed wardens of the said parishe alwayes for the space of fortie yeres & upward except one yere now last paste have sett & lette the standinges aswell againste the said church howse wall & upon the land therunto ^next^ adioyninge as in the said churche howse to the use of the ^said^ parishe [church crossed out] & that he himselfe this deponaunte beinge one of the hed wardens hathe lett & sett the same aswell withoute as within & hathe receaved the profites therof to the use of the parishe [as crossed out] aforesaid and also dyd sett the standynge agaynst the stere of the sayd churche howse who take the proffytts therof to the use of the paryshe as aforsayd.

5 Item to the fiveth intergatorye he saith that hee did here the said defendaunte promysse in the churche that he would doe as the reste of the feoffees did.

6 Item to the sixth intergatory he saiethe that the said defendant had kept the keyes of the said tenemente by the space of one yere or there aboutes & did take the profittes of the

[32] Tree Inn – originally Merchant's house?

[33] 1556 feofees, CRO, P216/25/137.

[34] Figure 7 shows land claimed, but not bound stones. See p.218.

f.8

churche howse & the said [standeth crossed out] standinges wherof hee hath not yet yelded accompte to the said parishe to this deponent[s crossed out] knowledge & that the said defendaunte hathe yet in the said howse divers tressells & bordes & other necessary thinges for standinges.

7 Item to the seaventhe intergatorye he saithe that the said defendant hathe withe in one yere laste paste divers tymes interrupted & letten the wardens of the said parishe [& crossed out] ^to^ lette [to crossed out] and sette the standinges agaynste the said churche howse & in the said howse & that the said defendaunte hath lett & sette the said standinges & taken the profittes therof to his owne use as this deponente thinkethe.

1 **Justynyon Jule** of the age of fyftye [seaven crossed out] eyght yeres or there aboute sworne and examyned saith to the first intergatory [sayeth crossed out]

f.9

that he knowethe the parties plaintiff & defendaunte and the churche howse menconed in that intergatorye.

2 Item to the seconde intergatorye he saieth that he knowethe some of the feoffees to whome the said land was geven namelie John Shorte, Nicholas Band, Thomas Call, John Yeo at Tree & divers others[35] and that the same was geven to thuse of the parishe as he hath harde & that the rentes & profittes therof was imployed to the mayntenantes of the ^churche^, releyffe of the poore & other necessary affares of the said parishe & the same hathe byn so imployed by the space of fortie yeres or upward to this deponents knowledge.

3 Item to the therde intergatory he saiethe that he hath harde by reporte of divers old men of the said parishe namely Thomas Hickett, William Bishoppe, John at Heale and John Uglo with others that the said feoffees menconed in

f.10

the said intergatory had [& crossed out] or ought to have fourtene foote of lande or there aboute withoute the said churche house walles & that he hath sene the bondes therof accordinglie by the reporte of the foresaid old men.

4 Item to the fowerthe intergatory he saithe that he certenly knowethe & remembreth that the churche wardens of the said parishe for the tyme beynge for the space of fortie fower yeres or ther aboute have usually frome tyme to tyme lett & sett the standinges againste the wall of the said churche howse & upon the grounde there unto next adioyninge at faires & markette[s crossed out] tymes & before & agaynste the staires of the said churche howse & have also taken the profitts therof as well for the standinges there as for the weightinge of yearne and wolle in the church howse aforesaid to the use of the said parishe.

f.11

5 Item to the fyveth intergatory he saith that hee did here by reporte that the said defendaunte had promyssed to doe as the reste of his feoffees should or would doe tochinge the land aforesaid.

6 Item to the sixth intergatory he saith that the said defendant doth kepe tow keyes of the said [defend crossed out] tenemente frome the said parishe and now doth & hathe done by the space of one yere laste paste & more taken the profits of the same howse frome the said parishe to his owne use as this deponente thinkethe & that the said defendaunte hath now at this presente divers boardes tressells & other provisyon for standinges in the said church howse.

7 Item to the seaventh intergatorye he saithe that the said defendaunte & one John Yeo at Stratton comonly called the great John Yeo have divers and sondrye tymes at faires & markets within the space of one yere & some what more now last

[35] 1576–77 feoffees, CRO, P216/25/137.

f.12
paste disturbed & interrupted the feoffees of the said lande & wardens of the parishe for ^the^ lettinge & settinge of the standinges agaynste the said churche house wall & to take the profittes of the same to thentente to defeate the feoffees [therof crossed out] of the same.

1 **William Heddon** of Stratton smithe of thage of fiftye sixe yeres or there aboute sworne & examyned saithe to the first intergatorye as Richarde Corrye & others have before said.

2 Item to the second intergatorye he saithe that he did knowe some of the old feoffees of the said tenemente or churche howse namely Thomas Heckette, Nicholas Judde & others who [reffeffed crossed out] ^refeoffyd^ the same to John Yeo at Tree, Peter Hallette & divers other yet lyvinge & that the same was geven to thuse of the parishe as far as this deponente

f.13
knowethe & that the profittes therof hath bin frome tyme to tyme imployed for the space of fortye one yeres or there aboute to the mayntenance of the churche, reliefe of the poore of the said parishe, wardens expenses [& crossed out] at visitatons & other necessary affaires of the said parishe.

3 Item to the third intergatory he saithe that he hathe hard by the reporte of divers old men namely Thomas Heckett, William Bishoppe, John Jule of Lunstone, Nicholas Symon & others that the said feoffees should have fortene foote of grounde withoute the churche house wall [belowe twentye crossed out] ^belowe and ten^ foote or there aboute ^above^ & that he hathe sene the bondes therof but the bonde belowe is taken awaye by whome he knowethe not, but the bonde above yet remaynethe to be sene.

4, 5, 6, 7 Item to the fowerthe, fyvethe, syxthe & seaventhe intergatoryes he saieth in every thinge as the aforesaid Justinyan

f.14
Jule hath aforesaid & deposed to the said intergatory.

1 **John Averye** of the age of fowrescore yeres or there aboute sworne & examyned to the first intergatorye he saithe as the aforesaid Richard Corrye & others have said & deposed.

2, 3, 4, 5, 6 Item to the [thirde crossed out] seconde, thirde, fowrethe [& crossed out], fyvethe [& crossed out] sixth intergatoryes he saith as the aforesaid Justinyan Jule & William Heddon have ^before^ said & deposed.

7 Item to the seaventhe intergatorye the said deponente saieth that Nicholas Rundell defendaunte [about crossed out] ^aboute^ St Andrues Tyde was twelvemonthe or two yeres at the faire there holden in Stratton did take upon him [did crossed out] ^to^lett & sette the standinges there withoute the churche howse walle upon the parishe land there & denyed the feoffees & the whole parishe of there right title & intereste therof & in the said tenemente or the rentes, revennewes & profittes of the said

f.15
tenemente & so interrupted & disturbed them at that tyme but who toke the profittes therof at that tyme he knoweth not but at Lentte nexte followinge this deponente did stand [thereof crossed out] there upon the said land to sell fish & the said defendaunt came unto hime & demaunded who did sett him there & he answered & said John Corrye and then the said defendaunte demaunded farther whose boardes & tressels they were & so departed & lefte this deponent remayne there quyetlye.

1 **Chrystopher Braye** of the age of fyftye fyve yeres or there aboute sworne & examined saythe to the firste intergatorye as the foresaid Justynion Jule hathe said & deposed.

2 Item as to the seconde intergatory he saith he knewe some of the olde feoffees of the said land namely Thomas Heckett and that it was geven to them & to theire heires to the use of the parishe & the rentes and profites of the same was for twentie fowre yeres

f.16

or there aboute imployed & bestowed by the wardens of the said parishe by the advise of the eyght men of the said parishe aboute the reparation of the churche, reparynge of the same howse & relieffe of the poore, provision of armor for the service of the prince, maintenance of bridges & other necessarye affaires of the said parishe.

3, 4, 5, 6, 7 Item to the third, fowerth, fyveth, sixthe & seaventh intergatoryes he saith in everi thinge as the forsaide Justynyon Jule hath said & deposed savinge that he hathe not knowne the lande aforesaid so many yeres as he hath afore menconed beynge fowertye fowere yeres but he remembreth for the space of twentye fowre or twentie five yeres or there aboute.

1 **Walter Rose** of the age of threescore [yeres crossed out] & syxtene yeres or there aboute sworne & examyned saithe to the fyrst intergatorye as the foresaid Richard Corrye & others have said.

2 Item to the second intergatorye he knoweth ^not^ who were the feoffees

f.17

to the said lande but as he hath herde the said landes of the churche howse in Stratton was geven to the use of the parishe & the yssues & profittes therof was imploied to the maintenance of the poore people of the same parishe.

3, 4 Item to the third & fowerthe intergatoryes he saithe as Justynion Jule & other hathe before deposed.

5, 6, 7 Item to the fyvethe, sixthe & seaventh intergatoryes he canne saye nothinge. [Item to crossed out].

1 **Thomas Beare** of the age of fyftye yeres or there aboute sworne & examyned saithe to the firste intergatorye as the foresaid Richard Corrye & others have deposed.

2 Item to the seconde intergatorye he saithe that he knowethe divers of the feoffees namelye John Yeo at Tree, Roberte Saunder, this deponente & divers others to whome the said tenemente was geven by some of thold feoffees to the use

f.18

for the maytenance of ^the churche^, relieffe of the poore, repayrynge of the same churche howse, providing of armorye for the service of the prince & other necessarye affares of the said parishe & that the profits therof hath binne imployed & converted to the same uses by the space of [thirthi crossed out] thyrtye yeres or theraboute by the churche wardens of the same parishe.

3 Item to the third intergatory he cann saye nothinge.

4 Item to the fowerthe intergatory he sayeth that he hathe knowen for the space of thirtye yeres or there aboute the churche wardens of the same parishe at faires & markettes ^holden^ with in the said ^said^ towne from tyme to tyme to sett & lette the standinges ^agaynst^ and by the walle of the said churche howse and upon the grounde thereunto adioyninge ^and^ before the said staires & have durynge their tyme taken the profittes of the same & of the churche howese to the uses aforesaid.

f.19

5 Item to the fyveth intergatory this deponente saieth that he and others beynge sente to the said defendaunte by all or the moste parte of the feoffees of the said land to knowe whether he would doe as the reste of the feoffees should or would doe tochinge the said land to whome the said defendaunte answered that he woulde doe in every thinge as the reste of the feoffees would or should doe touching & concerning the same.

6, 7 Item to the sixthe & seaventh intergatoryes he saiethe as the foresaid [July crossed out] Justinyon Jule hathe before deposed.

1, 2 **William Willys** alias Hele of thage of fyftye seaven yeres or there aboute sworne &

examyned saith to the firste and second intergatoryes as the foresaid Justinyon Jule hathe deposed.

3 Item to the thirde intergatorye he sayethe that aboute fortye fower or fortye fyve yeres sythens one William Bishoppe, Willyam

f.20

Payne, Thomas Heckette & divers other old [& crossed out] men of the said parishe did shewe unto this deponente & to dyvers other yonge men of the said parishe the bondes betwene the [londes crossed out] ^lordes^ of Stratton & the lands that the feoffees had bought of Trengeare which conteyned aboute fowertene [fortene crossed out] foote withoute the churche howse walle below & aboute tenne foote above & badd this deponente & the said others to remember there saynge touching the said landes & bondes.

4 Item to the fowerth intergatory he saiethe that for the space of xxx^tie^ yeres & upwarde this deponente hathe knowne that the said church wardens have from tyme to tyme sett & [le crossed out] lett the standings menconed in the said intergatory & have converted the profittes therof to the uses of the said parishe viz in repayringe the churche [& crossed out], reliving the poore of the same parishe and other necessarye affares of the said parishe.

f.21

5 Item to the fyveth intergartorye he said that the said defendaunte did promysse to doe in everi thinge as the resydew of the feoffees have done or should doe touchinge the said land.

6 Item to the sixth intergatory he [saieth crossed out] hathe harde saie that the said defendaunte dothe kepe the keyes of the said house & hath put into the said house divers tressells, boardes & other furniture for standinges for the space of one yere now last paste or more.

7 Item to the seaventh intergatory he saieth that he hath harde divers – of the parisheners reporte that the said defendaunte at divers faires & merkettes for one yere or more now laste paste hath disturbed & interrupted the feoffees of the said land & wardens of the said parishe for the settynge & lettynge of the said standinges & for taking of the profittes of the same.

[f.25]

Intergatories to be mynistred on the parte & behalf of Nicholas Rundell defendaunte to the bill of complainte of John Corrye complaynante[36]

1 *Imprimis* whether doe youe knowe the pleintiefe & defendaunte or any of them.

2 Item whether doe youe knowe the churche howse of Stratton menconed in the said bill of compl[aint].

3 Item whether doe youe knowe or have you hard that the said churche howse was geven towardes the mayntenaunces ^of the ^ parishe churche & poore [& crossed out] of the said parishe of Stratton or to what other uses & how doe youe know the same to be trewe.

4 Item to what uses were the rentes & profittes of the said churche house & other the lands of the said church belonginge imployed & converted to your rememberance or as youe have hard.

5 Item whether doe youe know the lande where the churche howse was builded [on crossed out] on before the house was builded & for what use the same served.

[f.26]

6 Item whether were there any standinges or bouthes pitched [on crossed out] on the said lande in tyme of markettes and faires & whether were the profittes therof paied to the use of one Trengeare then lorde of the same.[37]

[36] Two folios of interrogatories placed before depositions for defendant.

[37] CRO, P216/25/129. Rough notes in a later hand (as on plan a, see Figure 7) on back: '1599 / the 3 Julye there were teaken out 30 peces of writt[i]ng, 24 ux[illegible] delivered yarn, 17 writtenges & 2 boxes test. Nicholas Urll & 2 bond John Corye & John Yeo/. Delivered in all these./ Lente him & Water Yeo for the performans of the parishes leases./ Memorandum unto mi cossen Heale, 2 bonds of 30li everich that the vicar standeth bonde

[f.22]

[Depositions] ***Ex parte*** **Nicholas Rundell** ***defendentis***[38]

1, 2 **John Moryes** of Stratton gent of the age [three crossed out] ^fower^ skore yeres or ther aboutes sworne & examyined saith to the first & seconde intergatorye [& crossed out] that he did knowe the parties plentiefe & defendant & the churche house menconed in the second intergatorye & that he did knowe the grounde before the churche howse was builded.[39]

3 Item to the thirde intergatorye he saieth that he did knowe the said churche house ^was^ builded to the use of the parishe & to none other use to this deponents knowledge & that the parisheners did alwayes use to kepe there churche drinkinges in the same upon Rogacon Mundaye[40] & suche like dayes.

4 Item to the fouerthe intergatorye he saieth that the rentes & profittes of the said church & of other landes [& of other landes crossed out] of the said churche were & have bin from tyme to tyme by the space of three skore yeres & tenne or there aboute

[f.23]

imploied & converted to the use of the said parishe namely to the relieffe of the poore of the said parishe, reparacon of the churche & other necessarye affares & business of the parishe aforesaid.

5 Item to the fyvethe intergatorye he saith as before he hathe said.

6 Item to the sixthe intergatorye he saithe that he never knewe any standinges or boves [p crossed out] pight upon the said landes before the buildinge of the howse in tyme of markets & faires but he saith that the same place whereupon the howse is now builde was a comon filthy place & that the same was one Trengears lande but what profittes he tooke therof this deponent knoweth not.

1–2 **Jhon Copledycke** of the age of fowerskore yeres or ther aboute sworne & examined saieth to the fyrste &

[f.24]

second intergatoryes as the foresaid John Morys hath said in the same intergatoryes.

3 Item to the thirde intergatory he can saie nothinge.

4 Item to the foureth intergatory he saieth that the rentes and profittes of the said church house was comonlye taken by the Heighe Crosse wardens of the parishe of Stratton and that this deponent beynge on a tyme Highe Crosse warden[41] did receave fyve shillings for standinges againste the church howse wall [& crossed out] whereof eyghte pence was for waightinge of yearne at afaire holden at Stratton aforesaid which moneys he delivered unto the stocke wardens who did imploye the same to the mayntenauntes of the churche.

5 Item to the fyveth intergarorye he sayth that he did knowe the land before the said church howse was builded but to what use it was [builded crossed out] imployed he knoweth not.

6 Item to the sixthe intergatory he canne say no more then he before hath said.

Com[issioners] Richard Chamonde esquire,
John Kemthorne esquire & Digory Tremayne esquire//

with agremynt for wooll & lambes. 1 band of 10li & 3 contrepains of Straton, & a contrepane of Treburtell at John Yeo.'

38 Three folios.

39 Church house built c.1515.

40 After beating the bounds?

41 1548–49.

Glossary

Only a small sample of spellings is given below. The most common spellings, or those closest to modern form, are generally used, with a few examples given of words with detached letters. Only variants with a different first letter are cross-referenced, with etc. used to indicate this. Sources used: *COED* and see the Bibliography.

a boff above
a count (accompte) account
a genste (a gynnys) against, in honour of
a monse amongst
a pone upon
agayen again
agge, *see* **hagg**
albe (albys etc.) long white priest's robe
alers aisles
alyers (alers) alleys outside church
amletore ambulatory, aisle
amonthe amounts to
angells roof angels
anoyer, *see* **noder**
apurnes aprons for paupers
aquittans acquittance, pardon
archys arches
archysdekyn (archedecon, arsdecan, aschdekyn) archdeacon's held visitations
armiger esquire
armoure (armorye) armour, armoury
arrowes (aros) arrows
arrushees, *see* **russhe**
artykyls visitation articles?
artylcyre artillery
assen ashen planks
assies assise court
aulter (awtur etc.) altar
avyse advise
awnsur etc. answer
awyd owed
ayre, *see* **ire**

bacun bacon
badd bade, instructed
bake seat back
baker (bayer) baker, baking iron
banckyt banquet
bareles barrels for lime
barganyd contracted
barne burn
barrs window bars etc.
bason (besson) basin

basterd nail type
bawe boy
bayes (beyse) baize, coarse woollen material
baylyes bailiffs
be (bi) by
be quethe bequest
be twene between
beame rood beam
bede (beds) rosary beads
bede roll (bedroll, bedderoll) roll of people to be prayed for
bedman (beddeman) grave digger?
bedreden annual reading of bede roll
bekyn beacon
belcolers, *see* **colerys**
belluter (belefownder etc.) bellfounder
belropys bell ropes
belys (bele, bellys, boll) bells
bendyng (bendinge) book binding
beneght by night
bere (bear) funeral bier
berehurds bear-keepers
beren carrying
berethe carries weight of, contains
bestode given
besynes church business, rebellion
better more
beyse base, debased coinage
bhare bear
biggins children's caps
blake (brack) sute requiem vestments
blankette for pauper
blew (blwe) blue
blyssing (bressyng) blessing, consecrating
bobb of bell?
boce boss?
bock (bok, bucke etc.) book
bockell (buckyll) buckles for bells, armour
bofte bought
bokeram (bocram) buckram, fine open-weave linen cloth
bolle (bollyng) patching bell clappers
bondes boundary markers
bord (burd) board, table, type nail
borid borrowed
botens buttons
botte (but) archery butt/target, large cask
bottyll (botiles) for wine?
bouthes (boves) fair booths
bowes for archers
boxe pyx
bozth both
bradry gold for embroidering vestments
bras (brace) brass, bell supports
bred communion bread, breadth
brege (bryg) bridge

brent (bornd) burnt

broder brother

brodyer embroiderer

browerse hedge trimmings

brozft (brozt) brought

bruinge brewing

Brytton Breton

bukett (bockyte etc.) holy water bucket

bull neke for making coffer

bulringe tethering ring for bull?

bushull (bosshel, bz etc.) 8 gallons dry measure

butterie (botry) church house buttery

Bybell (Bebell etc.) Bible

byle (byll) hedging tool/weapon, document

bysshope (bosshopp etc.) bishop of Exeter visits and visitations

byynf buying

cace case for corporals or chalice

calender book

callever caliver, light gun

candeles (cundels) candles

canell bell canon, neck

canepy (canabe) high altar canopy

canne ale can

canves (chanvas) coarse hemp/flax

carag (caryeg) carriage goods

carped communion table carpet

carpenture carpenter

cathecheseme religious instruction books using question and answer

caunty county

cawse causeway

cay, *see* **kye**

cence, *see* **sence**

centerns (cynters etc.) framework for making arch

chalys chalice

chandeler (chendeles) candle stand

changyng exchanging

charies charges

chawnsell (chownsyll) chancel

chayne Bible/censer chain

cheld child

chepter ecclesiastical chapter court

cherche (chowrche, chruche, crych) church

cherchehowse (churchhows) church ale house

cherse kersey, woollen cloth

cherubyms, *see* **angells**

chese cheese

chesse abell chasuble

chesyl chisel

chowmber chamber

churcherd churchyard

churchstell, *see* **styll**

chymlye chimney

cinyng, *see* **singen**

clapare (claperys) bell clapper
clarcke parish/market clerk
clatch plaster
clats cleats
cler (chlere) clear profit
cleye clay to cast bells
clok (cholke, cloyc) clock
clothys (clathe, clozth) altar cloths, lead sheet
clyen clean
cock firearm cock
colers paints
colerys (colar etc.) collars
colys coal
compt, *see* **a count**
compulsior compulsion to serve the parish
comuning (comonyon) communion
constabells constables
contrepains counterparts, copies of leases
cooking stole cucking stool
cop (coppes) cope, semi-circular priest's cloak
cope (coupes etc.) communion cups
coper copper
corant current
corde for Lent cloth etc.
cordener cordwainer, shoemaker
corporys (carperas) corporal cloths for mass
corse coarse metal
cortens (curtayne) curtains
cortte legal court
cossen cousin
costage expenses
costlett (costhell, costilet) corslet, body armour
cotidiall every day
cott (coote) coat
covenants book book of sub-tenants' contracts
cowde could
cownesell legal advice
cowpartener co-partner
crescloth (clescloth) linen
crest (crestis) crested ridge tile about a foot in length
crewytts (cruyts) mass wine/water cruets
crobe etc. cob for building
croke cooking pot
croks crooks for gate, pothooks
crowder fiddle player
crownys 5-shilling coins
Crysmasse (Crecemas) Christmas
cumyn coming, arrival
cumyth (comyt) adds up to
cusshin (cosshynes) communion table cushions
custodye keeping
cutler knife maker

dachyng thatching

dafter (daufftes) daughter
dagars daggers
damaske silk/linen with raised figures woven in
darsessyd deceased
dayes (des) days
decease disseise, take back land
ded (dyd) did
dedes deeds
denar dinner
deseburse pay out
deske (dexis) desk, lectern
destybyt (distrubit) give out
dimidia half
dobelet (dublet) doublet
dole royal tax
doum dumb
dowlas (dowlys) coarse linen
dowre (dower) door
dowthe doth
drange drain
drawe haul
drayng (drowyng) hauling stone, taking down altars, drawing
drenk (dryncke, dryng) drink
dresen (dressin) preparing food, rubbing down armour
drinkinges church ales
dryyng seasoning wood
durnes doorposts
dystrayne distrain, confiscate goods

eat, *see* **yate**
eer, *see* **yer**
Egyppcions (Egepcyons etc.) gypsies, believed to Egyptians
ele, *see* **alers**
ellme elm tree
emanuel, *see* **manuell**
endentors etc. indented duplicate document
Erasmus (Eurasmus), *see* **parafrace**
ermerer armourer
ernest bargain penny, pledge
errows, *see* **arrowes**
erthe earth
erthyn earthen
est east
estatt estate, lands
Ester etc. Easter
evydens title deeds
exchekere Exchequer Court
excomunycatt excommunicate, deprived of sacraments
expencys etc. expenses
eyers curtain loops

facyon fashion
fader father
faketts faggots

falle monetary devaluation
fardens farthings, *see* **Peter's**
faste make fast, secure
fawnt font
fawtes faults
fayre (feare, fer) fair
fechinge (fetyng) fetching
fellynge (fyllyng) felling timber
felows fellows, Robin Hood's men
felvet, *see* **velfotte**
fenden finding
feofers feoffees
ferdelys etc. lime measure
fes (fie) fees
fethering feathering of arrows
feythement feoffment lands
flake hurdle
flaske powder flask
fleells flails
flowr (floyr) floor
flowre flour
floxe flock stuffing
fonoue funnel
foote (fose, fowte etc.) 12 inches, foot or furniture leg
forbor harness scourer or smith?
formys (fowrms) church house seats
fortenyzt fortnight
framys bell frames
frankenscens (francancens, frankence, frowkencens) incense
frethyng (frythyng) hedge trimming
frice (fries) frieze
frow from
frunts altar frontals
furen repairing
furnished complete
fyene fine

gaderyd collected
gage pledge
gawe gave
gaylles gallows
gefte (gyffte, gyzfte) gift, bequest
gellte (gyltte) gilt
gemes (gemys) door/gate hinges
gerdelys (gyrdells) girdles
gevyn given
glace (glas) glass
glassen (glasyn) glazing
glasyar (glacier etc.) glass fitter
glew glue
glovys gloves to seal bargain
godspels gospel book
goune (gownd, goyne) gown
grandmoder grandmother

grawe (grawff, grayff) church grave
grayle gradual book
greces (greysys) steps
gress/e (gres, gryse) grease
grette (greatt) great, grit

hacho long broad headed roof nail
hagg (hassyc, heg etc.) hedge
hally holy
hapes (hapsse) hasp, door/gate latch
harnyes (hernes) harness or body armour
haulls (holys) holes
hawne (havener) haven
hawssyn housing for bell
hawyn hewing
hayse hawser?
heades arrow heads
heddyn putting heads on arrows
helpyn helping workmen, choir
helyer (heller) hellier, roofer or slater
helyng (hallen, helyon etc.) roofing, slating
hepe grain heap
herrett heriot, best beast or fine due to the lord of the manor on death of tenant
hes his
heygh (hye, hyzght) high
hobys, *see* **albe**
hogs hed barrel for lime
holborne halberd?
hold, *see* **owlde**
holl whole
holond (howeland) holland, a linen cloth
holy water bucket, *see* **bukett**
hondart (hundrd) hundred
hondes hands
hongyng hanging
hony (huny) honey
hoper cooper
hoppys hops for brewing
horssemett horse food
hose (hossen) leggings
howess (howce, heowse, hoys) house
howsbond husband
howslyng (hosslen etc.) houseling, communion
hurdels scaffolding platforms
hurts damage, injury
hyer here, higher
hyere (heare, hyer) hire
hyerent chief rent
hyersse hearse, funeral bier
hyllts sword hilts
hymnor hymnal
hyzth height

Ierysche Irish

imagys statues
imprimis in the first place
in juncyon writ
intercloys enterclose, side screens
invitori inventory, list
ire (iar etc.) iron

jemys, *see* **gemes**
Jepsyons, *see* **Egyppcions**
jerkyn close-fitting man's jacket
jerre lamp oil jar
Jewes, *see* **Egyppcions**
jorney day work
Jule's book, Lord Bishop Jewell's *Apology*
juner joiner

kay (kee) quay
kepyn (kyepyng) looking after – clock, bells, register
kercher (kyerchars) kerchiefs, altar cloths
kersy, *see* **cherse**
kertell kirtle, underdress
kerver (kyrver) carver
keveryn covering books etc.
kiefe trough
klob, *see* **crobe**
knogys sheafs
knyllys (knollys, knyle) knell, funeral bell toll
koller, *see* **colerys**
konte, *see* **a count**
kop, *see* **cope**
kychin (kechyng, kyechyn) church house kitchen
kye etc. key
kyll (kell) kiln

laakyn (lakytt) lacking
laase lace
labare labour, work
lade lady
laft (laught, lofft) rood loft
lantrane (lantron) lantern
lasyn (lason) lacing
lates (lazth) laths
lawcurte law court
lazar (laser) leper hospital
leche latch, ledge, lych bell or gate, doctor
leche craft doctoring
lede (lides, lyd etc.) lead, leads
legentt service book
leggys furniture legs
lekeys (lwks) gold cloth of gold from Lucca
Lentcloth painted cloth to hang across chancel in Lent
lente (lonyd, londe) lent, loaned
letten latten, brass alloy
leyd laid

leyng (lyen etc.) laying in legal bills, tile
licens permission
lizt light, candle before statue
lode load
lokke lock
lokyng looking, viewing
longyng belonging to
lorde lord of manor, bishop's title
lyer book
lym (leme, lyem) lime
lyncloth (linclothe) linen cloth
lynne line

maken (mackinge, makyng) making
manuell (emanuel) sacrament book
marchands merchants
masbocke mass book
masonce (masyn) stonemason
Master gentleman, priest with Master's degree from Oxford or Cambridge
matens English matins book
matt (mettis) communion kneeling mat, window cover
mayd made, servant or girl
mayhamyd, meamed maimed
me my
medowys meadows
Mekelmas (Myghelmas) Michaelmas
mele grain for flour
mell mill
mellte (mollte, mylltt) melt
menden (mendyne, myddyng) mending
meneday (myndaye) mind day, obit
menys men's
mercer luxury cloth dealer
mercymentts amercements
merkettes market
messers (myssyers) masters/merchants at fair from messieur?
mete meet, suitable
mete (met, matytt) workman's food
mettill metal
metyn measuring
moder mother
mone money
more Bodmin Moor
mores (mote, moye) tree roots, bole
morestone (mourestonys) granite
morstryng mustering
moryon (morian, moryngs, murriones) helmets
mouster muster
mydell rome/church nave
mylward miller

nalb, *see* **albe**
nawter, *see* **aulter**
naylys (neales, nell) nails

nessecite poverty, hardship
newe (nu, nyew) new
noder another
norsynge nursing
nowtis organ notes
nowtyd noted
nyzght night

ob[ulus] halfpenny
obligacon contract under penalty
obys, *see* **albe**
obyte anniversary of death
occupyyng using
ode, *see* **wode**
oder other
offycall royal official?
offys office
oke oak
ord point or awl?
ordinaments church ornaments, requiem vestments?
organys (orgones) organs
othe oath
over plus profit
ovys eaves
owlde old
owre our
owtt out
oyer other
oyle (owle) lamp oil

paafmentt pavement
pac (packis, pake) pack, bundle of rushes
pagents rood loft scenes
palle coffin cloth
Pallme Palm Sunday
panne (panes) coal/lime pan
paper (paver) for books, music
parafrace of Erasmus New Testament commentary
parmittyng paving
parte divide
paryn cutting
pascall taper Easter candle
paspot (pasbote) pauper passes
passelle parcel, bundle
patrone pattern
paven paving
paver paviour
payented painted
payesture wood pasture
payns (payne) painstaking
paynters (penters) painters
payse pace, raised step for lamp
pease clock weights
peces (pesys) pieces

pecktors (pycktors) pictures
peeres bell piers, supports
pek (peecke, pyck) quarter bushel
peke (pychs) pike
pekyng pecking, tuning bells
pekyx (pycyse etc.) pick, pickaxe
pello pillow
penakyls pinnacles
penard pennyworth?
pentes (pentis, pentyse) church house pentice roof
per (peer) pair
performance fulfilment
Peter's (Petters) quarter, farthings papal tax paid to Elizabeth I
pettikotte peticoat, undergarment
pewys pews as Lady's pew
peyryll apparell
pight pitched
plaged plagued
planching flooring
plate church plate
platts plates, fixings
players travelling actors
ple plea
plesure pleasure, please
plumer (plommer) plumber
poche (putche) pitch for bell ropes
polle clock pole
polys (pole) pulleys
ponyon (punyon) corner of building
pore (pawre, pure) poor
posses posts
possession take land
possyng propping up
potyll (pottyls) pottle or half-gallon, ale, cider, oil
poutte put name on bede roll
pownde (pond, powne) 8 ounces weight
poynells type of nail?
poynsyn (poynshyn) puncheon for lime
poynten pointing walls
poynts (pontes) ties
prayer book The English Protestant Prayer Book
precepe precept, warrant
prest forced enlistment
prickyng writing music
prikesong music book for singing
pristes (pryst) priests
promys stick to bargain
prosessynall (presessinall) procession book
pulpytt pulpit
purse male money bag?
pyggs bell pegs
pylers pillars
pyne (pinnes) iron pins
pynyng fixing pillars, altars

pystels epistles book
pyte (pytt) church grave, bell pit
pyxke (pexce) pyx
pyys pies

quarte (quarrtt) two pints of honey, wax
quary quarry
queres (quear) four sheets or eight leaves of paper
quettance, *see* **aquittans**
quite quit
quyre (quere, qwyer) choir

raggs small slates
ratyfyed made valid
raunsom ransom
raze desk step
rebens ribbons to mend vestments
rebytts rebates
recetes (resett etc.) receipts
recevers general receivers
recevid (ressevyd) received
recoverye land recovery
redd (rede, rid) clean out
redenge (redyn, riding, ryddyng) ridding, cleaning out
regester (reiester) parish register
regestryng putting names on bede roll
relece (relese) of land
releyfe (releve) poor relief
remayneth (remenyght) remains in account
remeng rimming, tuning by removing bell metal
remlett remnant
removen removing
rengers bellringers
reppynge (ryppyng) tearing fur from gown or breaking locks
reryng putting up
rescull residue?
resters rafters, stay bars
restyt rests in account
revacachyn revocation
rewell rowell, wheel-shaped candle holder
reysyng raising, as roof
ringgs (renge, ryngs) rings for door, Lent cloth, lamp, bull
roble (roobell) rubble
rochetts (rachatts, rotgets, rotghydds) sleeveless surplice for baptisms
rode (rowde) rood, crucifix
rodelofte (redeloft, rowdlofte) rood loft
rods gun rods
rome space
rossin resin
roste roast
rowff (roff) roof
rowps (royp etc.) ropes
rowtyng uprooting tree
rubed robbed

russhe (rowshys, ryshes etc.) rushes
ryghtyng correcting bells

sacryng bell bell rung at elevation of sacrament during mass
saletts helmets
sarve serve, help
sarvyn (servynge) serving precept, helping workmen
satyn of burges Bruges satin
sauter psalter book
sawser saucer for communion bread
saye sea
schafyt (scaffetts) scaffolding
scharchyng searching
schelyng, *see* **helyng**
schelyngs shillings
schereffe (sheryfe) sheriff
schert (schurt, shart) pauper's shirt
scheryng shearing
schett shut, close off
scholers singing boys
scholmaster (scolemaster) schoolmaster
schope shop
schuyng shoeing horse
scope coal scoop
score twenty
scorer scourer
scrydos screeds, strips of wood used by plasterers
se view
secke sick
sefft (syft) sift
sege (seedge) pew
selen sealing documents
seler sealer of weights and measures
selyng (seylyng) ceilure
semys (seemes etc.) packhorse load
sence (sensys etc.) censer
sens since
sepulcar (sepullker) Easter sepulchre
ser (sur) sir, honorary title of priest, knight
serff serve
sertiffycats certificates
sertyne certain
server workman's helper
servyd served in place of
servyse (servece) being of service, church service
sessyans (sessyons) sessions
sesynyng seasoning wood
setts (setys) seats
settyn (syttyng) putting names on bede roll, fixing slates
seuyng (sawyng, sowyng etc.) sewing
seve (seffe) sieve
seyn seeing to bells
seynt (sent) saint
shammyles (shammylis) butchers shambles

Shere Shire court?
sherpynke sharpening
shewe sheaf
shootyng (schotyng, suyttyn) splicing bellropes
shote ammunition
shouwys (schowys, shose) shoes
showlle (schowle, soffel) shovel
shrowd (schorede, shrewde) shroud
shype (scheppe) ship-shaped frankincense container
singen (sygyne etc.) communion bread, singing
skabrydge scabbard
skoller scholar
skones sconce
skowryng (scoryng) cleaning candle stands, armour
slatts slates
slyves (slevys) for vestments, pauper
smoke pauper smock
smyzthe (smeythe) smith
sodre (sawder etc.) solder
somner summoner
sond etc. sand
songe psalm
sope (sowpe) soap
soper supper
souldiour (sawdiar) soldier
soune sang
sowthe church south aisle
spange of great bell wheel
speke speak, address
spering (spyryng) roof sparring
sponys spoons
spryngyll holy water sprinkler
spuks spikes, nails
spyll spill of clock, bell
stafe (staffe) staff, part of screen
stages organ loft
stamyn coarse worsted cloth
standen (stondyng etc.) fair stalls, statue, book or cruet stands
stape (stapell) for bells, doors
steare (ster) church house stair
stepell (stypyll) tower
stocke (stoke) parish store, bell stock
stolys long linen/silk strip worn over priest's shoulder
stonnes (stonis, stoanes) stones
stoockes stocks
stope stop
stoppyng filling holes
strapis for gluing boards/armour
strayned distrained
streate (streight, strett) street
strekyng thatching with unthreshed straw
stremer pennon of silk
strow straw
strynes bow strings

stwffe (stoffe) stuff
styll (stele) east and west churchyard stiles
subsyde subsidies, tax
suertyeshyp guarantor of debt
sueyt (sute etc.) suit, legal case, vestments
sunder (sondreye) sundry
supplication petition
suprovisers supervisors
surgent surgeon
surplesys (serpells, syples) surplices for clergy
swell for organs
swerd sword
sydemen sidesmen
syder cider
syftyng, *see* **zeften**
sylke (selk) silk
syneor senior
synternys, *see* **centerns**
syse (syys) assize
syssers (syssyers) assizers?

tabell communion or church house table
tabernacles canopied niches for images
taperes long candles for festivals
tarre tarry
taylder elder?
Te Deum part of English Matins
tember timber
tendyng attending
ter tar
tesels teasels for cloth finishing
testers (testrons) base coinage
testymonyall certificate of character
thackyng, *see* **dachyng**
thecke thatch
theire (thir) there
therde (thryd) thread, third
thongs for bell collars
thowsant thousand
thre three
toe to
tolswylt market toll
tonng tongues of bell collars
toppyng pollarding trees
tornyng turning bell
toryty authority, permission?
towe two
towle (towlys) to cover altar, houseling towel
towr church tower
trece (tresse) organ trace
Trenete (Trynyte) Trinity
tressells trestles for tables, stalls
tresys to bind scaffold
treys trees

trobel treble
truse tie up bell
trussys (trowsse etc.) bundles of rushes, straw
tuke coloured canvas
turny attorney
twyne for armour
twyste flat part of hinge attached to door
tychbocks (toche boxe) powder boxes
tyle floor tile
tyner byll tenor bell?
tynnyng bottyll tin bottle

unswere, *see* **awnsur**

vall., valle revaluations after debasements of coinage
vante, *see* **fawnt**
vawte vault
vax, *see* **wex**
veker (vycar etc.) vicar
velfotte velvet
verdells, *see* **ferdelys**
vernessen furnishing?
vesetacion (vycitacion, wisitacon etc.) examination of churches of diocese by archdeacon, bishop, archbishop etc., Visitation of the Virgin Mary
vestements (vesstments) vestments
vethem (vathem) fathom, measure for cord, rope, wire
vettyd checked
vewe view
vittles victuals
vote, *see* **foote**
vyare pan fire pan
vyce (vice) spiral staircase, rood stair
vycytors (vyseters) royal officials
vyllyng, *see* **fellynge**
vyne, *see* **wyn**

wache (watche) watch house
waggys (wadies, wheges) bell wedges
walche bord board from Wales
wardance (whardyns) wardens, church wardens
warde judicial decision, award
ware goods
warke (werke) work
warrant for arrest
wassen (whasheng, wyssyng etc.) washing church cloths
wasshed whitewashed
waste cote for pauper
wedow widow
wedyng (widynge) weeding
weghting (wighten, wortynge, wyztyng etc.) weighing yarn, bells
wekys (weck, wykyes) candle wick
wemen women
wendo (wyndays, wyndos) window
werkyng (wyrkyn) working

wex (waxe, weckes) wax
whasse was
whe we
whefyll (whevyll etc.) bell wheel
where wear
whittlymynge white washing
wobo, *see* **albo**
wode (owde) wood
wold, *see* **owlde**
woll wool
wone one
wosterd worsted
wretin (writtenge, wrytten) writing, document
wyff wife
wyk (weacks) week
wykeyerne candle wick
wyn (wyne etc.) wine
wynd beerds (wynd barge) weather boards
wyre (wyer) wire

yate (yeate) gate
Yearlond etc. Ireland
yefen given
yelde guild
yeles, *see* **alers**
yends ends
yeold, *see* **owlde**
yer (yair, yerrys etc.) year, *see* **theire**
yerd 3 feet, churchyard
yerne yarn
yerthe, *see* **erthe**
Yester, *see* **Ester**
yeve (yevyn) eve
yevery every
yewes use
ymagys, *see* **imagys**
ymnor, *see* **hymnor**
yndenters, *see* **endentors**
Yngglyssh English
yollo (yowlle) yellow
yoman yeoman
yonge young
yre, *see* **ire**

zande, *see* **sond**
zayng sawing
zeften etc. sifting
zemys, *see* semys
zodry, *see* **sodre**
zowing, *see* **seuyng**

Notes on People

Additional information from the Blanchminster Charity records, the 1520s–40s tax lists, the 1569 musters, c.18 Chancery Court cases etc. and over 20 wills from the 1590s to 1620 Poughill records etc. appears first in each entry. Stratton account material generally follows this additional information and can relate to either the High Cross or the two general receivers' accounts: BL, Add MS 32243, 32244; CRO, P216/5/25/208. Each section of information from the account material starts with the offices the individual held and then other information is summarised. Dates are mostly the accounting year, with dates of birth and death only accurate to within a year or two. Place names and some words are modernised. Surnames have been standardised using the first or most frequently used spelling, with key variants noted. A few occupational names are treated as surnames. An attempt has been made to identify individuals by occupation or residence, and the notations II–IV are used instead of older or younger. Likely occupations are noted in brackets. Multiple entries can relate to one person. For the sake of family historians, and completeness, some extra names that occur only in additional material have been added in square brackets. See index for a few more people not listed here.

Key to abbreviations used in the entries below

B Blanchminster Charity: CRO, P216/25/1–340 and Goulding, *Blanchminster Records*. Note B215–16 is appendix 1 and B140, appendix 4.

D Douch, *Cornwall Muster Roll*. *A* (archer), *B* (billman), *H* (harquebusier), *P* (pikeman), *S* (swordsman), *c* (catapult or sling), *d* (dagger), *g* (glide, a broad-bladed bill), *h* (helmet), *p* (poleaxe), *s* (splints, forearm protectors), *t* (staff), *u* (unknown) or value of goods or land.

E TNA, E134/16Jas1/East5, individual ages c.1617.

G Goulding, *Blanchminster Records*, pp.102–3, 1582+ general receivers.

I Ivall, 'High Sheriffs', p.179.

M Manors: Stoate, *Cornwall Manorial Rentals and Surveys*, p.41.

PC Poughill churchwardens' accounts, CRO, P192/5/1.

PR Poughill parish registers, CRO, P192/1/1.

R Rebellion: Rose-Troup, *The Western Rebellion*, pp.107–9, p.337fn; Pool, 'Stratton', p.502.

S Stoate, *Cornwall Subsidies* and *Devon Lay Subsidies*, and TNA, E179/87/130 (Stratton tax 1525).

T Tonacombe: Waddon-Martyn, 'Our Family History', p.7.

V Vicars: RIC, Henderson MS 10, pp.359–56.

W Wills, lost: Glencross, *Wills in the Archidiaconal Court*. Where wills survive full references are given.

Christian, *see* **ELYOTT**, **ELYT**
Edward, 1570 scoured harness.
Elizabeth, (d.1578) shroud.
Hellen, lame, of Warbstow, 1566 poor.
Johan, lame, (d.1547) knell.
Johane, poor. *See* **YEO**
John, Warden Our Lady Holmadon, 1537.
John, Sir, *see* **HODGE**
Mawte, 1538 kirtle for bede roll entry.

Nicholas, *see* **OLYVER**
Stephen, 1542 drank can of ale in church house. *See* **DAW**
Thomas, 1546 supplied two halberds.
Thomas, 1570 wife paid doctor, ordered to depart parish.
Thomas the younger, 1526 supplied wax.
Wauter, wife of the, 1581 poor.
William, 1535 gift to church.
William, Sir. *See* **MARTYN**

ADAM, John, CHYNG's man, 1573 bridge work.
AFERYS, Jone, (d.1569) shroud.
ALYE, John, 1568–69 received high rent for Treburtle, *see* LEY.
ALYN, Mawtt, 1530 bequest to church.
ANDERDON. *See* **UNDERDON**
ANDROW, John, 1521 rented church house stall.
ANTONY, ANTHONY
John, [merchant], 1543–69 £4–£20 goods(S+D). Tenant Sanctuary manor (CALMADY lessee) (M). Sexton 1539, warden High Cross 1545, general receiver 1547, 1575 and 1577. 1551–77 bought old church cloths, knell for Master CALMADY, supplied pyx timber and iron, doors, table boards, forms, clock pole; bought old stile material, borrowed slate; paid poor.
APRICE, APPRYS
Richard, [tiler], 1542 laid tile and rebates.
Thomas, 1533 weighed yarn.
ARCHER. *See* **ORCHARD**
[**ARSCOTT, John**, late Holsworthy, Devon. Landowner pre-1539 (TNA, C1/788/51)].
ARTHUR
Anthony, 1569*A*(D), rode to Bodmin before commissioners.
Humphry, 1577 worked on church house?
ARUNDELL, ARONDEL
Edward, (d.1527) knell, bede roll.
Lady, [Elizabeth?], 1527–28 paid knells and bede rolls.
John, knight of Trerice. Born Efford c.1496, buried Stratton November 1560. Lived at Gwarnick, St Allen, home of first wife. 1522–43 lands £80–£133 6s 8d(S). Witnessed Stratton chantry lease 26 November 1529 (B.83). Stratton church house used for his wake.
Mary, Mistress, 1571 bought church stuff (vestments?).
Richard, (d.1527) knell, bede roll.
Thomas, Master, esquire of Ley, Morwenstow (fl.1512, d.1574). Leased rectorial tithes Poughill and Stratton with KEMPTHORNE from 1537(T). 1525–43 lands £5–£20(S). Arbitrator for Treburtle 1541–45 (B93, 181–3). 1539–49 gave vestments and 26s 8d for chancel; supplied four hundred laths; dinner in honour; paymaster Helston company; bought velvet pieces.
ATKYNS, John, poor, 1578 passport.
ATTWYLL. *See* **WYLL**
AUGER, AWNGERE
——, **Mistress**, (d.1564) knell/grave.
George, 1525 goods £5(S). 1492–1539 tenant Popes Place, Heth parke etc., feoffee, rood loft contract-maker (B31, 77–8, 83, 215; TNA, C1/788/49–51). Warden High Cross 1519. 1525 name on bede roll.
Ralph, 1543 goods £4(S). Warden High Cross 1546, All Hallows guild 1547 and dole.
Richard[a], 1533 husband's grave, bede roll.
AUSTYLE, Thomas, 1572 borrowed 350 roofing slates.
AVERY
John, hellier (b.1503–83+). 1543 goods £2(S), 1569*Ahd*(D), 1576–83 literate witness, sold

fish in Lent (B137, 140). Poughill roof 1541–50(PC). Warden High Cross 1560 and 1578, general receiver 1567. 1540–66 paid family knells; worked on church, church house, pointed walls; wrote church goods inventory; set glass over organ; gave bell metal.

John II, hellier, (d.1607–8), 1569*A*(D). Literate church house lessee 1581–2 (B139, 144). 1593 left pan, platter dish, cloak, best leather doublet (CRO, AP/A38), 1583(G). Church warden 1577. 1563–81 church roof, clerk's chamber.

[**John III** (b.1543, d.1631), yeoman, witness 1617 tithe dispute(E), 1626 will, inventory £33 15s (CRO, AP/A184/1–2), 1620(G)].

BADCOCKE, Thomas, [merchant], (d.1594(W)), 1569*A*(D). Warden High Cross 1567, general receiver 1577. 1567–74 supplied pew planks, bought rood loft bits, borrowed church house stair granite.

BADLAM

Jasper, 1569*u*(D). 1588 warned parish of the Armada (B209). 1579–81 family paupers.

John, Sanctuary manor keeper 1575 (TNA, SC2/158). Sexton 1543. 1544–81 thatched chancel walls; mother's knell; bought bushel of wine; repaired butts; sick, poor.

[**Richard**, 1569*u*(D)].

Tamsyn, washed Johane COKE's clothes, 1579.

BAGYLL. *See* **BAYALL**

[**BALAMY, Philip**, 1569*u*(D)].

BALE. *See* **BOLE**

BALHATCHYT, BALACHAT

[**John**, 1525 goods £5(S)].

William, of Poughill, held offices, carried stones, communion book 1534–58(PC). 1554–66 rented stall, supplied roof crest, crocks distrained.

BANDE. *See* **BOND**

BARBOR, --, 1571 child's knell.

BARON, BARNE

John, (d.1600), literate feoffee 1562–92+ (B22, 26–7, 34, 36, 131, 136–9, 144–6). 1592, 1600(G). Causeway supervisor 1566. 1558–77 carried bell-house timber; acted re church house; paid John JUDD's grave, daughter's knell.

[**John II**, 1569*A*(D)].

William, (d.1563). 1543 goods £7(S). 1548–63 supplied slate; child's and other knells, bede roll; bought tree, gave bell metal, horses carried stones; grave.

BARRET, John, 1539 self and wife on bede roll, paid knell.

BARY, Robert, Sexton 1547. 1535 brought lime from Bideford.

BASTERD, ——, 1544–45 carried stone from Bodmin Moor.

BASTYAN (*see* **Basten LAWRENCE**)

——, (d.1577) [carpenter] 1547–77 repaired organ; made banner staff, communion table, seats; housed poor child, given gown, shroud.

Alice, 1580–81 poor.

BATYN, Alice née ROSE, 1548 left crock to church.

BAWDEN, Walter, 1538 daughter's knell.

BAWSE. *See* **BEWES**

BAYALL, John, 1543 goods £1(S), 1533 paid knell.

BAYE, Nicholas, 1581 received jerkin and breeches.

BAYLYE

Ralph, 1573 son's knell.

Robert, the taylder (elder?), (d.1568) shroud.

BEARE, BERE

Christian, 1548 husband and self on bede roll.

John, husband of Christian, father of Thomas. 1543 goods £7(S). 1529–45 reversionary lessee Hele (B83–4, 178, 180). Warden St George 1535, Trinity 1538, general receiver 1541, High Cross 1542. 1540 children's knells.

Thomas, (b.1533, d.1592(W)), cordwainer, of Ponte Hele. 1569*A*(D). Feoffee, church house witness 1563–86+ (B83–5, 130, 135, 137, 139, 140, 144, 178, 180). Churchwarden 1573, general receiver 1578. 1572–81 tenant Pont Hele, wood; child's knell; bell money

BEATYK. *See* **BYTTYCK**

BEAUCHAMP, Master [**John**], of Marhamchurch, 1543 lands £19(S). 1547 bought unused tile.

BEDLIME. *See* **BADLAM**

BEDNER, John, old clerk. 1562 half year's rent for chamber.

BELL, Ralph, 1559 gift to church.

BERYNG. *See* **BARON**

BESCHEPP. *See* **BYSSHEPP**

BESSE. *See* **BEYS**.

BEST, —–, wife of, 1579 poor.

BETEKE. *See* **BYTTYCK**

BETHELE. *See* **BADLAM**

BETTE

Elizabeth, 1534 Maiden.

Johan, 1534 Maiden.

Margery or Margaret, 1525–26 husband on bede roll, paid knells.

Robert, Warden High Cross 1524.

BEWES

Jone, 1576–81 given gown, smock, pauper with mother.

Robert, (d.1566). 1558–66 helped with bell; shroud.

BEYS

Johan, 1551 received 4d.

John, 1543 goods £3(S). Warden All Hallows guild and Sexton 1538, St George 1542, High Cross 1548. 1542–51 paid knells for HOCKYN and John BRYANT's wife; bought doublet, shirt; brought lime from Boscastle; supplied poles; gift.

Robert, 1528 on bede roll

[**Roger**, 1543 goods £1(S)].

BHARE. *See* **BEARE**

BLAKE, BLACKE

[**Robert**, 1569*u*(D)]

Thomas, 1522–25 goods £5(S). 1526 daughter's knell.

BLAKHYLL, BLACALL

Johan, (d.1555). 1543 goods £1(S). 1536–55 mother's bede roll, grave.

[**Richard**, 1543 goods £1(S). 1540 supplied wax(PC)].

Tomsyn, 1521 husband on bede roll.

[**BLUET, Harry**, witness 1570 (B79)].

BOLE, BOLLE

Elen or **Elnar**, (d.1577), Mother or Old Woman. 1558–77 washed Johan YEO's clothes; given gown, tended by WHALE's wife, shroud.

John, Old, 1569*u*(D). 1564–68 testimonial and shirt.

John II, 1577 paid knell; gave bell metal.

Thomas, 1574–81 worked on church house, bridge, butts; kept poor child thirty-one weeks, poor.

[**BOLLES, John**, esquire, landowner, plaintiff, detention deeds Binhamy and Stratton manor v. Thomas MARYS 1518×29 (TNA, C1/467/57). 1531 grant of Pinch (BL, Add Ch 74868)].

BOND, BAUDE

—–, 1545 sawed timber with brother.

Alson or **Alice**, 1543 goods £3(S). 1536 husband on bede roll.

John, Sexton 1512, Warden High Cross 1529. 1530 paid knells.

John, mason, 1588 lent horse against the Armada (B209). 1565–78 built bridge with sons, boarded with Jone COLE.

Nicholas, [mason] 1543 goods £2(S), 1569 £10–£20(D). Feoffee 1576–82 (B121, 135, 137, 139, 144). 1584(G). Warden High Cross 1551, general receiver 1576. 1547–81 used church house; rode to Helston against rebels and lost horse, lent his horse for Exeter trip; gift for child, paid knell; gave two crocks to bell, supplied lime, bridge and butts work; given breeches.

Robert, 1543 goods £2(S). Sexton 1538, warden St George 1544, High Cross 1557.

William, (d.1548), 1543 goods £1(S). Warden St Armel 1538. 1546–48 brass crock, knell.

BONFORTUN[E]

Jone, 1578 rent paid by John BADLAM.

[**William**, 1569*u*(D)].

BOSHELL. *See* **BUSCHELL**

BOSHOP. *See* **BISHOP**

BOWYES. *See* **BEWES**

BRAY, **BREYE**

Christofer (b.1528, d.1596(W)), arrived Stratton c.1558 (B140). 1569 £10–£20 goods(D). 1556–85+ feoffee, church house witness (B27, 34, 122, 130, 137, 139, 140–1, 144–6). Churchwarden 1561, general receiver 1570. 1561 answered for church lands.

Esbell, Maiden 1537.

John, 1569 £20–£40 goods(D). Feoffee 1556–77 (B130–1, 136). Sexton 1556, warden High Cross 1569. 1530–71 paid knells; supplied peck lime.

[**Nicholas** husbandman, Pinch, (b.1562, fl.1617)(E), 1602(G)].

Robert, (d.1609), will notes servant maid; musket, wool, beef, bacon, butter, cheese in £72 3s 8d inventory (CRO, AP/B13). 1592(G). Churchwarden 1581–82.

Thomas, 1525 goods with Jone JULE £4, 1543 £9(S). Witness 1534–40 (B78, 178), 1531 reversionary lessee for Pinch on death widow JULE (BL, Add Ch 74868). Warden High Cross 1527, general receiver 1531, 1537. 1540–48 family on bede roll; bought kirtle; buried servant Margery CRYMP, paid knells.

Thomas II, 1570 breakfasted Prideaux Place re church house.

William, (d.1587–88(W)), son of Thomas I 1531 (BL, Add Ch 74868). 1569 £10–£20 goods(D). Feoffee 1570–85+(B22, 27, 34, 131, 136). 1585(G). Warden St Armel 1541, churchwarden 1562, general receiver 1566, 1571, 1577. 1560–71 gift; horses brought stile stones, attended Launceston chapter court re rood loft; daughter's knell; rode Lostwithiel on church business.

[**BRETAYNE**, **James**, servant of JUDD, 1543 goods £1(S)].

BRODE

John, Master, 1543 goods £6(S). Sexton 1546, warden Our Lady and St George 1548.

Walter, 1567 kept wares in church house.

BROKE, **BROCKE**

——, mason, of Morwenstow?. 1543 made Stratton market cross.

[**John**, labourer, son of Jacobstow helyar, 1575–80 Exe tenant (B199).]

Thomas, 1571–72 owed money, cleaned drains.

BROWNE, **BROUNE**

——, 1579–80 sick, operated on by surgeon, poor family.

——, **Master**, 1555 attorney Exchequer Court, Westminster.

BRUSEY, **BRUZY**, **John**, of Week St Mary, 1525–43 £3 goods(S). 1518 Stratton work.

BRYANT, **BRAYND**

——, 1559–67 dinner when made stile, nails for children's seats.

——, 1573 mended timber under leads, nails.

Agnes, (d.1539), buried Poughill(PR). 1532 bede roll.

John, (d.1558), warden St Armel 1544. 1536–58 paid knells including wife; fetched Tintagel rag slates, served hellier, sawed church timber, grave/knell.

Thomas, 1543 £2 goods(S). Warden High Cross 1520, general receiver 1525, 1539. 1517–36 brought lime, rushes; son's knell and bede roll.

Walter, of Poughill, held offices, gave planks 1540(PC). Warden St Armel 1532. 1539 mother's bede roll.

BUSCHELL, BOSHELL, John [plumber]. 1558–68 supplied 84lb bell brass, looked at leads.
BUTTICK. *See* **BYTTYCK**
BUYS. *See* **BEYS**
BYLKE, Margery, 1517 on bede roll.
[**BYLL, William**, married widow Robert STRETCHELIE].
BYSCHEP, BOSSHEPP
William, (d.1542). 1522 25 goods £10(S). Feoffee, attorney, rood loft contract-maker 1529–34 (B21, 25, 78, 215). Warden High Cross 1533, Sexton 1535, general receiver 1536, Our Lady guild 1537. 1512–42 supplied bell ropes, wax, candles; paid knells; lent money; grave.
William, Leonard servant of, (d.1540) knell/bede roll.
William II, 1542 father and wife's graves.
BYTTYCK, BEATYK
——, mason's servant, 1544 chancel work, ridding, sieving.
Annis, (d.1575), shroud.
Walter, [plumber], 1569*u*(D). 1542–68 mended lead, cross, holy water bucket; laid lead, supplied bell brass, cleaned harness.

CALL
James, yeoman. 1543 goods £2(S), 1569*A*(D). Feoffee and attorney 1540–77 (B130–1, 136, 178, 184, 198–9). Sexton 1557, warden High Cross 1558. 1574 his man worked at bridge.
Johan, Maiden 1534, 1539.
Jone, 1574 supplied mason's board and drink.
Nicholas, (d.1602) (CRO, AP/C13). 1569*B*(D). Witness 1570–81 (B79, 139). Churchwarden 1564, general receiver 1568. 1554–72 supplied rushes.
Richard, smith, (d.1575), 1543 goods £2(S), 1569*B*(D). Feoffee 1556 (B130). Warden High Cross 1553, general receiver 1569. 1545–75 supplied lath nails, bell metal, items to truss bell, jambs, window iron, bell rings, collar reins, latten basin; repaired locks, picks; rode to Helston against the rebels; servant's knell; bought old iron, basin; bequest, grave.
Richard II, literate witness 1576–77 (B137). 1579 bell money.
[**Richard of Grove** (b.1559, fl.1617)(E), 1614(G)].
[**Silvester**, 1569*u*(D)].
Thomas, husbandman/yeoman, of Sanctuary, (d.1605). 1569*B*(D). Feoffee 1576–85+(B131, 136–7, 139, 144–6). Will 1602, inventory £70 12s 8d (CRO, AP/C109/1–2). 1585(G). Churchwarden 1580. 1570–74 child's knell; carried lime from Boscastle.
Thomas, smith, (d.1607), 1569*u*(D). Feoffee 1581–85+(B144–6). Held part of church house, left anvils to son Richard and widow, inventory £178 13s (CRO, AP/C139/1–2; 375/2). 1593(G). 1575–78 sharpened pickaxe, hammers; made and mended clock, armour.
William, 1525–43 goods £4–£6(S). Feoffee 1534–56 (B78, 84, 98, 121, 130, 140). Warden St Thomas guild 1535, High Cross 1537, St George 1538. 1515–48 bought doublet; made hedge, stile; gift, put MORGAN family on bede roll.
[**William II**, feoffee, witness 1576–85 (B137,139, 144–6) 1596(G)].
[**William of Bagbury** (b.1577, fl.1617)(E)].
CALMADY
Ann, Mistress, of Launcells, (d.1577), 1543 goods £8(S). knell/grave.
[**John**], Master, Launcells, (d.1557). 1525–43 goods £8–10(S). Sanctuary manor(M). 1535–57 supplied slate; knell.
Vincent, parish attorney 1555–76.
CALYGERNE, CALYGRYNE, Richard, 1525 goods £2(S). General receiver 1526. 1520–42 paid for grave, knells including wife.
CANNE, John, of Bradworthy, Devon?, 1525 goods £4(S). 1538 made rood loft door.
CAPRACYS, — daughter of, (d.1540) knell.
CARLYON, CARLIGHAN
Alsyn, 1558 supplied bell brass.

Elizabeth, 1539 on bede roll.

Richard, Master, (b.1471, d.1541), vicar of Stratton 1492–1541, Oxford-educated, related to John Carlyon, Launceston prior, 1507–21 (Orme, 'Cornish at Oxford', p.65; *L&P*, v, 1531–32, pp.397–8; xii, 1537). Also vicar of Lawhitton 1517–23, Morwenstow 1510–41, Marhamchurch 1523–41, Glasney canon 1492–1541 (Peter, *Glasney*, p.165). Witness, rood loft contract-maker 1529–34 (B21, 78, 215). 1539–41 bede roll; supplied lead for rood windows; loaned money; bequeathed lockable-coffer.

CARNSEW, CARNESOW, CRANESUYOW [William], Master, of St Kew. 1543 £20 lands(S). 1541 arbitrator (B181–3). Award re Treburtle 1541.

CARWETHAM, John, feoffee, rood loft contract-maker 1529–56 (B21, 33, 78, 84, 98, 121, 215). Warden High Cross 1525, Our Lady guild 1536. 1520–38 bought grave, old rood loft.

CATER

James, 1578, 1580 collector for Wadebridge and for the poor, St Ives rates and restoration Cornish heare custom.

Thomas, 1574 collector for Helland bridge.

CAWNTER, —–, Maiden 1544.

CHAMOND

Jane, Lady/Dame, of Efford (fl.1496, d.1551). Born GRENVILLE, married John ARUNDELL the elder and by 1513 Sir John CHAMOND. 1545 £50 lands(S). Will of 1 January 1551, buried Stratton south aisle between her husbands. John KEMPTHORNE was her servant and John LYLL her chaplain (RIC, Henderson MS 66, p.144). 1548 put John HARRY on bede roll.

John, Master and esquire, knight, (d.1544) of Efford, sheriff of Cornwall 1529 and 1537(I). 1522–43 lands £60–£100(S). 1531 witnessed deed (BL, Add Ch 74868). Witness, rood loft contract-maker 1531–41 (B21, 25, 78, 83, 178, 215). Warden High Cross 1518. 1534–44 gave alb and gown for vestments; letter to Penheale; ringers at funeral rewarded with bread and ale; rushes for obit.

John II, 1558 council at Mr Yeo's house.

John, Master, Mawte servant of, (d.1526) knell

Richard, Master, esquire of Launcells (b.1514, d.1599). Sheriff of Cornwall 1544 and 1563(I). 1569 £200–£400 lands and goods(D). Witness 1545–83 (B24, 98, 140). 1546–70 king's business (fighting in French Wars); expenses re feoffers' lands; provided harness, muster books; bought spare lead, laths.

[**CHECHESTER, James**, esquire, of Tawton, Devon?, landowner 1529×32 (TNA, C1/616/41)].

CHING. *See* **CHYNGE**

CHOLWYLL, COLWYLL

——, farmer (B224). 1578 discharged parish re Act for wearing caps.

John, carpenter, of Poughill, (d.1560(PR)). 1522–43 goods £12–£13 6s 8d(S), held offices, gave ewe for wife, hired black suit, carved tabernacles, banner staff, mended bell floor, bells 1528–54(PC). 1516–49 kept and mended bells; made new bier, chancel roof, pulpit, lamp.

John II, 1572 supplied nails to hang harness up.

Robert, (d.1573(W)) of Poughill, 1543 goods £8(S), held office(PC). 1557–58 fee to mend bells.

CHOPE

Jenken or Jensone, 1569*u*(D). 1567–76 made communion mats, hedge, given doublet when he and wife sick.

Johane, (d.1532) obit.

Matthy, 1579 bell money.

CHUBB, —–, wife of, 1580 poor.

CHULWYLL. *See* **CHOLWYLL**

CHYNGE, CHING

Isbyll, (d.1535) knell.

Johan, Maiden 1532.
John, baker, 1543 goods £1(S), 1569*B*(D). 1590–91 owed £30 by Kilkhampton man (TNA, C2/Eliz/B8/10/1). 1573–78 supplied wood to melt solder, cleats for butts.
[**John II** 1569*B*(D)].
[**John III** 1569*A*(D)].
Margret, Maiden 1548.
Walter, 1573 had servant John ADAM.

CITTOW. *See* **KETTOW**

CLARKE, CLERKE, CLARARTT?
Agnes, 1546 gave rosary beads.
Amy, 1580–81 poor.
Jone, 1558 mended old surplices.
Thomas [carpenter]. 1529–74 mended bell ropes, collars, seges, stile; made bell collar, watch house, coffers, cob wall behind church house, tapers, candles; greased and kept bells; uprooted tree; put up gallows; paid knell; filled two graves; cleaned out lych gate; given shoes when sick.

CLEVERDON
Ebott, (d.1559) knell.
John, of Poughill, 1569*A*(D), held offices 1533–42(PC). 1562–65 paid knell; bought songs at Bodmin.

CLOCKMAKER, Matthew the, 1558 clock work.

CLYFTON
Elyn, 1548 on bede roll.
Martin, possibly of Week St Mary. 1569 carried register book to Launceston; supplied injunction book.

COBELDICK, COPELDECKE
John, (b.1503). 1543 goods £3(S), 1569*B*(D). Witness 1583 (B140). Warden Our Lady Holmadon 1536, Sexton 1541, Our Lady & St George 1547, High Cross 1549. 1540–83 paid knell; bought lime barrels, supplied rushes, brass for bell; brought stones.
John II, 1590(G). Churchwarden 1578. 1574 bridge work.

COKE, COOKE (*see* **GRENDON**)
Alse, (d.1571). 1570–71 sick, shroud.
Cherite, Maiden 1540.
James, the cook, 1555 brought manual.
Johane, 1579 kept by BADLAMS when sick
John, Sexton 1512. 1547 wife paid.
[**John**?, 1569*AH*(D)].
Richard, (d.1559) knell.
William, 1573 fetched wine from Holsworthy

[**COKEHILL, John**, apprenticed to John COMBE, Stratton glover, 1504×15 (TNA, C1/297/98)].

COLE
Emate, (d.1534) knell.
John, 'old', (d.1569). 1565–69 helped bridge masons; shroud.

COLMAN
——, 1575 supplied laths.
James, (d.1566)(PPR) of Poughill, held offices, washed surplices 1543–54(PC). 1549 supplied roof crests.

COLWYLL. *See* **CHOLWYLL**

[**COMBE, John**, glover of Stratton, neglected apprentice; deeds taken in reprisal 1504×15 (TNA, C1 297/98)].

COMEN
John, 1543 wife's knell.
Margaret, 1575 poor.

CONCE, —, of Jacobstow. 1575 house burnt.

CONSTABELL, **Sir Thomas**, priest, 1513 paid knell, requiem.

COOPER, **COPAR**

Johan, widow of William GYST. In debt with second husband 1538×44 (TNA, C1/1030/37). 1546–48 made surplices; put Edward DRAPER's name on bede roll.

William alias WARMAN, 1543–5 goods £6–£10(S). Warden St Armel 1541, Sexton 1542, Trinity 1545. 1548 gave gown.

CORTER. *See* **COURTER**

CORTES. *See* **CURTYS**

CORY, **CORYE**

[**Harrye** or **Henry**, witness 1576–81 (B131, 136, 138)].

[**John**, c.1533×8 detained Whitstone and Stratton deeds (TNA, C1/918/21–4)].

John, [Master], Stratton, then Marhamchurch, gent (b.1547, fl.1617)(E), 1569 goods £10–£20(D). Literate feoffee, attorney, church house lessee 1556–92+(B26–7, 36, 130–1, 134, 137–40, 144). Trespassed in Sanctuary manor 1576 (TNA, SC2/158). Churchwarden 1571, general receiver 1574. 1564–81 made bills, feoffments re church lands, plague orders, passports; measured Exe ground; servant's knell; carried Bible to Exeter and back; brought communion cup, lime. Mended leads; bound singers books; supplied communion bread, wire, oil, lead for clock, roof spars, soldiers coats, flask. Bought bridge pool fish, bridge work with man, fed bridge builders, gave money to bell.

John, draper, 1576–81 supplied frieze for gown, coat cloth, baize for desk.

Richard, (b.1513, d.1583–84(W)). 1543–69 goods £19–£100(S+D), of Whalesborough, Marhamchurch. Plaintiff church house case 1583 (B140). 1541–43 wax, frankincense(PC). Warden St Andrew guild 1539, 1546, Sexton 1540, general receiver 1544, High Cross 1546. 1539–64 supplied scaffold rope, nails, pyx, posts, board, laths, stone; rode to Helston against the rebels and to Buckland Abbey re chalice, bought church plate and pictures.

[**Thomas**, witness 1581 (B138)].

William, 1513 supplied bell collar.

COTTON (alias) COTTELL, **John**, [smith] 1569*A*(D). Warden High Cross 1569. 1564–75 supplied nails, clock-house door lock, stapes, iron for clock/seat, lime, helliers' food; mended locks, keys, pickaxe, bell wheels, clappers; made bull ring, window bars; un-hung bells; bought surplus lead; lent bushel of lime.

COURTER, **Hew**, **Hugh**, **Hu** or **Heugh**, tailor of St Stephen's parish, Launceston, 1543 goods £7(S). 1527–42 made and mended church cloths, surplices, vestments; hired black suit; mended stile, hedge.

CRADOCK, **Johan**, Maiden 1541.

CRANESUYOW. *See* **CARNESOW**

CREMPE. *See* **CRYMP**

CROME, [**Thomas**], Master. 1578 viewed parish artillery.

CROSEMAN, **Jacob**, 1569*c*(D). 1558 carried stones.

CROSSE, **John**, of Bodmin, 1580 poor.

CROWDER, **John**, mason's servant. 1535 made wall over north aisle window.

CRYMP

Margery, Thomas Bray's servant, 1548 on bede roll.

Margret, 1559–61 kept poor Johane; sick, cut by surgeon.

Thomas, [tailor] 1529–42 paid knells; made stoles, mended vestments.

CURBONE, **John**, (d.1548) bede roll, knell.

CURRY. *See* **CORY**

CURTER. *See* **COURTER**

CURTYS, **CORTES**, **COWERTYS**

John, 1517–30 wife's grave, carried little bell.

John alias LAMERTON, 1543 goods £1(S), 1569*A*(D). Warden St Armel 1542, Sexton 1548, High Cross 1551, general receiver 1557. 1555–60 bought tree, supplied slates, weighed yarn.

Jone, 1564 gave mustard seed.
CUTTYNG, Robert, 1514 bell work.
CYMPTHORNE. *See* **KEMPTHORNE**

[**DAVERS, Thomas**, esquire, 1531 granted reversion Pinch (BL, Add Ch 74868)].
DAVYE
John, (d.1560). 1540–60 paid knell; cleared gutter; rode to Helston against the rebels, loaned horse to bridge; shroud cloth.
William, 1525 goods £2(S). Feoffee church house (B130). Warden High Cross 1515. 1516 supplied evidence box.
DAW, DOW
Anne, (d.1559) knell.
John, carver of Lawhitton. 1544 goods £4(S). 1531 contracted with John PARES to make rood loft (B215–16). 1534–43 supplied 'hache' nails; made loft, seges; set north roof; given gloves, acquittance, reward; child's knell.
[**Richard**, carver of Lawhitton, probably John's brother, bondsman 1531 (B216)].
Stephen, (d.1548), 1540–48 gave Irishman's white kersey; bought coat; supplied bread and cheese to Helston company; knell.
DAYMOND, DEYMAN, John, of Kilkhampton, 1543 goods £4(S). Warden St Armel 1534. 1535–42 helped mason, made wall over pillars; brought stone, image of Our Lady.
[**DEBS, Lewis**, 1569*u*(D)].
DENYS
Sir Richard, (d.1533). Parson of Powderham, Devon, vicar of Launcells. 1544 on bede roll.
William, feoffee 1492 (B77–8). 1529 bede roll with wife Margery.
DOBELL
Edward, 1569*B*(D). 1576–7 child's knell; made gowns.
John, of Poundstock. 1532 leased part of Millook with wife and daughter (B25). 1557–62 Millook tenant.
William, 1558–61 rented another part of Millook.
DOUNE. *See* **DUNNE**
DRAPER, Edward, 1548 on bede roll.
DRIN[NE]
Martin, 1567 helped with choir.
Peter, 1543 goods £1(S). 1540 wife gave kirtle to church.
DROMOND, DROMANT
Elizabeth, 1539 bede roll.
John, [hellier], 1525–43 wages £1–goods £3(S). Warden High Cross 1530, Trinity 1543. 1533–60 mended kitchen gutter, roof, stopped holes, pinned and hewed pillars; made aisle steps, rood stairs, holes to secure church house windows; remade high altar, Easter sepulchre; washed rood loft.
[**Nicholas**, 1569*A*(D)].
Walter, Sir, Stratton priest, 1528–39 read bede roll, names on same.
William, Master, 1525 goods £6(S). 1520–36 supplied honey, wax, pitch, mended church, made aisle steps, helyng work, set rags, pinned altars.
DUNNE, Edward, 1569*A*(D). 1573–75 bought cruets; paid knell.
DURDON
Flowre, 1520 bede roll.
Johan, 1526 gift.
DYER, Alsyn, 1540 gave kirtle.

EARE. *See* **YEARE**
EARL, ERLE. *See* **YERLY**
EDY. *See* **UDY**

ELLYS, ELIS
Margaret, 1581 poor.
Richard, the pedlar, 1578 testimonial.
ELYOTT, ELYT
Christian, (d.1536) kirtle/knell.
[**John**, 1529×32 detained Littlebridge deeds (TNA, C1/687/19–21)].
EVYN, John, 1565 suit against him.

FEARER. *See* **FRYER**
FEREMOUTH, William, 1557 paid Annys GERE for Treburtle hedge.
FOSTER, Richard, of Poughill, 1543 goods £9(S). Held offices, bought yarn, church house breakfast 1545–56(PC). 1543 carried stone to market cross.
FOTE, William of Tintagel, 1543 goods £9(S). 1548 collected for Tintagel quay
FRENSHE, John, 1574 received Millook high rent.
FRYER, FREER, Margaret, 1576–79 given shoes, sick, rent paid.
FYLYPPE. *See* **PHELLYP**

GARDE, GAD
Anthony, 1569*u*(D). Literate witness 1576–82 (B131, 139). 1573–79 brought passports to Marhamchurch constable; sick; carried prisoner to Launceston, gave money for soldier's powder.
Hare, 1512 mended bell rope.
[**GAROWE, William**, 1569*A*(D)].
GARRETT, —,1531 rented kitchen.
GAYE, —, of Lezant, 1574 house burnt.
GERY, GERE
——, 1541 Bodmin session expenses re Treburtle.
[**Alice**, tenant Treburtle 1558 (B187)].
Annys, widow, 1557 made Treburtle hedge.
GEST. *See* **GYST**
GETON, GETYN
John, 1512–19 family's bede roll.
Karitas, 1527 on bede roll.
GILBERT, GELBERD
Alsyn, 1520 son's knell.
[**John**, of Devon, esquire, landowner pre-1539 (TNA, C1/788/51)].
[**John alias JENSON**, free tenant, default suit, Sanctuary manor court 1575–76 (TNA, SC2/158)].
William, of Launceston, 1544 goods £3(S). 1536 gift to rood loft.
GLANFYLD, Stephen, 1545 chancel work.
GLAWEN, Thomas, Warden St Armel 1540.
GLYN, —, 1528 mended rochets, surplices.
GREBY, John, 1535 Robin Hood. 1538 mother's knell.
GRENDON (*see* **COKE**)
Agnes, Maiden 1537.
John, (d.1537) grave.
Thomas alias COKE, warden Our Lady Holmadon 1534, general receiver 1535.
GRENE, Sir John, priest. 1528–29 gave honey, washed corporals.
GRENVILLE, GRENDFYLD
——, **Mistress**, of Kilkhampton. 1528 supplied ribbons, bradry gold.
John, Master, of Buckland Abbey. 1549 demanded chantry plate.
Nicholas, Master, 1580–81 received Treburtle rent.
Richard, Sir, (b.1542, d.1591)(R). Held Stratton manor 1579×87(TNA, C3/216/29; /221/56). 1581 imprisoned two women.

GROVE

John, warden St Armel 1548.

William, (d.1575). 1543 good £6(S). Warden Christ guild 1537, High Cross 1540, Trinity 1541. 1548–75 supplied bread and cheese to Helston company; child's knell, mother's burial, grave.

GYBBYS, GYBS

——, (d.1516) knell.

John, paviour, of Week St Mary, 1569*B*(D). 1573 paved bridge.

GYST, GEST, GISTE

[**Edward**, (d.1590(W)), 1569*A*(D). 1576 fined for trespass at Sanctuary (TNA, SC2/158), 1579×85 owed Richard YEO £3 (TNA, C3/221/56)].

John, (d.1541). 1512–41 mended bell collars, rented church house, brought stones, paid knell, gift, grave.

John II, 1543 goods £2(S). Warden St Armel 1543. 1558 set bellfounder's house, communion table carpet.

John, of Poughill, held office, laid rags, rode to Lostwithiel, rented linhay 1546–55(PC). 1559 made stile.

Margaret, 1565 gifts.

Nicholas [smith], 1543 goods £3(S). Warden Our Lady and St George 1548, High Cross 1550. 1544–59 supplied lime, chancel nails, lady's pew nails, bell rings, buckles, spangs, twists, gate wedges; bought cloth of gold; mended coal scoop, picks, 3rd bell clapper bole; borrowed 300 slate.

Nicholas, Sir, priest (d.1545). Vicar of St Winnow 1538–45. Gift to Poughill 1540(PC). 1520–45 bede roll, bell money, gave chalice.

Roger, miller. Literate witness 1576–77 (B137). 1574 paid knell.

Simon, 1526 supplied bell wheels.

Thomas, 1553–68 wrote and audited account.

Walter, feoffee 1492 (B77–8). 1485–86 seised of messuage and 200 acres (TNA, C1/77/23). 1512 wife's grave.

William [merchant], (d.1540). 1522–25 goods £26 13s 8d(S). 1537 bought wood, madder, alum (TNA, C1/1030/37). 1539 leased Estwood from GILBERTS of Devon (TNA, C1/788/49–51). Feoffee 1529 (B21, 78, 131). Warden High Cross 1513 and 1533, general receiver 1534, All Hallows guild 1535. 1512–40 knells included mother and best cross; supplied wax, lime, surplice dowlas, vestment cloth, honey, church house window board, rood stair timber; old rood loft stored at house.

William, of Combe, Poughill, 1525 goods £2(S). 1512 made church stile.

William, Johan servant of, 1538 Maiden.

HACKER, HACKE

George, 1543 goods £1(S). Witness 1534 (B78). Warden Our Lady Holmadon 1535. 1539 paid knell.

John [carpenter]. Warden High Cross 1522. 1512–22 hewed church timber, propped up SANGWEN's house, made house for church timber.

HALLETT, HALLES, Peter, 1569*B*(D). Feoffee, witness 1569–85+(B22, 137, 139, 144–6). 1586, 1599(G). Warden High Cross 1567. 1573–78 paid penny for Exe, sought counsel re church house, bridge work with son.

HAMAT, HAMMET

John, 1569*A*(D). Trespassed in Sanctuary 1576 (TNA, SC2/158). 1571–74 daughter's knell; bridge work.

William, 1548 bede roll.

HARRY, HERREY

——, plumber. 1576 mended leads.

John, yeoman of Tremaine, (d.1548), 1544 lands £5(S). 1531–41 bondsman for rood loft (or father), made forcible entry on Treburtle with mother Joan and eight others leading to

settlement with Stratton parishioners (B180–3, 216); 1540–48 spoken to by John Hore at Marhamchurch, put on bede roll by Dame CHAMOND?
[**John**, 1543 goods £1(S)].
HAUGER. *See* **AUGER**
HAYNE
John, Warden High Cross 1521. 1523 mended stile.
Robert [mason] of Launceston, 1544 goods £2(S). Feoffee 1529–32 (B21, 25). 1535–38 made wall over north aisle window, rood loft stair.
HAYWARD. *See* **HEYWARD**
HECKET. *See* **HEKET**
HEDDON, HEDYNE
——, 1518 bought iron
——, of Pancras Week, Devon. 1544 brought CARLYON's gift.
Alsyn, 1515 paid knell.
John, 1525 wages £1(S). 1531–39 bede roll and gown.
John II [smith or carpenter], (d.1585–86?(W)), possibly of North Tamerton 1569*Ah*(D). 1562–67 mended forms, church house.
Nicholas [smith], (d.1546), 1522–25 goods £6(S). Coal supplier 1535(PC). Warden High Cross 1517, general receiver 1522. 1519–46 paid priest's wages, knell; bought broken iron; supplied lime, girdles, iron crock, hearse nails, twists, crook, tower window iron, bell buckles, bell and screen nails, surplice; made pyx, curtain and holy water bucket irons, north aisle windows, bells; mended clappers, stile, coal pan; gift/grave.
William, smith (b.1527–83+). 1569*Ahd*(D), church house witness 1583 (B140). Churchwarden 1580. 1558–77 paid knell; supplied shovels, lath and other nails, basin, bell iron; mended bell clappers; kept wares in church house; bought old iron.
HEKETT, HICKETT, HYCKYTT
John, (d.1589(W)), 1569*A*(D). 1570–80 child's knell, removed granite and jambs from market house.
Robert, 1528 crock for bede roll.
Thomas feoffee 1534 (B78–9). Warden St Armel 1537. 1537–42 supplied lock, made coffer.
Thomas [smith], (d.1572–73(W)), lived near causeway. 1543 goods £9(S). Feoffee 1540–63 (B84–5, 98, 121, 178, 180, 184, 198). Church work 1532–42(PC). Warden High Cross 1534, Our Lady guild 1539, 1540 and 1545, general receiver 1541, 1558 and 1566. 1528–73 paid knells, kept clock, supplied coffer, keys, locks, pyx, shovel, iron, gate nails, rood loft windows, hurdles, pulpit boards, lamp ring, slates, armour, stone, lime, iron staps, censer. Mended bede man's bell, church door, locks, clappers, clock. Helped make pentice, bought surplus bell metal, grave.
HELE, Tamsyn, 1572–81 made child's clothing, paid Mother Bole's rent, poor. *See* WYLL.
[**HELER, John**, detained CHECHESTER deeds 1529×32 (TNA, C1/616/41)].
HELYER, Robert the, 1574 roof work with man.
HEMAN, John, 1562 church work.
HERREY. *See* **HARRY**
HEWE, John, (d.1570). 1558–70 carried bell-house timber, knell/grave.
HEWETT, HUYTT, Thomas, glazier, of Bodmin (Mattingly, 'Who Made the St Neot Windows?'). 1525 goods £26 13s 4d(S). Lead supplier 1534(PC). 1545 chancel windows ironwork, glazing.
HEYGEYNES. *See* **HYGGENS**
HEYWARD, HAYWARD, Thomas, 1522–25 £13 6s 8d(S). 1512 hired black suit.
HOBBACOCK, ——, (d.1573) knell.
HOCKYN, ——, (d.1542) knell.
HODGE, HOGGE
Alson, 1517–18 straked straw for thatching; washed church clothing.
John, warden St Armel 1534.
John II, cordwainer, 1569*A*(D). Literate witness 1576–77 (B137). Churchwarden 1577. 1569 servant's knell.

John, priest, Sir, (d.1580), vicar of Poughill. 1580 took Chard collection to Camelford.
Thomas, witness 1570 (B79). 1578 bridge work.
HOLAFORD, HOLLEVER, George, 1576 and wife, sick.
HOLLODNER, John, 1529–30 gifts.
HOLMAN
John, of Philham?, Hartland. 1546 goods £16(S). 1544 supplied lead.
Margerye, 1580 made shrouds.
Simon, (d.1580(W)), 1569*A*(D). Feoffee 1576–77 (B131, 136–7). Warden High Cross 1565, general receiver 1571. 1553–79 rented church house chamber and table board; supplied arrows, laths, nails, lime, housel bread, soap, timber, shrouds; bought ladder, candlesticks; carried and cast bell brasses at Lostwithiel.
Tybot, 1549 used church house.
HOLMYS, William, bell-founder. 1539 mended great bell clapper.
HOOPER, HOPER
Michael, (d.1578–79(W)). 1566–71 made hedges, cob wall behind church house.
[**Nicholas**, 1569*u*(D)].
[**William**], of Burshill, Poughill, 1525 goods £5(S). 1534 gift(PC). 1535 gift.
HORE
[**Christine**, 1563 tenant Ponte alias Hele (B85)].
Crystoffer, 1569*Bh*(D). Churchwarden 1566. 1562–79 fine, Hele mill tenant, child's knell.
Harry, 1570 made churchyard wall.
Jenyt, (d.1518) grave.
Johan, 1534 husband on bede roll.
John, (d.1548), 1525–43 goods £3–£8(S). Feoffee 1540 (B130, 178). Warden High Cross 1511 and 1536, Trinity/St Thomas guild 1546. 1518–48 supplied lead, wax, went to Marhamchurch, knell.
John II, 1569*u*(D). Feoffee 1540–41 (B180, 198). Sexton 1540, churchwarden 1574.
Jone, (d.1576) knell.
Nicholas, 1569*ABhs*(D). Feoffee 1556–77 (B130, 135). Warden High Cross 1556, general receiver 1573 and 1581. 1556–75 paid knells including child, brought slate, bridge granite.
Richard, 1569*ABhs*(D). Warden High Cross 1553, general receiver 1557. 1557–74 tenant Pont Hele, wood; wife's grave, heriot, paid Elnar BOLE's rent.
Thomas, 1543 goods £2(S). Feoffee 1540 (B178, 180). Warden St Armel 1539, Sexton 1546. 1548 received 10s.
[**Walter**, literate witness 1576 (B131)]
William, (b.1523). 1543 goods £2(S), 1569*AP*(D). Witness 1583 (B140). Warden St Armel 1537, St George 1542, High Cross 1550. 1547–78 coat for grandparents' bede roll; fetched service books from Exeter, carried high altar stones; bridge work.
William of Upton, Sexton 1548. 1548 paid knells.
HORETOP, HORTOPPE
——, 1564–65 carried bridge stones.
Edward (d.1572–73(W)) of Upton 1543 goods £2(S), 1569*B*(D), lease from STRETCHELIES, but arrears 1558×73 (TNA, C3/18/47). Warden Our Lady Holmadon 1534, St George 1543, High Cross 1548. 1544–57 carried Lady chapel stones; paid knell; supplied lime from Boscastle, holy water bucket.
Martin, 1569*B*(D). 1571 went to Bodmin as soldier.
Nicholas, warden High Cross 1512.
Nicholas II, 1569*B*(D). 1570–79 made watch house; paid knell; carried prisoners' ransom money to Bodmin.
Thomas, 1557–62 hauled stone for high altar etc.
HOWGE. *See* **HODGE**
HUDDELL, Tamsen, 1580–81 poor.
HUTTON, Johan, 1548 Irish husband on bede roll.
HYELLYAR. *See* **HELYER**,

HYGGENS
Harry, warden High Cross 1568.
John, 1574 bridge work.
HYGHADON, **Robert**, 1544–46 carried stones, bought tree root, mended east church stile.

INGERAM ——, 1517–21 bells and clock.

JACOB, ——, **Master**, 1578 payment to.
JAGO, **Walter**, (d.1576) sick, shroud.
JAMYS, —–, 1579 family poor including mother-in-law.
JEELL. *See* **JULE**
JEFFRYE
——, 1566–73 children's knells.
Joane, (d.1576), 1571–76 shroud and for child.
Roger, 1577 carried artillery to Camelford.
JENKYN, ——, 1562–77 poor, gown. *See* also UDY.
JOCELYNG. *See* **PAYNE**
JOHN, **Gerens**, vicar of Stratton 1541–56, Glasney canon 1541–48. 1548 compulsion against him.
JOHNES, **Mr** ——, **preacher**. 1579–80 preached twice, borrowed and repaid money.
[**JOHNSON**, **Jone**, 1533×8 detained Whitstone and Stratton deeds (TNA, C1/918/21–4)].
JOLOW, —–, (d.1557) ale/knell.
JUDD, **JUDE**
Elizabeth or **Esabelle** or **Isbell**, (d.1584–85(W)), widow, 1562 reversionary lease (B26–7). 1553–81 supplied wine; tenant at Millook, meadows, heriot.
Isbell, Maiden 1532.
John, (d.1540) knell.
John II, (d.1571–72(W)), 1569 goods £10–£20?(D). Literate feoffee 1555–62 (B25, 121, 130). Warden St Armel 1544, general receiver 1555, 1562 and 1569. 1548–72 rented meadows, Millook; rode to Helston against the rebels and to London re chantry lands; rent rebate for vetting bridge, brought communion book from Exeter, attended Launceston, Week, Honiton, Camelford courts about rood loft, breakfasted at Prideaux Place re church house, lent church English Bible, grave.
[**John**, **Sir**, (d.1557), curate of Kilkhampton 1537, vicar of Launcells 1545–57. Nicholas's brother, Sir John LYLL, cousin].
[**Mariona**, 1525 goods £2 with Nicholas JUDD(S)].
Nicholas [smith], (d.1574), cousin Sir John LYLL, brother Sir John. 1525 goods £2 (with Mariona), 1543 £5(S). Feoffee 1529–46 (B21–2, 25, 33, 37). Bells and gutter work, wax(PC). Warden High Cross 1528–29, Trinity store 1532, Our Lady guild 1534, general receiver 1543, 1548 and 1570. 1526–74 supplied nails, Lent cloth rings, gate ironwork, slate, great bell cord tin; mended and made bell clappers, chancel window; bought old bell ropes, iron, brass, church plate; collected money for bell-founder, bridge; entertained clerk of market, breakfasted at Prideaux Place re church house; servant's knell, grave.
Robert alias SATERLEIGH, 1562–85 leased part of Millook (B26–7). 1574–77 arrested by bailiffs; paid knell; supplied shoes.
JULE, **JEWELL**
——, **of Bude**, 1568 fetched sand.
Alson, Maiden 1535 (*see* **WHEER**).
Edward, (d.1574(W)). 1543 goods £3(S), 1569*A*(D). Witness 1570 (B79). Sexton 1542, warden St George and Our Lady 1544–45, High Cross 1554.
Emma, 1580 poor.
George, mason's servant, (d.1547–48(PR)) of Poughill. 1543 goods £2(S). Held office, tower work 1541–45(PC). 1543–45 brought cross stone; worked on chancel, tiled, plastered.

Harry, 1569*A*(D). 21 July 1588 carried letter to Stowe (B209). 1577 collected Margaret FRYER's rent.

James, 1577 paid for gun.

Johana, 1533 husband's grave.

[**Joan**, widow, 1525 with Thomas BRAY £4 goods(S), 1531 tenant Pinch (BL, Add Ch 74868)].

John, 1525 goods £4, 1543 £6(S). Feoffee, witness 1529–45 (B21, 25, 78–9, 84, 98, 140, 178). Warden High Cross 1513 and 1534, general receiver 1547. 1517–57 thatching, supplied lime, measured Treburtle.

John II, (d.1614), 1569*A*(D). 1588 went to Stowe (B209). Inventory £33 4s 3d included book; garden with beans and peas (CRO, AP/J177/1–2). Churchwarden 1580. 1576 child's knell.

John, of Lynstone, (d.1580/83–4(W×2)). 1534–74 paid bede roll, drew stones and sand over cliff to bridge.

John, crowder, 1535 carried old rood loft to William GYST's house. *See* CROWDER.

[**John, miller**, witness 1576–77 (B137)].

John, tailor, 1569*A*(D). 1548 paid knell.

Justynyan or **Justyne**, merchant, (b.1525). Witness 1583 (B140). Churchwarden 1563. 1564–65 paid knell, crock for bell.

Mary, 1574 bridge work.

Richard, 1543 goods £3(S). Warden St Armel 1534, St George 1538, Our Lady Holmadon 1542, High Cross 1547, general receiver 1560.

Richard, of Lynstone, (d.1590–91), 1569*Ad*(D). Trespassed at Sanctuary 1575–76 (TNA, SC2/158). Feoffee 1570, 1588 lent horse against the Armada (B79, 209). Constable 1572–73 and 1577–78. 1572–80 collected bridge money, poor relief, wheat rate, muster expenses; entertained clerk of market; bought lead; supplied bell metal; took down rood loft.

Roger, 1529 repaired churchyard hedge.

Thomas, 1522–25 goods £5(S). Feoffee 1529–34 (B21, 78). Warden High Cross 1521.

Thomas II, 1569 £10–£20 goods(D). Warden High Cross 1555, general receiver 1573 and 1579. 1553–76 bought firepan, old harness, rope; supplied collar, horses, man, meat, drink, lime, clock timber; paid knells.

Thomas, merchant, 1569*A*(D). Feoffee 1576–91+ and literate, built cellar at Stoneland (B33–4, 99, 131, 136–9, 145). Churchwarden 1561. 1570–77 wife sold cloth; daughter's knell; weeded Hele wood; supplied timber, ladder.

Thomas, cordwainer or shoemaker, reversionary lease with wife Margerie and daughter Joan, 1556; 1588 horse carried armour against the Armada (B33, 209). 1565–81 tenant Popes Place at Stone, held half bz lime; attended Bodmin sessions; wife's grave, daughters knell; took rubble out of church house.

Walter, vicar of Launcells (d.1560) knell paid by Alison WHEER.

William, smith, Warden High Cross 1522. 1512–27 mended stape, clapper, bede roll.

William, 1555–62 supplied slates; received coat cloth.

William, crowder (fiddler), 1520–25 cleaned church house; mended coffer.

JYLBERT. *See* **GELBERD**

JYST. *See* **GYST**

KALL. *See* **CALL**

KELLY, [Teage], 1532–48 took altar cloths to Bodmin, coat for bede roll.

KEMPTHORNE, KYMTHORNE (*see* **LEY**)

John, Master, esquire of Tonacombe, Morwenstow, MP (d.1566). 1543–45 goods £18(S). Lady CHAMOND's servant, literate. Leased Poughill and Stratton rectorial tithes with Thomas Arundell from 1537(T). Made obligation between Master Fortescue and Poughill 1545(PC). Witness 1534 (B78). 1540–57 dinner re parish goods; made bill, obligation, award, Treburtle release; brought king's money for chancel; paid for chancel roof repair.

John II, of Tonacombe, Morwenstow, esquire, MP, JP (b.1533, d.1591). 1569 lands £66 13 4s–£100(D). Steward Sanctuary manor 1575–76 (TNA, SC2/158). Took depositions 1583 (B140). 1570 precept taken to him.

KETTOW, KETE
Johane/Jone, 1564–81 built house on church lands, poor.
John, 1574 rented church house kitchen.
Margery/Margaret, 1568–70 poor, blanket and bread while sick, looked after by wife of Red ROBERT.

KNIGHT, KNYZGHT, Edward, mason (d.1575). Lodged with Jone CALL. 1571–75 made wall behind church house; money to wife when sick; roofed church house, mended tower leads, bridge work; shroud.

KYNDYSMAN, Roger, of Launcells, 1543 goods £3(S). 1548 paid knell.

KYNE, John, 1580 took out granite.

KYNG
James, 1543 goods £1(S), wax supplier 1544–47(PC). Warden St George 1543. 1540 paid knell.
John, 1527–44 bought crock, took stone to church house.
Nicholas, 1539 fetched image.

LAKE, Thomas, 1576–77 church house work, slating church.

LAMERTON. *See* **CURTYS**.
——, (d.1514).
John, of Marhamchurch, 1543 goods £4(S). 1547–62 paid lame Johan's knell, supplied wood to melt bell metal, workmen's meat; worked on gate? wall.
[**William**, literate witness 1576 (B131)].

LANE, LENE
Alice or **Alison**, 1577 kept WHALE's wife when sick.
John, 1562–68 supplied lath nails; paid knell; made hedge; mended ladder, stile; cast drain.
William, 1539 bede roll.

LANG, LONG
Alexander, witness first payment to John DAW 1531 (B215).
Anneta, wife of Nicholas, 1533 bede roll.
Hamifre or **Humphrey**?, 1529 work on stile.
Johan, 1537 bede roll.
Johan, Maiden 1541.
John, 1543 goods £6(S), 1569*B*(D). Warden St George 1536, High Cross 1538, general receiver 1540. 1536 paid knell.
Mawtt, Maiden 1545.
Nicholas, general receiver 1522. 1533 on bede roll.
Thomas, warden St Armel 1547.
William, 1543 goods £5(S). Witness 1540 (B178). Warden Our Lady Holmadon 1535, All Hallows guild 1536, general receiver/Trinity 1539, High Cross 1541. 1540–49 paid knells, bede roll; supplied slate.

LANGDON,
Johan, 1545 name on bede roll.
John, 1557–77 Exe tenant.

LANGFORD, LANGFORTH
Johan, widow 1525 goods £1(S). 1523–36 husband's grave, house used for church ale.
[**John**, 1543 goods £3(S)].
Walter, **Master**, feoffee church house c.1515 (B130). Warden High Cross 1514. 1512 paid knell.

LARDER, Walter, Master, 1547 hired black suit.

[**LASCALL, Nicholas**, witness 1581 (B144)].

[**LAUMPHREY**], [**Johane** and **Richard**, mother and step-father of John COKEHILL, 1504×15 (TNA, C1/297/98)].

LAWRENCE, Basten, witness 1556 (B130). 1560 made communion table. *See* BASTYN.

LENE. *See* **LANE**

LEPPE, Johane, 1575 relieved Joan PARTEREGE.
LEY, LYE (*see* **ALYE, KEMPTHORNE**)
[**John**], **Master**, 1555–74 of Launceston, office searched for charge to make plea by; made indentures; received Treburtle high rent.
LIGHE. *See* **LEY**
LILL. *See* **LYLL**
LOBBYS, Richard, 1512 hired black suit.
LONG. *See* **LANG**
LORD, [**Richard**], of St Dominick, 1543 goods £4(S). 1543–44 supplied lime.
[**LOYER, Dennis**, 1569*u*(D)].
LUCAS, LUKYS
[**John**, witness 1581–82 (B139,144)].
Raynburne, 1574 bridge work.
LYE. *See* **LEY**
LYLL, LYELL
Esbyll, 1535 gave kirtle.
John, left wax 1534–40(PC). 1548 on bede roll.
John, Sir, (d.1554), chaplain to Dame Jane CHAMOND 1551, rector of Plymtree, Devon, 1521–54. Will 1554 left parcel-gilt and silver salt, spoons of Jesus, apostles etc., two gold rings, two great taches and a silver pin, silver rosary beads, broken silver, pieces of groats etc. in coffer at cousin Sir John JUDD's house, Launcells (TNA, PROB 11/36/377). 1521–54 parents on bede roll; gift 20s, knell.
Marion, 1518 church house board.
LYMSCOTT, ——, wife of, (d.1526) of Kilkhampton?(S). 1526 knell.

MABYN
Davy, feoffee, literate witness 1581–85 (B138–9, 144–5), 1574–75 kept clock; supplied flock stuffing.
Edmund, of Launcells, 1543 goods £4(S). 1544 brought Hartland lead.
John, (d.1573(W)) [plumber], 1569*A*(D). 1563–73 kept and mended clock, organs; cast lead to fasten church house window bars.
MAGER, MAIOR. *See* **MAYGAR**.
MARK, MARK[E]S
——, 1556 rented higher church house.
John, (d.1609). Will and inventory £23 3s 8d included wool. 1573 paid knell.
[**Nicholas**, 1569*u*(D)].
Richard [glover], (d.1602). 1569*A*(D). Will 1601, inventory £69 12s 8d–white leather and gloves (CRO, AP/M17/1–2). 1587(G). 1566–72 wool in church house, gift.
MARTYN, MORTON
Alson, 1561 smock cloth for.
Joane, 1573–76 passport for, brought from Orchard to Boro', sick.
Johan, 1523 mended surplice.
John, (d.1528). 1525 goods £6(S). 1528 grave.
John, 1525 wages £1(S). Warden St George 1532. 1537 helped with bells.
John II, 1577 brought home artillery from Camelford.
Margaret, wife of John, 1518–48 made surplice; washed church cloths; sold wood of Robin Hood's house; husband's name on bede roll.
Thomas, 1569*A*(D). Witness and literate 1577 (B137). 1548–81 rode to Helston against the rebels, horse to bridge; made hedge; lent ladder; goods distrained.
William, Sexton 1557. 1555–70 cleaned kitchen; paid knell; gift when in gaol.
William, Sir, curate of Stratton 1537–38, vicar of Linkinhorne (CHAMOND benefice) 1550–56, vicar of Stratton 1556–81. 1533–48 alb, read bede roll in vicar's absence.
MARYS, MARRYS, MORYS
——, **Master**. 1578 rode to Launceston for catechism book; made subsidy acquittance. *See* **John**.

——, **Mistress**, husband's grave 1536.

Elizabeth, (d.1552), Thomas's widow, refused to pay son's marriage portion c.1534×8 or seal lease (TNA, C1/856/14; /714/15). 1543 goods £3(S). 1542–52 bought churchyard wood; grave.

[**Francis**, gentleman, feoffee, witness 1540–45 (B84, 98, 178), evicted UNDERDON? c.1534–35 (TNA, C1/714/15)].

John, Master, gentleman (b.1503). £13 6s 8d marriage portion not paid c.1534x8, so 1543 goods only worth £4 (TNA, C1/856/14; S). Literate feoffee, church house witness 1556–83 (B22, 130–1, 134, 140, 178, 180–3, 189). 1536 Robin Hood, warden Our Lady Holmadon 1538, High Cross 1542, 1549, 1561, 1565 and 1575, general receiver 1543, St Andrew guild 1544. 1530–73 rented church house, stalls, chamber, weighed yarn; rode to Bodmin sessions and Exeter about Treburtle and chancel, collected king's dole, high rent collector Binhamy and Exe, went to Week St Mary to see king's visitors, rode to Helston against the rebels; bought old church cloths; mother's grave; went to Camelford, Launceston, Week, Honiton etc. re rood loft and church goods, and Exeter when parish excommunicated, breakfasted at Prideaux Place re church house, carried register to Launceston. Bought Lady chapel timber, Hele wood faggots, roof angels; sold church stuff to Mistress Mary ARUNDELL; supplied lime; made first church goods inventory; paid soldiers' expenses at Bodmin, sent man to Ireland, rated parish for harness, collected money for Colyton Haven, Devon.

Thomas, (d.1534×6), feoffee, rood screen contract-maker, witness 1488–1534 (B25, 129–30, 215). 1518×29 detained Binhamy manor deeds (TNA, C1/467/57). 1531 witnessed deed (BL, Add Ch 74868). Warden High Cross 1518, general receiver 1525, St Andrew guild 1534. 1512–34 hired black suit, paid knells, servant's grave; supplied slate; blessed altar cloths; rented church house kitchen.

[**MATTOLE, John**, Breton, 1543 goods £1(S)].

MAYGAR, MAYOR

George, 1543 goods £2(S), 1569*Bd*(D). Sexton 1537, warden Our Lady of Holmadon 1539, High Cross 1545, general receiver 1548. 1547–51 paid knell Martin MAYOR; bought old church cloth.

George II, 1569*u*(D). 1568 supplied Easter rushes.

John, warden High Cross and Christ's guild 1539, Our Lady Holmadon 1540. 1542–5 supplied ARUNDELL wedding rushes; made alleys around church.

John, of Poundstock, (d.1592–93(W)), carpenter-joiner. 1543 goods £4(S). 1562–78 kept and mended stocks, turned great bell; mended church stile, tower windows, church house wall, sparring; took down rood loft; made new door on leads, north aisle pews, gate; viewed bridge; carried stone from Bude; supplied nails; boarded with Jone CALL.

Martin, (d.1547) knell.

Walter, 1525 Warden High Cross.

William, 1517 supplied rushes.

William, husbandman, feoffee 1581–92 (B27, 36, 144–6), 1584(G). Churchwarden 1575.

MAYNARD, MENARD, John, (d.1572). 1537 owed 56s 8d by William GYST for wood, madder, alum (TNA, C1/1030/37). 1572 knell.

MAYOW, MEYO

Johan, of Kilkhampton, 1543 goods £2(S). Family on bede roll 1540.

John, of Kilkhampton, 1536 brought synterns for north arches.

Roger, 1548 rode to Helston against the rebels.

MEAGER, MEJHER. *See* **MAYGAR**

[**MERCHAUNTE, Nicholas**, 1569*u*(D). *See* YEO]

MERMAN, William, warden Our Lady and St George 1547.

MERYFIELD, MERAFELD

Alson or **Alice**, (d.1545) of Poughill, held office, gave ewe 1529–34(PC). 1539–45 put names on bede roll, knell.

Johan, 1531 paid knell.

[**John**, 1543 goods £1(S)].

MEYER. *See* **MAYGAR**

MOCKE, MOKE

——, 1546–53 made desk; mended lead; kept bells. *See* **Nicholas**

——, 1568 served hellier.

——, **Master**, 1580 laid tiles; cleaned church.

John [carpenter], warden All Hallows guild 1537. 1536–51 made synterns, clock tower, leads, gallows; pulled down Lady chapel, reared chancel; cut trees; supplied glue, organ notes; set up my Lady's pew; scoured candle stands, censers; helped glazier; sheared hedge; sewed and mended church cloths.

Jone or **Joone**, (d.1571). 1567–71 given shirt, shroud.

Nicholas, 1537–46 helped with bells; covered king's book; mended vestments; reared chancel; supplied reed; sawed elms; served masons.

Nicholas II, 1571–81 scoured armour, carried arrows to Poundstock; levelled chancel; helped mason and hellier; cleaned church house; tended men working on pentice and BROUNE; sick, got shoes, shirts.

MORE, MOWRE

Andrew, 1578 bridge work.

Annys, (d.1561) shroud.

Joan, 1571–77 poor.

John, 1569*u*(D). 1545–76 cleaned chancel, fetched grit, rooted tree, mended stile, with horse, supplied sand, bought oak by church house, lodged Jone PARTEREGE's child, sick.

John II, 1569*u*(D). 1580 and wife poor.

Jose, 1558 carried clay, made post holes for bellfounder's house.

MOREMAN, JOHN (b.1490, d.1554), Master Doctor, born Hartland. Vicar of Menheniot 1529–54. 1547–53 imprisoned for Catholicism(R). 1535 hired black suit for requiem.

MORES. *See* **MARRYS**

MORGAN, MORYAN

Johan, Maiden 1544.

Johan, wife of William, 1548 on bede roll.

William, 1543 goods £1(S). Work 1530–32(PC). Sexton 1537, warden Our Lady Holmadon and St George 1538. 1548 names on bede roll.

MORSE, ——, mason, possibly Richard MORS of Launceston, 1569*B*(D). 1563 bridge work.

MOURTON, Simon, vicar of Poundstock, (d.1549). 1549 rebel. Hanged in Stratton market-place, 13 October, buried 18 October(R)

MOYSE, MOYYES

——, 1545 grave.

William, (d.1540). Warden St George 1536, St Andrew guild 1538, High Cross 1539, general receiver 1540. 1529–40 mended collars; pecked and greased bells; knell.

William II, 1542–51 kept bells, mended collars.

MUSSELL, [John], of Minster, 1569*u*(D). 1564 brought home from France.

MYLL

Johan, 1525 goods £3(S). 1526 gift.

Mychael, (d.1520). Warden High Cross 1519. 1515–20 bought old bell rope; bede roll names; supplied candle stand; gift, grave.

NEALE, NELLE

[**John**, literate witness 1577 (B137)].

Robert, 1569*p*(D). 1582(G). Sexton 1559, warden High Cross 1565. 1555–80 paid grave Johan BLAKHYLL, boys fetched keys from Stowe?, collector for poor; made butts.

NICHOLSON, NYCHOLLSON, Thomas, 1524 goods £2(S). Attorney 1540–41 (B178). Warden High Cross 1527. 1528–41 supplied frankincense; paid knell; at Launceston, Bodmin about Treburtle.

NORDON, NORTHYN, William, fl.1439–92+, Chantry benefactor (B69–77). 1523–47 obit.

[**NORMAN, Anthony**, 1543 goods £1(S)].

[**NYCOLL, John**, 1569*u*(D)].

OBLIN

Nicholas, churchwarden 1573.

Richard, 1572 roofed church.

OGLOW. *See* **UGLOW, WOGLLO**

OLYVER, OLLVER (*see* **alias RUNDELL**)

Agnes, (d.1576) knell.

Elizabeth, widow, gave Stratton manor messuage to Emote PRIST to settle debt <1579×87 (TNA, C3/216/29). 1569 supplied communion wine.

Johan, Maiden 1543.

Johan I, 1542–45 husband's gift, supplied rubble stone.

Johan II, 1548 on bede roll with husband.

John, 1543 goods £6(S). Attorney 1540 (B178). Warden St Armel 1539, Trinity 1547.

[**John II**, 1543 goods £2(S)].

John alias RUNDELL, yeoman, (d.1628). 1581 went to London for Richard Yeo's lease, but not paid expenses (TNA, C3/287/5). 1588 lent horse against the Armada (B209). Held two tenements (CRO, AP/R491). 1599(G). 1577 supplied soldier's sword.

Nicholas alias RUNDELL, 1543 goods £1(S), 1569*A*(D). Feoffee 1569–85+, defendant church house case 1583, literate (B22, 136–7, 140, 144–6). 1579×87 claimed mother's messuage against Emote PRIST (TNA, C3/216/29). 1591(G). 1569–80 paid Thomas OLYVER and wife's graves; supplied shroud for Jone AFERYS, clock timber, child's shirt cloth, sword girdles, gunpowder, canvas, thread for helmet lining; helped choir, reimbursed for highways, gave shirt to MOCKE.

Nicholas, of St Ives, 1570–71 sick, supplied *Te Deum* song.

Richard, attorney 1556 (B130). 1548 St Armel warden. 1548–70 rode to Helston against the rebels, collector for poor; paid paver.

Thomas, (d.1569). Sexton 1557, warden High Cross 1559. 1548–69 paid knell; borrowed slates; mended hogshead; supplied frankincense, books, clock wire, laths, nails; grave and wife.

[**Thomas II**, feoffee 1576, 1588 fought against the Armada (B131, 209).]

William, 1525 goods £4(S). Warden High Cross 1537. 1516–37 supplied Welsh board, rope, lime, slate; paid masons; bede roll.

ONGER. *See* **AUGER**

ORCHARD

Richard, 1576 supplied rushes.

William, clerk, from Week St Mary 1569*A*(D). Witness 1576 (B131). 1572–81 gift; boards lent to him; kept clock; wrote register; supplied singing books.

[**OSBOURNE, Thomas**, 1569*u*(D)].

OULLOCOTT, —–, carpenter. 1556 unspecified work.

PALMER, PAYLLMAR

——, hellier's servant 1529.

——, priest or clerk. 1533 rochet; mended church floor.

William, Sir, writer, witness 1576–77 (B131, 137). 1577–78 brought home discharge for wearing hats; kept register book.

PARCYVALE, PERCIVAL, [Tomasine], Dame or Lady, born Week St Mary (Hull, 'Endowment of a Grammar School'). 1513 four priests at obit.

[**PARES, John**, of Northlew, Devon, carver, 1543 goods £13 6s 8d(S). Contracted for rood loft 1531 with John DAW (B215–16)].

PARTEREGE, Johan, 1575 sick, child kept by John MORE, passport.

PAYLE. *See* **POLE**

PAYNE (*see* **JOCELYNG**)

John, of Launcells, 1520 bede roll.

John, 1522–43 goods £5–£9(S). Feoffee Treburtle, rood loft contract-maker, 1529–40 (B21, 25, 33, 215). Warden High Cross 1512 and 1534–35, general receiver 1536 and 1545. 1517–58 made scaffolding; greased bells; supplied and carried lime, leather, stone, slate; lent money; gave Agnes CLERK's rosary to church; dined with Mr UNDERDON.

Mark, literate feoffee 1569–82 (B22, 131, 136–9, 144–6). Churchwarden 1576. 1573–75 supplied lead for clock, lead cloth; loaned keeping stones.

[**Mark II**, (b.1551, d.1618–19) yeoman of 'Yellowleigh' and Legh woods 1616(G), will and inventory £391 10s, twenty-six cattle, mare, Bible, books (CRO, AP, P343/1–2)].

William, 1543 goods £9(S), 1569*A*(D). Feoffee, literate witness 1540–70 (B180, 184, 189, 198). Free tenant Sanctuary default suit 1575 (TNA, SC2/158). Warden St George 1544, Our Lady 1545, Sexton 1547. 1547–66 Went to Launceston before commissioners; feoffment and writings re church land; supplied bell brass.

PAYNTER

George, the, 1577 drew Ten Commandments.

Johan, 1513 bede roll names.

PEARSE, PERYS, PIRSE

——, joiner, 1575–80 made barrows, pews, cucking stool; took down rood loft.

John, 1528 mended vestments.

John II, joiner, 1581 goods distrained.

Roger, 1577 mended church gate.

William, warden High Cross 1570. 1570–75 served mason and hellier for churchyard wall, made hedge; paid knell.

PENFOS, PENVOS

Alexander, [labourer], 1522–35 goods £5(S). 1530 distrained goods at Exe. Feoffee 1540 (B97, 177–8). General receiver 1524. 1529–36 supplied wax, rushes.

[**Nicholas**, 1525 goods £2(S)].

[**Richard**, witness 1545 (B98)].

PENGELLYE, Davye, 1578 bridge work.

PENWELL. *See* **PYNWELL**

PERDE, ——, of Welcombe, Devon. 1573 non-payment stall rent?

PERIS, PERYS. *See* **PEARSE**

PERY, PERE

John, (d.1564?). 1525–43 goods £4–£8(S). Feoffee 1531–55 (B78, 84, 98, 121). Warden High Cross 1528 and 1558, St Andrew guild 1535 and 1537, St George 1540. 1522–55 paid grave, gift, bede roll; carried lime, stones; on bede roll and wife, father's grave, knell.

John II, (d.1580(W)). 1543 goods £1(S), 1569*g*(D). Feoffee 1563–76 (B85, 137). Warden St Armel 1536, Sexton 1543. 1557–76 attended visitation; children's knells.

Nicholas, 1569*A*(D). Feoffee 1540–56 (B178, 180, 184, 198). Warden St Armel 1546, churchwarden 1563. 1564 father's grave.

Richard, 1569*B*(D). 1565–81 supplied sand; carried stones, kiln mortar; hurt leg, poor.

Tomsyn, Maiden 1539.

William, (d.1537?), 1522–25 goods £10(S). 1513 paid priest.

[**William II**, 1569*A*(D)].

[**PERYN, John**, 1525 goods £5(S)].

PETHECK, PEDOKE

Alson, Maiden 1548.

Emmet, 1562–64 poor, given gown, blanket, smock cloth, shoes.

PHELLYPE, PHYLLIP

John, husbandman, of Egloskerry, 1543 goods £1(S). 1540 disseised feoffees at Treburtle (B180). 1540–41 evidence shown to John KEMPTHORNE and John MARYS who copied deed.

Rysse or **Ryce**, 1559 house rented for poor Johan.

Thomas, 1561–77 paid knell; supplied ode for bell; daughter's knell.

PIRSE. *See* **PEARSE**

POLE, POWYLL, POYLE

——, **Mistress**, 1564 husband's knell.

Jamys, 1524 on bede roll.

Martin or **Martye**, Master, (d.1565), witnessed will of Dame Jane CHAMOND. 1544–65 gave old purse, gilt buttons, bell brass; gift.

Simon, 1512 on bede roll

POOTH, John, (d.1562) knell.

PRIDEAUX, ——, **Master**, of Prideaux Place, Padstow. 1570 entertained five men to breakfast re church house.

PRINE, PRYN, John, trespassed in Sanctuary 1576 (TNA, SC2/158). 1575 relieved Joan PARTEREGE.

PRIST, PRUST, PRYSTE

[**Emote**, before c.1579×87 sold two sheep, wool, fleeces to Elizabeth RUNDELL and claimed messuage in lieu of debt (TNA, C3/216/29)].

Genkyn, 1514 gift.

Hew, 1517 supplied lime.

Johane, widow of Thomas, 1525 goods £4(S). 1524–32 bede roll, husband's grave.

John, 1530 knell.

John II, 1577–80 brother's knell, gave poor money.

Richard, Sir, priest. 1539 bede roll entries.

Richard, 1573–79 bought coffer; gave BROWNE victuals.

Thomas, (d.1524), feoffee 1492 (B77–8, 178). 1519–24 refused to be High Cross warden; bede roll, grave.

William, of Morwenstow, 1560 gift.

PRYER, PORE, Peter, 1569*A*(D). 1570 brought lime home.

PUDDENER, PUDNER

Alson/Alice, widow, 1543 goods £3(S). 1528–33 husband's grave, bede roll; rent owing.

John, 1522–25 goods £5(S). Held office, slate supplier 1539–56(PC). Warden High Cross 1526. 1538–48 supplied quarry stone; shirt for bede roll.

Robert, of Poughill, 1543 goods £3(S). Held offices 1528–38(PC). 1546 paid knell.

Roger, 1548 shirt for bede roll.

PYLE, Richard, 1516 on bede roll.

PYNE, Alson, (d.1541) knell.

PYNWELL ——, hellier. 1581 mended church.

QUYCKE, QUIKE

Jane, 1580–81 poor.

Peter, Warden High Cross 1568. 1558–73 paid knells including Richard COKE; supplied alder tree; songs from Bodmin; hung bell stocks.

[**Robert**, (d.1583–84(W))].

RAD. *See* **RODDE**

RATENBURY, John, of Marhamchurch, 1525–43 goods £2(S). 1562 church work.

RAW, Alexander, 1525 knell.

RAYNOLL, RAYVELL, RAYNER

Harry, Master, witnessed first payment to John DAW 1531 (B215). 1526–29 pricksong book for grave, but did not pay child's knell/grave.

Richard, millward. General receiver 1533. 1528–38 used church house; put name on bede roll.

Thomas, 1563 paid by four men.

[**William**, witness 1534 (B78)].

RECARD, —, hellier, 1517 work.

REDE

Johan, 1543–46 husband's knell; mended church clothing.

John, (d.1543?). 1535 supplied lime from Bideford.

REGG, **William**, 1530 knell.

REGYLL, **REGELL**

Ame, widow, (d.1515), grave.

Edmund, (d.1575). 1569*Sd*(D). Warden St Armel 1535. 1560–75 weighed yarn; gift, grave.

John, (d.1515). Feoffee 1492 (B77–8). c.1504×15 seised with wife Amice of two messuages and garden (TNA, C159/33). Warden High Cross 1511. 1514–15 knell/grave.

Robert, (d.1545). 1543 goods £1(S). Feoffee 1529–32 (B21,5). Warden St Armel 1532, Sexton 1534, St George 1538. 1533–45 wife's grave; carried grit; grave.

RENALL, **RENELL**. *See* **RAYNOLL**

RESKAROCKE. *See* **ROSCARROCK**

ROBERT

[**John**, 1569*u*(D)].

Red, ——, **wife of**, 1568–70 poor, kept Margaret KETE half year.

RODDE

John, 1531 witness to first payment to John DAW? (B215). 1573 William RODDE brought him to St Leonard's hospital, Launceston.

John, of Bridge, 1569*A*(D). Attorney, witness 1576–77 (B137). Lynstone tenant who sublet in 1590. Brother George cut down unripe onion seed, beans and teasels in garden out of spite? (TNA, C3/229/33). 1594(G). General receiver 1574, warden High Cross 1578. 1571–75 wife and father's graves; rented stall; worked on bridge; carried boards, granite.

Jone, (d.1575) grave.

William, (d.1574?), 1543 goods £1(S), 1569*A*(D). Warden Our Lady Holmadon 1537, St George 1541, Christ guild 1546, High Cross 1550. 1548–74 paid knells; lent mare; bought cloth of gold, rood loft material; supplied bell brass, rushes, lime; took down organs; took John RODDE to Launceston hospital; Hele wood arrears; bridge work.

ROLAND. *See* **ROWLAND**

RONELL. *See* **RAYNOLL**

ROSCARROCK, **John**, **Master**, of St Endellion. 1564 helped MUSSELL.

ROSE, **ROOS**

Alice, *see* BATYN.

John, 1525–43 goods £2–£9(S), 1569*A*(D). Feoffee, literate witness 1541–77 (B130, 137, 178, 180, 198). Warden High Cross 1520 and 1542, general receiver 1524, 1537, 1548 and 1562, Our Lady guild 1535 and 1546. 1514–58 paid grave, knell; cleaned church house; supplied pitch, wax, honey, window mat, bell metal; bought part old rood loft; paid CHOLWYLL; made loan; rode to Launceston re Treburtle.

John II, warden St Armel 1545.

Matthe, 1525–43 wages £1–goods £5(S). Warden High Cross 1536, general receiver 1542, St Andrew guild 1545. 1527–45 knells including mother, bede roll; bought old rope; served mason; supplied and carried lime, sand, grit; made mortar for market cross; sold wood of Robin Hood's house.

Michael, (d.1548) knell.

Richard, 1576 received money?

Thomas, 1543 goods £2(S). Attorney 1534 (B78). Former messuage 1558×79 (TNA, C3/201/47). Warden Our Lady Holmadon 1541. 1534–48 used church house, paid knells including Michael ROSE.

Walter, (b.1507). 1569*A*(D). Witness 1583 (B140). Warden St Armel 1538. 1544–81 hauled stones; gave sister Alice BATYN's crock to church; used and cleaned church house; swept gutters; carried paver's stone, levelled chancel; sick and poor, wife's shroud.

ROUCKE?, ——, paver, 1575 paved church porch.

ROWCLYFF, **ROWCLUFF**, **John**, mason, of King's Nympton, Devon?, 1525–43 goods £3–£10(S). 1535–39 bargained for tower and north aisle, servant pinned old pillars, made pillar and north window.

ROWLAND

John, [carpenter], (d.1570). 1543 goods £5(S). 1558 made bell collars(PC). Sexton 1535, warden Our Lady Holmadon 1536, All Hallows guild 1540, general receiver 1559. 1530–70 mended and made collars; kept bells; bought old church cloth; supplied slate, canopy, carpenter's meat and drink, gate? timber, bell crock, kiln stone; grave.

John II, Warden St Armel store 1536, Sexton 1541, St George 1544, High Cross 1547. 1539–49 gave John HEDDON's gown, supplied boards for lead casting, leather and thongs for bell collars; paid knell.

[**Nicholas**, tanner, (d.1629). 1569*A*(D). Attorney, feoffee, literate 1576–85+(B131, 139, 141, 144–5), inventory £136 10s included feather beds in chamber and parlour, tan troughs (CRO, AP/R497).].

RUNDELL. *See* **OLYVER**

RYGELL, **RYGYLL**. *See* **REGYLL**

SAMPSON, **SAMSON**

—— [mason] of Kilkhampton? 1569 dinner when bargain made; pointed tower.

Agnes, 1543 goods £1(S). 1548 put name on bede roll.

SANGWEN, **SANGUYN**

——, 1517 house mended.

Agnes, 1539 bede roll.

Andrew, (d.1592(W)), 1569*Bd*(D). 1589(G). Warden St Armel 1547, churchwarden 1564. 1572–81 gift, son's grave; rented Hele Wood.

John, warden Our Lady Holmadon 1532. 1557 measured Treburtle.

John, (d.1577) knell.

Mary, (d.1577) knell.

Richard, 1539 on bede roll.

[**Thomas**, owed money to Richard GRENVILLE c.1579×87 (TNA, C3/221/56)].

William, 1540 knells for self and children.

SATERLEIGH. *See* **JUDD**

SAUNDER

John, 1521–37 supplied wax; made upper tower door, church house windows, wooden gate; mother's bede roll.

John II, (d.1589(W)), 1569*A*(D), feoffee 1576 (B131). Church warden 1576.

John of Lynstone. Feoffee 1577–83 (B136–7, 139, 144–6).

[**John**, smith of Stratton, feoffee, held part church house 1576–83 (B137, 139, 141, 144–6) 1603(G)].

Lewis, (d.1571(W)), 1569*A*(D). 1571–72 child's knell; bought boards.

Nicholas, cordwainer (d.1606), 1569*A*(D). Will noted shop and chamber 'wherein I have wrought' (CRO, AP/S85/1–2). Churchwarden 1562, general receiver 1565, collector for poor 1576. 1566–80 made staple; mended third bell clapper, shovel; supplied brass, nails, timber for barrows, sword hilts, seat nails; paid knell.

Robert, (d.1599) yeoman, of Colebroke, 1569*Ah*(D). Feoffee, witness 1569–86+(B22, 79, 131–2, 136–9, 144–6). Will 1598 bequests to Stratton and Poughill poor, apprentices, servant, godchildren etc. beds, silver salt, spoons, brass crocks, queen's privy seal, two cows, thirty sheep and Summerlease bought from WARMINGTON (TNA, PROB 11/94/426). 1588 and 1596(G). Churchwarden 1566, general receiver 1572 and 1580. 1569–80 Hele wood and mill tenant; supplied shoes, wheelbarrow timber; relieved poor; went to queen's visitation at Launceston; horses carried bridge material; paid clock maker.

[**Thomas**, 1569*A*(D)].

SCHORTT. *See* **SHORT**

SCOT

John church house interest (B131–2). 1576 counsel re same.

[**William**, literate witness 1576 (B131)].

[**SELLER**, **John**, 1543 goods £1(S)].

SERVYS, **Richard**, 1543 goods £1(S). Sexton 1544, warden Our Lady and St George 1546, High Cross 1556. 1548–63 paid knells, poor.

SHARSELL, **Lewis**, [of Kilkhampton]. 1574 went to St Lawrence, Bodmin.

[**SHEPYNGHAM**, **Agnes**, widow, (d.<1575), heirs fined for non-attendance, Sanctuary manor court, 1575 (TNA, SC2/158)].

SHORT, **SCHURT**

John, (d.1534) of Poughill, 1525 goods £6(S), held office 1528–29(PC). Warden High Cross 1531. 1530–31 paid knells.

[**John II**, feoffee 1532 (B25)].

John III, (d.1603). Literate 1582, 1588 horse carried victuals (B136–9, 209). Will included chamber at 'boards end in the hall' where John the younger dwelt, inventory £29 7s (CRO, AP/S29/1–2). 1592(G). Warden High Cross 1557, general receiver 1563, 1578, one of four men 1569. 1559–81 supplied coffer bull necks, Alse COKE's meat and drink; went to Boscastle for subsidy and harness rates; bought two little stones; mended sege; rented Glebe, paid fine of meadows; wife's grave.

Margery, (d.1565). 1543 goods £4(S). Supplied meat and drink to Alice Luke of Poughill 1551(PC). 1534–65 husband and another's bede roll, gifts, grave.

Robert, 1572 led church singing.

[**Silvester**, cordwainer, (d.1619), Lickham woods, witness 1581–2 (B139, 144), will and inventory £332 6s 8d, included shoes, tallow, working tools and specialities in shop book].

SINCOCKE, **Roger**, [of Morwenstow], 1581 supplied organ swell; mended bull ring stapes.

SKENARD, **SKEYCARDE**, **SKYBERD**

[**John**, 1569*c*(D)].

Margaret, (d.1571), 1561–71 sick, blanket, shroud.

SKYR, **Thomsyn**, 1539 put on bede roll by Elizabeth DROMOND.

SMALE, **SMALL**

Ede, 1564–69 sick, poor.

[**John**, 1525 wages £2(S), held office, hoop, kieve supplier 1554(PC)].

Stephen, 1525 goods £2(S). held offices 1537–56(PC). Warden High Cross 1532. 1517–31 assisted thatcher; paid knell.

Stephen II, of Poughill, (d.1574(PR)), 1569*A*(D). 1561–73 rented Glebe.

William, 1569*u*(D). 1572–81 made cob; sick, poor.

SMYTHE

Thomas, 1569*A*(D). Churchwarden 1580.

William, feoffee 1540 (B178). 1534 rented church house.

SNELL, **Henry**, 1580 removed granite.

SNOWE, **Thomas**, 1564 paid knell.

SONDER. *See* **SAUNDER**

SOWDON, **Ame**, 1548 on bede roll.

SPARKE, **SPERCK**

Agnes or **Amys**, 1558 reversionary lease Treburtle (B187). 1572–79 tenant.

[**Elizabeth**, 1525, with William, goods £4(S)].

Robert, 1526 cleaned church house.

[**Walter**, 1522–25 goods £1–£5(S)].

William, (d.1572(W)), 1522 goods £5, 1525 with Elizabeth £4, 1543 £1(S), 1569*A*(D). Feoffee 1529–63 (B21–2, 25, 33, 37, 78, 85, 98, 121, 187). Warden St George 1534, High Cross 1535, general receiver 1545 and 1558, highway supervisor 1566. 1525–71 Treburtle tenant; made alleys around the church, causeway; reimbursed surplus bell metal; father's grave, gift, knells.

SPAYVER, **Thomas**, 1527 spliced bell ropes.

SQUANS, **Richard[a]**, Maiden 1542.

STAWFORD, **STOWFORD**

[**Richard**?], mason, of Buckland Brewer, Devon?, 1543 goods £16(S). 1545 tower windows, walls(PC). 1544 took down and made new chancel.

STEVEN, **Robert**, 1563 paid knell.

STRECK, STRYCKE
[**John**, 1569*A*(D)].
Pett[er], 1572 set up board in church house.
[STRETCHELIE, STRACHELEY]
[**Margaret**, widow of Robert, married William BYLL by 1558×73]
[**Robert**, gent, of Ermington, Devon. Landowner, held Upton after GILBERTS and Edward HORETOP his tenant by 1558×73 (TNA, C3/18/47; CP25/1/34/44)]
[**William**, esquire, of Strashleigh, Ermington, Devon, landowner with wife Ann, refused to seal lease 1558×79 (TNA, C3/201/47)].
SUTTON, Nicholas of vill, warden High Cross 1538.
SWEPER, William, 1569*t*(D). 1573–81 rented stalls.
SYMON
Margaret, (d.1570). 1543 goods£1(S). 1542–70 husband's and son's graves/bede roll, grave.
Mary, Maiden 1545.
Nicholas, of Burwood, 1525 goods £4(S). Feoffee 1529 (B21, 25, 33, 37). Warden High Cross 1523, general receiver 1535 and 1555, St Andrew guild 1536. 1517–40 supplied lime, crock; on bede roll; bought old rood loft bits; paid knells.
Nicholas, 1543 goods £8(S). Warden St Andrew guild 1540, general receiver 1559. 1531–58 supplied honey; knells including brother; attended Launceston law court; bought kirtle, church cloths; dined with Mr UNDERDON.
[**Thomas**, 1525 wages £1(S)].
Walter, 1543 goods £2(S). Warden St Armel 1540, Sexton 1544, Our Lady and St George 1546, High Cross 1552.

TACKELL. *See* **TOWYLL**
TAYLOUR, TAYLDER, TALAR
Ebot, (d.1559) grave.
Isbell, 1517 supplied wax.
Margaret, (d.1558) grave.
Moris, tailor, 1512 made stole.
[**Thomas**, feoffee 1476–92 (B75–6)].
Thomas II [merchant], (d.1564). 1522–25 goods £6(S). Feoffee 1534–50 (B33, 78, 84, 98, 189), supplier vestment buckram, wax 1528–50s(PC). Warden St George 1538, general receiver 1546 and 1557. 1521–64 supplied wax, frankincense, clock wire, stole material, dowlas, thread; wife's grave, grave.
Thomas, wife of, (d.1536) grave.
Thomas III, esquire, 1543–45 goods £21–lands £30(S). Feoffee 1529–56 (B21–2, 37, 121, 130, 178, 180, 198). Warden High Cross 1523, general receiver 1530 and 1538, Trinity 1535, St Armel 1546. 1536–42 supplied lath nails, slate, bell brass; lent money; made tiles; went to Week to see king's visitors; father's grave.
Thomas, old, (d.1563) grave.
[**Thomas, of Launcells**, feoffee 1562 (B26)].
[**Thomas, of Tawstock**, gentleman, literate feoffee 1576–77 (B134). Free tenant of Sanctuary and did not attend manor court, 1575 (TNA, SC2 158].
Walter, 1536 gift.
TEHELLA (*see* **WYLL alias HELE**)
TERELL, ——, mason, 1573 stopped water at bridge.
THAYLOUR. *See* **TAYLOUR**
THOMAS, Gylberd, 1538 bede roll.
THORNE
———, **Master**, 1531 requiem, knell.
John, 1572 carried letter to plumber.
TOCKER, TOCAR
[**John**?], of Poughill, 1543 £2 goods(S). Church house tenant 1551?(PC). 1555 paid knell.

Peter [hellier], 1572 worked with Richard OBLIN.

TOME, John [fletcher] of Poundstock 1569*A*(D). 1573 supplied arrows, bow string, feathered old arrows.

TOWYLL, TAKYLE

Esbell, 1580 poor.

Nicholas, 1551 bought rood cloth.

Thomas, 1569*B*(D). 1572–79 supplied lime; rented buttery; child's shroud, poor relief for wife.

William, 1517–18 sheared hedge; cleaned church house.

TREBARFOOT, TERBARFOTTE, William, of Poundstock, 1525 goods £18(S). 1531–32 bede roll.

TREMYLL, TRIMBLE

Christopher, 1569–71 set up church house boards; wife paid BARBOR's child's knell; made choir.

John, literate witness 1576–77 (B137). 1572 child's knell.

Thomas, 1581 poor.

William, 1548 knell.

William II, 1575–81 supplied lath nails; given shoes, gown, shirt as poor.

TRENGER, TRYNGER, [John], (d.1522–23?) benefactor, held 1,340 Cornish acres when he died (Tucker, *Penfound Manor*, p.10), gave church house site 1488 (B129–30). 1515–23 expenses; obit.

TREVELYAN, TREVELAN

Cheryte, Maiden 1539.

John, (d.1550/51)(executors). 1525–43 goods £3–£4(S). Feoffee, attorney 1529–46 (B37, 178, 198). Received 4d 1542(PC). 1531 witnessed deed (BL, Add Ch 74868). Warden High Cross 1528, general receiver 1532, Trinity 1537, All Hallows guild 1545–46. 1520–51 supplied wax, lime, books, including English matins; made wax, tapers, bede roll; bought old rood loft staff; acquitted parish; wrote new bede roll, Treburtle feoffment etc.; paid grave, gift, bede roll, knells, gift.

[**Thomas**, feoffee 1540 (B178, 180)].

TREWEKE, John, (d.1605). 1569*A*(D), inventory £9 (CRO, AP/T89/1–2). 1570 child's knell

TRIWEELL. *See* **TREMYLL**

TRYPPLET, Elizabeth, 1560 knell.

TUNNYNG

Elyn, 1548 family on bede roll.

William, 1548.

TURVELYON. *See* **TREVELAN**

UDY, UDE, EDEY, EDE, EDYE

——, of Otterham, 1543 goods £3(S). 1544 carried granite.

John, of town (fl.1500, d.1564/65), 1543 goods £3(S). 1546–56 leased Pope's Place near sea in Stone with wife Margaret and son George (B31, 33, 37). Warden High Cross 1524 and 1540, St George 1535, Trinity and Christ guild 1536, general receiver 1544. 1527–64 Stone land tenant; bede roll; gave doublet, shirt; knells including servant; supplied lime; bought churchyard wood; carried chancel granite; horse carried bridge materials.

John II, 1543 goods £1(S). Warden St Armel 1534.

John, ——, servant of, (d.1548) knell.

John, alias JENKEN, 1561–63 poor.

[**Walter**, 1569*u*(D)].

UGLOW, OGLOW, WOGLLO

——, **old**, of Marhamchurch, (d.1559) knell.

Christina, (d.1545). 1543 goods £6(S). 1538–45 grave, gift of six silver spoons.

Elizabeth, of Marhamchurch, 1559 gift.

John, (d.1581(W)), 1543 goods £3(S). Warden Our Lady Holmadon 1532, St George 1537, High Cross 1544. 1533–68 paid knell; supplied lime, straw; carried grail books from Bodmin; parish brought case against him at Launceston.

Jone, 1569–72 Hele Mill tenant.

Nicholas [merchant]. 1543 goods £6(S). Warden High Cross 1517, general receiver 1526. 1517–39 carried lime; supplied stone, bell ropes, collar, dowlas, crests, iron bars, wax, clock wire, Lent cloth, little bell cords etc.

Robert, 1522–25 goods £20(S). Feoffee 1529–34 (B21, 78). Warden High Cross 1526, St George 1532. 1527–37 servant mended bell collar; bede roll, knell, gift, grave, wife's knell.

Thomas, 1558–68 tenant part Hele Mill.

William, (d.1535). 1522–25 goods £5(S). Feoffee (B83,130). Warden High Cross 1515. 1520–35 supplied wax; heriot.

UNDERDON, ANDERDON

[**John**], **Master**, of Launcells 1569 £5–10 land(D). 1558–78 parish counsellor; drew up writing; dinner at Mr Yeo's house; passport for Jone MORTON etc.

[**Richard**, wife Margaret and son William agreed lease with Elizabeth MARYS, but she refused to sign 1534×8 (TNA, C1/714/15)].

VEVIAN, VYVYAN, Richard, 1569*c*(D). 1558–78 knell; bridge work.

VOLER, Robert the, 1556 bought a cask.

WADE

Johan, 1544–48 supplied workmen's meat and drink; paid Amy SOWDON knell/bede roll.

John, 1543 goods £6(S). Warden St George 1537, Sexton 1539, Our Lady Holmadon 1541, High Cross 1544, general receiver 1546. 1530–44 bede roll including brother; helped with church house.

John II, 1569*A*(D). Churchwarden 1571. 1570–74 child's knell; drew seams of stone over cliff for bridge.

Robert, feoffee 1493 (B77–8). Warden High Cross 1514.

Thomas, 1543 goods £3(S). Feoffee 1540 (B178, 198). Warden St Armel 1535, All Hallows guild/Our Lady Holmadon 1539, High Cross 1543. 1544 supplied meat and drink for CHAMOND's knell.

Thomas, ——, female servant of, 1540 kirtle for bede roll.

WADYN

Avys, (d.1520) grave.

Robert, (d.1515) grave.

WALKYE

Davy, 1569*u*(D). 1570–81 carried justice's precept to KEMPTHORNE; made cob for wall behind church house; maiden and self received poor relief.

Richard, (d.1596(W)), 1569*B*(D). 1571–77 daughter's knell; made gown and sleeves for William CLARK's child.

WALSHE, Richard, 1544 supplied lamp.

WARMAN. *See* **COOPER**

WARMENTONE, WARMINGTON

[**Robert**, of Poughill, 1569*A*(D)].

[**Walter**, (d.1614(W)), of Crabbe, Poughill, reeve Sanctuary manor 1575 (TNA, SC2/158)].

William, of Poughill, 1569*ABh*(D). Sold Summerlease to Robert SAUNDERS <1599 (TNA, PROB 11/94/426). 1566–70 supplied bell brass, gift to bell; slate carried to him.

[**WATERMAN, William**, 1569*u*(D)].

[**WATTES, Robert**, (d.1585(W)), 1569*A*(D)].

WERENG. *See* **WRYNG**

WESTCOT,

[**Elys**, 1569*u*(D)].

William, 1563 sick at Candlemas.

WESTLAKE

[**Nicholas**, literate witness 1576–77 (B137), 1597(G)].

Richard, of Poughill, (d.1531) knell/bede roll.

WHALE

[**Isot** or **Esit**], 1579–81 poor.

William, 1569*u*(D). 1575–79 to leave parish, sick, wife tended old woman BOLE, Alice LANE tended wife, received gown and waistcoat for children.

WHEER

Alsen, 1560 paid Walter JULE's knell.

[**Richard**, 1569*u*(D)].

[**Thomas**, 1569*A*(D)].

WHORE. *See* **HORE**

WHYTE, WHITE

Elizabeth and **Esbel**, 1580–81 poor and sick.

John, bellfounder [of Bristol?], 1558–78 took down, weighed bell, given drink, hung bell up, supper with servant, cast another bell, Trinity Sunday dinner, hung up bell.

John, Thomas servant of, bellfounder's servant, reward, supper 1559.

Thomas, 1569*B*(D). Sexton 1559. 1559–76 made tapers; borrowed slates; bought Hele Wood faggots; rented butts; distributed relief in time of sickness.

Thomas II, 1572–73 helped choir, bought music.

William, 1531 held requiem, gift to Our Lady warden.

WHYTHED, Tomsyn, 1523 bequest to church.

[**WHYTINGTON, Thomas**, esquire, granted reversion Pinch 1531 to BRAYS (BL, Add Ch 74868)].

[**WHYTSTON, William**, landowner Whitstone and Stratton 1533×8 (TNA, C1/918/21–4)].

WILL. *See* **WYLL**

WILLCOCKE, WYLCOK

Johane, 1579 poor.

[**Thomas**, 1543 goods £1(S)].

WODEMAN, Sir William, Week St Mary priest 1537–38, 1556 rector of Helland(V), 1545 discharged parish at visitation.

WODEWARD, [William], (b.1505, fl.1559) Poundstock priest 1537–38(V). 1535 on bede roll.

WOGLLO. *See* **UGLOW**

[**WOLCOTT, John**, 1569*B*(D)].

WOLFE, WULFE

John, of Poughill [merchant], (d.1534–35(PC)). 1522–25 £18–20 goods(S). Held office, wax and tabernacle linen cloth supplier 1528–35(PC). Feoffee 1492–1534 (B21, 77–8, 83, 97). 1512–35 supplied wax, cloth; hired black suit, on bede roll.

John II, of Poughill, (d.1579(W)), 1543 goods £8(S). Held offices, ceilure boards (still extant) and rags supplier 1534–54(PC). 1551 laths.

John, tailor, [of Poughill], 1524 paid knell.

John, of Northcott, 1524 gift.

Mensyn, 1539 hired black suit.

WRYNG

——, *see* Richard.

Richard, 1543 goods £1(S), 1569*B*(D). Coverlet 1551(PC). Warden St George 1540, Our Lady Holmadon 1542, High Cross 1549. 1548–71 paid knell; bridge work with horse; kept, mended and greased bells, collars.

WYER, Thomas, 1558–61 supplied bell brass; expenses.

WYETT, WYOTT, John, of Bodmin, 1543 goods £3(S). 1540–45 paid knell; set up lamp step.

WYLCOK. *See* **WILLCOCKE**

WYLL (*see* **HELE**)

Alson, 1542 Maiden.

John, feoffee 1492 (B77–8). 1512–17 paid knell supplied lime.
John II alias HELE, 1543 goods £1(S). Warden Our Lady Holmadon 1540. 1535–46 paid knell; helped pave chancel, loft.
Nicholas, (d.1569). 1525–43 goods £2–£8(S). Feoffee 1534–63 (B78, 84–5, 98, 121, 178, 180, 198). Warden High Cross 1530, general receiver 1532 and 1563, St Thomas guild 1534 and 1536. 1540–69 paid knell; reimbursed when priest sued for books; rode to Launceston re Treburtle; carried harness from Launceston, laths from Holesworthy, put Johan LANGDON on bede roll, paid John BRYANT's grave/knell, grave.
Nicholas II alias HELE, 1569 goods £10–£20(D). Feoffee, literate witness 1576–85+(B136–7,145). 1597(G). Churchwarden 1572, constable 1578–80. 1573–81 rented church house kitchen; provided Ten Commandments boards; child's knell, mother's grave; responsible for eight men working on Bude quay; went to Camelford muster, carried butts, pressed men as soldiers; worked on bridge; paid poor; rented Hele mills; entertained clerk of the market.
Richard, Sir, priest, 1565 gift via William WYLL.
Thomas, 1544 paid knell.
William alias HELE, 1569*Bh*(D). Feoffee 1576–85 (B135,137,144–6). Mediator who detained deeds 1579×87 (TNA, C3/221/56). Warden St Armel 1545, churchwarden 1560, Sexton 1565, general receiver 1580. 1560–80 rented part Hele mills; before commissioners at Launceston, bought psalter book at Bodmin; mother-in-law and wife's graves, gift for John LYLL priest; lent horse; council with Peter HALLETT about church house; child's knell.
William, ——, wife of, (d.1571) mother's and own grave.

WYLLIAMS
——, Master, 1555 counselled parish.
[**William, tailor**, 1569*u*(D)]. *See also* **WYLL**

WYLSON, ——, (d.1537) John ROSE paid knell.

YATE, Edmund, (d.1525) grave.

YENGRUM. *See* **INGERAM**

YEO, YOE, YOWE
Agathe, Maiden 1540.
Andrew, 1569*A*(D). 1574–75 bridge work.
Joane, 1560 supplied communion bread, wine.
[**John II**, feoffee, witness 1540–56 (B22, 98, 130, 180, 185, 198)].
[**John, husbandman**, 1569*AP*(D). Feoffee 1569–76 (B22, 135)].
John, merchant, gentleman of Tree, Stratton, and then Burwood (d.1607). 'the great John YEO' (B130). 1569 £20–40 goods(D). 1569–83 feoffee, literate witness. 1581–83 pulled down timber building by church house and interfered with letting of fair stalls (B22, 27, 34, 79, 132, 135–9, 140–1, 144–7). By 1558×79 held messuage from STRETCHELIES but they refused to sign lease (TNA, C3/201/47). Will and inventory only 8s 4d for trunk, sword and red child's blanket. Appraisers claimed goods distrained and brothers held Burwood, Howard mill, Pyworthy, Devon etc. (CRO, AP/and3/1–2)]. 1590, 1597 and 1603(G). Churchwarden 1577. 1569–83 supplied communion bread, smock canvas, linen, shrouds for old COLE, Irish child, Alse COKE, poor Elizabeth, cloth for CLARK's child, nails, great armour buckles which he kept and carried to muster, bell stock timber, bars, wheelbarrows, communion cup cover and Bible, stones, lath nails, bell metal. Bought chest; made bell indenture, wrote supplication to bishop etc.; rented stall, church house.
John, husbandman of East Bridge, (d.1614), 1581–86 feoffee (B138–9, 144–6), 1595(G). Will and inventory £80 included cheese rack and wring (CRO, AP/Y7/1–2). 1578 bridge work.
——, Mistress, 1569–71 supplied communion wine. 1571 husband's grave.
Nicholas, 1543 goods £9(S), 1569 £20–40(D). Witness, feoffee 1540–86+(B131, 134, 137, 145–6, 178). Warden Christ guild 1534 and 1548, High Cross 1541, general receiver 1542, 1567 and 1579, one of four men 1569. 1536–81 paid knell, bede roll; bought trees, sepulchre and painted cloths, barrel of lime; rented church house; rated parish for harness; breakfasted at

Prideaux Place re church house and at Launceston re rood loft; fetched barrels lime from Bideford; carried stones, earth to bridge, butts.

[**Nicholas II**, witness 1576 (B134)].

[**Nicholas, merchant**, witness 1576–77 (B137). 1583, 1589 and 1617(G). Free tenant Sanctuary manor, 1615(M)].

Peter, 1559 borrowed slates.

Richard, merchant. Literate feoffee 1576–85+, 1574 High Cross scribe (B136–7, 139, 144). 1581 leased Sanctuary manor property, but failed to pay Nicholas RUNDELL's expenses, and claimed that £6, ox hide value 18s and deeds detained (TNA, C3/287/5, C3/221/56). 1578 churchwarden. 1572 gift.

Robert, 1548 rode to Helston against the rebels.

Roger, 1543 goods £2(S). Literate witness (B130). Warden St Armel 1542, High Cross 1544. 1549–69 supplied the Prayer Book, wax, slate, frankincense, shroud cloths, shirts, blankets, communion bread; bought two blue cloths, rood cloth; paid Alsen GYST and children's knells, Thomas TAYLOUR's and another's grave; collected harness money.

[**Thomas**, nephew of Nicholas 1585–86 (B145–6)].

Walter, [merchant/shopkeeper] (d.1621) 1569*AHB*(D). Literate feoffee 1569–81. 1588 lent horse against the Armada (B22, 27, 34, 131, 136–9, 144, 209). Will 1619 left £126 13s 4d and six silver spoons to daughter Jone, inventory £337 1s 6d included Bible, 'victuals in the salt', hall, parlour, kitchen, buttery with two chambers over, new house, and shop. Yeo's shop sold cloth, nutmeg, saffron etc. (CRO, AP/Y14/1–2; North, 'Fustians, Figs and Frankincense', pp.62–3). 1602(G). Churchwarden 1575, general receiver 1581. 1570–78 expenses at Camelford before queen's commissioners; bought basket, armour; supplied stones, shroud and doublet cloth.

William, (d.1570(W)), 1569*BS*(D). Warden High Cross 1558, general receiver 1560 and 1568. 1548–67 paid Helston company; went to visitation; house used for parish meeting; slate brought to same; shop by stile; lent two trestles to fair; supplied lath, stones; paid Mrs AUGER's knell,

William II, 1569*A*(D) feoffee 1581–85 (B144–5). 1573–80 paid HOBBACOCK's knell, distributed money to poor.

YERE, YEARE, Harry, (d.1580) 1569*u*(D). 1572–80 made and cleaned church house; hewed granite; sick, shroud.

YERLY, YERELL

Nicholas, 1542–55 drank can of ale at church house; helped bellfounder.

Thomas, 1525 goods £3(S). Warden High Cross 1513.

YNGERYS, Ralph, (d.1558) grave.

YNGRAM. *See* **INGERAM**

Bibliography

Primary sources

British Library, London

Add Ch 64216, 74868 Deeds of Pinch 1531, 1538.
Add MS 32243 Stratton High Cross wardens' accounts 1512–78.
Add MS 32244 Stratton general receivers' accounts 1531, 1534–49.

Cornwall Record Office, Truro

AP/A38, 184; B217; C13, 109, 139, 375; J177, 271; M17,144; O70; P343; R491, 497; S29, 85, 374; T89; Y3, 7, 14: early-seventeenth-century wills, inventories and administrations for Stratton
B/BOD/245; /314/2–6: Bodmin churchwardens', general receivers', and town receivers' accounts, c.1473–1553
FS/2/54 Microfilm of the Stratton High Cross wardens' accounts, 1512–78 (BL, Add MS 32243).
P7/5/1 Antony churchwardens' accounts, 1538–84 (transcript only).
P/19/5/1 St Breock churchwardens' accounts, 1529–98.
P27/5/2/1 Camborne churchwardens' accounts, 1535–79.
P102/1/1 Kilkhampton parish register, 1539–1782.
P102/5/1 Kilkhampton churchwardens' accounts 1563–1603.
P144/5/2, /3/1–2 Menheniot churchwardens' accounts, 1555–1681.
P167/5/1 North Petherwin churchwardens' accounts, 1493–1591.
P192/1/1 Poughill parish register, 1537–1812.
P192/5/1 Poughill churchwardens' accounts, 1525–98.
P216/2/71 Notes on Stratton church restoration, 1887.
P216/5/1 Stratton churchwardens' accounts and vestry minutes, 1789–1921.
P216/25/1–340 Blanchminster Charity Records including:
/25/140 Church house depositions and two plans, 1583.
/25/208 Stratton general receivers' and stockwardens' accounts, 1557–81.
/25/215–16 Stratton rood loft contract and bond, 1531.
P221/5/1–5 St Thomas Launceston churchwardens' accounts, 1479–1559.
TA, TM/216 Stratton tithe apportionment and map, 1842.

Devon Record Office

DRO, 303A/PW1 Uplyme churchwardens' accounts, 1632–99.

The National Archives (formerly the Public Record Office), Kew

C1/77/23; /159/33; /297/98; /467/57; /616/41; /687/19; /714/15; /798/49–52; /856/14; /918/21–4; /1030/37: Chancery Court cases, c.1504–44.
C2/Eliz/B8/10 Chancery Court case 1590–91.
C3/18/47; /201/47; /216/29; /221/56; /229/33; /287/5: Chancery Court cases, 1558–1616.
E134/16Jas1/East5 Tithe case 1619, E179/87/130 Lay subsidy, 1525.
PROB 11/36/377; /94/426: wills of John Lyll, 1553; Robert Saunders, 1598.
SC2/163/9; /158/42: 1539–41 County Courts; 1574–5 Sanctuary Manor Court.

Royal Institution of Cornwall

Henderson MS 10, pp.359–56: list of Cornish clergy, 1537–38.
Henderson MS 66, p.144: extracts from lost will of Dame Jane Chamond, 1551.

Hennessy's Institutions 1456–1877, MS: notes on Cornish incumbents.
Toms, H. N. W., ed., 'Stratton with Bude Haven Cornwall Church Records 1611–1860 including the Parish Registers' (typescript, 1977).

Printed primary sources

Binney, J. Erskine, ed., *The Accounts of the Wardens of the Parish of Morebath, Devon, 1520–1573* (Exeter, 1904).
Burgess, Clive, ed., *The Church Records of St Andrew Hubbard, Eastcheap, c.1450–c.1570*, London Record Society 34 (1999).
— ed., *The Pre-Reformation Records of All Saints' Church, Bristol*, II: *The Churchwardens' Accounts*, British Record Society 53 (2000). www.bristol.ac.uk/Depts/History/bristolrecordsociety/publications/brs53.pdf (accessed 24 January 2017).
Chynoweth, John, Nicholas Orme and Alexandra Walsham, eds, *The Survey of Cornwall by Richard Carew*, DCRS new ser. 47 (2004).
Cornish, Robert, ed., *Kilmington Church Wardens' Accounts MDLVV–MDCVIII* (Exeter 1901) babel.hathitrust.org/cgi/pt?id=coo1.ark:/13960/t.83j41w5f;view=1up;seq=25 (accessed 24 January 2017).
Dils, Joan, ed., *Reading St Laurence Churchwardens' Accounts 1498–1570*, Berkshire Record Society 19–20 (2013).
Douch, H. L., ed., *The Cornwall Muster Roll for 1569* (Bristol, 1984).
Dunstan, G. R., ed., *The Register of Edmund Lacy Bishop of Exeter, 1420–1455*, vol. 1, DCRS new ser. 7 (1963).
Fox, H. S. A., and O. J. Padel, *The Cornish Lands of the Arundells of Lanherne, Fourteenth to Sixteenth Centuries*, DCRS new ser. 41 (1998).
Glencross, R. M. ed., *Calendar of Wills, Administrations and Accounts relating to the Counties of Cornwall and Devon in the Connotorial Archidiaconal Court of Cornwall*, Part I: *1569–1699* (London, 1929).
Goulding, R. R., ed., *Records of the Blanchminster Charity in the Parish of Stratton* (Stratton, 1898).
Graham, Frank, ed., *A Topographical and Historical Description of Cornwall by John Norden* (Newcastle upon Tyne, 1966).
Hanham, Alison, ed., *Churchwardens' Accounts of Ashburton, 1479–1580*, DCRS, new ser. 15 (1970).
Hays, Rosalind Conklin, C. E. McGee, Sally L. Joyce, Evelyn Newlyn, *Records of Early English Drama – Dorset, Cornwall* (Toronto, 1999).
Hingeston-Randolph, Revd F. C., ed., *The Register of Edmund Stafford (A.D. 1395–1419)* (London, 1886).
Kitto, J. V., ed., *St Martin-in-the Fields: The Accounts of the Churchwardens 1525–1603* ([s.l.] 1901), *British History Online* www.british-history.ac.uk/no-series/churchwardens-st-martin-fields/1525-1603 (accessed 24 January 2017).
Kowaleski, Maryanne, ed., *The Havener's Accounts of the Earldom & Duchy of Cornwall 1287–1356*, DCRS new ser. 44 (2001).
Litzenberger, C. J., ed., *Tewkesbury Churchwardens' Accounts, 1563–1624*, Bristol & Gloucestershire Archaeological Society, Gloucestershire Records Series 7 (1994).
Middleton-Stewart, Judith, ed., *Records of the Churchwardens of Mildenhall: Collections [1446–1454] and Accounts [1503–1553]*, Suffolk Records Society 54 (2011).
Northeast, Peter, ed., *Boxford Churchwardens' Accounts, 1530–1561*, Suffolk Records Society 23 (1982).
Orme, Nicholas, ed., *Cornish Wills 1342–1540*, DCRS, new ser. 50 (Exeter, 2007).
Osborne, Francis Mardon, ed., *The Church Wardens' Accounts of St Michael's Church, Chagford 1480–1600* (Chagford, Devon, 1979).
Palmer, Anthony, ed., *Tudor Churchwardens' Accounts*, Hertfordshire Record Society Publications 1 (1985).

Peacock, Edward, 'On the Churchwardens' Accounts of the Parish of Stratton, in the County of Cornwall', *Archaeologia* 46.1 (1880), pp.195–236.
Pool, Peter, ed., 'Cornish Parishes in 1753: I: St Issey', *OC* 4.8 (1965), pp.366–8.
— ed., 'Cornish Parishes in 1753: IV: Stratton', *OC* 6.11 (1966), pp.500–3
Pounds, Norman J. G., ed., *The Parliamentary Survey of the Duchy of Cornwall, pt. II*, DCRS new ser. 27 (1984).
Price, Revd W. H. and E. A. B. Barnard, eds, *The Churchwardens' Accounts of the Parish of Badsey with Aldington in Worcestershire from 1525 to 1571* (Hampstead, 1913).
Ravenhill, Mary R. and Margery M. Rowe, eds, *The Acland Family: Maps and Surveys 1720–1840*, DCRS, new ser. 49 (2006).
Smith, Lucy Toulmin, ed., *Leland's Itinerary in England and Wales*, 5 vols (London, 1964).
Snell, Lawrence S., ed., *The Chantry Certificates for Cornwall* (Exeter, 1953).
— ed., *The Edwardian Inventories of Church Goods for Cornwall* (Exeter, 1955).
Stallard, Arthur Dudley, ed., *The Transcript of the Churchwardens' Accounts of the Parish of Tilney All Saints, Norfolk 1443–1589* (London, 1922).
Stoate, T. L., ed., *Cornwall Manorial Rentals and Surveys* (Bristol, 1988).
— ed., *The Cornwall Military Survey 1522 with the Loan Books and a Tinners Muster Roll c.1535* (Bristol, 1987).
— ed., *Cornwall Subsidies in the Reign of Henry VIII 1524 and 1543 and the Benevolence of 1545* (Bristol, 1985).
— ed., *Devon Lay Subsidy Rolls 1524–7* (Bristol, 1979).
— ed., *Devon Lay Subsidy Rolls 1543–5* (Bristol, 1986).
Winnington-Ingram, A. J. 'The Early Parish Registers of Stoke Edith', *Transactions of the Woolhope Naturalists' Field Club* (1949), pp.19–43.

Secondary sources

Bainbridge, Virginia R., *Gilds in the Medieval Countryside: Social and Religious Change in Cambridgeshire c.1350–1588* (Woodbridge, 1996).
Baker, J. H., *An Introduction to English Legal History* (London, 1979).
Balchin, W. G. V., *The Cornish Landscape* (London, 1983).
Barnwell, P. S., Claire Cross and Ann Rycraft, *Mass and Parish in Late Medieval England: The Use of York* (Reading, 2005).
Barton, Allan B., 'The Ornaments of the Altar and the Ministers in Late-Medieval England', in *Mass and Parish in Late Medieval England: The Use of York*, ed. P. S. Barnwell, Claire Cross and Ann Rycraft (Reading, 2005), pp.27–40.
Beacham, Peter, and Nikolaus Pevsner, *Cornwall* (New Haven and London, corrected repr. 2014).
Benham, Hugh, *Latin Church Music in England 1460–1575* (London, 1977).
Bere, Rene, and Brian Dudley Stamp, *The Book of Bude and Stratton* (Buckingham, 1980).
Beswetherick, Kathleen, *The Aclands and Budehaven: The Story of a Devon Family and a Cornish Town* (Bradworthy, 1995).
Blake, Hugo, Geoff Egan, John Hurst and Elizabeth New, 'From Popular Devotion to Resistance and Revival of the Holy Name of Jesus and the Reformation', in *The Archaeology of the Reformation 1480–1580*, ed. David Gaimster and Roberta Gilchrist (Leeds, 2003), pp.175–203.
Bond, F. Bligh, and Dom Bede Camm, *Roodscreens and Roodlofts*, 2 vols (London, 1909).
Brown, H. Miles, *Cornish Clocks and Clockmakers* (Newton Abbot, 1961, rev. 1980).
Burgess, Clive, 'The Churchwardens' Accounts of St Andrew Hubbard, Eastcheap, and their Implications', *Transactions of the London & Middlesex Archaeological Society* 50 (1999), pp.61–6.
— and Eamon Duffy, eds, *The Parish in Late Medieval England*, Harlaxton Studies 14 (Donington, 2006).

Byng, Gabriel, 'The Contract for the North Aisle at the Church of St James, Biddenham', *Antiquaries Journal* 95 (2015), pp.251–65.

Carter, Paul, and Kate Thompson, *Sources for Local History* (Chichester, 2005).

Catchpole, Antonia, David Clark and Robert Peberdy, *Burford* (Chichester, 2008).

Coldstream, Nicola, *Medieval Craftsmen, Masons and Sculptors* (London, 1991, repr. 1993).

Colvin, Howard, *Essays in Architectural History* (New Haven and London, 1999).

Cotton, Simon, 'Medieval Roodscreens in Norfolk: Their Construction and Painting Dates', *Norfolk Archaeology* 39.3 (1986), pp.44–54.

Cox, J. Charles, *Churchwardens' Accounts from the Fourteenth to the Close of the Seventeenth Century* (London, 1913).

Cresswell, Beatrice, *The Churches of Exeter* (Exeter, 1908).

Drake, Michael, ed., *Population Studies from Parish Registers* (Matlock, 1982).

Duffy, Eamon, *The Stripping of the Altars: Traditional Religion in England c.1400–c.1580* (New Haven and London, 1992).

——, *The Voices of Morebath: Reformation and Rebellion in an English Village* (New Haven and London, 2001).

Dunkin, Edwin H. W., *Monumental Brasses of Cornwall* (Bath, 1882, repr. 1970).

Dymond, David, and Clive Paine, *Five Centuries of an English Parish Church: 'The State of Melford Church', Suffolk* (Cambridge, 2012).

Elphick, George, *The Craft of the Bellfounder* (Chichester, 1988).

Farmer, David H., *The Oxford Dictionary of Saints* (Oxford, 1978, repr. 1987).

Finberg, H. P. R., *Tavistock Abbey: A Study in the Social and Economic History of Devon* (Newton Abbot, 1969).

Fletcher, Anthony, and Diarmaid MacCulloch, *Tudor Rebellions*, fifth edition (Harlow, 2004).

Fraser, Angus, *The Gypsies* (Oxford, 1992, repr. 1995).

Gaimster, David, and Roberta Gilchrist, eds, *The Archaeology of the Reformation 1480–1580* (Leeds, 2003).

Gant, Andrew, *O Sing unto the Lord: A History of English Church Music* (London, 2015).

Gilbert, C. S., *A Historical (and Topographical) Survey of the County of Cornwall*, 3 vols (Plymouth 1817–20).

Gray, Todd, *Devon's Fifty Best Churches* (Exeter, 2011).

Haigh, Christopher, ed., *The English Reformation Revised* (Cambridge, 1987).

Harvey, John, *English Mediaeval Architects: A Biographical Dictionary down to 1550* (Gloucester, 1987).

Henderson, Charles, and Henry Coates, *Old Cornish Bridges and Streams* (Truro, 1928, repr. 1972).

Holt, J. C., *Robin Hood* (London 1982, rev. 1989).

Hull, Peter, 'The Endowment of a Grammar School at Week St Mary by Dame Thomasine Percival', *JRIC*, new ser. 7.1 (1973), pp.21–54.

Humphreys, Caroline, *A List of Cornish Manors* (Truro, 1990).

Hutton, Ronald, 'The Local Impact of the Tudor Reformation', in *The English Reformation Revised*, ed. C. Haigh (Cambridge, 1987).

— *The Rise and Fall of Merry England: The Ritual Year 1400–1700* (Oxford, 1994).

Ivall, David E., 'The High Sheriffs of Cornwall – A Provisional List', *JRIC*, new ser. 2, vol. 1, part 1 (1992), pp.171–93.

Langdon, Andrew G., *Stone Crosses in North Cornwall* (Wadebridge, 1992).

— *Wade-bridge: Notes on the History of the Fifteenth-century Bridge* (St Agnes, 2012).

Lysons, Revd Daniel and Samuel, *Magna Britannica Being a Concise Topographical Account of the Several Counties of Great Britain*, III: *Cornwall* (London, 1814).

MacCulloch, Diarmaid, *The Boy King: Edward VI and the Protestant Reformation* (Berkeley and Los Angeles, 1999, repr. 2002).

Mattingly, Joanna, 'Built to Last? The Rise and Fall of the Church House', *The Local Historian* 42.2 (2012), pp.107–18.

—, 'Going a-riding: Cornwall's Late-medieval Guilds Revisited', *JRIC* (2005), pp.78–103.

—, *Looking at Cornish Churches* (Redruth, 2005).
—, 'The Medieval Parish Guilds of Cornwall', *JRIC*, new ser. 10.3 (1989), pp.290–329.
—, 'Who Made the St Neot Windows? Some Tudor Glaziers in Cornwall', *DCNQ* 40 (2010), pp.227–32.
Middleton-Stewart, Judith, 'Parochial Activity in Late Medieval Fenland: Accounts and Wills from Tilney All Saints and St Mary's, Mildenhall 1433–1520', in *The Parish in Late Medieval England*, ed. Clive Burgess and Eamon Duffy (Donington, 2006), pp.282–301.
North, Christine, 'Fustians, Figs and Frankincense: Jacobean Shop Inventories for Cornwall', *JRIC* new ser. 2, vol. 2, part 2 (1995), pp.62–3
Orme, Nicholas, *The Church in Devon* (Exeter, 2013).
—, 'The Cornish at Oxford, 1180–1540', *JRIC* (2010), pp.43–82.
—, *Cornwall and the Cross: Christianity 500–1560* (Chichester, 2007).
—, *English Church Dedications with a Survey of Cornwall and Devon* (1996).
—, *The Saints of Cornwall* (Oxford, 2000).
—, *The Victoria History of the Counties of England: A History of the County of Cornwall*, II: *Religious History to 1560* (London, 2010).
Padel, Oliver, *A Popular Dictionary of Cornish Place-Names* (Penzance, 1988).
Palliser, D. M., *The Age of Elizabeth: England under the Later Tudors 1547–1603* (London and New York, 1983).
Peter, R. and O. B., *The Histories of Launceston and Dunheved in the County of Cornwall* (Plymouth, 1885).
Peter, Thurstan C., *The History of Glasney Collegiate Church, Cornwall* (Camborne, 1903).
Polsue, Joseph, *A Complete Parochial History of the County of Cornwall*, 4 vols (Truro, 1867–72).
Powell, Susan, ed., *Saints and Cults in Medieval England*, Harlaxton Studies 27 (Donington, 2017).
Rendell, Joan, *Old Bude* (Glasgow, 2001).
Richards, Raymond, *Old Cheshire Churches* (London 1947, repr. 1973).
Rose-Troup, Frances, *The Western Rebellion of 1549: An Account of the Insurrections in Devonshire and Cornwall against Religious Innovations in the reign of Edward VI* (London, 1913).
Rosewell, Roger, *Medieval Wall Paintings in English and Welsh Churches* (Woodbridge, 2008).
Rowse, A. L., *Sir Richard Grenville of the 'Revenge'* (London, 1937, repr. 1940).
Schofield, R., '"Crisis" Mortality', in *Population Studies from Parish Registers*, ed. Michael Drake (Matlock, 1982), pp.97–108.
Slack, Paul, 'The Local Incidence of Epidemic Disease: The Case of Bristol 1540–1650', in *The Plague Reconsidered*, ed. Slack et al. (1977), pp.49–62.
— et al., eds, *The Plague Reconsidered: A New Look at its Origins and Effects in 16th- and 17th-century England*, Local Population Studies (Matlock, 1977).
Symonds, R. W., *A History of English Clocks* (London and New York, 1947).
Taylor, Steven J., *The Parish Church of St Andrew, Stratton: A Brief History* (church guide, 1991).
Tucker, Kenneth and Doris, *Penfound Manor* (Liverpool, n.d.).
Vallance, Aylmer, *English Church Screens being Great Roods, Screenwork and Rood-lofts of Parish Churches in England and Wales* (London, 1936).
Vivian, J. L., *The Visitations of the County of Cornwall* (Exeter, 1887).
Voigts, Linda Ehrsam, 'Plague Saints, Henry VII, and Saint Armel', in *Saints and Cults*, ed. Susan Powell (2017), pp.101–23.
Westlake, H. F., *The Parish Gilds of Mediaeval England* (London, 1919).
Whiting, Robert, *The Blind Devotion of the People: Popular Religion and the English Reformation* (Cambridge, 1989, repr. 1991).
Wordsworth, Christopher, and Henry Littlehales, eds, *The Old Service-Books of the English Church* (London, 1904).

Wylie, J. A. H., 'Observations upon the Distribution and Spread of the English Sweating Sickness (Sullor Anglicus) in Devon in 1551', *TDA* 112 (1980), pp.101–15.

Unpublished secondary works

Waddon-Martyn, W. H., 'Our Family History – "Waddon-Martyn"' (nd).
Williams, Michael Aufrère, 'Medieval English Roodscreens, with special reference to Devon', Exeter University PhD, 2008.

Websites

Clergy of the Church of England Database, 1540 1835: www.kcl.uk/artshums/depts/history/research/proj/clergy.aspx (accessed 2 February 2017).
Gazetteer of Markets and Fairs to 1516: Cornwall section: www.history.ac.uk/cmh/gaz/cornwall.htmail (accessed 23 February 2015).

Index of People and Places

Places beginning with St are generally indexed as St but alphabetically under the second part of the place name due to their frequency in Cornwall. Christian names have been modernised, though Joan and Johanna remain problematic and are indexed as they appear in text. The glossary and maps have not been indexed and the Notes on People section has been indexed selectively. Only people's names and local place names (often not listed otherwise) have been indexed here. A few additional names not included in Notes on People also appear in this index. Note that multiple references can occur on a page.

Index of Subjects

The glossary has not been indexed and the Notes on People section has been indexed selectively. Only occupations and a few select subjects from Notes on People are indexed here. Note that multiple entries can occur on a page.

DEVON AND CORNWALL
RECORD SOCIETY

(Founded 1904)

Officers 2017–18

President: Dr. S. Roberts BA, MA, PhD, FSA, FRHistS

Chairman of Council: Dr T. Gray BA, PhD, FRHistS

Hon. Secretary: E. Babbedge BA Hons, Dip AA, PGCE

Membership Secretary: K. Osborne BA MA PhD AMA

Hon. Treasurer: M. Billings MSc, BA, PGCLT, FCA

Hon. Editor: Professor A. J. Thorpe BA, PhD, FRHistS

The Devon and Cornwall Record Society promotes the study of history in the South West of England through publishing and transcribing original records. In return for the annual subscription members receive the volumes as published (normally annually). For further details see http://www.devonandcornwallrecordsociety.co.uk/

Applications to join the Society should be sent to The Membership Secretary, Devon and Cornwall Record Society, Devon Heritage Centre, Great Moor House, Bittern Road, Exeter, EX2 7NL, or emailed to membershipDCRS@btinternet.com

DEVON AND CORNWALL
RECORD SOCIETY PUBLICATIONS

Previous volumes are available from Boydell & Brewer Ltd.

A Shelf List of the Society's Collections, ed. S Stride, revised 1986

New Series

1 *Devon Monastic Lands: Calendar of Particulars for Grants 1536–1558*, ed. Joyce Youings, 1955

2 *Exeter in the Seventeenth Century: Tax and Rate Assessments 1602–1699*, ed. W. G. Hoskins, 1957

3 *The Diocese of Exeter in 1821: Bishop Carey's Replies to Queries before Visitation, Vol. I Cornwall*, ed. Michael Cook, 1958

4 *The Diocese of Exeter in 1821: Bishop Carey's Replies to Queries before Visitation, Vol. II Devon*, ed. Michael Cook, 1960

5 *The Cartulary of St Michael's Mount*, ed. P. L. Hull, 1962

6 *The Exeter Assembly: Minutes of the Assemblies of the United Brethren of Devon and Cornwall 1691–1717, as transcribed by the Reverend Isaac Gilling*, ed. Allan Brockett, 1963

7 *The Register of Edmund Lacy, Bishop of Exeter 1420–1455, Vol. 1*, ed. G. R. Dunstan

8 *The Cartulary of Canonsleigh Abbey*, ed. Vera C. M. London, 1965

9 *Benjamin Donn's Map of Devon 1765*, Introduction by W. L. D. Ravenhill, 1965

10 *The Register of Edmund Lacy, Bishop of Exeter 1420–1455, Vol. 2*, ed. G. R. Dunstan, 1966

11 *Devon Inventories of the 16th & 17th Centuries*, ed. Margaret Cash, 1966

12 *Plymouth Building Accounts of the 16th & 17th Centuries*, ed. Edwin Welch, 1967

13 *The Register of Edmund Lacy, Bishop of Exeter 1420–1455, Vol. 3*, ed. G. R. Dunstan, 1968

14 *The Devonshire Lay Subsidy of 1332*, ed. Audrey M. Erskine, 1969

15 *Churchwardens' Accounts of Ashburton 1479–1580*, ed. Alison Hanham, 1970

16 *The Register of Edmund Lacy, Bishop of Exeter 1420–1455, Vol. 4*, ed. G. R. Dunstan, 1971

17 *The Caption of Seisin of the Duchy of Cornwall 1377*, ed. P. L. Hull, 1971

18 *The Register of Edmund Lacy, Bishop of Exeter 1420–1455, Vol. 5*, ed. G. R. Dunstan, 1972

19 *A Calendar of Cornish Glebe Terriers 1673–1735*, ed. Richard Potts, 1974

20 *John Lydford's Book: the Fourteenth-Century Formulary of the Archdeacon of Totnes*, ed. Dorothy M. Owen, 1975 (with Historical Manuscripts Commission)

21 *A Calendar of Early Chancery Proceedings relating to West Country Shipping 1388–1493*, ed. Dorothy A. Gardiner, 1976

22 *Tudor Exeter: Tax Assessments 1489–1595*, ed. Margery M. Rowe, 1977

23 *The Devon Cloth Industry in the 18th Century*, ed. Stanley D. Chapman, 1978

24 *The Accounts of the Fabric of Exeter Cathedral 1279–1353*, Part I, ed. Audrey M. Erskine, 1981

25 *The Parliamentary Survey of the Duchy of Cornwall*, Part I, ed. Norman J. G. Pounds, 1982

26 *The Accounts of the Fabric of Exeter Cathedral 1279–1353*, Part II, ed. Audrey M. Erskine, 1983

27 *The Parliamentary Survey of the Duchy of Cornwall*, Part II, ed. Norman J. G. Pounds, 1984

28 *Crown Pleas of the Devon Eyre 1238*, ed. Henry Summerson, 1985

29 *Georgian Tiverton, The Political Memoranda of Beavis Wood 1768–98*, ed. John Bourne, 1986

30 *The Cartulary of Launceston Priory (Lambeth Palace MS.719): A Calendar*, ed. P. L. Hull, 1987

31 *Shipbuilding on the Exe: The Memoranda Book of Daniel Bishop Davy (1799–1874) of Topsham, Devon*, ed. Clive N. Ponsford, 1988

32 *The Receivers' Accounts of the City of Exeter 1304–1353*, ed. Margery Rowe and John M. Draisey, 1989

33 *Early-Stuart Mariners and Shipping: The Maritime Surveys of Devon and Cornwall 1619–35*, ed. Todd Gray, 1990

34 *Joel Gascoyne's Map of Cornwall 1699*, Introduction by W. L. D. Ravenhill and O. J. Padel, 1991

35 *Nicholas Roscarrock's 'Lives of the Saints': Cornwall and Devon*, ed. Nicholas Orme, 1992

36 *The Local Port Customs Accounts of Exeter 1266–1321*, ed. Maryanne Kowaleski, 1993

37 *Charters of the Redvers Family and the Earldom of Devon 1090–1217*, ed. Robert Bearman, 1994

38 *Devon Household Accounts, 1627–59, Part I: Sir Richard and Lady Lucy Reynell of Forde House, 1627–43, John Willoughby of Leyhill, 1644–6, and Sir Edward Wise of Sydenham, 1656–9*, ed. Todd Gray, 1995

39 *Devon Household Accounts 1627–59, Part II: Henry, Earl of Bath, and Rachel, Countess of Bath, of Tawstock and London, 1639–54*, ed. Todd Gray, 1996

40 *The Uffculme Wills and Inventories, 16th to 18th Centuries*, ed. Peter Wyatt, with Introduction by Robin Stanes, 1997

41 *Cornish Rentals and Surveys of the Arundell Family of Lanherne, Fourteenth to Sixteenth Centuries*, ed. H. S. A. Fox and O. J. Padel, 1998

42 *Liberalism in West Cornwall: The 1868 Election Papers of A. Pendarves Vivian MP*, ed. Edwin Jaggard, 1999

43 *Devon Maps and Map-makers: Manuscript Maps before 1840*, ed. with Introduction Mary R. Ravenhill and Margery M. Rowe, 2000

44 *The Havener's Accounts of the Earldom and Duchy of Cornwall, 1287–1356*, ed. Maryanne Kowaleski, 2001

45 *Devon Maps and Map-makers: Manuscript Maps before 1840*, ed. with Introduction Mary R. Ravenhill and Margery M. Rowe, 2002

46 *Death and Memory in Medieval Exeter*, ed. David Lepine and Nicholas Orme, 2003

47 *The Survey of Cornwall by Richard Carew*, ed. John Chynoweth, Nicholas Orme and Alexandra Walsham, 2004

48 *Killerton, Camborne and Westminster: The Political Correspondence of Sir Francis and Lady Acland, 1910–1929*, ed. Garry Tregidga, 2005

49 *The Acland Family: Maps and Surveys 1720–1840*, ed. with Introduction Mary R. Ravenhill and Margery M. Rowe, 2006

50 *Cornish Wills 1342–1540*, ed. Nicholas Orme, 2007

51 *The Letter Book of Thomas Hill 1660–1661*, ed. June Palmer, 2008

52 *Collecting the New, Rare and Curious: Letters Selected from the Correspondence of the Cornish Mineralogists Philip Rashleigh, John Hawkins and William Gregor, 1755–1822*, ed. R. J. Cleevely, 2011

53 *Robert Furse: A Devon Family Memoir of 1593*, ed. Anita Travers, 2012

54 *The Minor Clergy of Exeter Cathedral: Biographies, 1250–1548*, Nicholas Orme, 2013

55 *The Chancery Case between Nicholas Radford and Thomas Tremayne: the Exeter Depositions of 1439*, ed. Hannes Kleineke, 2013

56 *Elizabethan Inventories and Wills of the Exeter Orphans' Court*, Vol. 1, ed. Jeanine Crocker, 2016

57 *Elizabethan Inventories and Wills of the Exeter Orphans' Court*, Vol. 2, ed. Jeanine Crocker, 2016

58 *Devon Parish Taxpayers, Vol. 1, Abbotskerkwell to Bere & Seaton*, ed. Todd Gray, 2016

59 *Devon Parish Taxpayers, Vol. 2, Bere Ferrers to Chudleigh*, ed. Todd Gray, 2017

Devon Maps and Map-makers: Manuscript Maps before 1840. Supplement to Volumes 43 and 45, ed. Mary R. Ravenhill and Margery M. Rowe, 2010

Extra Series:

1 *Exeter Freemen 1266–1967*, ed. Margery M. Rowe and Andrew M. Jackson, 1973

2 *Guide to the Parish and Non-Parochial Registers of Devon and Cornwall 1538–1837*, ed. Hugh Peskett, 1979, supplement 1983